Deschutes
Public Library

D0371966

The Hero's Way

Also by Tim Parks

Fiction
Tongues of Flame
Loving Roger
Home Thoughts
Family Planning
Goodness
Cara Massimina
Mimi's Ghost
Shear
Europa
Destiny
Judge Savage
Rapids
Cleaver
Dreams of Rivers and Seas
Sex is Forbidden (first published as The Server)
Painting Death
Thomas and Mary
In Extremis

Non-fiction
Italian Neighbours
An Italian Education
Adultery & Other Diversions
Translating Style
Hell and Back
A Season With Verona
The Fighter
Teach Us to Sit Still
Italian Ways
Where I'm Reading From
Out of My Head
Italian Life

Tim Parks

The Hero's Way

Walking with Garibaldi from Rome to Ravenna

W. W. NORTON & COMPANY
Independent Publishers Since 1923

Copyright © 2021 by Tim Parks
First American Edition 2021

All rights reserved
Printed in the United States of America

For information about permission to reproduce selections from this book, write to
Permissions, W. W. Norton & Company, Inc., 500 Fifth Avenue,
New York, NY 10110

For information about special discounts for bulk purchases, please contact
W. W. Norton Special Sales at specialsales@wwnorton.com or 800-233-4830

Manufacturing by Lake Book Manufacturing

Library of Congress Cataloging-in-Publication Data

Names: Parks, Tim, author.
Title: The hero's way : walking with Garibaldi from Rome to
Ravenna / Tim Parks.
Other titles: Walking with Garibaldi from Rome to Ravenna
Description: First American edition. | New York : W. W. Norton & Company, 2021.
Identifiers: LCCN 2021013011 | ISBN 9780393866841 (hardcover) |
ISBN 9780393866858 (epub)
Subjects: LCSH: Garibaldi, Giuseppe, 1807–1882—Travel. |
Italy—Description and travel.
Classification: LCC DG552.8.G2 P275 2021 | DDC 945/.083092—dc23
LC record available at https://lccn.loc.gov/2021013011

W. W. Norton & Company, Inc., 500 Fifth Avenue, New York, N.Y. 10110
www.wwnorton.com

W. W. Norton & Company Ltd., 15 Carlisle Street, London W1D 3BS

1 2 3 4 5 6 7 8 9 0

For Eleonora, *garibaldina*

ACKNOWLEDGEMENTS

Warm thanks must go to all those who read the book as a work in progress, Eleonora Gallitelli first and foremost, my brother John, Chris Greenhalgh, Edoardo Zuccato, James Bradburne. Also to the historians David Kertzer and Alessandro Barbero, whose work was particularly illuminating and who were kind enough to correspond. To John Ochsendorf of the American Academy in Rome for his warm hospitality and to the historian Claudio Fracassi, who generously showed us round the battleground on the Gianicolo. And, more generally, to all our B & B hosts, the waiters, hoteliers and café proprietors who offered succour on the way.

CONTENTS

AUTHOR'S NOTE

One version of my life story might be that I met an Italian woman in 1978, married, moved to Italy and have lived here ever since. Without really choosing the place or it choosing me. But a happy curiosity of my 'Italian destiny' was the way it was foreshadowed in adolescence. Faced with the need to choose a special subject for my history A level, I chose the Risorgimento, the process by which the various Italian statelets freed themselves from foreign domination and became, in 1861, a single unified nation. Under the guidance of a passionate teacher, we read a book of original documents from the time and learned of the four great artificers of modern Italy: the revolutionary republican Giuseppe Mazzini, who spent his entire life fomenting armed insurrections that invariably failed; the Machiavellian prime minister of Piedmont Camillo Cavour, who ably exploited rivalries between France and Austria to further Piedmontese expansionism, making his state the core of the emerging nation; the blundering but strangely effective Vittorio Emanuele II, King of Piedmont, who played a double game between his prime minister on the one side and the revolutionary patriots on the other; and finally Giuseppe Garibaldi, the extraordinary guerrilla warrior with a South American past who in 1860 astonished the world by taking a thousand rebels to the west coast of Sicily, capturing the island from a 20,000-strong Bourbon army, crossing to Calabria and driving north through Naples, gathering volunteers as he went, Rome bound, until he met the

Piedmontese army racing south to stop him and handed all territorial gains to Vittorio Emanuele, creating the unified Italian state by fait accompli.

A year after those studies, in 1974, I took advantage of the newly introduced Interrail Pass to visit Italy for the first time and discovered in the process that I already knew a good percentage of the country's street names. Viale Cavour, Via Mazzini, Corso Vittorio Emanuele, Piazza Garibaldi – the four patriots are everywhere, their exploits celebrated in countless monuments, statues and plaques. By far the most attractive, both on the page and in stone, is Garibaldi: the deep-set eyes and bearded severity, the manly bearing beneath soldier's cap and gaucho's poncho, still transmit a powerful charisma; the words *ROMA O MORTE!* inscribed beside the many balconies around the country where he pronounced his famous rallying cry still thrill the heart. Shame that the history books have him down as an ingenuous fellow, a tool in the hands of others, a lucky simpleton.

I began to doubt this description a decade later when asked to review biographies of the hero. Manipulated he may often have been, but simpleton he was not. He was canny, highly organized, creative. And if there was luck, which he acknowledged, it was luck he worked for. The injustice is interesting. Passionately local, ever divided into clans, factions, lobbies and corporations, Italians are not a people inclined to unity. Suspicion, conspiracy theories, cynicism abound. Infighting is the norm, defeatism is rife. Garibaldi, most unusually, set these negative qualities aside, and with them his republican ideals, to focus on a single goal: unity at any cost. He believed it could be achieved in his lifetime and, exhorting others to forget their differences and fight, even die, together, he achieved it. He thus becomes a challenge, even an accusation, for all those who like to feel that courage is futile and progress impossible. To make matters worse, he lived to tell the tale. Despite collecting a dozen bullet wounds over forty years of fighting, the hero died in his bed in 1882 at the age of seventy-four.

All the same I did not fall in love with Garibaldi till I came across *A Diary of Events in Rome in 1849* by Gustav Hoffstetter. Hoffstetter was a Bavarian officer who volunteered to fight for the short-lived Roman Republic which replaced papal rule in February 1849 and fell to French troops after a two-month siege in early July. Garibaldi was one of the commanders in that battle, a battle he knew he could not win. However, it was not so much the doomed siege that moved me as the description of the hero's extraordinary retreat from Rome through central Italy together with his Brazilian wife, Anita, and 4000 volunteers. He had sworn never to surrender to foreign soldiers on Italian soil. Arguably, it was what the hero learned and the example he set on that calamitous 400-mile march that would make his future triumph possible. Hoffstetter was his aide-de-camp. Rarely, reading his account, have I wished so much to live in a different time and another man's shoes. Or boots.

In 2019, 170 years after those events in Rome, I bought a pair of trekking shoes, persuaded my partner Eleonora to do the same and set off, in July, to retrace their steps.

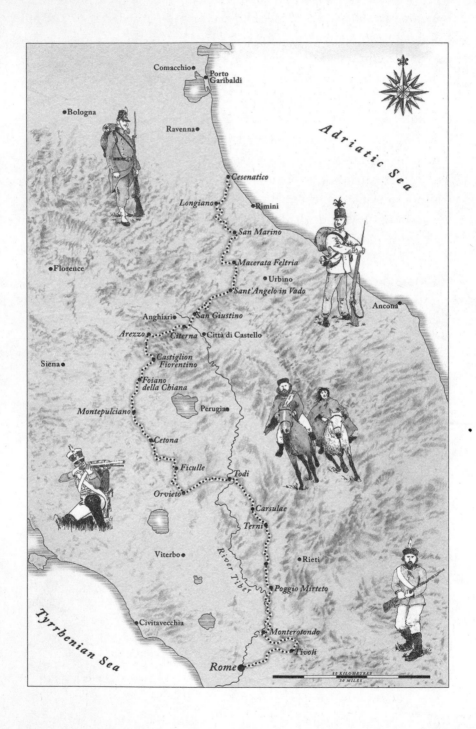

Comacchio

Porto Garibaldi

Bologna

Ravenna

Adriatic Sea

Cesenatico

Longiano

Rimini

San Marino

Macerata Feltria

Florence

Urbino

Sant'Angelo in Vado

Ancona

Anghiari

San Giustino

Arezzo

Citerna

Città di Castello

Castiglion Fiorentino

Siena

Foiano della Chiana

Montepulciano

Perugia

Cetona

Ficulle

Todi

Orvieto

Carsulae

Terni

Viterbo

River Tiber

Rieti

Poggio Mirteto

Civitavecchia

Monterotondo

Rome

Tivoli

Tyrrhenian Sea

50 KILOMETRES
50 MILES

A WORD OF ADVICE

Aside from this principal map, it would be wonderful to pack this book with sketches and routes and plans. It's a tale of movement through a magnificent and varied landscape. A story of flight and pursuit. Cat and mouse. Or rather cats and mice. There are times when you need a sense of where everyone is in relation to this or that geographical feature, the mountains, the rivers, the sea. But maps are expensive and one would need so many. And these days most of us have the most wonderful and versatile maps right in our pockets. So, whenever you feel a little lost, as we often felt very lost along this trip, I suggest you pull out your phone. Each chapter, each day, opens with the names of the two, three or four towns or villages we passed through. Tap the names into Google Maps. Use the satellite view, the terrain view, the street view. I will do my best with the words, but they may be more alive and exciting if you know where we are.

PART ONE

Flight

DAY 1

2 July 1849 – 25 July 2019

Rome, Tivoli – 22 miles

He had forty-eight hours to prepare for the journey. We've been thinking about it for a year and more. Four thousand infantry had to be
organized. Eight hundred cavalry. Mules, carts, munitions, food, medical services. A cannon. He was disappointed, having hoped for 10,000.
We always knew it would be just us two, with our backpacks.

Still, we are leaving from the same place. Piazza San Giovanni in
Laterano, Rome. The white facade of the basilica looms in the dark,
its huge stone apostles silhouetted against the sky. He set out at sunset
and had his men march through the night. No smoking was allowed.
Orders were whispered down the lines. The enemy must not get wind.
Our main enemies, we reckon, at least on this first stretch of the journey, will be traffic and heat. The forecast is for thirty-seven degrees,
so the cool of the night is tempting. But to walk along fast roads in the
dark would be suicidal. So we leave at 4.30 a.m., hoping to cover the
twenty-mile hike before the sun is high.

The square is dead at this hour; San Giovanni isn't lit up. Our selfie
on the steps shows only shadowy masonry behind wired-up smiles.
No one has come to see us off. Garibaldi and his men were cheered on
their way by a big crowd. The American journalist Margaret Fuller
was there. 'Never have I seen a sight so beautiful,' she reported, 'so
romantic and sad ... I saw the wounded ... laden upon their baggage
carts, I saw many youths, born to rich inheritance, carrying in a handkerchief all their worldly goods.'

Garibaldi, Fuller says, was distinguished by a white tunic. Other
observers have him wearing the red shirt he made an emblem of the

struggle for Italian nationhood. And a poncho, relic of his time in South America. Anita, six months pregnant with their fifth child, followed him on horseback at the head of the column. Seeming entirely 'a hero of the Middle Ages' Fuller wrote, Garibaldi 'went upon the parapet and looked upon the road with a spyglass, and, no obstruction being in sight, he turned his face for a moment back upon Rome, then led the way through the gate.'

That was 2 July 1849. One hundred and seventy years later Eleonora and I followed him under the same sixteenth-century arch. Unlike Garibaldi and his men, we knew we had a month's walking ahead of us. Naively, we were thinking of it as a holiday.

A hundred and seventy years and twenty-three days to be precise. We're leaving Rome on 25 July 2019. It's irritating; we would have liked to leave the same day, but I had to be present at a graduation exam in Milan. There was some cause for celebration, though; that had been my last professorial duty. I had resigned my job after twenty years and more. Italian friends sought in every way to dissuade me from doing this. You're taking a big risk, they told me, throwing away a reliable income. On no account must I end up alone and vulnerable, outside organized society.

Garibaldini was the word Italians came to use for the men who volunteered to fight with Garibaldi. It was understood that they were of a type. Soon enough the name escaped its specific historical context and took on the more general sense of someone bold and idealistic, someone who takes risks, perhaps ingenuous, even rash. So even today you can say, 'She's a real *garibaldina*! God knows what will become of her.'

Do Eleonora and I want to think of ourselves as *garibaldini*? Is that why we're here in the empty Roman square at this godforsaken hour with twelve pounds of gear on our backs? Eleonora gave up her steady job a couple of years ago. She wouldn't accept a life of dull constriction. Or not without a fight. The problem with this approach, of course, is that a risk really is a risk. And a fight a fight. You can end up badly. 'The flower of Italian youth were marshalling in that solemn place,' Fuller wrote of the *garibaldini* in Piazza San Giovanni that evening. 'They had been driven from every other spot where they had offered their hearts as bulwarks of Italian Independence; in this last stronghold they had sacrificed hecatombs of their best and bravest in that cause; they must now go or remain prisoners and slaves.'

So the men we're following were traumatized, in denial perhaps; they had lost a war but were refusing to surrender. Others who might have joined them that fateful evening had been locked in their barracks by commanders who thought the project folly. Others simply chose not to. The Lombard Bersaglieri, the most disciplined of Rome's defenders, had promised to be there; only a handful turned up.

Garibaldi had called his rendezvous for six o'clock; now he waited, trusting more would come. But with every minute the risks were growing. At eight o'clock, exactly as he decided enough was enough, a group of Bersaglieri arrived to announce that, after much consideration, no, they weren't coming. We're only in the square to say goodbye to our friends, they said.

Were these renouncers wiser than the *garibaldini*? Margaret Fuller doesn't mention them. She doesn't say that the march began with a sense of disappointment and betrayal. It didn't fit with the romantic picture she was painting for the *New York Tribune*.

Selfie taken, we set off under lamplight through deserted streets, past neglected monuments and shuttered cafés, across dry thirsty grass where destitute men and women turn fitfully on stone benches. The air has that brooding staleness of summer nights in times of drought. To our right the recently renovated Historical Museum of the Sardinian Grenadiers is flying the Italian tricolour, something you would have been imprisoned for under papal rule. Following a long bend, we arrive at the Aurelian Wall, a mass of Roman brickwork dividing a shabby waste of cracked tarmac and faded road markings.

What a tangle of ancient and modern Rome is! In the space of a couple of minutes we pass beneath ancient imperial arches then under a grim concrete viaduct carrying the high-speed rails that brought us into the city from Milan a couple of days ago. Iron fencing, urine smells and sodium lamplight. Stazione Termini is to our left. Needless to say it wasn't here in 1849; Pope Gregory XVI had dubbed railways the work of the devil; the Papal States were among the most backward territories in Europe.

An early bus has RISORGIMENTO glowing up front. Meaning Piazza Risorgimento, not the historical movement. Does any Italian heart warm to the word these days? Three passengers getting off are all immigrants of different ethnicities, the people the minister of internal affairs, right-winger Matteo Salvini, loves to blame for Italy's decline. Before the battle for Rome began in April 1849, Garibaldi caused a stir when he rode into the city with a black man at his side. Uruguayan child of African slaves, Andrea Aguyar would be much admired for his courage in battle, in particular his ability to pull enemies off their horses with his lasso. But he did not join Garibaldi in the piazza on 2 July; he had been killed by cannon fire in Trastevere two days before.

OMIO DANTE GARIBALDI, announces a poster rather mysteriously as we swing into the Via Prenestina. We've quickened our pace now; we need to move fast while it's cool. But what does Dante have to do with Garibaldi? 'For sure it takes courage to unite Italy,' runs the poster's text beneath images of trains and planes, 'but now you can finally buy all your rail, bus and air tickets in the same place. OMIO.' They give a website address. I'm still not sure how this justifies bringing in Dante, but we don't have time to stop and reflect. The sun is rising and through the cluttered, post-industrial cityscape of Rome's eastern suburbs we get a first glimpse of the distant hills in low silhouette, tinged with red. Garibaldi knew he had to be on those slopes by dawn.

But how did this all begin? To understand where we'll be heading in the next few weeks, we need to know where the people we are following were coming from.

The city of Rome and the territory then known as the Papal States, stretching north to Bologna and Ferrara, east to Ancona on the Adriatic coast and south to Terracina, declared itself a republic on 9 February 1849. As such it was the last of the ephemeral revolutionary states that emerged across Europe from the liberal uprisings of 1848. The hope was to make Rome the capital of a united Italy, since at the time the country was seriously fragmented and largely governed by foreign or despotic powers.

The road to this republican declaration was complicated. In 1846 the newly elected Pope Pius IX had looked favourably on the movement for national unity, even encouraging patriots to think of him as a future Italian monarch and granting his subjects a constitution in March 1848. This allowed for an elected chamber of deputies and for government ministers who would not be priests but competent laymen, a move that infuriated Rome's bishops and cardinals. When Pius further allowed a hybrid army of papal troops and patriotic volunteers to go north to support the Piedmontese in their attempt to liberate Lombardy and the Veneto from the Austrians, there was a surge of excitement. Forty thousand men volunteered. *Viva Pio Nono! Viva l'Italia! Viva l'unione! Libertà!* was their battle cry.

But a little freedom whets the appetite for more. Frightened by the clamour for further reform, Pius grew nervous, then openly hostile. He withdrew support for the war against Austria and tried to put a lid on the new chamber of deputies, appointing a shrewdly conservative ex-diplomat, Pellegrino Rossi, as his prime minister. Unpopular with reactionaries and reformers alike, Rossi was assassinated in November 1848, and Pius fled the city for the protection of the Kingdom of Naples.

Nobody knew what to do. Having set up his court in exile just south of the border in the coastal town of Gaeta, the Pope declared the government of Rome illegal but did nothing to replace it. The chamber of deputies sent envoys begging him to return and resume his papacy. They promised to be loyal; but he refused and after a month-long stand-off the chamber called for the election of a constituent assembly to decide the future shape of the state's institutions. On 9 February the new assembly declared the end of the Pope's temporal rule and the establishment of a republic. In response Pius called on four Catholic powers – Austria, France, Spain and Naples – to recover his realm by force.

Given that only the previous June the Austrians had had to fight a papal army in alliance with Piedmont, this was quite a turnaround. But it suited Austria fine. They had already defeated the Piedmontese

7

and retaken Lombardy and all of the Veneto but for Venice. These territories were part of their empire. On 18 April, only four days after the Pope's appeal, Austrian imperial troops crossed the border from the Veneto and took the papal town of Ferrara. They then proceeded to lay siege first to Bologna, then Ancona, bombarding the two towns into submission over many days with considerable loss of life. Meantime, in early March, Giuseppe Mazzini, the great ideologue of Italian unity and republicanism, left his place of exile in London, came to Rome and at once told the constituent assembly, 'After the Rome of the Emperors, after the Rome of the Popes, will come the Rome of the People ... We may have to wage a holy war against the only enemy that threatens us, Austria. But we will fight it, and we will win.'

Mazzini was wrong on various counts. On 24 April a French army disembarked at Civitavecchia, Rome's port, fifty miles to the northwest of the city. On 29 April a Spanish army landed sixty miles to the south. The Neapolitan army was also mobilizing. So much for one enemy. In response, the republic formed an emergency triumvirate, headed by Mazzini. Thousands of patriots had been gathering to defend the city. They needed to be organized, and what military protection they could offer would have to be integrated with the new state's diplomacy. All this would be the task of Mazzini, who had no military or diplomatic experience.

By far the most prominent of the new arrivals was Giuseppe Garibaldi. Born in 1807, a seaman by trade, sentenced to death in 1834 by the Piedmontese authorities for insurrection, Garibaldi had spent many years in exile in Brazil and Uruguay, where he established a reputation as a courageous and effective soldier for liberal causes. He had dedicated his life, he said, to freeing people from oppression. But the cause he cared for most was Italy. Excited by news of revolutions in Europe and reassured by a Piedmontese amnesty for those previously convicted of political crimes, Garibaldi returned to Italy with sixty of his comrades in June 1848. He at once offered his assistance to the Piedmontese king, who was fighting the Austrians in Lombardy, but was turned down. He then fought briefly for the independent Republic of Milan, which soon collapsed.

Wandering around central Italy and recruiting volunteers in the hope of playing a role in the liberation of his country, he was in Ravenna in November 1848 when news came that the Pope had fled Rome. He hurried south and spent some months in Rieti, forty miles north-east of the city, training 1200 men whom he called the First Italian Legion. Not the Piedmontese, the Milanese or the Venetian, but the Italian. It was an important signal.

Let's take a breath and think about this. Returning to his country after fourteen years away, with no paymaster or supporting political organization, a man moves from town to town openly inviting people to join his private army and fight for a cause. He then has to feed those men, arm them, find uniforms for them and places to sleep, train them and organize them. The fact that such a hothead isn't immediately arrested suggests a certain recognition that his cause is legitimate. Or it could mean the country is sinking into anarchy.

The further fact that this man, who suffers from frequent bouts of malaria and paralyzing attacks of rheumatism, nevertheless persists in these illegal recruiting activities even after certain towns in Tuscany and Emilia force him to move on and papal troops are sent to Bologna to deter him, suggests a deep personal need to be doing what he is doing. Garibaldi cannot imagine accepting life without a united Italy. Or more generally without a cause. Constantly on the move, offering his services right and left, he appears to be yearning for a home, a community where he can settle. But before he can settle anywhere, that place must be free.

This obsession with freedom is the key to understanding Garibaldi. Freedom from foreign powers dictating the laws of your country, freedom from religious institutions telling you how to behave or simply social conventions telling you how to dress. Garibaldi always dressed and wore his hair and beard absolutely as he wanted, with no regard for etiquette or common practice. Ponchos, sombreros, red shirts, white tunics, hats of many kinds: he wore what took his fancy or would send out the message he wanted to send. And when, aged thirty-two, sailing into the Brazilian port of Laguna, he had focused his telescope on a seventeen-year-old girl standing on the shore, he knew at once he wanted her. Fortunately, when they met, she wanted him too. Anita. That she was married was not an obstacle. She left her family and went with him, bore his children, made his wars her wars, fought beside him in the thick of battle, was imprisoned and escaped, rode through forests with her newborn son in her arms. How could Eleonora and I help but admire their boldness? We too are an unconventional couple in our way; the age difference between us is exactly twice that between Garibaldi and Anita. We've faced a few disapproving frowns.

This is the secret of Garibaldi's charisma. He roused people to fight for a specific political cause, Italy, but the deeper cause was freedom. A freedom he embodied. 'I couldn't resist him' was the typical comment of one young man whose life was changed when he heard Garibaldi speak. Thousands felt this. 'We all worshipped him, we could not help it.'

Yet, at first, the Roman Republic did not want him. Mazzini had delegated the organization of the defence to Carlo Pisacane, an ex-soldier from the Neapolitan army. Garibaldi's men were a rabble, Pisacane thought. Tanned, dirty, long-haired, bearded. Their so-called uniforms were ridiculous. Their officers were chosen on the basis of courage and performance, with no regard to education or class. Their cavalrymen saddled and fed their own horses, like brigands or cowboys. They could stay outside Rome and defend the provinces, Pisacane decided.

But as the French army, 7000 strong, approached the city, a new minister of war was appointed. Giuseppe Avezzana had fought in the Napoleonic wars and in Mexico. He summoned Garibaldi at once. The First Italian Legion marched into town through Porta Maggiore on 27 April with Garibaldi on a white horse. 'I had been dreaming of this since childhood,' he later wrote. Andrea Aguyar was at his side. Behind them marched 1500 men sporting a bizarre assortment of military cast-offs, extravagant caps and hats, unlikely weapons. The Romans were thrilled. At once, in the teeth of etiquette and convention, it was understood that Garibaldi was the city's hope.

Avezzana assigned the new arrival the defence of the Colle del Gianicolo above Porta San Pancrazio, on the city's western side. It was a crucial vantage point. Anyone controlling the hill could bombard the city at will. Garibaldi had just two days to examine the area. He realized at once that the three or four large villas outside and above the city walls would be decisive and had them occupied. He now had 2500 men, and was allotted a reserve of another 1800. In all, Rome had some 9000 soldiers to throw into the battle, but they were thinly spread around the city's many gates and walls.

The French attacked on the morning of 30 April, expecting a stroll. They chose a gate slightly to the north of Garibaldi's position, Porta Pertusa, not realizing it had been walled up years before. Forced to move along and beneath the walls to the next gate, they were surprised to find themselves under heavy musket fire. Garibaldi didn't wait for the enemy to come to him; he used the men he had placed outside the walls in the villas to encircle the French and attack. For many of his volunteers it was their first fight. The French were experienced and organized. Fighting in gardens and vineyards, they pushed the Italians back and took two of the key villas. Garibaldi called in his reserves and led a cavalry charge himself. The villas were retaken. After hours of sporadic fighting, the French fell back. They had lost about 500 men, dead or wounded. The Italians 200. There were 365 French prisoners. Garibaldi himself took a bullet wound in his side that would cause him much pain in the months to come.

This was the first time Italian volunteers had defeated a professional army in the field. The Romans were euphoric. Support for the republic intensified. All over Europe, politicians and diplomats were astonished. But Garibaldi saw it as a missed opportunity. He felt he could have chased the French all the way back to the sea. Mazzini stopped him. France was a republic, he insisted. And now that the French had seen the Romans were ready to fight, they surely wouldn't want to destroy a fellow republic to bring back a despotic pope. The 365 prisoners were well treated and released.

But already a Neapolitan army, 12,000 strong, was approaching Rome from the south-east. On 5 May Garibaldi was sent to deal with it, taking his own Legion and the Lombard Bersaglieri, a group of middle-class student volunteers from Milan, led by the charismatic, twenty-three-year-old Luciano Manara who had fought courageously in the defence of Milan the previous year. Garibaldi zigzagged this way and that, spreading false rumours as to his intentions. On 9 May he took up positions on the high ground above Palestrina, twenty-five miles outside Rome. The Neapolitans attacked; initially they made progress, but after three hours of intense fighting they were beaten back and put to flight. Garibaldi was ordered not to chase them; he must return at once to the city.

Mazzini had begun to fear the French might attack again after all. Instead they asked for a truce. Delighted, Mazzini believed they now planned to negotiate a peaceful solution. In fact, they were waiting for reinforcements that would bring the army up to 30,000 men, equipped with modern siege artillery. Exploiting this lull, on 16 May the republic's army was sent out to attack the Neapolitans again. Some 8000 men, including Garibaldi and his Legion, were placed under Commander in Chief Pietro Roselli, an ex-major in the papal army. Roselli had the advantage of being a native Roman. He had never seen battle.

Roselli followed the military manual, aiming to bring all his forces to bear on the enemy simultaneously. Given this intention, it was a mistake to send Garibaldi ahead as advance guard. Garibaldi's notion of war was to be in perpetual motion, forcing the enemy to guess, testing his flexibility, his communications, his awareness of the territory, never allowing him to settle. When he came into contact with the Neapolitans in Velletri and sensed they weren't in good spirits, he ordered an attack and called on Roselli to join him as soon as possible.

Once again initial failure was followed by a successful charge of the reserves, with Garibaldi at their head. But this time, as he tried to stop the disorderly retreat of his own advance cavalry, Garibaldi was overwhelmed and went down 'in a heap of men and fallen horses'. The Neapolitans were all around with their bayonets and sabres. Garibaldi was saved by his reserves. Mostly adolescent boys. Afterwards, it was some time before he could get to his feet 'feeling arms and legs to check if anything was broken'.

The Neapolitans retreated into the town of Velletri, but the main body of the Roman army didn't show up to finish the job. Roselli said his men couldn't move without food supplies. Garibaldi had disobeyed orders, he complained. They would attack the Neapolitans the next morning. But the next morning Velletri was deserted. The Neapolitans had fled in the night.

The French had now built up their forces around Rome. Before leaving, Garibaldi had suggested that the villas on the Gianicolo be fortified with trenches and defensive walls. On return he found nothing had been done. On 26 May, Mazzini asked him his opinion of their chances of defending the city. Garibaldi replied aggressively: he could only serve the war effort, he said, as a dictator with unlimited powers or as a common soldier. 'You choose.' Mazzini called his bluff, and Garibaldi carried on as before: a popular hero, but without overall command, always criticized, always called on in a crisis.

General Oudinot, leading the French forces, announced that the truce would end on 4 June, allowing two days for French citizens in Rome to leave. In fact he attacked the key position of Villa Corsini on the night between 2 and 3 June. Roselli had inspected the outpost earlier the same evening, assuring its defenders that no action should be expected for another day at least. The main body of the army was billeted below, in the town, on the other side of the Tiber, with many of its officers sleeping in private houses and unable to respond swiftly. Garibaldi himself was in Trastevere, in serious pain from his wound of a month before. He would wake to one of the worst days in his life.

The problem was Villa Corsini itself. Built right on the top of the hill, it had been designed to defend itself against an attack from the city, not the surrounding countryside. High stone walls channelled any attack uphill towards a narrow gate with the villa right behind. On the other side there was a regular perimeter wall around the extensive grounds. The French were able to get right up to that wall under cover of darkness, blow a hole in it, occupy all the vineyards and gardens and take the villa almost without a fight.

Alerted at 3 a.m., Garibaldi gathered what forces he could. He knew it was crucial to retake the house and hilltop before the French could set up their artillery and start pounding the city walls below. He considered a flanking operation, but that meant going around the villa's wall with the French already in place behind. He decided on a head-on assault. It was 5 a.m. The men raced uphill towards the gate with no cover from heavy gunfire.

Had Garibaldi's attack simply failed, that would very likely have been the end of it. But the villa was taken, albeit at the expense of heavy losses. Taken, but impossible to hold. The French had their cannons. They had overwhelming numbers and plenty of cover. The Roman reserves hadn't yet arrived. The villa was lost again. The reserves arrived. It was won again, but then lost again, then won again. Lost again. Each time, throughout the long hot day, hundreds of men died. But the prize was the war itself. Once the French were allowed to consolidate the game would be up.

Garibaldi had repeatedly told Mazzini that Rome's volunteer army would be far more effective operating outside the city. He believed in momentum. One must take the initiative. Trapped within the ancient walls, they would be surrounded and starved. Mazzini, on the other hand, believed in the symbolic value of Rome, the Eternal City, and the need for martyrs to create a national myth. The besieged city, he thought, would become an object of pathos and admiration for civilized Europe, a glorious bloodbath. He was right. And on 3 June Garibaldi, in desperation, gave him that bloodbath. When night fell the army had lost a thousand men, including many of its finest officers. The French held the villa, the hilltop, the vantage point overlooking the city. They were in control.

The day before we set out on our walk, Eleonora and I visited the battlefield. You're struck at once by how small the area is; a grassy slope perhaps three hundred yards long at the southern edge of the Gianicolo park, with Porta San Pancrazio, where Garibaldi's men gathered, at the bottom, and the Villa Corsini, destroyed in the battle, at the top. A monumental arch has now replaced it. The place is called Piazzale dei Ragazzi di 1849.

We stood at the top and looked west over the shimmering city, vast and vulnerable beneath us. It was a hot Roman day with tourists all around, eating ice creams and enjoying the shade of the elegant umbrella pines. Back at the bottom of the slope, in the wall of another villa, you can still see, and touch, a black French cannonball embedded in the masonry. Moving on into the Gianicolo, a long path is lined with white busts sitting on low plinths. Hundreds of them. They are the men who fought. Engraved on the low wall of the parapet to the right, in capital letters, stretching for yards and yards, is the text of the Constitution of the Roman Republic. SOVEREIGNTY IS THE ETERNAL RIGHT OF THE PEOPLE, it begins.

One bust shows a handsome, earnest young man, his head turning slightly to one side above the high collar of his uniform. Goffredo Mameli was the poet who wrote Italy's national anthem, 'Fratelli d'Italia'. He was wounded on 3 June and died after a month of agony, aged twenty-one. Apparently his nurse read Dickens to him to pass the painful hours. *Oliver Twist.*

Close to the busts is a small statue of a bare-chested twelve-year-old boy, Righetto. The French cannonballs were in fact small bombs, with burning fuses designed to explode shortly after impact. The republic, short of munitions, offered a reward to anyone who managed to recover an unexploded cannonball. Women and children rushed to the falling bombs with damp cloths to extinguish the fuses. Which is how Righetto met his end, and became a symbol of civilian resistance.

Righetto died on 29 June, more than three weeks after the battle for Villa Corsini. It had seemed Rome must fall at once, but if nothing else the mad assaults to retake the villa gave the defenders time to consolidate their positions below. Paradoxically, the terrible losses increased rather than diminished their resolve. And though Garibaldi's critics would always point to his failure on 3 June, he was more popular than ever among the soldiers and people. He had fought in the thick of it himself. The goal had seemed possible. The men believed in their cause. Morale was surprisingly high.

For four hot weeks the defenders hung on as the French pounded the walls and the city and kept up constant sniper fire on the Roman defences. Many artworks were destroyed, many civilians killed. In his refuge in Gaeta the Pope was furious about the delay, convinced that the French were not trying hard enough. General Oudinot urged

Mazzini to surrender, to avoid more loss of life. He did not want to go down as the man who had destroyed Rome. Mazzini insisted they would fight to the last man.

Meantime, the military leaders argued. Pisacane wanted Garibaldi to encircle the French in order to recover Villa Corsini. He refused. He felt it was impossible. He proposed to take a thousand men out of the city and move at will, attacking the French wherever it made sense. This Roselli would not allow. On 21 June the French made a first breach in the outer defensive wall and moved forward. This time Garibaldi refused to try to push them back. It would be another massacre. Again and again he had to change headquarters when buildings collapsed under cannon fire. The city was crumbling around them. Ironically, on 28 June the uniforms that Mazzini and Pisacane had insisted the men of his Legion must wear were finally delivered. Garibaldi had chosen simple red shirts, similar to those he had used years ago in the siege of Montevideo. On that occasion he had come across a shipment of red cloth intended for abattoir workers. The red hid the blood.

On 29 June the French blasted through the second line of defences. This time Garibaldi led a determined counter-attack. He fought 'like Leonidas at Thermopylae', remembered the historian Candido Augusto Vecchi, who battled beside him. Luciano Manara was killed. Andrea Aguyar was killed. The situation was hopeless. At midday on 30 June a truce was arranged. Meeting in the Capitol, the republic's constituent assembly debated whether to surrender or fight on. They summoned Garibaldi for his opinion. He arrived direct from the battle line, soaked in sweat, plastered with dust. Mazzini was urging that they throw up barricades and fight in the streets. Garibaldi told them the French would simply use their cannons and destroy everything; instead the army should break out of the city and take to the hills. Again Roselli would not allow this; not unreasonably, he observed that the army was demoralized and exhausted. How could they take the war to the countryside? Eventually the assembly agreed 'to cease a defence that has become impossible, but nevertheless to remain in its place'. Mazzini, disgusted, resigned.

The situation was confusing. The assembly hadn't actually surrendered, nor had the government resigned. Roselli and Garibaldi retained their commands; any action they took on behalf of the republic would be legitimate. On the other hand, negotiations were under way to allow the French to enter the city. During these hectic hours, the American chargé d'affaires sought out Garibaldi to offer him safe passage to New York. He declined. Instead, he announced that he would speak to the people on the morning of 2 July in St Peter's Square. The Dutch painter Jan Philip Koelman recalled the scene.

In the midst of the throng surging into the piazza we saw the black feather of Garibaldi's cap. His officers were lost in the crowd and he was surrounded by civilians, many women, pressing all around him. Only slowly and with great effort did he reach the Egyptian obelisk in the centre of the square. There he stopped and turned his horse, and when his men had gathered round him, he raised his hand to stop the cheering. After a few moments a deep silence fell on the crowd.

Garibaldi kept it brief. 'The fortune that has abandoned us today will smile on us tomorrow. I am going out from Rome. Anyone wishing to fight on against the foreigner should come with me. I offer neither pay, nor quarters, nor food; I offer hunger, thirst, forced marches and all the perils of war. Let him who loves his country in his heart and not just with his lips, follow me.'

A hundred and seventy years late for the appointment, Eleonora and I are doing just that: following. Do we love the country? In our hearts? I've been here forty years, yet remain residually English. Eleonora is from Taranto, Puglia, a part of Italy many feel gained nothing from unification. On the other hand, I've never had any desire to go back to England, and she's never felt tempted to join the tens of thousands of young Italians who have left the country in this last decade of economic decline. So I think we do love it, yes.

Certainly we love the Blu Bar, which appears towards 7 a.m. in the suburban wasteland just before the Grande Raccordo Anulare, the great circular road that marks the end of the city. Garibaldi's men walked non-stop through the night. We've been going two and a half hours and are hungry and thirsty and discouraged by heavy traffic, gritty streets and piles of uncollected rubbish.

But we can't complain. The burly proprietor of the Blu Bar swiftly produces two tall glasses of freshly squeezed orange juice, creamy cappuccinos and plump croissants. Bringing them outside on a tray, he lays them before us on a white plastic tabletop with the air of a butler serving a lord. His other clients are all van drivers and factory workers, in a hurry to start the day. No one else is sitting down. Yet he seems pleased to take the time to squeeze our oranges and bring our tray to the table. At no extra cost. Only when he sees our shiny new backpacks and the map we've spread on the table does he allow himself a quizzical smile. What in God's name are two hikers doing in a place like this?

It's a fair question. The fact is that though we know where Garibaldi went, we don't know how he got there. Two of his officers, Egidio Ruggeri and Gustav von Hoffstetter, kept diaries of the march and published accounts in the 1850s. In 1899 the patriot Raffaele Belluzzi collated their versions with details gleaned from letters, unpublished manuscripts and interviews with surviving witnesses. In 1907 George Macaulay Trevelyan added information from other correspondents in his book *Garibaldi's Defence of the Roman Republic*. But there's no agreement on the route the men took, particularly in the first two days, and this is very likely because Garibaldi's main concern was to fool everyone as to where he was going.

The French had penetrated Rome from the west, the side nearest the sea. Leaving from Porta San Giovanni, Garibaldi gave the impression he was heading south, yet the following morning his men would be settling down outside the hilltop town of Tivoli, twenty miles due east. No one is sure where they changed direction. Ruggeri says they quickly circled through the town to the Via Tiburtina, which runs straight out to Tivoli. Belluzzi believes they marched south-east to the Alban Hills and the small town of Zagarolo, fourteen miles south of Tivoli, and only then turned north. Trevelyan agrees, since this is the only way, he claims, they could have fooled the French. But that would mean, I calculate, a march of thirty-two miles, and Hoffstetter, who had professional military training, observes that 'while a good walker can keep up a speed of three miles an hour, a marching column of soldiers, whether by night or in the torrid heat of the day, with the dreadful dust of the road, in general won't do more than two miles an hour'. On this occasion they marched for ten hours. So twenty miles at most.

I have spent months thinking about this. One day it dawns on me that Hoffstetter's miles might not be my miles. Sure enough, I discover there is, or was, an Italian mile which amounts to 1852 metres or 2025 yards. That means Hoffstetter's two miles an hour would actually be 4050/1760 yards = 2.3 English miles, so that ten hours walking (non-stop!) becomes 23 miles. But that still isn't 32 miles.

Why am I so taken by this idea of walking *exactly* the route they took? Isn't this a form of constriction, the opposite of the freedom Garibaldi stood for? The more you look at a book of history, the more you realize how many gaps there are, how much is being glossed over. Narrative in general is a gloss, as every novelist knows. For example, historians agree that the *garibaldini* left Rome around nine in the evening and arrived in Tivoli at seven the following morning, but since in the nineteenth century people didn't move clocks forward in summer time, wouldn't that have been ten in the evening and eight in the morning our time? Then none of the books I have read on the Roman Republic mentions the size of Rome's population at the time, which I finally discovered was a mere 170,000 in 1848, as compared to today's 2,900,000. So the *garibaldini* would have been out of town in a matter of minutes, whereas we're still walking through a suburban haze of carbon monoxide after two and a half hours.

You can't reconstruct the past. We would like to walk to Tivoli through Zagarolo, but we know we'd never manage thirty-two miles on our first day in a temperature of thirty-seven degrees. We've done some training in recent weeks, mainly in the flat country south of Milan, but we've never walked more than twenty miles. After much fussing, we decide that since our sources disagree, we're free to take any route that makes sense. For example, the Via Tiburtina, the short-est. At least we know the Tiburtina was already there the night of 2 July 1849. It's been there since 286 BC.

But does this route make sense? No one leaves Rome on foot these days, that's the truth. There are no footpaths and only short stretches of cycle track. Once out of the centre, there are no pavements. As well as our paper maps, we've invested in the 'professional' version of a path-finding app that seeks out every possible pedestrian route. But sitting in the Blu Bar just a hundred yards from the sign that has ROMA with a red slash through it, our app can't find anything pedestrian-friendly.

Packs on our backs again, the capital's rush hour is upon us. In the underpass beneath the Grande Raccordo there's barely space to walk between a faded white line and the wall. Headlights rush towards you. Trucks rumble. It's frightening and certainly far more dangerous than marching through the countryside 170 years ago. Then comes a tangle of slipways and connecting arteries as we work our way north towards the Tiburtina. We move circumspectly, pressed against crash barriers. By eight, the sun is warm. We're behind schedule. Brambles stretch out from behind the crash barriers to pluck at arms and ankles. We're walking on detritus: broken glass, road kill, syringes and plastic; plas-tic in every shape and form.

On the approach to an autostrada overpass we meet some walkers coming the other way, the first and last we'll see all day. They're Gyp-sies, another group of people Minister Salvini loves to hate. Enviably relaxed, they advance in single file, the women in their long dresses and headscarves, the men heavily moustached. Passing by, they salute us with wry smiles, but the last in the line, a young boy stops. 'You be careful,' he says. 'It's dangerous here.'

To walk, it seems, is to shed your class, to strike new alliances.

As if determined to prove its worth, our app begins to suggest off-road alternatives, through the scrub of an autostrada embankment for example, or along the fence by a railway line. For almost half a mile we force our way between barbed wire and prickly shrubs. I begin to wonder when Eleonora will rebel. She'll tell me the whole project is crazy and we'll give up before lunch.

Finally, we arrive at the Tiburtina where it crosses a small place called Setteville. Not seven villas, as the name would suggest, but rows of ten-storey red-brick blocks over a ribbon of pizzerias, hardware stores and low-cost supermarkets. We follow the Tiburtina to the end of the high street and realize it's hopeless. The 2000-year-old route is now a thin strip of tarmac thundering with heavy commercial traffic.

As we stand there staring, a passing driver honks at Eleonora and waves his hand out of the window in an unequivocal gesture. The third in an hour.

Is this the moment to take a bus? Eleonora has quickly established herself as the expert with the app. She coaxes it into proposing a detour: a cycle track to the north followed by a maze of minor roads. It adds four miles to the hike. We've been walking five hours. We drink some water, spread more sun cream on arms and legs, then, finally, the circumstances offer a little fun.

The road we're walking down is called Via G. Leopardi. It's a tic the Italians have, to put celebrated names on road signs in exactly the way names are written in school registers or legal documents. Via D. Alighieri. Viale M. Buonarotti. High culture and bureaucracy. It always makes us laugh. I have a photo of Eleonora standing by G. Leopardi – our favourite poet – among weeds and broken asphalt, sun powering down on her hat, and she's smiling broadly, utterly confident of our success. A real *garibaldina*. Anita, Ruggeri writes of Garibaldi's wife, always tried to cheer the men up, however bad things got. 'Better times will come,' she would tell them.

But not yet. When we get to the cycle track, it's enclosed between the crash barrier of another busy road and a tall fence; we have traffic racing to our left and scorched fields of harvested corn to our right. The fields are beautiful to look at but inaccessible. At no point in an hour and more's walking is there any sign of a track or footpath or any break in the fence. We pass just one cyclist, so amazed to see us he stops to talk and tells us that he carries a pair of secateurs with him in case of brambles.

Here's an irony then. We are walking through the political reality that so many patriots in the 1800s yearned for, a free united Italy.

We'll have no borders to cross in our long hike through the country. We won't have to show our papers to foreign soldiers or pay duties at customs posts. Yet the freedom to walk, or to walk safely, is gone. At least on the outskirts of Rome. And our first attempt to get close to the experience of the *garibaldini* has actually taken us away from them. Plunging my forearms in cold water in the bathroom of a petrol station, I realize I haven't thought of their march for an hour or more.

Tivoli, Hoffstetter writes, is 'surrounded by woods' and 'delightful waterfalls'. 'The sacred groves of ancient times,' he adds. He was an educated man. At 7 a.m., alerted in the early hours by an advance party of cavalry, the good citizens came out of the town to greet the tired soldiers as they approached, bringing bread, meat and wine in abundance. I imagine horses galloping through the night, clattering on cobbles at the city gates, soldiers banging on doors to wake people up. Again, when you start to picture things, you realize how much has been glossed over. Were the people of Tivoli really happy to be woken and asked to rustle up a meal for getting on for 5000 men? Hoffstetter insists they were. In any event, campfires were lit and soon the men were cooking and eating. Then they slept in the shade of a wood below the city walls while Garibaldi and his staff set about organizing the infantry into two legions of 1800 men, each legion then being divided into three cohorts and each cohort into six centuries. Officers were allotted, groups merged and divided. The problem was that, aside from his own soldiers in the First Legion, Garibaldi had little idea who had chosen to come with him or what he could expect of them. Counting them in the early morning beneath the walls of Tivoli, it became clear there had already been scores of desertions. Many had sneaked off in the dark.

How I sympathize! With the sun at its zenith, we are still zigzagging across the torrid plain in the early afternoon, past sand pits and stone quarries, over rivers reduced to trickles, taking occasional refuge under a fig tree. The landscape is distinctive here. Moving east out of Rome the flat land ahead of you ends in a solid north–south line of dark green hills. To your right is a scorched expanse of grassland and suburban sprawl. But to the left, the north, three burned brown hills rise abruptly from the plain. Each with a town on top. Monterotondo, Mentana, Montecelio. At a distance, there's something shabbily exotic about them. Not picturesque but grittily real, in a very foreign way. And they preside, somehow, these conical hills, over our long walk, as if we will never quite get beyond them, until at last we hit the steep slope up to Tivoli.

Closing the day's walk with a sharp climb will be a constant in the coming weeks. The towns of central Italy are mostly atop hills. Garibaldi sought them out for their defensive potential. A fast stream rushes down the approach we've taken. It's channelled in a conduit against a stone wall, lively, bubbling water that invites you to take your shoes off and dip your burning feet into its freshness. Except there's no shade to stop in. And the sun is frightening now. We're in difficulty. I'm feeling quite dazed and strangely detached when finally we pass through the city gate into the relative cool of Tivoli's narrow streets, panting for breath, heart racing from the climb. But strangely elated too. And even more so when we discover *he* is there to greet us. Yes, a small be-hatted bust, no doubt long removed from some more prominent position, has been hidden away behind railings among children's swings and slides in the public gardens. Uncannily, we spy it at once – Garibaldi! – and at once the flowing hair, deep-set eyes and thick beard conjure up that mood of stern serenity you find in so many statues of the hero. Across the road, on the wall of a deconsecrated church, a plaque reads:

Terror of his Enemies,
Admiration of the People,
Garibaldi rested here with his brave men,
3 July 1849.

We rested too. We found our B & B, gave up trying to explain to the logorrheic landlady that we had walked from Rome – too bizarre an idea for her to cope with – and listened patiently to interminable instructions for parking a hypothetical car. I wondered how she could not see the pitiful state we were in, clothes sodden with sweat, skin grimed and scratched.

'Since we're walking again tomorrow,' Eleonora interrupted an equally interminable explanation of breakfast procedures, 'we'll be leaving around 5 a.m., so we won't be here to eat.'

The good lady struggled with this.

'Perhaps you could leave something on a tray,' Eleonora proposed.

Later, under an icy shower, examining sore toes and sunburn, we learned what the history books do not tell you, that the first duty of the soldier is to look after his body for the battle to come. Or her body. I needed to lance a blister; Eleonora had sores on her collarbones where the straps of her pack rubbed. '*Coraggio*,' she announced. 'We knew this would be the toughest day.'

Tivoli

Dump the carts and switch to mules. This was Garibaldi's decision, Hoffstetter tells us, while mulling things over in Tivoli. Only as the days went by would I realize how profoundly that choice would shape our summer.

But who was Gustav von Hoffstetter? It's hardly an Italian name. We need to get to know the people we'll be travelling with.

Born in 1818 in Bavaria (thirty-one, then, at the time of our expedition), Hoffstetter had attended the military academy in Munich, served in the Swiss army in 1847 and seen action on the winning side in the Swiss civil war of that year. In 1848 he had thrown his professional career to the wind, taking the side of liberal revolutionaries in southern Germany. The liberals were crushed and Gustav forced to flee, first back to Switzerland, then Italy.

Once in Rome, he offered his military expertise to the republican cause and spent May and June as assistant to Luciano Manara. When Garibaldi asked Manara to become his aide-de-camp, Hoffstetter was part of the package, and when Manara was killed on 30 June during the last battle of the siege, Garibaldi asked Hoffstetter to replace him.

Why? The German brought traditional military know-how and organizational skills into the volunteer mix. He was reliable. He knew how to secure a camp, how to seal off a town, how to use cavalry to cover the flanks of a marching column. He never forgot the men's need for food and water and somewhere to sleep. He was always thinking ahead, sharing his ideas, making proposals. Garibaldi would listen to him, then do something quite different. But not always. And when the General did what he proposed, Gustav was thrilled.

But this wasn't just a military mind. Hoffstetter was a romantic too, ready to go into raptures over a fine landscape or gloomy ruin. Here he is on arrival in Rome.

The object of my first outing was the Capitoline Hill. What a change to be suddenly transported from the hubbub of military assemblies and the variety of 19th century city clothes to the ruins and few remaining columns of this venerable shrine of a great people! Even in their decay, those ruins are proud, magnificent. In the calm, quiet evening, I felt as though the old ghosts of Rome were walking among the fallen stones in their togas, excited to hear that their oppressed descendants had finally taken up arms and rebelled.

Again and again along our walk, as Eleonora and I look back at the *garibaldini* who went before us, we will find that they were looking back at others. And those others perhaps looked back at others again. We each have our day and measure ourselves against a past as alluring as it is elusive.

Hoffstetter's romanticism, however, didn't ignore modern Rome and in particular the city's women. 'Come evening,' he tells us, 'the streets fill with people, and I would stroll up and down the *corso* admiring the noble faces and splendid shapes of the Roman women.' It wouldn't have been proper of him to tell us how much he got to know those women, but here's a diary entry from the early days of the siege.

Today two girls turned up, eager to join the Legion (already 5 or 6 have enrolled and distinguished themselves for their courage in battle). One, Carolina, was very shapely, but they were both too delicate to handle a rifle; so we proposed they help with catering at Headquarters. We had them dressed up in fine fashion, officially enrolled and given a salary, their main job being to prepare a good black coffee every morning and make sure there was a constant supply of cigars. For a while all went well, but then Carolina, who had seemed so submissive, turned out to be quite dangerous. Manara fired both of them, not wanting to set a bad example at headquarters.

Dangerous to whom? Gustav doesn't explain, but it's interesting he remembers, and repeats, only the 'shapely' girl's name. Carolina.

What most endears me to the German, though, is his prickliness about his accent when speaking Italian. He hates to be criticized. On 9 June, as the siege was beginning to bite, Manara organized an evening sortie to unsettle the French cannon positions. Hoffstetter was to be in charge and had spent many hours devising a complex two-pronged attack. However, at lunch – and they were eating well so as to have plenty of energy for the battle – a junior officer passed a comment about his Italian. Everyone laughed. The German observed that it was hardly polite to make fun of a foreigner who was risking his life for their cause. They kept laughing. Hoffstetter stalked off without his coffee. Worried about bad blood between the men, Manara removed the German from his command. Without him, the attack was botched.

I too am sensitive about my accent. Over the years Eleonora and I have noticed that when we order drinks in certain cafés, the price will be higher if I do the ordering and the barman picks up my foreignness. Which was why, in Tivoli, when we finally found the energy to get off the bed and go out and eat something, it was she who ordered for us both at a *tavola calda* – tomatoes stuffed with rice and flavoured with garlic, mint and basil, a Roman speciality, for which we paid an extremely modest price. Small victories.

I have to confess I had bad thoughts about Italy in Tivoli. And about our trip. The small town is a mix of narrow streets and steep steps – Rome's antiquity in miniature – then more modern, open, nondescript areas, for which we must thank some heavy Allied bombing in 1944.

Overall, the feeling is of a place imperfectly spruced up for tourists, entirely focused on marketing its key assets, those wonderful villas and waterfalls.

Away from the central pedestrian areas, the traffic is oppressive and the road king. We had imagined ourselves exploring the town through the afternoon and evening, visiting its picturesque castle, moving at ease through graceful piazzas and shaded gardens. In the event, footsore as we are, our curiosity takes us no further than Piazza Garibaldi, which turns out to be a deserted, sun-scorched expanse dominated by a twisting arch of steel and bronze some twenty feet high by sixty long. A plaque tells us that this is THE ARCH OF THE FOUNDING FATHERS, made in 2009 by the sculptor Arnaldo Pomodoro.

Contemplating this incongruous structure, you wonder if anyone passing by is ever prompted to think of the seventy-five founding fathers who wrote Italy's post-war constitution. Why should they be? Why isn't the statue of Garibaldi in Piazza Garibaldi?

'I'm beginning to worry about our walk,' I tell Eleonora. 'I'm afraid we'll never get away from the traffic. We'll blow the whole summer in a haze of carbon monoxide.'

She laughed and took me to a *gelateria* and back to the B & B to rest, and it was there, booting up the mini-computer that has all our source materials stored in it, that I read again of Garibaldi's decision in Tivoli. Dump the carts. Use mules.

Why?

Garibaldi had left Rome determined to keep a flame alight and revive the bonfire of revolution in the provinces. But reviewing his men on 3 June, he had to recognize that this was not the army he had hoped for. The night's desertions were a wake-up call. Nor, for all their generosity with food and drink, were the people of Tivoli queuing up to join the fight. Barely out of Rome, Garibaldi realized his project could soon end in fiasco. On the other hand, he was committed now. If some men had sneaked off, thousands of others were looking to him for a way forward. What to do?

Buy time. Keep the enemy in a state of confusion as to your whereabouts. The French army would soon be after them from Rome. Over the Apennines to the east a Neapolitan army was busy reasserting papal power in Abruzzo. There was also a considerable Spanish army to the south of Rome. Garibaldi was not ready to fight them.

Egidio Ruggeri, whose account is much shorter than Hoffstetter's, claims that Garibaldi had letters from Florence, 'promising, in the liveliest colours' that the whole of Tuscany was on the brink of insurrection. As a result the General, as his men always called him, decided to turn north, leaving Tivoli in the afternoon after just a few hours' rest and spending the night near Montecelio eight miles to the north. This is the route you see on maps in history books and museums.

Hoffstetter is more detailed. Having slept off their food, they left Tivoli at four, he says, taking the road to Naples, southwards; at nightfall they stopped and slept some more, then, in the small hours, set off again turning sharply north. This to deceive any informers in Tivoli. By the following evening they were settling down in the grounds of monasteries in Mentana and Monterotondo, twelve miles to the north-west.

But Trevelyan disagrees. Poor Hoffstetter had no idea where he was, he says. He quotes the German's account of an extremely arduous climb into the hills when the men turned off the road from Tivoli, the ground so steep and the path so poor they had to use ropes to haul up their one cannon and a few remaining carts over rocks and spurs, in the dark; 'an inhuman effort of heaving and pulling, blaspheming and whipping'.

There are no such hills on the route Hoffstetter thought they took.

'So where are they?' Eleonora asks.

We're going to bed early – it's barely 9.30 – anxious about the morning to come. We've promised ourselves we're going to do this march in the same time Garibaldi's men took. But our morale is low too, and if our sores and blisters get worse, our project like theirs risks ending before it has properly begun.

'Trevelyan says they went through San Polo dei Cavalieri.'

One nice thing about our hiking app is that it gives contour lines and altitudes.

'Quite a climb,' Eleonora observes. 'Two thousand, two hundred feet.'

At last I see the obvious: the General had to dump the wheeled carts in order to go where no one imagined an army could go. In order to *disappear*. Except, with so much luggage and too few mules, he couldn't dump all of them at once.

We contemplate Trevelyan's route, based on notes made by Colonel Gaetano Sacchi, whom Garibaldi had put in direct command of the First Italian Legion, notes later used by a certain Generale De Rossi for an article published in the *Cavalry Review* in 1902. Whatever the truth of the matter, it makes the trip to Monterotondo, which we intended as our second destination, twenty-two miles instead of fourteen. Twenty-two mountainous miles.

Still, we hadn't booked a place to stay as yet. We were free to stop where we liked, when we felt we'd had enough. And while a direct walk from Tivoli to Mentana and Monterotondo would be all busy roads under blazing sun, the path to San Polo would be earth and grass and rocks and trees and oxygen.

'Perhaps even a breeze,' Eleonora reflected.

The decision was made.

DAY 2

3 July 1849 – 26 July 2019

Tivoli, San Polo dei Cavalieri, Marcellina, Montecelio (Villa dei Romani) – 15 miles

San Polo dei Cavalieri

We had thought we were so organized. We had bought nice pastries for our 4.30 breakfast. In our room there was a brand new Nespresso machine with a generous variety of coffee pods – *Arpeggio*, *Levanto*, *Capriccio*.

The alarm does its cruel job. We dress quickly, pack our bags and drink our juice.

But the Nespresso doesn't work. The machine won't turn on. No amount of changing plugs, pressing switches helps. No little red light.

Eleonora refuses to give up. An army marches on its caffeine, she declares. She resorts to Google. Nespresso's online manual comes up on her phone. At 4.45 a.m.

'You're sure you have the right model?'

'Of course I'm sure.'

In the event it's 5.30 before we stumble down the stairs and let ourselves out into the dark. Coffee-less. But the pre-dawn hush quickly reconciles me to Tivoli. Everything is softly solemn in the shadowy streets, the air sweet and cool.

'You just like it now because there's no one around,' Eleonora observes.

We drop down to the road by the river, the Aniene, that feeds the town's fountains and waterfalls, and set off east, as if towards Abruzzo and the Adriatic. This is the road that Hoffstetter thought was heading south because it leaves from the southern part of town. Then, following Trevelyan, following De Rossi, following Sacchi, we strike abruptly north, leaving the valley and tackling the viciously steep hillside on what looks like an old mule path, an underlying stone base now mostly broken or covered with debris. Could anyone ever have pulled a cannon up here? 'Others said it was impossible,' Hoffstetter writes. He had been sent ahead to reconnoitre. 'But I knew what the General expected of me.'

We climb in silence, ducking under wet leaves, brushing cobwebs from our mouths as the day comes up and the light steals through bushes and pines, turning a grey world to green. When the path comes out of the trees to round a spur, we find Tivoli already precipitously below us, a warm cluster of arches, columns, terracotta and stucco; then the pink haze of the plain beyond, and Rome.

Another half-hour and we top a ridge that allows us to look east towards the Apennines proper, where the Neapolitan army awaits. First a broad patchwork of fields and woodland, then rising lines of dark mountains with the sun climbing behind. The sheer scope of the vista feeds a sense of achievement. We're feeling good.

When Eleonora is startled by a noise.

A white cow struggles to its hooves in the underbrush and trots off, clattering long horns on low branches. There are others too, lean and melancholy before another day of purgatorial heat. Hoffstetter was surprised and admiring when Garibaldi explained they would be bringing cows along with them on their march, so they could slaughter and eat them as required. The German had never seen this done in a regular army. Garibaldi learned the trick in Brazil.

'So they would have been dragging cows up here with them?'

Eleonora and I are vegetarians.

'They had twenty or so cows. And, at this point, thirty-seven mules. Two for Garibaldi and Anita's personal stuff. Five for the pots and pans. Two for what they called "the ambulance" – stretchers, bandages, medicines. Then rifles, munitions, clothes.'

Following a steep path through dense thickets of oak, we try to imagine 4000 men and hundreds of horses, mules and cattle swarming up the mountainside. Garibaldi, Anita and Ugo Bassi rode at their head. Bassi was a priest and poet whom Garibaldi had met in Bologna in the months before coming to Rome. Garibaldi loathed priests as a rule, but Bassi was entirely committed to the national cause. 'Our souls have been conjoined,' the cleric wrote. 'Garibaldi is the Hero most worthy of poetry I can ever hope to meet.' Bassi's 'soft eyes,' Hoffstetter observed, 'his high forehead, curly hair and beard, eccentric clothes and fiery speeches, surprised everyone. No handshake ever did me so much good as his.'

When it came to battle, Bassi moved in the thick of it with total abandon. 'He saddens me,' Garibaldi complained. 'He makes it so obvious he wants to die.' But perhaps this was the General's fault. 'Nothing would please me more than to die for Garibaldi,' Bassi enthused. 'Garibaldi is Italy.'

Raffaele Belluzzi, who loves to give every possible detail, has Bassi in a black shirt with a cross swinging from his neck riding a lively horse that had belonged to the British ambassador in Rome. But of the three up front, the best rider was doubtless Anita, who is supposed to have schooled Garibaldi himself in this department. In his memoir Garibaldi tells us she'd had her hair cut the same afternoon they left Rome, so she could look like a man. Other observers report her hair was long. 'Dressed like an Amazon,' Hoffstetter says, 'Garibaldi's wife road a fine roan and wore the same cap with an ostrich feather as everyone else. She wasn't usually armed but when we were expecting danger she wore a light sabre that she had used in Brazil.' Belluzzi has her wearing a red shirt and carrying a pistol and a dagger. All the men had daggers in their belts, he says.

The only weapon we have with us is a brand new Swiss pocket-knife, which I use to slice up a peach for a snack. We've reached 1500 feet now and there's a broad clearing where four paths meet. Exposed to the sun, the grass is a parched grey-green, but there's shade around the edges, and putting our packs down I strip off my shirt and hang it on a branch to dry the sweat. Not woollen like the shirts of the *garibaldini* – how hot must that have been? – but a marvellously light grey-blue fabric that according to the boasts of its manufacturers shifts the sweat off your body through its tiny holes into the air. It works fine for a while, but there are limits to what tiny holes can do when your body is streaming.

We have light trekking shorts too, while the *garibaldini* wore grey woollen trousers with a red stripe. And we've discovered elasticated, anti-rash athlete's underwear, for which I am immensely grateful. What wonderful progress has been made in fabrics over the last two centuries! Did Garibaldi's men even have underwear? I fear not. The more alert I'm becoming to all the places where skin is rubbing, shoes pinching and pains lurking, the more extraordinary their determination seems. I try to picture the men sprawled around the edge of the clearing here, examining their toes, their heels, finding sores, taking precautionary measures. I have a small silicon tube that fits over the fourth toe of my right foot, which is prone to blisters. I suppose they wrapped bits of cloth round theirs. And we have invested in the lightest possible trekking shoes, and the very best walking socks. Just occasionally, our various chroniclers touch on the problem of the *garibaldini* not having good boots. Socks are never mentioned. In general, the word *disagi* – discomforts – is made to do a lot of work.

We follow a long flat path winding through dense woodland, blissfully shaded and alive with birdsong. Then at last, through a break in the trees, San Polo appears. We had thought we were almost there, our app had promised a walk of just two and a half hours; instead the little town is still dramatically above us, tower, turrets and sun-soaked facades outcropping from dark green foliage the other side of a deep gorge.

How beautiful and how disappointing. We've already walked more than three hours. Obviously the software doesn't take sufficient account of the ups and downs and the quality of the paths. Garibaldi's men were not even told where they were going, never mind how long it would take to get there. They just walked.

It's that time of the morning now when the heat intensifies, and in a matter of minutes the quiet countryside is transformed by the urgent clamour of the cicadas. One strikes up in a tree above us, a rasping rhythmic whir, then another and another and another, until a harsh, hypnotic chorus fuses with the oven-hot air in one vast summery stupefaction.

I have a pair of trekking poles attached to my pack. I've never used poles, but friends insisted they would be useful. Eleonora thought them a pointless expense and unnecessary weight. I unhook them now and adjust the length without really knowing what it should be, and start to use them without really knowing how. At once I think of pilgrims and shepherds in children's picture books, never without their elegant sticks or crooks, and I wonder if the *garibaldini* were sometimes tempted to use their rifles for support. Probably not. They were too precious. For me the poles are a revelation. It's a pleasure to swing the arms and push down hard on the rocky ground. Energy surges with the roar of the cicadas.

'We have to get you a pair,' I tell Eleonora as we swing into San Polo at quarter to ten. 'Like it or not. General's orders.'

The *garibaldini* had no backpacks. There hadn't been time to find them. They carried their day's ration of bread tied to a string round their necks. Arriving in a village, they could hardly expect the local hostelry to serve all of them. Fortunately we can travel light because we know there'll be sustenance along the way. Our only fear, approaching a place as small as San Polo, is that the café we're counting on may not materialize, and our first question, on coming across a native, is Where is the piazza? since that is where the café will surely be.

But San Polo is not so small after all. Its piazza is generous and breezily elegant. And it has two cafés, not one. We turn this way and that, considering. Invariably two cafés in an Italian piazza will distinguish themselves by one being upmarket, one down, one for the sophisticated folks and one for the rough and ready – *borghesi* here *contadini* there. It is received wisdom that the Italians, unlike the English, have little sense of class distinction. How this notion gained currency I can't imagine. It takes no more than two seconds in San Polo to spot on the one side the unshaven men in vests playing cards around early glasses of wine, on the other the shabby chic of well-to-do housewives still drinking their breakfast coffee.

We choose the smarter bar, for its terrace, which has dazzling white sunshades and offers the opportunity of looking down over a parapet across the landscape we've just walked through. Inside, a pleasant lady promises freshly squeezed, fridge-cold oranges. 'It'll take a while though, because I do it by hand.' In the event, it's fifteen thirsty minutes before the juice is brought out together with coffee and pastries on a tin tray carried by a dreamy, distracted boy.

As our young waiter retreats, we call to ask if he could bring some sugar for the coffee, but he doesn't hear. He doesn't hear another customer call either. Barely fifteen, he has gone to stand at the parapet and gaze out across the wide world. Very likely if Garibaldi passed now, he would sign up in a trice. He's waiting for the call, any call. There were hundreds of adolescents among Garibaldi's men. They formed a group called the Compagnia Speranza. Hope Company. French boys, in particular. They were excellent soldiers, Garibaldi felt, even when fighting their own countrymen. Fervently idealistic, never complaining. While we eat and drink in the gentle breeze of the terrace, Eleonora turns the pages of a local newspaper and points to an article complaining about teenage motorcyclists using the hairpin bends between San Polo and the neighbouring Marcellina as a racetrack. It's something we're going to have to get used to over the coming weeks: young men in possession of fabulous technology and as ready to die, it seems, as Ugo Bassi, but for no other reason than boredom.

Marcellina

The world is full of surprises. The territory is never as you imagined. Your app tells you to take a short cut along a pretty-looking path. You proceed pleasantly enough, steeply downhill, until all trace of the path is lost amid waving grasses and dense brambles. You climb back up the hill under the pitiless sun, cursing. But then, around the long bend that your short cut was meant to avoid, an extraordinary sight awaits. Built against a rock wall that rises sheer from the road is a huge grey-brown industrial complex including a half-dozen cylindrical silos, each a hundred feet high. And on the rounded concrete surfaces of these now abandoned structures someone has painted six enormous black and white images of workers' faces. The effect, as these faces loom twenty feet above us, staring away over our heads, is eerily striking. The whole area, it seems, has for centuries been quarried for stone to crush into lime for cement. When Mussolini ordered the construction of extensive new suburbs in Rome, this cement factory was built to meet demand. It closed in 1975.

The inevitable explanatory plaque is long enough to fill two pages and comes complete with a garbled English translation. The artwork on the silos is entitled *The Gold Mine*. 'With an alchemical idea, artist Romolo Belvedere turns these stones into gems of gold. To all those who pass by, it will be difficult to take their eyes off. The golden-mine is blinding!'

This is not the case. Shaded by the hillside, the cement works are the only gloomy element in this otherwise dazzling day. Speaking of gold, though, there is an awful lot of glittering going on. Looking back to San Polo, now high above us, or down to Marcellina, a couple of miles below, we are constantly aware of intermittent gleams of light, as if the sun were catching scattered mirrors, dozens of them, but fitfully or perhaps rhythmically. It's an unsettling effect and seriously undermines that picture-postcard look one's learned to expect of ancient Italian towns.

Entering Marcellina, the mystery is solved. Almost all the chimneys have been fitted with spinning stainless-steel chimney cowls. Turning in the breeze, their shiny blades catch the light on and off. What can one say? In a flash, as it were, a simple industrial product transforms an ancient landscape. Garibaldi, Hoffstetter tells us, was immensely careful about not attracting attention from afar. Fires must not be lit at night. Cigars must not glow. Bayonets must not glint in the sun. Meat must only be barbecued in daylight. He would have abhorred the revolving stainless-steel chimney cowl.

In Marcellina we grab a drink in the Roxy Bar. It's 12.30. WIN FOR LIFE invites the lottery advertisement, in English, on the window. *Spensierati e sistemati* (Carefree and sorted). One can't imagine a more alluring message for a tired soldier. Inside, the bar is pleasantly air-conditioned. A calamitously overweight woman is squatting at a low table trying to help her little girl with some summer homework. Above the two, the TV plays a song by the singer Nek, an entry (so Eleonora tells me) at this year's Sanremo Song Festival. *Mi farò trovare pronto*, he sings – I'll make sure I'm ready. Not for the General's call, but for love. It's the typical, slightly hoarse, earnestly straining voice of the Italian male singer-songwriter, virile and vulnerable.

Sono pronto, sono pronto, A non esser pronto mai. Ready never to be ready. Garibaldi, we discover in his memoirs, was having serious misgivings about Italian masculinity in the first days of this long march. He wondered if his men would ever be ready for the task ahead. 'When I compared the constancy and abnegation of those South Americans I'd lived with,' he remembers, 'men who put up with any kind of food, or none at all, forsaking every comfort to survive for years in forest and desert ... with my faint-hearted, effeminate fellow citizens, who couldn't go a month in the wild without a city-dweller's three meals a day, I felt ashamed to belong to this degenerate progeny of a once great people.'

Hard words. But the General never showed his disappointment to his men at the time. By all accounts he was constantly praising their fortitude, galloping up and down the long column of marchers, always seeking to encourage and inspire. He worked with what he had.

'Two *cedrata*s, please.'

Child of the south, Eleonora chooses a southern drink. It's a refreshing, faintly soda-like concoction made from the Calabrian *cedro*, a large yellow citrus fruit, and served in a small bottle that you pour into a glass crackling with ice. I've had a couple of *cedrata*s before this trip, but never in the overheated state I'm in now. I raise the yellow swirl to my lips and, wham! Citrus-sharp, ice-enhanced ecstasy. The world is what you bring to it. Come with your hunger, and the most modest food is exquisite. Bring parched lips, and the *cedrata* is elixir. Pampered city-dweller that I am, I'm going to be wanting more of these.

One learns from one's mistakes. And makes others in the process. It had been an error, we decided, to try to hurry to Tivoli yesterday, before the sun was hot. We had been anxious and neurotic. Today we would take things as they came, accepting the heat, stopping more often, drinking more, resting in the shade and only booking a place to stay, from our phones, when we were sure how far we could get. But we had reckoned without the fact that Marcellina, Montecelio, Mentana and Monterotondo are not tourist towns. Checking Booking. com and Airbnb in the bar in Marcellina, we could find nowhere to stay along our route.

It was a problem. We could hardly, like Garibaldi's men, simply walk into a monastery and tell the monks we were going to sleep in the grounds.

'Villa dei Romani,' Eleonora eventually proposes. 'Artistic, bohemian atmosphere, it says. Only two miles off our route, south of Montecelio.'

Montecelio

So now, having dragged carts and cannon, cows and mules and 4000 men up to San Polo dei Cavalieri, then down to Marcellina, Garibaldi turns west back across the Roman plain towards the Tiber. If you're struggling to get a grip on all these movements, think of a horseshoe. Hold it up sideways with the curve to the right and the points to the left. We have gone first east, out of Rome along the bottom side of the shoe, then curved up, north, into the hills, and now, having disappeared from everyone's view, we're walking back along the upper side of the horseshoe, travelling west, so that when we arrive at our B & B this evening we'll be no more than four or five miles to the north of the road we struggled on from Rome to Tivoli.

No doubt some of Garibaldi's men must have wished they'd taken a short cut and saved themselves thirty exhausting miles. Nevertheless the effect of this ruse, in an age when there was no satellite surveillance, was extraordinary. On receiving reports that Garibaldi had left Rome at night from the city's southern gate, a French army set off towards noon to catch him in the Alban Hills. Overwhelmed by the heat and finding no trace of the rebels, they gave up in Frascati.

The Spanish, stationed to the south, seeing that the rebels had not arrived, assumed that Garibaldi must be heading for the Adriatic, perhaps planning to commandeer a ship and escape to Venice, where the liberal government was still holding out against the Austrians. They sped east into the hills south of Tivoli to cut him off at a town called Subiaco. The Spanish were renowned for their speed and resilience over rough terrain, and it is true that had Garibaldi headed east from Tivoli, he would have passed through Subiaco. But he didn't.

Garibaldi compounded the confusion by a madly intensive use of his 800 cavalrymen. The precise Hoffstetter with his military-school training begged his General to keep the cavalry close by the infantry, to protect the men from surprise attack. Instead Garibaldi split his horsemen into bands of fifty or even fewer and dispatched them on missions twenty, thirty and even forty miles away. There were cavalry in the Alban Hills to lead the French on. There were cavalry on the road to Subiaco, and again on the road to Rieti, forty miles due north of Subiaco. There were small parties of cavalry on all the roads leading east and north from Rome, to watch the enemy's movements. And all these men spread the news that Garibaldi was coming and that huge quantities of rations must be prepared. This to give the impression that his army was larger than it was. When they came into contact with the French or Spanish they rode off in directions that led away from the main body of infantry. So the Spanish set off to Rieti from Subiaco, travelling much faster than Garibaldi's men could, but in the wrong direction. On arrival they were so exhausted they hung up their boots for a week.

'When it came to saddles and weapons,' writes Generale De Rossi for the *Cavalry Review* in 1902, 'Garibaldi's cavalry was poorly equipped, to the point that it would not have been much use in battle.' But none of the General's enemies had any experience of such a systematic use of misinformation. Since he didn't tell any of his cavalry officers what orders he was giving to the others, the only person who knew what was going on overall was Garibaldi himself.

One of the positive sides to this, as far as our walk is concerned, is that even when we can't be sure that we're walking where he and his men walked, or even when we know perfectly well that we're not, we can always feel consoled that his cavalry probably passed this way. We're outriders, I tell Eleonora, in time and space.

The walk to Montecelio was challenging. *Bollino rosso* the newspaper in San Polo said. Red alert. Hottest July on record. Forty degrees. Infants and old folks should stay at home. We had our water bottles of course, which we filled at fountains in San Polo and Marcellina. We had our hats, our sun cream, our sunglasses. But these are winding roads through low olive groves and grey, bone-dry soil. You could dive into shade from time to time, but most of the walking was in direct sunlight.

At three in the afternoon we face the steep climb up to Montecelio itself. First hawthorn hedges, shrubs and stunted trees, then shabby little villas with faded awnings over peeling balconies. At a corner I lean on my poles. Am I old enough to be one of those the authorities warn to stay at home? All around not a soul in sight. Everyone hiding from the despotic sun. The heart pounds. The sweat runs down your lenses. Eleonora is way out in front now. Her blue shorts and orange shirt shimmer in the heat. I take off my hat and empty my water bottle over my head.

At this critical point we realize that the town has two centres, or seems to, one far above to the right, the other far above to the left. Both seem attractively dark and shady in the afternoon glare. But far away. At last we're in the streets. No pavements here, no frills. Stone, iron, brick. Rusty garage doors. Laundry hanging limp in the air above. Gratings on low windows. Then a wide area of cracked asphalt. With petrol pumps. And a bar. Bar di Montecelio. This time there's no question of hesitation or choice. We dive in.

'That's all we've got left, *signori*! But take it all! Whatever you can eat!'

Two heavily tattooed young men preside, all tight T-shirts and bulging muscles. They joke and laugh in strong local accents over our

40

miserable state, but in a kind way, hurrying to put things on the table, extravagantly chivalrous to Eleonora, eyeing me up ironically. A litre bottle of near-frozen water is gone in a trice. Yes, one says, he often goes running up around San Polo; lovely paths, quite a climb. But not in this heat! No one goes out in this heat. No one goes up to San Polo from Tivoli then down to Marcellina then up again to Montecelio. Who would do that?

'Garibaldi.'

'The man was mad.'

This was the moment when I learned how quickly the body can recover if only you give it food, water and shade. I had thought I was in trouble, that I might not make it. And in just five minutes of liquids, sugar and soggy pizza, there I am again, up and running. I presume it's an experience Garibaldi's men were familiar with.

I help myself to a Cornetto from the fridge and look round the room. Polished wood furniture. Tiled floor. A clock on the wall says four when it's five. They're still in nineteenth-century time. Aside from ourselves, the only other customers are four men playing cards, beer bottles in hand, enjoying their Friday afternoon.

'What language are they speaking?'

Eleonora listens. 'Romanian.'

Young Romanians have flocked to Italy since their country joined the EU in 2007. More than a million. Mainly building workers. In the same period the financial crisis has reduced the Italian building industry to half its previous size.

Eleonora asks, 'Were there any Romanians among Garibaldi's men?'

There weren't. But there were Poles. It's amazing how many Polish military men got around Europe during the 1848 revolutions. A group of 200 fought for the Roman Republic, and what survivors there were joined Garibaldi's retreat. It's curious too how the struggle for Italian nationhood was fought idealistically by a multinational, multilingual army. You couldn't accuse the Risorgimento of being isolationist or excluding. It was a Polish cavalryman, Major Emil Müller, who was given the task of completing French confusion over Garibaldi's whereabouts. When the 'horseshoe manoeuvre' terminated at Monte-rotondo on the east bank of the Tiber, just fifteen miles north-east of Rome, Müller and fifty cavalrymen rode on westwards, as if the plan had always been to circle the city to the north and head due west for the Tyrrhenian coast, perhaps to cut off the French supply line at the port of Civitavecchia.

Müller and his men left at nightfall and swam the Tiber in the dark. The bridges were all guarded. Alerted to their presence around Lake Bracciano, twenty-two miles north-west of Rome, the French set off after them in force. Müller led them even further west. The upshot was that Garibaldi was entirely free to move the main body of his men due north up the Tiber from Monterotondo, towards Umbria.

'How much is it?' I'm at the counter.

'Five euros forty,' says the big young man, flexing his tattoos.

My eyes must have widened, because he laughs and asks, 'Too little?'

I don't know what to say. I'd expected at least double.

He laughs heartily, as if I were the butt of some joke that only he and his fellow barman understand. Then he leans forward and says quietly, 'We get by, *signore*. It's a struggle here, but we do get by. Happy walking.'

Villa dei Romani

Our learning curve was steep those first few days. Steep as the Sabine Hills. We had imagined ourselves checking into friendly B & Bs and testing the temperature, as it were, of the country, mentioning Gari-baldi and hearing what people thought about the Risorgimento now. Instead, on arrival at Villa dei Romani, a surprisingly gracious house perched on a dry knoll in the middle of nowhere, our only craving was to collapse in our room. It was the merest sense of duty that led me to mention our project to our landlady, and I was immensely relieved when she just nodded vaguely and handed over a key.

It was exactly the reception we wanted. Still, there is a limit to how early you can hit the sack. To one side of the house the sun was setting in pink over Rome, illuminating Tivoli to the left, Montecelio to the right. We slipped quietly down to the garden to get a better look.

The grounds, perhaps an acre or so, were utterly barren but for a few gnarled trees and thick fleshy cactuses. Between these stood half a dozen large sculptures of body parts. Villa dei Romani, it turned out, was first and foremost an artists' retreat that paid for itself with the B & B. There was a scatter of ten-foot-tall hands, made of bright white concrete. With their wrists planted in the ground and fingers spread in the air, they seemed to invite comparison with bushes and trees. On another side of the house an impressive semi-erect stone penis had been given the dimensions and demeanour of a cannon (the scrotum its carriage) and placed so as to thrust out across the plain towards Rome. How could we not be reminded of the cannon Garibaldi's men were so valiantly dragging around with them? How much does a cannon weigh? Three tons? Four? 'Our light four-pounder,' Hoffstetter says, was designed to be drawn by four horses, though the men often ended up using their shoulders to heave it over the uneven terrain.

Fortunately, Villa dei Romani's stone penis doesn't have to be moved anywhere, or shoot at anyone. We smile and take a silly selfie beside it and are just sneaking back to bed when a robust little man emerges from the bushes and is suddenly upon us. We can't escape.

If only he had known that we were interested in Garibaldi, he cries. Yes, yes, he is the artist who sculpted the hands and there is something he absolutely must show us. 'Garibaldi's men stayed in the cellar here!'

I look around. The house looks old enough. But Villa dei Romani is some way off the route that—

'Not in '49! Later. After the battle of Mentana.'

Mentana is the town we will be heading for at dawn. When Italy was united in 1861, Rome was not included in the package; the Pope kept it for himself. In 1867 Garibaldi led a volunteer army to try to take the city, but was beaten by combined French and papal forces near Mentana.

'Some of the men hid in the cellar here, after the battle. They made drawings on the wall.'

Intrigued, we follow him into the house and downstairs to a low cellar. The walls are a rough grey limestone, the raw rock of the hill. One area, perhaps four feet by three, is enclosed by a white wooden frame. Inside the frame there are deep scratchings in the stone. Perhaps a few letters in the centre, which someone has tried to rub out with an abrasive and someone else has painted over in white. They're still visible but not legible. In the bottom right of the frame is a drawing, a vaguely pyramid shape, which our host tells us must be a nearby church.

'To remind themselves where they'd hidden their rifles,' the artist thinks. 'If they weren't caught with their weapons they could always claim they weren't *garibaldini.*'

Later, in the early hours I wake with a start and can't get back to sleep. We have the two windows wide open and outside the crickets are whirring in the warm air. The sound comes in waves, a rising and falling melancholy. I find myself thinking about the men who holed up in the cellar. Not the same men we're following of course. Though some did serve in both campaigns.

But even imagining that those graffiti were scratched by someone who had also been with Garibaldi back in 1849, can we really suppose that that takes us any closer to the earlier drama? Such a man would be different, eighteen years on. Garibaldi himself was quite different in 1867, long since transformed from most wanted villain to most popular hero. He'd been saluted by adoring crowds all over Europe. Met the world's leaders. And was physically in pretty poor shape. Pushing sixty, Garibaldi could not have done the walk that I'm doing at sixty-four. His rheumatism was so severe, he had to be lifted onto his horse. Yet he could still command an army, which I never could.

The General celebrated his forty-second birthday in Monterotondo, where we hope to arrive by midday tomorrow. Hoffstetter describes him standing with 'a good telescope' on a vantage point beside a monastery, gazing down across 'a landscape of hillocks, lush with vines and crops, beyond which, from afar, the dome of St Peters rose majestically'.

I'm eager to find this place and to see Rome from where he saw it. The expression on Garibaldi's face, according to his faithful aide-de-camp, was *addolorato*, sorrowful; perhaps he was wondering whether he would make it to forty-three or live to see the birth of the child his wife was carrying. Or perhaps, as Trevelyan prefers, he was grieving over Rome, wondering if the city would ever be free of popes and foreign armies. 'From the vineyard beside,' recounts Hoffstetter, 'a boy was singing one of those yearning melodies so typical of this country.' And hopefully more convincing than Nek's Sanremo entry.

But the more I think about all this, lying in Villa dei Romani with the crickets whirring outside the window, the more convinced I am that these are sentimental projections. Whenever he had a spare moment, Hoffstetter was jotting down notes, turning each day into a story. Trevelyan too was deep in his own romantic evocation of Italy and of Garibaldi. And I myself am always looking for the detail that will spin and catch the light.

But Garibaldi lived in the moment. Looking through his telescope towards Rome, he would have been studying the lie of the land, watching for enemy activity, calculating how quickly bread could be baked to get his men on the road. That sorrowful look very likely had to do with finding more mules to replace their last carts. Garibaldi was interested in doing, not recording what had been done. Which is why the whole of this extraordinary march gets only a half-dozen cursory pages in his memoirs, full of imprecisions. He can't remember; it isn't important.

And it was because he was so concentrated on the moment that he was always a step ahead of his enemies. Right now, after two days on the road, he is about nine miles ahead of us, but tomorrow we will catch up with him, because, as Ruggeri says, the first days' marches had been 'devastating'; the men were desperate for rest; and then, to force the General's hand, the bakeries in Monterotondo couldn't deliver to the deadline he demanded. It takes a while to produce 4000 rations of bread.

DAY 3

4 July 1849 – 27 July 2019

Montecelio, Mentana, Monterotondo, Tenuta Gran Paradiso – 17 miles

Mentana

The pleasure of leaving before daylight. The household still asleep. Sneaking down the stairs, shaking the dust from your feet. You don't have to have disliked the place. You're not avoiding any chores. It's simply freedom. I'm going. And going too early for the grind of goodbyes.

Or rather *we're* going. Accomplices. Free *together*. Taking with us the boiled eggs the landlady left for breakfast. Two portions of apricot jam. Did Garibaldi's men feel something of this? The joy of moving on. Not knowing what the day would bring, but knowing it would not be the same as yesterday. Free in the wide world to savour the elegance of the bulrushes and the blue of the cornflowers, the smells of lavender and mint, the bray of a donkey. Striding towards distant hills, at dawn.

Maybe they did. Or maybe they were just cursing to be prodded from their sleep in the early hours. 'Getting going is the toughest moment,' Hoffstetter writes.

Today we have a list of places to visit. To start with, the monastery just outside Mentana where Anita and Hoffstetter told the monks that the men of the rearguard would be arriving soon. The monks were 'frightened out of their wits', having been warned how fierce and evil Garibaldi was, hence were relieved to discover that providing food and wine and floors to sleep on were all that was required. Anita checked the rooms and grounds and decided who would go where, an

46

illiterate Brazilian mother telling the learned celibates what was what. In her approximate Italian. Beside the German officer, with his German accent. In the name of Italian freedom, Italian unity.

But when we arrive in Via del Conventino on the outskirts of the town, the monastery is now a hotel, a picturesque pile behind a high wall, glimpsed through a thick cover of pines, oaks and magnolias. It's 8.20. We could press a buzzer on the gate, of course, and ask to be let in. We could walk up the drive to Reception, explain that we're conducting enquiries into a thousand and more guests who checked in without a booking on the evening of 4 July 1849, etc. But I feel discouraged. It's just an old monastery turned hotel. Where is the piazza! Where is our coffee?

This had been an easier walk, which is to say a gentler climb, through varied farmland and fast criss-crossing roads. There were horses in the fields and monumental piles of cylindrical straw bales, golden in the early sunshine. On the uncultivated slopes the vegetation is a massed collage of light and dark greens, gloss and matt, rounded volumes and spiky thrusts, watched over at strategic points by tall, sombre umbrella pines, angular and aloof. Gathering and unfolding as you progress, always more depth than surface, this endlessly varied plant life soaks up and satisfies the walker's attention in a way that is wonderfully calming.

But once in the ramshackle clutter that is Mentana, there's not a piazza worthy of the name. Behind the town hall, the so-called Piazza Garibaldi is no more than a gritty cul-de-sac where the Birra del Borgo serves us coffee and croissants. No orange juice. We eat up fast and move on to the next place on our list, the Mentana Garibaldino Museum, which we have reason to believe opens at nine. And so it does. Monday to Friday. But not on Saturdays. On Saturdays it opens at 3 p.m.

It's Saturday. We console ourselves with a large mural in a steeply sloping cobbled street – Via Roma – that shows Garibaldi alone on a white horse, riding into Mentana. The town is clustered Cézanne-fashion towards the top of the painting while Garibaldi in a red shirt, his white poncho transformed into a wizard's cloak, has neither weapons nor saddle and seems too big for his horse, his body bent and broken, mouth glum. The consequent aura of victimhood is vaguely reminiscent of Christ on his donkey riding into Jerusalem; it's a pathos that has more to do with current taste than history.

Around the corner a road sign points to the State Middle School G. Garibaldi. In the main street a plaque rather too high up on a stuccoed facade reads,

> These the hills of Mentana,
> Here the unequal fray,
> Here the anguish of
> GIUSEPPE GARIBALDI,
> in 1867.

We hurry on. Mentana, it seems, has nothing to boast but this one lost battle. The hero's previous passage through the town is forgotten.

Monterotondo

Where once towns began with outlying monasteries, then walls and bastions, Monterotondo is announced by superstore and shopping mall, walls of steel and glass rising behind slopes of dry grass and bamboo. Never mind. The town centre is as gracious and hospitable as Mentana was shabby and discouraging. A deliciously shady walk through a garden, typically mixing children's playground and war monuments, leads us to a piazza where two tall *cedrata*s are already winking on a yellow tablecloth before we realize we are sitting in the Caffè Garibaldi. Impossible to escape the man.

As we shoulder our packs to leave, a voice accosts us: 'How can you walk in this heat? And carry all that stuff!'

It's an elderly woman. She falls into step with us, wearing a summer dress on a thin frame, shins and ankles mottled with age, a bulging carrier bag in her hand. 'The summers didn't use to be so hot,' she says. She's eager to talk. 'I remember hoeing all day under the sun out in the fields. Now I have to run home and hide.'

When Eleonora tells her where we're going, the woman shakes her head in dismay. 'You young people! Do be careful, please.' For me this comes as the first sign that we are growing used to the heat. It's not so bad. The key is to keep moving. A steady pace generates the slight refrigeration required not to shrivel up and die. Never stand still in the sunshine.

A quarter of an hour later we're at the famous convent whence Garibaldi stared at Rome through a telescope. It's on a south-facing slope just beyond the old centre, and no doubt there would be a view across 'rich vineyards', as Hoffstetter puts it, all the way to Rome, were it not for the fact that the town has spread out and all we can see are the white walls and orange-tiled roofs of brash little villas strung beside the road. When at last a corner opens up the view southward, Rome is invisible in a simmer of pollution. There is nothing to feel here except the foolishness of having imagined there might be anything to feel.

Through the gates of the monastery you can see the splintering in the white stone door surround caused by a papal cannon ball in 1867, when Garibaldi camped here for the second time. The Pope's men shelled their own church to get at him. But there is no sign or mention of the place where eighteen years earlier – 4 July 1849 – a man was executed. Hoffstetter reports the event thus: 'Today we resumed the severe response to insubordination: a soldier was shot. But during the execution something displeasing happened; the criminal broke free and tried to escape. The guard at the convent gate stopped him and he had to die despite the most desperate resistance.'

Something displeasing? During an execution?

Belluzzi, who loves Garibaldi with the blind love of the convert, tries to make the incident more palatable and justifiable. Insubordination in his version becomes 'extremely serious insubordination'.

What is going on here? Why is Garibaldi, who loathed the Church, obliging us to visit all these monasteries? Why did he so often billet soldiers with monks? And why, given his lifelong belief that capital punishment should be abolished, was he having a man executed?

49

The General, as we've seen, was trying hard to put off a battle with his enemies, hoping the tide would turn in his favour. But beyond the military conflict, there was a propaganda war to be waged, a battle for hearts and minds. The Pope had come out strongly against a liberal state and a united Italy; such ideas were not compatible with his temporal sovereignty over a large part of the peninsula. This forced the Church and all its faithful into an alliance with the conservative foreign powers propping up the Pope and occupying the country. Consequently, Italian patriots must be presented as evil, a rabble of common criminals whose only purpose was to steal and kill.

Pulpits were a good place to launch this kind of attack, the tens of thousands of pulpits in provincial Italy. The country priests, Garibaldi knew, commanded the minds of the peasants and encouraged them to spy on him. It was a Christian duty. Every time the *garibaldini* arrived in a town, they had to seal it off for the duration of their stay, partly to prepare against attack from outside but mostly to prevent informers, very often priests, from reporting their presence. This was one of Hoffstetter's jobs. It meant keeping dozens of men from their rest, and stringing sentinels along approach roads to intercept each and every traveller.

At the same time, friction between the volunteer army and the local people had to be avoided at all costs. It would play to the Church's narrative. The easiest way to do this, Garibaldi told Hoffstetter, was to billet the men just outside town. People could then bring food out to them, rather than have the soldiers invade their streets and homes. None of the authors who describe the march has a single word to say about sanitary arrangements, but these too must have been a concern. Four thousand soldiers are four thousand people who need to pee and crap. If the likes of Belluzzi and Trevelyan don't want to mention it, Garibaldi certainly had to think about it. Heaven knows, Eleonora and I have to think about bodily needs often enough. But two people alone can pick their secluded spot in the countryside. Or synchronize bowels and cafés. An army is a different matter.

The monasteries presented an obvious solution. They were usually situated on the outskirts of towns. They were large, with extensive walled grounds, easy to defend. They had bread and wine, vegetables and fruit. And sanitary facilities. There were no women. Case closed.

However, billeting the men in monasteries was a risk. To upset or offend the clergy would only invite them to step up their anti-Risorgimento rhetoric. They could present themselves as victims. On the other hand, if one could convince the monks that this was no rabble but a well-organized group of idealists fighting for a just cause, then some might be won over. Ugo Bassi, himself a Barnabite monk, was often at the fore when it came to announcing to the holy fathers that they had guests. Likewise Father Stefano Ramorino, another priest marching with the *garibaldini*.

The General's quandary was he did not know his men. When recruiting his Legion in the autumn of 1848, he had conducted personal interviews with volunteers. But there had been no time to vet all those who had turned up that evening at San Giovanni in Laterano. Many might have been criminals eager to get out of the city before papal law was reimposed. Hoffstetter describes how Garibaldi, entering a monastery, would immediately place an armed guard on the vegetable gardens and wine cellar. He did not trust his men not to steal.

On 5 July, in the early hours, as the column was about to set out on the road north, Garibaldi dictated an order of the day that ran to three pages: 'Although I have frequently had cause to remind you' – he wrote, and his officers would have read the words out loud to their battalions – 'to be rigorously respectful towards all people and property in the places we're passing through, this for many reasons, but most of all so that you can show yourselves true sons of that republican principle that we all wish to advance at the cost of our lives, nevertheless, I find myself obliged once again and with great regret to recall this duty ...'

Some soldiers had been stealing livestock and selling the animals on for money, some selling rifles, some taking food without leaving payment. Such actions were 'unworthy of the name we must all be proud of, the First Italian Legion, a name that is and shall be a great glory for us'. And the General issued a warning: 'Anyone guilty of theft of any

51

object of whatever kind or value will render themselves subject to the death penalty.'

Was the soldier executed in Monterotondo guilty of stealing? Hoffstetter calls him a *delinquente*, a criminal. If so, who had he stolen from, if not the monks? In which case the execution would serve as a demonstration to the monks that a republican Italy would defend their rights.

'His soldiers fear him with the same intensity that they love him,' Hoffstetter noted in his diary on the following day. 'They know he has only two punishments: reprimand or death ... He would have them shot without so much as taking the cigar from his mouth.'

The General's order of the day was stamped with the official seal of the Roman Republic, 'God and the People'. It was important for Garibaldi to believe he had a legitimate mandate for his actions. But thinking the whole thing over as we look through the gates into the monastery, trying to imagine the hectic circumstances in which that execution took place, what strikes me is the absolute confidence of Garibaldi's decisions and rhetoric. Here is a band of men on the run, last survivors of a failed revolution. They are surrounded by armies far greater than their own. No one is financing them. No one is going to come to their aid. Very likely they will soon be crushed, annihilated. But Garibaldi insists on discipline. And in the teeth of the evidence he declares that one day the First Italian Legion will be a title to be proud of. Glory will come, not in heaven but here on earth.

And he was right. It did come. Heading back through Monterotondo to pick up our journey north, hugging the meagre shade of a stuccoed wall, we look up and see the sign 'Via Ciceruacchio – Garibaldino Martyr, 1800–1849.' Here is another of those walking beside us, and one of the many who will not survive our trip.

Ciceruacchio is a nickname with the sense of Chubs or Chubby. Angelo Brunetti was the man's real name. Born to a labourer's family in 1800, he had built up a carting business, bringing wine and farm produce into Rome from the Alban Hills. It was he who guided Garibaldi's men out of Rome on the first night's march. He knew the territory. He also ran a busy tavern. But most of all Ciceruacchio was the charismatic, undisputed leader of Rome's *popolino*, the mass of ordinary people who became passionately involved in politics in the months leading up to the declaration of the republic. 'He can hardly read or write,' Florence Nightingale wrote to her family from the city in 1847, 'sells firewood to all the English, has not genius, but a common sense almost amounting to genius, and can turn the whole Roman people round his fingers.'

Vivacious, explosive, expansive, persuasive, throughout the 1840s Ciceruacchio settled local disputes, organized festivals and demonstrations. 'He is Rome's first citizen,' observed the Piedmontese ambassador. 'He exhorts, pontificates, keeps the peace.'

When the Pope reneged on his promises of reform, Ciceruacchio was at the centre of the popular protests that followed. Later he was suspected of conspiring to have the Pope's prime minister, Pellegrino Rossi, assassinated, and even of convincing his eldest son to do the deed. These are suppositions, but we do know that after the Pope left Rome, Ciceruacchio was involved in vandalizing churches and burning confession boxes. Mazzini was appalled, but Ciceruacchio was untouchable; he fought hard throughout the siege and was always in the thick of it.

So this champion of the people is up there at the head of our column, beside Anita and the General and Ugo Bassi, with his chubby face, goatee beard and wavy moustache. His two sons are travelling with him, the elder under a false name with false papers; the younger is only thirteen years old. All three depend absolutely on Garibaldi, since, should they be caught, summary execution is the only outcome. Yet despite the man's fame and charisma, our accounts of the march barely mention Ciceruacchio. Ruggeri recalls him generously sharing what little water he had in his canteen at a moment of great thirst. Belluzzi quotes a witness who, forty years on, remembered Ciceruacchio losing his temper with a priest and picking up a rifle to scare him. But that's about it. Perhaps, at nearly fifty, he was feeling his age, exhausted by the long hours on the road and difficult sleeping conditions. Or perhaps he was appalled by the collapse of all his hopes, the many bereavements, the perils ahead.

Paradiso

There is a word Italians no longer use, *viandante*. On a July night in 1817 the adolescent Giacomo Leopardi opened what was to be a 4000-page diary with: '*Palazzo Bello* [the house where he was staying] *Cane di notte dal casolare, al passar del viandante*' – Dog in the night from the farmhouse, as the wayfarer passes. 'Wayfarer' is not much used these days. The authoritative Treccani dictionary defines *viandante* as 'A person who goes (*andare*) along the way (*via*); in particular someone who goes on paths outside towns, travelling by foot, to reach distant places.' And adds, 'No longer current.'

First the figure fades, ghost-like into the mists of the past, then the word with it. An aura of the archaic spreads like a mould. Old poems, old diaries. Then a host of things that sustained that figure wither away too. The roadside water fountains are mostly gone, the wells, the taverns and hostelries where you could eat and sleep along the way. Who needs them now? So once again Booking.com and Airbnb offer almost nothing along our route today. But there is a place off the wayfarer's path, a different kind of place, not designed for sleeping the night and moving on, but a world entire unto itself. Gated luxury. We're going to be finding more and more of these hideaways from here on, not taverns or hotels but projections of the perfect holiday retreat. This one, which also caters for wedding receptions and 'grand events', is aptly named Paradiso. Eleonora reads me the description from its website. In English: 'Tenuta Gran Paradiso, lovely Villa at a glance away from Rome, it is immersed in the quietness of the suggestive Tiber valley ... with his being a chameleon, it will make all your unforgettable event.

'There's a swimming pool,' she adds and shows me a blue photo.

'Book it!'

'Dog in the night from the farmhouse,' Leopardi wrote, meaning barking presumably, 'as the wayfarer passes.'

Wayfarers may be no more, but the dogs remain. They've multiplied. The fewer wayfarers, the more dogs. And they go on barking across the centuries. German shepherds, mastiffs, Dobermanns, Rottweilers, protectors of the fearful proprietors of pretentious provincial villas. Or hunting dogs in farmyards: pointers, setters, spaniels and beagles. Working dogs out with the sheep: collies and Labradors. Fancy dogs on balconies: poodles and terriers and miniature pinschers. Dogs that tear back and forth between hedge and fence as you pass. Dogs wriggling heads through balcony railings. Dogs that strain at the ends of chains. Dogs that leap up behind a remote-controlled gate, panting loudly, pink tongues out in the heat. Dogs that dash into the road to confront you. Or follow you. All without exception barking, yapping, snapping, snarling, growling. Day after day, house after house, as we pass. Ferocious, festive or frightened, they all seize this now rare opportunity to justify their existence: the passage of a wayfarer. And when one dog begins, others soon join in. Spirit of the pack. Canine carolling. Across the road, along the valley. There are moments when it seems the whole Italian landscape is barking.

Eleonora is terrified of dogs. She was mauled as a child. Dauntless when facing trucks on the Tiburtina, she jumps with fright when a dog bursts out of bushes to slam itself against a fence, barking wildly. Throughout this trip I am tensed for the moment – it will surely come – when we are confronted by loose dogs in open country. For now I merely observe, 'So much for the quietness of the suggestive Tiber valley.'

To tell the truth, it doesn't feel like a valley. Just pleasantly undulating countryside, tall white drought-stricken grass set off by the resilient greens of shrub and olive. I remember a narrow chalky track downhill between dry thistles so tall their thistledown waved above our heads. Then a raspberry-stuccoed farmhouse, cactus to one side, fig tree to the other, with these words handwritten in white over the door: *Formaggio e ricottina, la mangi da Michelina.* Cheese and ricottinas, you can eat at Michelina's.

Once again, this is not quite the road Garibaldi took. Assured by his returning horsemen that he had shaken off the French and Spanish and still burdened for the moment with a number of carts, he took the main road north up the meandering Tiber. But that road is still the main road. More than ever the main road. Having learned now how to use Google Satellite and Street View, we inspected a few miles of it online and came to the conclusion that it is not a place you would want to walk. Dogs may bark and even bite, but they will not flatten you.

So we're outriding, on tiny parallel tracks to the east of Garibaldi's column. An elegant but broken tower on a hillock to our right is the so-called Grotta Marrotta, a medieval ruin in what was once a rich and populous village. Regular signs warn us we can only hunt if 'authorized'. Hunt what, one wonders, having seen no animals but dogs. The occasional hawk, turning high above, perhaps. A few sheep on the hills. Lizards everywhere, dozing on warm white stones or rustling off in the thistles. Crows pecking in stubble. Nobody hunts crows.

Now another sign – glossy blue and yellow – informs us that we are on the Via Francigena, St Francis' Way, the old pilgrim route from Canterbury to Rome. But in two hours along this particular track we meet no pilgrims. We are absolutely alone in the scorched fields. It's discouraging. A people once doggedly attached to the land – 'I hoed all day under the sun' – have been freed to sit in air-conditioned environments following events on TV and computer screen. The whole drift of modern life, from the actual to the virtual, opens the question of why emotions of loyalty and identity should any longer be attached to a physical territory. That once unshakeable connection – place/identity – that so galvanized and justified nineteenth-century liberal nationalism is now fast coming undone.

All the same, it's fun to think of Garibaldi's path overlapping with a pilgrim route: the devout Christians going to bow their heads before the Pope; the patriot in flight from the Eternal City but still hoping to wrest it from papal clutches one day. And the two meet on this dusty road; or rather the pilgrim plodding south stands aside to let the soldiers marching north pass by. The meeting and mixing, or non-mixing, of these two mindsets lies at the core of Italy's precarious identity.

Also looking precarious are our plans for afternoon swimming. As always with these long spells of intense summer heat, the moment comes when the storm clouds gather, the air grows stiller, the clamour of the cicadas louder. We're not entirely surprised. Like Garibaldi we cannot choose our weather, but unlike him we can type 'Roma meteo' or 'Monterotondo meteo' into Google and get a two-week forecast. The websites spoke of a storm in the night, but the clouds are already here at one o'clock.

The *garibaldini* took a swim that afternoon. They set up camp at midday after eight hours' walking and bathed, Hoffstetter tells us, in the Tiber by an old stone bridge. All of them? Thousands of men piling into the sluggish muddy stream? You imagine them sprawled nude on the banks to dry off in the sun – no swimming trunks of course – waving away hornets and wasps, looking for herbs to treat a rash.

Did Anita turn away? Apparently she and Garibaldi – José, she called him – rode their horses across the water and rested in the shade of a little cliff.

By the time we slip into our costumes the sun is hidden behind thick cloud, and as we arrive at the Paradiso's blue pool the air stirs and a breath of wind ruffles the water. Most of the blessed have withdrawn to their bowers. Only four or five remain, lounging poolside. An older man is reading *La Gazzetta dello Sport*. A couple of young women are in the water, their elbows hooked onto the side, talking to two others on deckchairs. Loudly. About a friend's relationship.

Eleonora goes to the ladder and dips a foot. I'm a dive-in sort of person, so I've done a couple of laps before she's properly in. But what's a lap of fifteen yards, however cool and clean? I'd prefer the muddy challenge of the river. We splash about for a while, but the breeze is tugging the fringes of the sunshades now. The old man has to fight the pages of his *Gazzetta*. The oleander hedge that shelters Paradise from the wilds beyond is suddenly a shivering panic of white and pink. The women gather their towels and lotions. We follow, disappointed.

But I should have told you about Angelino and Massimo, the Gran Paradiso's guardian angels. St Peter was not on the gate as we turned off the road. Nor was he sorting through keys at the reception desk. Looking for someone to judge our worthiness, we had to wander, packs on backs, damp sunhats still on our heads, into a spacious restaurant, a sea of white tablecloths, where a dozen sparsely scattered guests were winding up their Saturday lunch. Finally we had the attention of the waiter, who approached us, wiping hands on his apron.

'Heavy going, hey?' Wiry and thin, he grins broadly, lantern-jawed, black bowtie on black shirt. You understand immediately that he's a wag. A Ciceruacchio perhaps. Leading us round the building outside, he stops, sighs and – 'You don't mind, do you?' – lights a cigarette, cupping his hand against the breeze. But where on earth are we walking with these heavy packs? Madness! Complete madness! 'I'm a runner,' he declares. 'You're passionate about walking. I'm passionate about running.' He takes a deep drag of his cigarette. 'Much deserved!'

He leaves us in Reception and goes through a dark door to the kitchen. Eventually, a burly man in a chef's hat appears, tall, stooped and abundantly bearded. His black shirt makes me think of Ugo Bassi. 'We're short-staffed today,' he admits. 'Of course you'll be dining here, won't you? Yes, we do have dishes for vegetarians. We have everything. Best food in the world.' The other man comes back. 'Tim-oh-tee;' he reads my name from my ID. 'I'm Angelino.' He wipes a hand and offers it. 'This is Massimo. Our magician.'

We're led through a maze of low buildings, bungalow apartments with brick-paved terraces. POMEGRANATE, PEACH, CHERRY, OLIVE. Each little dwelling has a pretty name and every space is marked off by bright white railings lined with fake classical vases held up by intertwining cherubs and ablaze with geraniums. 'Massimo's a genius,' Angelino is telling us. Truly. 'Everything is home-made. Haute cuisine.'

It's extraordinary how eager Angelino is to talk, to draw us into an atmosphere of excited complicity that somehow has to do with his smoky fingers and glassy eyes and a faint smell of grappa. He and Massimo are a team, he says. 'He's so meticulous. You know. I'm a bit more laissez-faire. He keeps me in line, I make him more human.'

He might be a newly-wed enthusing over his bride.

'You want to leave early in the morning? No problem.' A breakfast basket will be brought to our apartment after dinner. 'But you can't walk tomorrow, my friends, it'll be wet. Haven't you seen the forecast? Why not stay another day? You look like you need a rest.'

What we actually need is to take a shower. Which at last, suddenly remembering other duties, Angelino leaves us free to do. One thing is clear, however: we will have to eat in his restaurant this evening, and we will have to do justice to Massimo's cooking. Any thoughts of resistance would be folly.

With an early bed in mind, we went along as soon as the restaurant opened and chose to sit outside, which meant we were alone and Angelino could stop by and regale us with his personal history. His time in London. The English girlfriend who taught him English. 'Not wishing to offend, you know, but I didn't really like the place.' Very soon he felt he had to get back to Italy, to Rome. 'These are our *frittelline*,' he says, setting down gleaming plates. The white cloth over the arm of his black shirt makes a handsome picture. And a little later, 'This is our *formaggio semi-stagionato pastellato e fritto*.' He watches us tuck in. 'A writer, are you?' With Massimo being such a good cook, he expects the two of them will end up on television one day. 'I suppose celebrity could be exciting, but to be honest I couldn't put up with the Bangla. You know? I'm happy as I am. Here is our polenta. You'll love it. Here is our *parmigiana*.'

At no point were we shown a menu. The plates just kept coming. How could we not like what he brought? It was exquisite. Washed down with a Castelli Romani wine, the same that Ciceruacchio carted to Rome from the Alban hills.

'Did he really say "Bangla"?' I asked.

'He did.'

'Bangladeshis?'

'I think he means if they got famous, they'd have to move in some slick international environment, with foreigners. Bangla.'

'Here is our *sformatino di zucchine con ricotta e noci*.'

Of course living in the city had become impossible, Angelino was laughing. 'Not to be racist, you know, even though I probably am ... Out here it's wonderful.'

As he departs with another set of plates, Eleonora reminds me that this whole area – Montecelio, Mentana, Monterotondo – voted for Salvini's xenophobe League in the recent European elections.

'Here are our *gnocchi con funghi porcini zucca e tartufo*.'
I'm way beyond my limit.

Meantime, down by the Tiber, Hoffstetter had his first chance to see South American slaughter techniques. A Uruguayan soldier selected eight cows and tied them in a circle round a tree. The soldiers held the animals still with ropes. Then this man, a 'child of the pampas', took the dagger from his belt and 'with the greatest rapidity struck one beast after the other in the heart; almost at once the animals collapsed to the ground. As you can imagine, this strange spectacle gathered quite a crowd.'

The meat was then cut up – a complex process – and an officer charged with distributing portions to the men, though only after the tenderest pieces had been reserved for the General and his wife. Fires were lit. 'The soldiers cut their portions into thin slices, skewered them on green sticks and held them obliquely to the flames. We were resting on our saddlecloths round the fire, cutting the cooked meat with our daggers. But you could see from some men's faces that they missed their olive oil and salt, and Anita went round smiling and consoling everyone with the thought that things would soon improve.'

Towards evening, Garibaldi addressed his men. It was the first time he had talked to them all together since the piazza in Rome. You wonder how it was done, with 4000 soldiers by the riverbank. And you wonder what was said. We don't know. But Hoffstetter describes it in terms of sustenance, as if it were part of the barbecue; 'a juicy talk', he calls it.

Replete, the soldiers slept, but the cavalrymen had to feed their horses. The problem was that even though they had managed to find oats and beans they had no nosebags. 'Men fed their horses from handkerchiefs, or dug little holes in the ground. I stood for hours with my two horses,' Hoffstetter tells us 'feeding them out of my cap'.

I put my cap on again because the evening at the Gran Paradiso is suddenly cool. Once again a breeze is rising. And I'm eating so much I fear I won't sleep. 'Here is our *semifreddo alla pesca*!' Angelino announces. I begin to worry they are planning to hit us with a huge bill.

Now there is a bottle of limoncello on the table. Eleonora declines. Angelino pours her a glass anyway. 'Our home-made limoncello!' She lifts it to her lips, but the level in the glass remains the same. And when the bill arrives, it's truly modest. Massimo comes out of the kitchen to pump our hands. A group selfie is taken. In the distance a first rumble of thunder has the two of them begging us to stay tomorrow. I feel mean for having doubted their genuine enthusiasm for serving us some of the best food I've ever eaten. Back in our room, a hamper is waiting on the table, with breakfast inside. You can see at once that it will cover lunch as well. What can we do but collapse on the bed and wait for the storm?

DAY 4

5 July 1849 – 28 July 2019

Gran Paradiso, Passo Corese, Ponte Sfondato (Le Murene) – 19 miles

Passo Corese

It comes towards two in a gust of wind. We rush out on the terrace to sort out a pot that has blown over and is rolling around. The sky flickers and splits. The rain descends in drenching sheets. At once a tension develops. Eleonora is for turning off the alarm and starting later. Or not at all. I'm reluctant to change plans.

The *garibaldini* also faced marches in the rain. On three occasions. All 'ruinous for morale', Ruggeri complains. The first time, ten days into the journey, was particularly dramatic, since they were walking in the pitch dark, through open country, in close proximity to the enemy. Having read all my authors' accounts of that terrible night at least twice, I've been assuming that we too will walk that section in the wet. Our weather will follow theirs. Instead, the rain is upon us now, at 2 a.m., on day four, the exact hour when Garibaldi's men resumed their march under quiet moonlight after their long break by the river. 'In excellent order,' Hoffstetter enthuses, 'one of our most beautiful marches, thanks to the General's talk.'

For Hoffstetter, a march is an aesthetic experience.

At five the rain is still falling, in thundery bursts. But after seven there's a lull. Eleonora agrees to get going, and I feel guilty for pushing her, which makes me aware that deep down I actually want us to get caught in the rain. Yes, torrential rain. I want some extreme experience. To test the gear we've brought? The waterproof covers for the packs? The dry bags? I don't think so. We're getting to the heart here, I sense, as we swing out of Paradise and along the misty road, of why

I've become obsessed with this journey. I could never have such a sublime goal in life as Garibaldi had – fighting for liberty, the making of
a nation – but I do want to share something of his enviable purpose-
fulness, his derring-do.

A great wet cloud is held up at the corners above olive groves and
gravel pits, like a sagging sheet. It must burst soon. We have a mile or
so of main road to walk, back towards the Tiber, before turning off
on a tiny track to link up with the main body of Garibaldi's column
at a town called Passo Corese, seven miles to the north. 'No, it's too
early to stop,' I tell Eleonora as we pass a service station with a big
café. Two minutes later, the wet sheet splits, the heavens open, and
we're dashing back.

This is the first of a number of occasions over the coming weeks
when we're prodded to think of providence – the café right there, a
single isolated building in an expanse of open country, *exactly* as we
needed it. 'I've always had some faith in luck,' Garibaldi admits in his
memoirs. And 'when it comes to war, you need luck on your side, or
a very superior genius'.

With no claims to genius, we're sugaring espressos contemplating a
steady downpour through plate glass. The scene in the café is familiar.
The Italians are avid Sunday trippers. They rise early, move straight
from bed to car and grab themselves a quick breakfast standing at the
counter. Not having a car to escape in, we sit at a table studying maps
and weather forecasts. Eleonora observes that there's a mile or so along
the route our app is proposing that doesn't appear on Google Maps.
The satellite image just has a broad stain of dark green. It's odd.

Cut now to an hour later and two figures standing on a narrow road
under a makeshift shelter. The rain is coming down so hard that the
drops bounce merrily about their feet. Each uses one hand to hold up
a trekking pole whose point passes through an eyehole in the corner
of a plastic groundsheet stretched above their heads; the other hand
pulls the sheet down behind them, so that the water runs off the surface in a chuckling trickle beyond their ankles. Fortunately, the only
car that passes them in twenty minutes slows down and veers away.

Even so the spray tickles their shins. 'Thank God there was no wind,' the woman remarks when finally the rain eases and they can fold the soaking groundsheet.

Another mile down the road, and the sheet is stretched over the trekking poles again as the couple press their backs against the wall of a barn. Thunder rolls over low hills. Through the teeming rain they spy the same car returning. It's moving cautiously, wipers racing. This time it stops; the window slides down. '*Buon giorno*. Can I offer you a lift?'

It's 9 a.m. Sunday morning. The driver is wearing a suit and tie. On his way to mass.

It's our first temptation. To abandon the quaint pathos of the *viandante*, out under all weathers, and return to the contemporary convenience of the combustion engine and the warm sedan.

'We're fine,' Eleonora says. 'We're walking.'

'I'm afraid you'll be soaked. Let me take you to the village at least.'

I'm not sure which village he means. It would take a while to explain to him about Garibaldi.

'No thanks.' We shake our heads. And he shakes his; he seems puzzled.

'*Buona domenica*,' we all sign off.

Towards 10.30, with hints of sunshine brightening the clouds, it looks like we've got away with it. The road is flat, empty, easy, the landscape a relaxing palette of dull greens framed by distant hills. We are planning to walk twenty and more miles today. To Poggio Mirteto. All good, then, until a yellow sign with bold black lettering announces, ZONA MILITARE. LIMITE INVALICABILE. In short, No Entry. However, the sign is old and faded. There's no fence or barrier to block our progress.

The hell with it.

Another hundred yards and the road deteriorates. Asphalt crumbles to clay. We're skirting brown puddles. More signs appear, with interesting variations. ZONA MILITARE. DIVIETO ASSOLUTO DI ACCESSO. Not just forbidden, but *absolutely* forbidden. ZONA MILITARE, SORVEGLIANZA ARMATA. Armed surveillance. Why didn't our app know about this? But to turn back now would mean retracing our steps a mile and more to take the road by the Tiber with its heavy traffic.

Once invested in an attack, Garibaldi comments, even if you realize it was a mistake, the only thing to do is to go on. Eleonora is hesitant; those signs are so threatening. But they're also very old, I point out, rusty even, and we haven't seen any hint of military activity.

We enter the woods. This is the enigmatic green stain on Google Satellite. The path begins to climb. Bushes and brambles narrow in. Cobwebs cling. Branches spring in our faces. I'm using the trekking poles to beat a way through now. Water sprays off the leaves. Beneath our feet the path is becoming a ditch, a stream. Nobody has been this way in years. Why? Are we about to come across some top-secret installation? Or will it be target practice? Could we plead that we didn't see the notices, we were so concentrated on our app? Will the military men be interested in our enthusiasm for Garibaldi, who after all gave his name to any number of Italian battalions and regiments? Though it has to be said the hero himself was categorically opposed to the existence of professional armed forces. Armies, he thought, should only be formed ad hoc to confront a despot or foreign invader. 'I would fight against the Italians themselves,' the General declared, 'if they tried to deprive another people of their liberty.'

I can't imagine getting into all this, should a shot ring out.

Eleonora's cheerful gameness amazes me. I'm so ready to feel like a bully, if only she would complain. But she won't. Not even when her hair snags on thorns. We're fighting through a jungle now, climbing over fallen tree trunks, ducking under low branches. Any hope of staying dry has long since been abandoned. A brown foam swirls and bubbles over our trekking shoes. 'You don't want waterproof shoes,' the expert in Milan told me. 'They're so much hotter.'

'How much further?' she asks. I reach in my pocket to consult my phone. But it isn't there.

MY PHONE ISN'T IN MY POCKET!

My left pocket. I always put my phone in my spacious left pocket. It's not there.

This is not the same as being shot at, but nevertheless a bombshell. Aside from all the normal problems when one loses one's phone, there are the photos I've been taking, any number of photos, which amount to my notes on the trip. Not backed up anywhere, since my Google photo allowance has long since been exceeded.

Eleonora is calling my phone from hers. It doesn't ring. The rain is getting heavier. As I scurry back down the path – where did I last consult the thing? – not even bothering now to avoid scratches and soakings, it crosses my mind how carefully Hoffstetter and Ruggeri and Gaetano Sacchi must have looked after their diaries on that march, kept them in safe dry places, never abandoned them even in extreme circumstances.

The phone is in a black case, which hardly makes things easier, given the gloom under the thick vegetation. I stop, panting, turn 360 degrees, then go on. I poke in some weeds. I feel I'm in the zone. I'd been checking the thing every ten minutes.

THERE IT IS.

Oh, the pleasure of finding something you feared lost! My dear dear Huawei, all the way from China to the Tiber valley. As I pick it up, it starts to ring. Sweet sound! I don't give a damn that my feet are soaked, my knees bleeding, my jacket torn. I have my phone, my photos.

'Got it, Ele!'

And onward. The vegetation begins to thin, the path broadens. True, there are more stern warnings that we absolutely oughtn't to be where we are, but as long, I decide, as there isn't a fifteen-foot barbed wire fence between us and the road when we get there, all will be well.

Just as we turn a bend into a last steep slope, the dogs appear. Two great white Dobermann-type creatures. They are standing on the track above us looking down. For some reason, the fact that they are not barking makes them all the more ominous. As if they were professionals, informed of our imminent, unlawful arrival.

Eleonora grabs my arm. The dogs seem in no hurry. They are studying us, predatory heads pointing, smelling the air. There's a static, dreamlike feel to the scene. As if we had conjured it from our fears.

'It's completely fine,' I announce. 'They're just two dumb dogs.' Shaking off her hand, I walk straight at them in the rain.

They don't move. Big animals. White with pinkish noses and eyes. They seem fascinated by my effrontery. I advance at a steady pace, stupidly remembering that the Austrians wore white uniforms. Always have your enemy understand that you are absolutely determined, Garibaldi insists. You will not turn back, whatever your losses. The white dogs watch me approach with growing interest. *Calmly* determined, Garibaldi qualifies, *lucidly* determined. One animal begins to paw the ground.

I'm ten yards away when a voice calls from the distance, off to my right. It's a man's gruff voice from beyond the trees where a meadow is opening up. The dogs hesitate, as if caught between competing duties, then race off. A moment later I glimpse two men with shotguns.

Five more minutes and we're at the end of our track, where, sure enough, defended by a high fence, there is a long low military building. But this is to our left. There is no obstacle to our reaching the road on the right. LOGISTICAL ARMY COMMAND, reads a large notice. POLYFUNCTIONAL EXPERIMENTATION CENTRE. There are no soldiers on sentry duty. Hoffstetter would be appalled. The path, it seems, has been closed for no reason at all.

By Italian standards Passo Corese is a recent settlement. It grew up where the Rome–Florence railway crosses the river Corese, a tiny tributary of the Tiber. There would have been next to nothing here in 1849. When we ask two passers-by Where is the piazza? they respond, Where exactly do you want to go? The main piazza, we say. They give complicated instructions. Second on the right, a flight of steps, first left, then ask somebody else. We can't find the steps. It seems the piazza must be at the top of a kind of hillock in the middle of a maze. We have to ask three times. Under their umbrellas, people are puzzled. But why do you want to go to the piazza? We want to see the church, Eleonora offers. There are wry smiles.

The steps, when we find them, are many and steep. Arriving, we discover, yes, there is a piazza, and a church, but no café. It's a big space entirely given over to a car park, which is empty because mass is over. The church is a modern brown brick pile. The Lego–like bell tower reminds one how beautiful such buildings used to be.

Back at the bottom of the hill, we're barely through the doors of a spacious modern café when a monstrous deluge explodes, something that will radically alter walking conditions for days to come. As the rain pours down we slip into the bathroom to change into dry clothes.

Ponte Sfondato

'The winners tell one story,' says an elderly man in the grocer's in Ponte Sfondato, 'and the losers another.'

It's now mid-afternoon. Five miles on. The grocer's in Ponte Sfondato doubles as a bar. With just two tables.

'The truth is,' the old-timer proceeds, 'Garibaldi didn't beat the Bourbon army in Sicily. The soldiers had been bribed not to fight.'

It's also a newsagent's, and a tobacconist's.

'He would never even have landed in Sicily if he wasn't protected by Jewish bankers and English lords.'

Once again providence has provided us with a refuge from the rain.

'How can you believe,' our man spreads his arms 'that he took the whole of southern Italy with a thousand men? It's a fairy tale!'

Needless to say, we're responsible for having sparked off this tirade. But first let's get our bearings. As we said, the *garibaldini* marched nine miles due north beside the Tiber from Monterotondo to Passo Corese, which was where I suspect they had their swim. After that the Tiber drifts off north-west, while the General proceeded north to Poggio Mirteto, a further ten miles on, in the direction of the larger and more distant town of Terni. This walk took them through the hamlet of Ponte Sfondato, where Trevelyan is convinced they had their swim, in the Farfa, not the Tiber. It hardly matters.

Ponte sfondato means broken bridge, and this is odd because in 1849 the famous bridge, or rather geological feature – a huge natural arch of stone created by the erosion of the little river that passes under it – was still very much intact. Indeed the road to Terni ran over it. The bridge only collapsed in 1961, having featured in various films, including *The Return of Don Camillo* and *Totò and Carolina*. Even the retreating Germans crossed it in the summer of 1944. The name

Ponte Sfondato actually derived from the older Monte Sfondato – Broken Mountain. A change of one letter to draw attention to the only interesting feature of the place. A couple of centuries later, when the bridge, alas, fell into the river, there was at least the consolation that the *sfondato* now made sense.

One curiosity of the walk from Passo Corese has to be mentioned. We found a country lane that climbs away from the town between olive groves and tall electricity pylons. At a corner, a large sign pointing to our left declared, AMAZON. Not a reference to Anita, but to the Amazon Logistics Centre, a development of over 700,000 square feet employing more than 2000 people which sends millions of products all over Italy. So this nondescript provincial dead end is in fact at the nerve centre of a billion clicks, as people from Trieste to Taranto seek what they want in cyberspace and wait until someone in Passo Corese slips it into a package so that it can be whisked off to the nearby autostrada and rail connections. Five hundred hectares of olive grove and archaeological park were levelled to build the facility, which is at once the biggest local employer and a powerful expression of modern society's aspiration to be done with any reliance on the local. Here I must confess in passing that we bought all our clothes for this trip online. And they all come from abroad.

But speaking of clothes, we can't afford to get wet again, since we're only carrying one change. So when, just as we are leaving the grocer's in Ponte Sfondato, the rain comes down again, we turn back inside. The proprietor, a morose woman in slippers and crumpled housecoat, eyes us from behind her counter. I order a glass of wine to keep her sweet. For one euro fifty she fills me a whole tumbler of something sharp and sour. Later, when I head for the bathroom, feeling nauseous, one of the older men at the only other table takes the opportunity to move in on Eleonora.

The man's excuse, I later intuit, was to draw her attention to two photos on the wall showing the old stone bridge before it collapsed. A matter of local pride. Upon which she told him of our Garibaldi project. As I return, he retreats rather abruptly to his seat and his game of cards, and the four men begin to discuss Garibaldi, without addressing us but knowing we can hear them. Which is odd. Their assumption seems to be that we know nothing and need enlightening. Of the four, all in their seventies, one is the type Italians call a *dietrologo*, a conspiracy theorist.

Garibaldi, this man tells his mild companions, as he deals out the cards for another game of *scopa*, was at best an ingenuous frontman for international banks and Anglo-Jewish scheming. At worst a bandit. The fanciful story of his conquering the south of Italy was invented to cover up a Masonic plot to destroy the Bourbon monarchy and place the south under the ruthless sovereignty of the north, which then proceeded to bleed its economy dry and even embarked on a campaign of genocide.

Taking breaks to throw down cards and protest over his bad luck, or raise a glass of sour wine to his lips, the man goes on and on. None of what he says is new to me. It is part of a now popular revisionism that seeks to rubbish the 'myth' of the Risorgimento. Quite why these people want to do this isn't entirely clear. Initially, you might suppose they were pushing for some new division of Italy into four or five autonomous states, but there's little real appetite for that these days. Even the once separatist Northern League has now become just the League and looks for votes in the south like any other national party. Perhaps what the proponents of this version of events most enjoy is the thought that there never was any heroism or idealism in the world, a conviction that releases them from the burden of emulation.

Where Eleonora comes from – Taranto, on the south coast of Puglia – revisionism is particularly strong. The south was miserably governed and much exploited after unification. The bandit bands – the brigands as they're called – were ruthlessly suppressed; Gaetano Sacchi, once accused of being a brigand himself, would be a leading figure in that suppression. A recent movement that refers to itself as the *Neoborbonici*, the New Bourbons, talks up the Bourbon kings of Naples and claims that a flourishing and entirely viable southern economy was deliberately destroyed by the north. Here there is some truth and much exaggeration, but again, crucially, there seems to be no political direction to this movement. It constructs a moral high ground from

70

which to lay claim to victim status and disclaim responsibility for the dire state of the south as it is today. We can't do anything because the south was destroyed by the Risorgimento, in which Garibaldi was a key figure.

'He did it for money!' our man in Ponte Sfondato exclaims. There's a derisive tone to his voice. 'Why else? He was a desperado! They stole from churches. Carried off all the gold and silver. What do you think he bought his island hideout with?'

'Don't,' Eleonora says. She covers my hand with hers, which has a couple of fresh scratches above the knuckles.

She's right. There's no point reminding them of the famous letter of 1845 in which Garibaldi rejected all payment for his long service to the government of Uruguay in their fight for independence, this while Anita was raising their children in a shack with no chairs to sit on. No point explaining, to these men over their Sunday afternoon card game, that the farm on barren Caprera, off the north coast of Sardinia – Garibaldi's home from 1856 on – was bought with a small legacy and loans from friends. No point telling these men that after handing over half of Italy to King Vittorio Emanuele in 1861, Garibaldi returned to Caprera with a sack of seeds, three horses and a barrel of stockfish.

'Just don't go there,' Eleonora repeats.

Fortunately, the rain is easing. We can leave. A few hundred yards on, crossing the new bridge that replaced the old, we look down into a steep drop where a muddy stream runs through thick vegetation, but of the great stone arch across which Garibaldi led his long column of men, mules, horses, carts and cannon 170 years ago, there is no sign.

Le Murene

Nettare la camicia. Wash your shirts. So began one order of the day. The General wanted his men clean. Obediently, we make this our first task every time we reach our destination. As soon as we're through the administrative preliminaries and have the door closed behind us, no matter how tired we are, it's clothes off and into the sink. They're so grimy. Our socks in particular are full of burrs and seeds and itchy

71

arrows of dry grass that spear their way through the aerated fabric of the trekking shoes to tickle and torment the feet. Today, following our adventures in the military zone, it takes a good ten minutes to get all nature's fertile stickiness out of the thick wool. Then ten more to wash and rinse everything thoroughly. And ten more again to find the wherewithal to hang everything up to dry, maybe on coat hangers dangling from window catches or balcony railings, or over the backs of chairs, or on the points of trekking poles wedged between bits of furniture. More and more, what we imagined as a holiday feels like a military operation. But at last we're ready for dinner, and in for a very different experience from last night's. With no pretensions to paradise, this place calls itself Le Murene – The Eels.

Once again we've had to change plans to suit the availability of accommodation. There was nothing in what Trevelyan calls 'the remote Poggio Mirteto', where Garibaldi's men are now safely camped. But there was the even more remote Le Murene, a couple of miles before Poggio. It's an *agriturismo*, a holiday farm. Not gated opulence, but a place to bring your children to discover the joys of goats, geese, pigs and sheep, and to enjoy some rustic cuisine. Strictly *biologico*.

Of the last stretch of walk on that long rainy day I remember only endless peaches glowing luminous red under stormy skies in the orchards along our path. And to the left, beyond the Tiber, the strange form of Monte Soratte, an isolated mountain that rises 2300 feet straight out of the plain and looks like a triangle with the top half removed, or like Siamese volcanoes joined by a long horizontal ridge. It looms there, lonely and glum amid the rain clouds, and will remain there for much of tomorrow, always on our left, in the west. Behind and beyond that mountain, Garibaldi's returning horsemen informed him, the French army had now realized its mistake and turned north, presumably intending to intercept the column at some point. The rebels would have to hurry.

We hurried, because it was already late in the afternoon, and found as always that a steep hill had to be climbed through thick woods to arrive at our goal. 'The storm has blown away everything,' the young woman who greeted us complained at once. Chairs and sunshades were scattered every which way. The terrace was awash with mud and wet leaves. Even the three big black-and-white goats seemed to be shaking their heads over it all. Our hostess was clearly upset that we should see her beautiful farm in this state. And no, she was sorry, but the restaurant wasn't open; they'd had a big party for Sunday lunch, which was upset by the rain, but we were the only guests this evening and she had to be off home soon. We must go to Poggio Mirteto to eat.

Eleonora explained our situation.

'On foot!' She was astonished. 'Twenty miles in that rain!'

She took pity. She took interest. She was someone, she said, who wished people could be more involved in the land. She would leave us some leftovers in the conservatory, she said.

It was perfect. This low glass structure ran the length of the farm-house and featured two long tables, each with twenty and more places. On one our landlady had left a litre of ice-cold water, a full carafe of sparkling wine, a basket of fresh bread, a platter of local cheeses, a bowl of fruit and a dish of cooked vegetables: aubergines, zucchini, peppers.

Why do I like this kind of food so much more in the end than the fancy fare of Paradise? We just felt so happy to be there. And how cheering to discover, dipping into Hoffstetter after dinner, that if our holiday sometimes seemed like a military operation, the *garibaldini*'s military operation could sometimes seem like a holiday. Here is the German talking about their evenings.

Garibaldi ate a frugal meal to which his close staff were always invited. Usually it was at this time that citizen deputations would come from nearby towns and Garibaldi would talk to them with extreme politeness, gleaning from them with great guile news of every kind; in return he would give them fake news about where we were headed and what we planned to do. Then, if he wasn't too tired, the entertainment would go on late into the night with the General telling stories about his past. One evening he recounted this adventure from his American life ...

'Once I found myself after several fierce cavalry battles with just 400 infantry and 400 cavalry. We were attacked by an enemy much stronger than ourselves and after some ferocious fighting we were routed. I escaped into some woods with just 400 men. My wife had been fighting on the left side of the battle and it all went wrong for her. Her hat took a bullet, then her horse was shot from under her and she was taken prisoner and tied up. But during the night, while the enemy was sleeping, the courageous woman was able to wriggle out of her ropes, grab a horse and take off. Some cavalrymen came right after her, but she plunged into a wide river and, grabbing the horse's tail, managed to make it to the other side despite all the shots they fired after her. Yes, *signori*, my wife is a valiant woman,' the General wound up, reaching out a hand to her and sending her a warm look. Her face lit up with joy and pride.

We also felt moderately proud of the day's achievements. Albeit upstaged by Anita. And relieved not to have to think of the death of 400 companions.

DAY 5

6 July 1849 – 29 July 2019

Le Murene, Poggio Mirteto, Cantalupo, Vacone – 16 miles

Poggio Mirteto

Poggio means hill and turns up in many Italian place names – Poggio Bustone, Poggio Catino, Poggioreale, Poggibonsi – so we knew what to expect. However, at the top of this hill, steep as ever, in a pretty central piazza, there was a surprise waiting, something that moved me quite unexpectedly and reminded us of a huge difference between the *garibaldini*'s journey and ours: we know where they are going and how it will end. They had no idea.

Realizing our shoes would take time to dry and with a promise of breakfast at seven, we had made a late start. Hopefully the heat would not be a problem after such a deluge. At 6.30 the view from our balcony was yellow sunshine over an ocean of dense vegetation and wisps of white cloud lying in the Tiber valley below. The landscape had been rinsed clean by the rain. We felt lucky.

But we were wrong about the heat. By nine the temperature was already touching thirty. As ever the walk turned out longer and more complicated than we imagined. Map and territory never seem to match. So our ten o'clock coffee felt well deserved. Hoffstetter, who never missed a chance to drink a proper coffee, talks of there being just one café in Poggio Mirteto, whose owner, he was delighted to discover, was Swiss and could speak German to him.

We found a number of cafés around Piazza Martiri della Libertà and chose the smartest, with white tables and yellow sunshades, partly because I wanted to find relief in the bathroom. But there was no lock on the door. I didn't feel I could sit there with no lock. Check, Eleonora suggested, to see if there's a piece of string. I went back through the café's elegant lounge and, sure enough, in the bathroom there was a string attached to the handle. Pulling it tight, to keep the door shut while I sat, I had time to reflect that all my reading on Garibaldi had produced just one mention of such issues: while captain of the steamship *Piemonte*, on his way to land in Sicily in 1860, the General was seen sitting with his backside over the stern rail dropping his business directly into the deep.

After our coffees we wandered up and down Piazza Martiri della Libertà, which is actually more of a street opening up into a tree-lined oval than a square. But it's all expensively paved and laid out, with a garden and war monument, pretty facades and awnings, a baroque church and a lovely old town gate complete with vigorous yucca tree thrusting out of its masonry at ground level. This nobly named but actually rather modish piazza is set off by decidedly poorer surroundings: narrow alleys crisscrossed with drying laundry and old folks in slippers smoking on doorsteps.

I was ambling back and forth, taking photographs, reminding myself to push my phone deep in my pocket each time I put it back, when I looked up and saw, beneath the blue shutters of an open window, a white stone plaque. Twisted wire cables sagged across the top, and a water pipe ran up the left-hand side. It said:

In this house of the Lattanzi family,
ANITA GARIBALDI,
from 6 to 7 July 1849
was lovingly welcomed
and found rest and solace.
In her heroic heart,
together with the throb of motherhood,
the dream of Rome lived on.
And perhaps, like the light of the setting sun,
she foresaw her death.

Why these words hit me with such force, I have no idea. For a few seconds it was as though the figures we were shadowing, and above all the brave woman Garibaldi had talked about at dinner last night, were right there behind that shuttered window. I had only to push open the door – yes, it was ajar – and I could call to her up the stairs. 'Anita! Don't go on. Have your baby here in this pretty house where these kind people will look after you.'

Then my eyes fell on the last line of the inscription, in smaller letters: *Poggio Mirteto – nell'anno Garibaldino X dell'era Fascista* – heroic year ten of the Fascist Era. Which is to say, 1932. The plaque was part of the Fascist attempt to appropriate the Garibaldi story, to the point that the word *garibaldino* had become a synonym for the embattled heroism Mussolini always encouraged – 'Better one day lived like a lion than a hundred years like a lamb.' The Duce had had those words engraved on every 100-lire coin.

Garibaldino year ten. I stared at the inscription and shook my head. How disorientating it is when one layer of history lies over another, evoking and distorting it. There was nothing Fascist about Garibaldi, or the *martiri della libertà* who died for the Risorgimento. Fascism was the opposite of liberty. Nevertheless, I couldn't help feeling there was something heartfelt in this tribute to Anita. *Perhaps, like the light of the setting sun, she foresaw her death.* Below the plaque, by the door to the house, a sign in fashionable Euro-English, read BARBER SHOP.

The *garibaldini*, who notoriously wore their hair long, arrived in Poggio Mirteto at 10 a.m. The men camped on the slope; Garibaldi had a sun shelter built for himself with poplar branches. He thought it best to stay close to the men. Anita was given a dress by the Lattanzi family and continued to work on sewing a tent for herself and José. The mayor's wife had food sent to the soldiers' camp – including 'the most exquisite fruit, in particular some big black figs'. She even came along to serve at table 'in the politest possible way'. How jolly it all sounds. But all afternoon Garibaldi was focused on making sure enough pack saddles and baskets could be found for his mules. And the column was on the road again at 2.a.m. From front to back it was three miles long.

Mixing long marches and short. Setting out at different times of the day and night. Leaving a rearguard far behind or sending an advance guard far ahead. Joining the main road in full view of any spies, only to leave it again an hour later. Taking longer paths where shorter ones were available, or splitting the column over parallel paths. Ordering 6000 rations when there were only 4000 men. Camping over large areas with no discernible order. These were Garibaldi's methods for keeping everyone guessing. But he did at last confide to Hoffstetter that their immediate goal was Terni, thirty miles to the north, because in Terni he was intending to meet up with an Englishman.

Ex-British army, settled in Siena, forty-year-old Colonel Hugh Forbes wore a white top hat, shaved carefully every day, and was a fervent supporter of the Italian national cause. In 1848, together with his twenty-year-old son, he had fought for the Venetians against Austria; in 1849 he moved south to the Roman Republic, which assigned him a force of 900 men to garrison the strategic town of Terni. With the fall of the republic in Rome, these men, a mix of Swiss volunteers and ex-papal soldiers, were at a loose end. It made sense to join forces.

So from Terni onwards, Hugh Forbes will join Ugo Bassi, Ciceruacchio and Anita at the head of the column. I suppose, as an Englishman myself, it's good to have a compatriot as company, though Forbes is not the kind of Englishman I usually feel comfortable with. Where Garibaldi has little interest in rank, Forbes is obsessed by it, especially his rank. Where the General is always sensitive to the reactions of the local populace, Forbes demands people obey orders, in particular his orders. The citizens of Terni will be glad to see the back of him; he lives in the most expensive hotel in town and expects others to make sacrifices. But whatever we think of Forbes, when the Austrian hussars burst into the picture, when the bullets fly and the sabres swing, this prickly Englishman will be right there in the thick of it, risking his life and his white hat. For liberty. 'A courageous and most honest soldier,' Garibaldi remembered.

The road to Terni leads straight up a long valley, but the towns on the way are on hilltops either side. Garibaldi's men needed to climb up to them, because they had wells, and water – there is no river in this valley – and for safety too. The French army was now only a day's march over the hills to the west, the Spanish army a day's march over the hills to the east. The nightmare scenario was a coordinated attack, and the point of maximum vulnerability was the small town of Vacone, halfway along, since immediately south of Vacone there is a valley opening out to the west and immediately north a valley opening to the east. Vacone is where we plan to spend the night, if only we can find a bed there. There are few places to stay near Vacone, our websites tell us, and they are all fully occupied.

I have positive memories of the small town of Cantalupo, because this is the first time I feel comfortable, even happy, with a steep climb in blazing sunshine. Not only are we getting used to the heat, but we are growing stronger. I now raise my eyes to walls high above and do not feel daunted. But we are both suffering from sunburn on our thickening calves. A long tunnel of tall feathery bamboo, the elegant canes leaning in from both sides of the road, provides the sort of delicious shade where you can stop and apply some cream. At one corner, an enormous grey-green agave plant seems to be waving tentacles to grab you. Aside from the puddles left by yesterday's rain, there is definitely a different feel to this morning's walk. We have finally escaped Rome's orbit. Even at the Gran Paradiso, the metropolis was still exerting its pull. Now it has fallen away. We're in the heart of the heart of the country.

At the heart of the hilltop pile that is Cantalupo we find Piazza Garibaldi, where the only place open at 1.30 is Bar Garibaldi. The town is deserted, paralyzed by the day's blue dazzle. The barman is forlorn. The piazza somehow combines the chic and the cemeterial. All the *palazzi* and even the church have been freshly stuccoed, pink or beige. The white stone paving is new and rigorously swept. Carefully trained oleander trees have been arranged at regular intervals and massive white concrete pots are lined up in perfect symmetry, sprouting other trees, young as fresh graves. The five or six shops all have the same regulation cream-coloured awning, so that between CARNI SALUMI FORMAGGI on one side and MICKEY MOUSE, GIOCATTOLI, EDICOLA, CARTOLERIA on the other, the sign ONORANZE FUNEBRI – Funeral Directors – looks entirely reassuring. Just another shady doorway where you might take refuge from the sun.

The barman brings out our drinks and decides to help us find a place for the night. He makes four or five phone calls but draws a blank. When I ask him why his café is called Bar Garibaldi he says it's because the Piazza is called Piazza Garibaldi. He doesn't know the hero passed this way. Very likely a myth, he says. He doesn't know of any way to walk to Vacone except along the main road and won't believe that our app might know paths that he doesn't. But it does. When I show him the little screen he peers and frowns and scratches his ear.

Big tech knows more about your neck of the woods than you do; that's the truth. The local may not be quite as dead as the wayfarer, but you can't help smelling decay in the air in Cantalupo. Turning the piazza into some kind of decorous memorial – just three years ago, the barman tells us – has only given an impression of expensive embalming. 'They wanted to encourage young people to value their home town,' he says. 'Because so many are leaving.'

Vacone

'Magnificent,' enthuses Hoffstetter, 'is the road from Cantalupo to Terni. Enormously rich in wine.'

It doesn't look quite like that as we start to wind our way down the hill. Perhaps wine production is concentrated elsewhere these days. The landscape spreads out like a vast uneven quilt where each section is a little hill, some with castles on top, or villas, or villages. There's a patchwork of colour too – woods and fields, wheat and pasture. But the patchwork only occasionally corresponds to the quilting and the hills. The overall effect is of intricacy, density and movement. A rich smell rises off the soil, dry and honeyed. Filling your lungs, you feel drawn in.

Meantime it's mid-afternoon and we still have nowhere to stay. But we do have full water bottles, topped up at the fountain in Cantalupo. We carry about a litre each and are learning to drink regularly. Don't wait until you're thirsty and then gulp it; it will go down the wrong way and you'll splutter and cough. Garibaldi's men were not so lucky. Few had bottles, and when they did they couldn't carry more than a pint or so. 'We were marching in the most oppressive heat, and found not a drop of water all day long,' Hoffstetter recounts. 'Those who have walked along these roads,' Trevelyan observes, 'from fountain to fountain, will realize what the army must have suffered when the usual springs were dry.'

Water. How important it suddenly becomes when you realize you are running out. The tongue grows drier and saltier. The saliva thickens. A growing urgency overtakes all other concerns. At every corner or roadside shrine, you look out for those fountains Trevelyan mentions, or simply water taps in stone walls. There are still a few around. When you spot one, the relief is immense. You drink and soak your hat and splash the water over your head. You fill your bottles to the brim. The weight doesn't matter.

Over the coming days we will visit local museums in Todi and Orvieto and various Tuscan towns from Montepulciano to Arezzo. Invariably there is a fine collection of artefacts from pre-Christian times, Etruscan, Greek and Roman. As regular middle-class museum-goers, we move between the display cases thinking aesthetics, history of art, anthropology. We read captions that fill us in on trading routes and cultural influences, colonization and burial practices. Only in Arezzo will it finally occur to me that almost all these artefacts were designed to hold water, or wine, or oil – vases, pots, pans, urns, perfume bottles, medicine phials, amphorae, ewers, jugs, bowls, craters, carafes, demijohns – as if the supreme concern of any human being and goal of all technology must be to preserve a supply of liquid.

Finding no water in Cantalupo and none in Torri in Sabina, the next village along the way, the *garibaldini* approached Vacone, the point of maximum military danger, in a state of some desperation. Parties of cavalry had to be sent back to gather up stragglers. Then, in Vacone, which really is a stinker of a climb, the town's one stream was dry and the fountain reduced to a trickle.

We too are experiencing some minor desperation. Minor for me, major for Eleonora. The web has failed to turn up any place to stay. At the bottom of the climb to Torri in Sabina a woman standing at the open door of an isolated building turns out to be a doctor doing her surgery hours. No one has turned up. We ask her if she knows of any B & Bs. Like the barman in Cantalupo, she starts to make phone calls. Evidently it's a pleasure to show a stranger that you have acquaintances who can help. But her friends just give her other numbers to call, to show that they too have their connections. We're wasting time.

We walk swiftly now through a golden-green landscape still shiny with yesterday's rain, and I remind Eleonora that we do have a tiny, superlight tent with us. 'It'll be exciting!' But she has read that this is an area where wolves are thriving again. 'Why is Cantalupo called Cantalupo?' Sing wolf. Not to mention wild boars. She won't even consider sleeping out.

This seems mad to me. Dogs may be dangerous, but a quick search on Google will tell you no man has been killed by a wolf in Italy since forty-nine years before the *garibaldini* started their march. The year 1800. Nor do wild boars look for trouble with people in tents. Hoffstetter, Ruggeri, Belluzzi, Trevelyan never mention these animals. But Eleonora is adamant. She's not sleeping outdoors.

To keep us off the main road as we approach Vacone, our app suggests we turn left into the valley whence the French might attack, then right up a narrow lane which eventually becomes a stony track climbing steep as a staircase to a dilapidated jumble of brick and terracotta perched on the top of a darkly wooded hill.

Just before turning into this track, we pass a poster advertising Villa dei Fiori, a holiday farm. I call the number, but no one answers.

As we climb, last energy ebbing, a low stone structure built into the hillside appears to our left. An arch and a shadowy grotto with water trickling steadily into a deep stone basin, green with moss and slime. A plaque tells us that this same spring was the subject of a poem written by Horace over 2000 years ago. The verses are inscribed on the wall, in Latin. It's the kind of curiosity that Eleonora insists we stop and decipher, even at an anxious moment like this. Fortunately, Horace is right on theme. The Latin is a struggle, but here's a rather twee translation from the nineteenth-century American poet, Eugene Field.

> FOUNTAIN of Bandusia!
> Whence crystal waters flow.
> With garlands gay and wine I'll pay
> The sacrifice I owe;
> A sportive kid with budding horns
> I have, whose crimson blood
> Anon shall dye and sanctify
> Thy cool and babbling flood.
>
> O fountain of Bandusia!
> The Dog-star's hateful spell
> No evil brings into the springs
> That from thy bosom well;
> Here oxen, wearied by the plow,
> The roving cattle here
> Hasten in quest of certain rest,
> And quaff thy gracious cheer.
>
> O fountain of Bandusia!
> Ennobled shalt thou be,
> For I shall sing the joys that spring
> Beneath yon ilex-tree.
> Yes, fountain of Bandusia,
> Posterity shall know
> The cooling brooks that from thy nooks,
> Singing and dancing go.

If there were cooling brooks when Horace wrote his poem, there certainly weren't any when Garibaldi's men passed. Perhaps in 1849 the summer Dog Star had indeed cast a hateful spell. It's curious too, in this poem, how blood and water flow together; the goat must be killed to thank the gods for the gift of water. As if life had to be paid for with other life. But these are weighty matters and we too must 'hasten in quest of a rest' that for the moment is far from certain.

The sun is dipping below the horizon as we step onto the cracked cobbles of Vacone. It's the least promising of the towns we have seen. We follow a twisting alley through dingy housing and eventually reach an open terrace that looks back over the countryside, pink with a goat's-blood sunset. Miraculously, there are people here. Three to be precise. Two women, one old, one young, mother and daughter perhaps, sitting on a low wall with their backs to the panorama, and a man in his sixties astride an ancient scooter. Opposite the women is a poky little grocery and above that a tower with a coat of arms under a big clock, which surprises us by showing the right time. Late.

'*Buona sera*. Is there a café?'

'*Buona sera*. No.'

'Really, no café?'

'There is a bar, but it opens later in the evening. For the men to play cards.'

Eleonora explains our predicament − on foot with nowhere to stay − and the Garibaldi project that got us in this mess. The three locals are entirely uninterested in Garibaldi but very eager to show off their knowledge of possible accommodation in the area. The problem is, the older woman explains, that all the B & Bs and holiday farms down in the plain have been occupied by a group of Americans. 'Archaeologists,' says the man, his face red with the sinking sun. 'They come here for the summer and take all the places available.' 'They are digging,' says the younger woman. 'In a Roman villa.'

'Horace's villa?' asks Eleonora.

They don't seem familiar with the name.

All three launch into the rigmarole of phone calls to friends and relatives whose friends and relatives may know other relatives and friends who have a B & B. Or whose mothers or aunties have B & Bs. As they talk, a little girl dashes onto the terrace from some hidden aperture in the general stoniness and rushes to be hugged by the older woman. '*Zia!*' she shouts. '*Gioia mia!*' the woman cries. The girl runs off again.

The sun is almost gone. The calls go on. And now a little boy comes running down the steps beside the clock tower and goes straight to grab the older woman's knee.

'*Zia!*'

'*Gioia!*'

The older man, straddling his scooter, shakes his head from his phone call to the younger woman who shakes her head from hers. Despairing, Eleonora leaves me to it and goes into the grocery for some food. The younger woman follows since it turns out she is the shopkeeper. A rather older boy strides onto the terrace and shouts, '*Zia!*' '*Gioia!*' she replies.

'*Complimenti,*' I tell her. As if to say, what a lot of nephews and nieces.

'All the children call me *Zia,*' she explains.

'And you call all of them *Gioia.*'

'Yes.'

Another phone call comes to nothing. 'There was an advertisement,' – I decide to get involved – ' for a holiday farm, Villa dei Fiori. We saw it down on the road. I called the number but the phone was off. Perhaps I should call them again. Do you think?'

They are unimpressed. Obviously they know the place, but would never have thought of sending us there.

I make the call anyway. A woman's voice answers at once.

'*Pronto?*'

'*Pronto.* Do you have a room for the night? For two?'

'Yes.'

'Where are you exactly?'

'Via dei Casali.'

The road we came up.

'How long will it take us to walk from Vacone?'

'Twenty minutes.'

Easy as that. Our helpers look a little peeved. When I question them, they won't tell me anything about Villa dei Fiori. They don't want to talk about it.

Emerging from the dark cave of the shop with bread, ricotta and tomatoes, Eleonora is delighted we've found a place. 'We should celebrate,' she says, 'except the only beer they have is warm. So I didn't bother.'

I go straight back to the shop and tell the young woman we'll take a beer anyway.

'Oh you don't want it warm,' she says.

'Perhaps there's one in the fridge, then.'

She hesitates, then bends to open something under the counter. She gets on her knees and moves things around in the dark down there. When her head reappears, it's shaking.

'Sorry, we only have a big one.'

How do these people make a living?

I take the big icy bottle back up to the terrace and we finish it off in ten minutes. Meantime our welcoming party regroups to watch us eat. They seem fascinated by the clumsy way I use my penknife to slice tomatoes and peaches.

Between mouthfuls, I ask, 'So what do people do in Vacone of an evening?'

The younger woman answers promptly: 'We sit on the terrace and talk.'

'When we have time,' the older woman adds.

'Looking for Villa dei Fiori?'

A tall slim man with red face and very white teeth looks up from the engine of one of those three-wheeled vans Italian artisans use for moving scrap iron and the like.

'Place of last resort!' he says cheerfully. 'Had a cyclist last week; he'd given up all hope.'

There are big dogs at the door, but we're able to circle round them and enter the scrubbed gloom of a ground-floor flat, furnished, it

86

seems, with the relics of long-dead relatives. The black-enamelled sideboard is right in line with the day's funereal theme.

The landlady appears, in her early forties, holding a small can of beer. 'I thought you might be thirsty.' We have no cash and she has no credit-card facility, but surprisingly we manage to organize an electronic funds transfer, me rushing out and running the gauntlet of the dogs to get a signal on my phone in the wide open marvel of the starry night.

Despite our evident tiredness, the landlady sits at the kitchen table to talk while we sip the beer. Yes, she's from Vacone, she says, but her husband isn't. He doesn't really fit in.

'Where is he from?'

She mentions a village and explains, 'Ten kilometres over the hill.'

They work in a factory and keep hens and chickens and sheep and goats. And the B & B, of course. When people stop. Her son works in the factory too and has a passion for mountain biking. She worries that it's dangerous.

'Perhaps he likes to be free,' I suggest.

'Yes.' Her eyes light up. 'He says he feels free on his bike.'

Eleonora explains the purpose of our trip and wonders what Vacone was like in 1849.

'I don't know about the past.' The woman shakes her head sadly. 'I didn't have grandparents.'

She says it with quiet dignity, resignation and a certain air of mystery, as if with this admission she'd given a clue to understanding her existence, her alienation from the community up on the terrace under the clock tower.

She stands to leave. 'By the way, did you see any wolves? They say there are quite a few these days.'

As soon as the door is shut, Eleonora is triumphant.

'There are wolves!'

I have to think fast. 'Good job I found a place.'

But now we're sorted for the night, what of the *garibaldini*? Have they slaked their thirst? In bed we read about tomorrow's route.

Disappointed in Vacone, Garibaldi rode ahead with Hoffstetter to Configni, a name that means border, the border between Lazio and Umbria. The locals had told them it was only three miles when in fact it was five. 'Configni is just one hostelry,' Hoffstetter observes, 'but there was a spring with plenty of water and hay in abundance.' A couple of hours later the main column arrived and 'all crowded round the natural drink. The horses were the most frantic, thrusting their front hooves into the trough. My black horse was the worst, pushing its head up to its eyes in the water. I'd always thought that drinking so immoderately was dangerous. But it didn't have any unhappy consequences in this climate. We didn't lose a single horse the whole march.'

Hoffstetter, you often feel, was more concerned about the horses than the men. Nothing is said of the mules.

Lights out, Eleonora reflects that our landlady was telling us she was a *trovatella*, an abandoned child adopted by others. That's why she 'didn't have grandparents'. She was cut off from the past. And the community. She hadn't run about as a little girl shouting *Zia* and being called *Gioia*.

What amazes me is that Eleonora could have come to this conclusion. Nothing in my experience would have got me there.

DAY 6

7 July 1849 – 30 July 2019

Vacone, Configni, Stroncone, Terni – 21 miles

Configni

How easy to fall out when you're hot and weary. Perhaps bicker over trivial issues of power and control. Garibaldi had made Hoffstetter his chief of staff, but the ambitious Colonel Marocchetti, who was fourteen years his senior and had fought with Garibaldi in Montevideo, was upset and refused to take orders from the German.

What to do about a petty conflict like this in the context of a desperate march by a weary volunteer army shedding deserters by the hour, and much in need of enthusiasm and solidarity?

Garibaldi explained to Hoffstetter that he would make Marocchetti officially chief of staff while in reality everything would continue as before. After which, Hoffstetter tells us, Marocchetti was charm itself, and whenever anything went wrong Garibaldi would laugh with the German and shake his head saying, 'What's this about, is it Marocchetti's fault?' And Hoffstetter would reply, 'Yes, General, all the chief of staff's mistake.'

Differences were not so easily settled with Colonel Ignazio Bueno, a Brazilian and another old comrade who had travelled to Italy with Garibaldi in 1848. Bueno was as close to the General as anyone ever was. In February he had carried him on his back into the constituent assembly in Rome when Garibaldi was immobilized by rheumatism. But the big Brazilian was also undisciplined, unpredictable and perfectly capable of disobeying orders. A bear, Hoffstetter calls him. The two avoided each other.

89

In reality, the whole column was alive with possible conflict. The men hated it when an old battalion was obliged to integrate with the fragments of another, or others. They liked their old friends and the security of knowing who was who. They were frustrated over the lack of combat and the uncertainty of the expedition's aims. These were 'long, ruinous marches', Ruggeri remembers, and by the time they arrived in Terni the men were 'shattered and bruised by discomforts and privations'. It was around Vacone, Belluzzi warns us, that the terrain was too much for many of the men's boots, which began to fall apart.

My feet are in trouble too. Our trekking shoes are too light for the rockier paths. Perhaps this feeds into a certain tension that is developing between us over who chooses the route. Eleonora has the paid-up version of the navigation app on her phone. This gives her a certain control. The app produces and records a red line, which is the actual way we're walking, and she has to make sure that line coincides with the blue line, which is the route we've chosen to take.

This sets her up for making mistakes. You can't hold a phone in your hand all the time. The paths are twisty and full of turns. The app doesn't distinguish between a broad track and what may seem no more than a rut in the ground. We miss turns. We have to go back and forth. So I demand to see the screen, and she feels I'm accusing her of being stupid. I start to rely on Google Satellite as a confirmation of what she's telling me. I suggest we take Google routes which are more direct. The navigation app is capable of adding a mile of thorny thicket and slimy riverbed to avoid a couple of hundred yards of moderately trafficked road. A situation develops where we each champion the different apps we're using, as if promoting rival products. Then we notice this and burst out laughing. But when the sun is at its fiercest and we have to turn back a second or third time, a few sharp words are inevitable. We're under pressure.

Yet the day couldn't have started better. Dawn was still to break when we passed some remnants of white stone walls criss-crossing a rough pasture. It was Horace's villa. Shortly afterwards we glimpsed an approaching figure carrying a red lantern in the half-dark. How romantic! Except, as he grew nearer, it turned out to be a transparent red water bottle that somehow gathered and reflected what little light there was. A young man heading for shift work in a factory, we supposed. But a hundred yards on, here was another, in jeans and T-shirt with backpack and water bottle. *Buon giorno*, we said, but he was wearing headphones. And now another. And another. All men, all young, at intervals of fifty yards or so, in this narrow lane with thick hedges either side, as the day was dawning. *Buon giorno*, we said to the fourth or fifth, and this time the young man removed his headphones and said *Buon giorno* with a strong American accent.

There must have been thirty of them. A little group walking together included three young women. Eleonora felt it was only polite to address them first in Italian, to give them a chance to show off what they knew. But they knew nothing. When we laughed and told them they had hogged all the decent accommodation in the area, they were relieved to hear English but astonished by our accusation. They knew no more of the area they were staying in than of the language they couldn't speak. In a sense they had no idea where they were. They were specialists, archaeologists, or studying to be so, flown in from 4000 miles away to examine the artefacts of 2000 years ago. Much as Bueno and Anita had travelled 7000 miles to fight for freedom without speaking Italian or knowing anything about Rome, let alone Vacone or Horace. Garibaldi, it has to be said, spoke four languages fluently – Italian, French, Spanish and Portuguese – and could get by in English and German. A citizen of the world, he called himself.

Climbing up to Configni towards eight, an open door in a dilapidated grey facade invited us to poke in our noses and discover a tiny church. You would never have guessed. A fresco over the altar showed Saint Sebastian cheerfully resigned to his arrows. Perhaps, experienced soldier as he was, the saint sensed he would survive to die another day, another way. We will have a similarly astonishing tale of survival to tell towards the end of our adventure, and, for the record, back in South America Garibaldi himself survived a bullet that penetrated behind the left ear, crossed his throat and lodged under the right ear. Perhaps we are all rather hardier than we imagine.

Configni is still, as Hoffstetter described it, a one-hostel town. The Osteria della Cuccagna has a bead curtain on the door to keep out flies. Inside, a quotation from Julia Child has been painted in sharp black calligraphy on the white wall, in English. PEOPLE WHO LOVE TO EAT ARE ALWAYS THE BEST PEOPLE. Can that be true? Outside, from our table, we can read other announcements, expensively inscribed on freshly stuccoed walls round the piazzetta. *L'artista è un uomo*. The artist is a man. *Vissi d'arte, vissi d'amore*. I lived on art, I lived on love.

Eleonora, whatever I sometimes think of her map reading, is enviably erudite and quickly identifies these as lines from operas, Leoncavallo's *Pagliacci* and Puccini's *Tosca*. They have been put up, the café proprietor tells us enthusiastically, as part of the music festival held in Configni every summer, bringing much-needed business. 'May the Singing of Birds Fuse With the Sweet Sound of the Oboe,' one event is titled. To be held in the tiny Church of San Sebastiano.

By now a pattern is becoming clear. To keep these small places alive – only 700 people now live in Configni – they must be transformed into centres of upmarket culture, their centuries-old stone and stucco prettily refurbished, their cracked paving replaced with quaint fans of porphyry. This at great public cost, encouraged by ex-residents now based in some nearby town but eager to preserve their or their parents' birthplace as some sort of shrine or holiday home.

Unlike the boldly lettered operatic announcements all around us, the plaque that tells you where Garibaldi stayed the night, on the wall of a house twenty yards from the café, is so faded as to be barely legible. Actually he didn't stay the night here. He slept under linden trees at the top of the hill, 'where we were horribly mistreated by the ants', Hoffstetter tells us.

Beyond the house is the area with the spring where the men and horses drank so thirstily. There's a steep slope of palm trees, weeping willows, beech hedges, magnolias. Also an ugly monument to the war dead. From Saint Sebastian to Second World War partisans, there are no end of combatants, no end of monuments. Often you have to get close to see which war is being remembered. Here, in bas-relief, an angel with large round breasts gathers up a dead soldier whose tin hat did not save him.

In respectful memory, we fill our water bottles from the fountain, standing in a thick patch of dandelions and columbine. Now all we have to do is walk the twelve miles to Terni, and we will at last have caught up with our heroes, sleeping in the same place as they did and on the same day of the journey.

Stroncone

'A good, wide road,' Hoffstetter calls it. And it still looks good, though hardly wide by modern standards. The traffic is moving fast. Our app proposes crossing the valley from west to east and climbing to the town of Stroncone. It only adds a mile or so. It's 9 a.m. We're up for it.

This walk is breathtakingly beautiful, back-breakingly arduous. First the downward slope through dusty pasture and thick copse, then a stream to ford, with slimy stones under your toes, then an old mule track to climb. Everywhere the ground is rutted and scored by the rain of two days ago. A hillside of deep dry grass must be crossed, but with areas of swampy mud. Huge puddles must be skirted. It takes time. The sun climbs faster than we can. At burning midday, in a lane sunk between high banks of bush and bramble, we stumble upon the miracle of a *lavatoio*, a spring channelled into long stone troughs for washing clothes.

We take off our shoes and socks and sit on the edge with our legs in up to the calves. Again you're aware how discomfort affords the intense pleasure of its alleviation. A plaque beside tells us that *per fatale disgrazia* – by fatal misfortune – in the flower of youth, Virgilio Giusti died here in 1948, aged eighteen. Italians love these sad memorials, flowers forever refreshed at the point where a foot slipped or lightning struck. There will be a name, a date, a few words. They spin a sticky web of sentiment across the landscape. For some reason Eleonora is convinced that the expression *per fatale disgrazia, nel fiore degli anni* hints at suicide.

Uno dei Borghi più belli d'Italia, a sign boasts as we approach Stroncone. A *borgo* is a fortified medieval town or village. Vacone is a *borgo*. And Configni, and Cantalupo. There is now an official certification of *i più belli*, the most beautiful, which permits the *borgo* to display this sign. To attract tourism. There is even an official online 'top-ten' classification of the most beautiful *borghi* in each region. A beauty contest. We will be seeing more and more of these signs as we march through Umbria into Tuscany. I always feel sorry for the towns that applied for certification and were rejected. I wonder if the people of Vacone bothered. Or even knew about it.

Stroncone deserves its award. A fairy-tale skyline of battlement and bell tower. A café – Bar del Castello – spilling onto a terrace with a stunning view back across the valley. Cheap sandwiches, *cedrata* in abundance. As we drink and eat and congratulate ourselves, blissfully unaware of the trial the afternoon has in store, a young man comes to sit at a table near our own and orders a beer. He is the only other customer. He is not Italian. Romanian perhaps. Or Albanian. Lean, tanned and unshaven, carrying a battered backpack. When the barman returns with a bottle, the stranger explains that he is looking for work. The barman sighs, shakes his head, talks about a restaurant some miles into the hills that just might ... you never know. It crosses my mind that this young man is a wayfarer. Or a deserter. In the wrong century anyway.

The afternoon's difficulties begin when we find we can't get out of Stroncone. Ten minutes of surreal disorientation ...

It should be so simple. The topography is obvious. The village is stretched, ribbon-like, along the side of a steep spur running north–south. What can go wrong if you know you have to head north?

Your app.

I suggest we walk down a narrow cobbled passage, parallel to the road and full of fascinating old bric-a-brac, coats of arms, water troughs. No sooner have we gone twenty yards than Eleonora tells me we're going the wrong way. The app's red line is striking off in a different direction. We walk back and forth, first to the square, then this way and that, up and down, trying to get blue and red lines to meet, me protesting that it's obvious where we have to go, Eleonora shaking her head, the app creating fancier and fancier squiggles as we go round in circles. And of course the sun is hot, our packs feel heavy after lunch, and the third time we pass the tables of Bar Castello, arguing excitedly, I see our wayfarer raise an ironic eyebrow.

'It's gone mad. We'll have to follow our noses.'

And we do. Beyond the maze of the town's stone walls the red line calms down and starts to behave again. This wonderful piece of software that makes it possible for us to cross the Italian countryside without using busy roads is vulnerable to agglomerations of stone. Never trust blindly.

Garibaldi of course had no app and didn't rely on maps. In every place he came to, his first task was to find a guide to get him to the next place. It was hard to find these men, he complained – shepherds, woodsmen, hunters – because the priests warned them it was a sin. And when found it was hard to explain to them his unusual requirements, hidden paths one day, the fastest road the next.

No sooner had a guide agreed to work for the General than he was placed under armed guard. He mustn't talk with anyone. If he led the army into a trap he could have no illusions what his fate would be. On the other hand, for the whole length of the march this man would have the honour of Garibaldi's company. In the 1890s Belluzzi tracked down a number of surviving guides. They had only fond memories of the experience.

The Austrians and French, on the other hand, used maps. The Austrians in particular were proud of their meticulous military mapping. It was blind faith in their maps that would let them down when the chase was at its most intense.

Terni

Beyond Stroncone the road down to Terni turns out to be even more dangerous than the road in the bottom of the valley: narrow and fast, with tight bends and no place to walk. Again we plot a new route that stays in the hills to the east, dropping down into the big town only at the last.

A steady climb is followed by a sudden plunge. Then the same again. Avalanches of sharp brown stones. Their jagged spikiness felt through our soles. We miss one turn, then another, and another. We backtrack. The sun at its zenith. Hawthorns, furze and gorse. Tiffs, irritations. We've arranged to meet the man who's renting us a flat in Terni at three. We'll never make it. We phone to tell him four. We phone again to tell him five. The water is running out. The path is still climbing. And plunging. Eleonora slips and goes down. It's a wake-up call. A twisted ankle and our trip is over. How many of the *garibaldini* were limping or hobbling? At times, walking downhill, gauging boulders, roots and puddles, through sunglasses trickling with sweat, it seems the mental attention required is even more tiring than the physical effort climbing.

'Long, ruinous marches …' 'The soldiers' poor shoes began to break …'

Still, what a pleasure, finally to reach a high ridge and for the first time look down, rather than up, to the place where we are headed, a brown and grey sprawl quivering in the haze where two valleys meet. There are even skyscrapers.

A band came out to greet the *garibaldini* as they approached Terni. Crowds waved the tricolour. The men were led to the Carmelite monastery, just short of the centre, where a camping space had been prepared for them in the gardens. After which, on this occasion, they were allowed into town. Here is Hoffstetter.

Since Tivoli we'd done nothing but wander around side roads and tiny *borghi*. Now it was a pleasure to stroll about spacious neighbourhoods, with big hotels and cafés, leading to lovely gardens outside the city walls. Terni has ten thousand inhabitants and is one of the Papal States' prettiest cities. Burghers, peasants and soldiers mingled together and livened up the streets. There was no need to fear trouble at moments like this since intemperance with drink is almost unknown among Italian soldiers. They enjoyed the chance to sip a lemonade, or a coffee, or even a sorbet, to rest in the cool shops and admire the pretty girls. The General had decided on a day of rest here, much needed by both men and beasts.

And by ourselves. Taking off my filthy socks and counting the new blisters the rough paths have brought, I feel I would have had to take a day off whatever the General decided. Eleonora on the other hand, who always gets the most vicious blisters when she wears smart shoes, has none at all. Only headaches from the sun and stomach cramps. No sooner have we showered than I hurry out to find a pharmacy.

Pharmacies are places you can rely on in Italy. Rely on to be exactly the same from Turin to Trapani. A triumph of unification. The same bright white spaciously antiseptic atmosphere. The same studiously diligent staff in white coats. A hint of old-fashioned apothecary in the neat stacks of shiny wooden or steel drawers that climb the walls behind the counter. The same invitingly prurient images of flourishing young women rubbing anti-cellulitis creams into voluptuous thighs. Soft greens and blues dominate. There's not a speck of dust. It's a safe, expensive place. And there's always a queue. Because Italian law does not allow you to buy even the simplest medicines – aspirin, Alka-Seltzer – in the supermarket or, God forbid, the tiny grocers of Vacone and Cantalupo. To live in a little *borgo*, however *bello*, is to have to travel to town for a pack of paracetamol. Protected and enriched by a thousand restrictive regulations, the good pharmacists can usually be persuaded to break the rules and sell you a prescription-only drug, if you insist. After all, they're obliged by law to be graduates in pharmacy. People like to ask advice, explain their problems, at length. I arm myself with *santa pazienza*.

Never did I imagine I would become a browser in the pedicure section, but here I am examining products for cracked heels, corns and calluses, toe-blister plasters, underfoot-blister plasters, bunions, warts. Feet are suddenly extremely interesting to me. Connoisseur status beckons. In particular I'm looking for tubular toe protectors. In vain.

Seeing my perplexity, a young lady pharmacist putting the shelves in order comes to offer advice.

'Of course the best thing is to rest your feet.'

I explain that we have been walking a week and expect to be walking at least a couple more.

'The Via Francigena?'

When I tell her about Garibaldi, she is delighted. 'Did he really stop here? In Terni?'

It's interesting how none of the six or seven people marooned in the queue seem upset by this leisurely conversation the pharmacist is enjoying.

'There are two plaques in the main piazza,' I tell her. 'He stayed about forty-eight hours.'

'Longer than most tourists!' she laughs. Now she drops her voice and confides, 'It's awful isn't it? Terni. I mean, for an educated person like yourself. From outside.'

'In the early eighteen hundreds it was thought one of the prettiest towns in the Papal States.'

She shakes her curls. 'I really envy you your walk. I'd love to go away.' And she reaches deep into the display where shiny little boxes dangle by cardboard hooks from chrome rails and pulls out a hidden product, which isn't quite what I'm after, but almost. A silicon tube you can cut into toe lengths. It will have to do.

My young pharmacist was right. Terni is no longer the jewel it was a couple of hundred years ago. Exploiting its favourable position, its millwheels and water supply and easy accessibility, the town became a major manufacturing centre after Unification, to the point of being described as the Manchester of Italy. Steelworks, guns, textiles, chemicals. Then in the Second World War it paid the price for that success when the Allies bombed it heavily, destroying much of the ancient centre. But there are still some noble buildings here and there, and spacious squares, and a good atmosphere in the streets.

Certainly we struck lucky with our accommodation; all the more so since we're staying two nights. We're met by a brisk young man in a bright silk shirt who takes us up to the seventh floor of a 1950s build-ing and shows us round a four-bedroom flat with two lounges and a huge terrace that runs the length of the building, complete with tables, garden chairs, loungers and a thousand plants.

His mother will come and water the plants tomorrow evening, our host says. 'Not to worry, she's discreet.' He speaks ten to the dozen, in a hurry to be away. 'You'll find cakes in the fridge for a snack.' A heavy door with elaborate security locks clunks after him.

The perfect host. Except, oddly, there's no soap. Eleonora phones him. She doesn't say we need something to wash our clothes. 'We don't supply soap,' the young host tells her. As if it were corporate policy. But he will text us, he says, the address of a good restaurant.

Rooting in our packs, we find some shampoo sachets salvaged from Paradise. Teabags from Villa dei Romani. We make tea – there's a china teapot – sit out on the terrace, shaded by broad eaves from the blazing sunshine, enjoying a local cake with thick icing on top. Inside the flat, the furniture is upmarket 50s retro. Wall-fitted cupboards with doors designed to look a century old. Polished floors of red and white stone scattered with Persian rugs. It's another flat left empty by deceased relatives. I imagine a student of mid-twentieth-century decor booking him- or herself into B & Bs all over Italy to produce the definitive report.

And we go to bed. For two blissful hours. Then hobble to a restaur-ant. It's an odd thing about blisters that once you've really got going they don't seem too bad. But take a break and you might as well be walking on hot coals.

Our host's choice of restaurant is hidden behind a rundown farmhouse on the outskirts of town. Trattoria da Carlino. But it has a garden, and pink tablecloths. The place is busy, but a young waiter appears immediately and points us to a corner. A table of six is tackling full plates of steaming meat. 'But there are vegetarian choices, *signori*.' *Penne con burrata e pomodorini* for me. *Ciriole alla ternana* for Eleonora, which is to say, thick spaghetti made from semolina flour and served in a garlic and tomato sauce. There are mosquitoes too, round my ankles. But I manage to ignore them, discussing Garibaldi's contempt when, on arriving in Terni, he found that the rich folk who supported the Pope had fled. He ordered that their property be confiscated for the use of the town council.

Ruggeri provides this info. Perhaps Hoffstetter was too busy exploring the town's cafés to notice. In the end nothing was confiscated because none of those in power in the town wanted to alienate the rich folk, who would surely be back. No one believed the revolution would last.

We order a carafe of Trebbiano. Meanwhile darkness has fallen and the evening air has a mothy summeriness to it.

'What did Ruggeri think of Hoffstetter?' Eleonora asks.

'He never mentions him.'

'In his whole book?'

'It's only sixty pages.'

'And Hoffstetter of Ruggeri?'

'He never mentions him. In five hundred pages. They have completely different feelings about the march.'

'But they do go through the same towns!'

'In the same order.'

'And Belluzzi?'

'Belluzzi mentions Ruggeri's diary in passing and says Hoffstetter exaggerates his own importance. But he takes at least half of his details from him. Without acknowledgement.'

'They were jealous of anyone close to Garibaldi.'

'I suppose so. They wanted all the limelight for their hero. Trevelyan too. Even Anita is only tolerated because she makes Garibaldi greater.'

'Her passion and loyalty a measure of his charisma.'

'The irony is that Garibaldi was modesty itself. Everyone who met him said as much.'

We're puzzling over this enigma – a hero without hauteur – when a new figure of evident charisma appears on the scene. A wounded soldier, no less, with two women in loyal attendance to enhance his greatness.

A wheelchair is pushed through the gate but is too wide to move between the tables. A one-legged man is helped onto crutches and lurches towards the table next to ours. He's young, tall and ruddily corpulent. A fleshy grin shows gleaming teeth and a mood of happy sensuality. He seems to have stepped, or hopped, straight out of a Rubens; a satyr in a white shirt.

Leaning on one crutch, the man raises the other to salute friends here and there. *Forza!* someone calls. Our efficient waiter has the menu in his hand the moment he's settled. Wine appears on the table. The man launches into stories to entertain his adoring escorts, an elaborately tattooed blonde and a prim brunette. At once the blonde is in stitches. A peel of giggles shifts the mood of the restaurant. Followed by another. And another. It's time for us to go. When the waiter brings our bill, a flicker in his eyes tells me he understands. There's a hint of the expression, *pazienza*, and of the sentiment, *poveretto*. Poor guy. What a pleasure, these moments of unexpected complicity!

Later, I wake in the night and my body is on fire. My feet are ablaze. It's intolerable but strangely pleasing too. I'm ripe with summer sun. I almost *am* the summer, after these long hours trudging the warm earth in the vegetable fervour of oaks and vines and brambles and olives. Summer stretched on a bed. Insomniac summer.

We have the big windows to the terrace open and the night air stirs in the room. I think about the fat sensual man who had lost his leg. How alive he was despite his handicap. Or perhaps because of it. And I think of all the men who lost limbs defending the Roman Republic. Volunteers. Why did they do it? There were only 2500 *garibaldini* left, Ruggeri reckons, when they arrived in Terni. Fifteen hundred desertions. Those who found themselves near their homes were particularly prone to go. The Second Legion more than the First. But why did the others hang on?

For this glowing body perhaps. I remember our sore feet in the soothing water of the *lavatoio*. I imagine the pleasure the men took in the cafés of Terni after that ordeal by thirst the day before. They were *in* life, and in it together. Which is maybe a way of saying they risked life, as a community, for a cause. 'They danced in the bullets,' Hoff-stetter reports of the battle against the Neapolitans at Palestrina. Drunk on the pungent precariousness of it all, the men actually celebrated the arrival of enemy fire.

I sit up in bed. Eleonora looks beautifully relaxed, sleeping on her side. I go to the kitchen to pour myself a glass of cold water then sip it in an armchair on the terrace looking out over the quiet city.

DAY 7

8 July 1849 – 31 July 2019

Terni

Six days they walked and the seventh they rested.

That was the plan. But we both woke to emails requiring urgent work. I had an article to proofread. For London. Eleonora a few pages to translate. For Milan. In 1849 a man marching through the Italian hills was where he was. At most a horseman might gallop up with the news that an Austrian army was approaching Foligno just thirty miles to the north. Or that the French had passed Civita Castellana heading towards Orvieto forty miles to the north-west. But it was unlikely he would get letters discussing website servicing, or inviting him to subscribe to magazines. Today you have to work hard really to be where you physically are. The temptation is always to spread yourself across the globe, checking on news that doesn't affect you: Trump, Syria, cricket scores. Or WhatsApping photos to family in London or New York. We decided to take a look around the town in the morning and spend the afternoon with our minicomputer and our work.

Our apartment is slightly to the north of the centre. The monasteries where Garibaldi's men camped are a half-mile beyond the river Nera, which circles the old centre to the south. The rivers in this part of Italy are disappointing, at least in summer, little more than muddy trickles. Despite the recent rain, the Nera is no exception. Fortunately, just beyond it there is an excellent sports shop where the owner, a genuine mountaineer, talks us through trekking poles and trekking socks.

Just as yesterday in the pharmacy, I find a new fascination in browsing products I've barely thought about in the past. I see the importance of the way a trekking pole handle is shaped, the way it telescopes, how easily and securely you can fix its length. Meantime, the owner is thrilled by our Garibaldi project. He calls the other members of staff to the till. 'These two explorers are mapping out a new walking route! They're going to write a guidebook. And it passes through Terni! Right by our shop!'

Everything comes down to business in the end. Eleonora tucks her new poles under her arm as we say goodbye.

The Delle Grazie monastery is now an old people's home, but the gracious public park around it still has more than enough space to sleep 2000 men. It's a pleasure imagining them in their red shirts milling around us on the dry grass, among the cypresses and lindens, as we walk across to the second monastery, about a mile away, where the cavalry slept. 'Marocchetti and I thought we might take advantage of the mattresses in the rooms,' Hoffstetter remembers, 'but we soon realized we were no longer used to such things. I slept fine on the bare earth: for each of my three horses I had a cloak and a big fur, with which I made myself the most enviable of beds. One horse stayed saddled, just in case, while one saddle served as a pillow. My boy, Ramussi, fared even better; he slept on the forage with a blanket and one of my cloaks.'

Two fast roads have to be crossed to get from the park to the Basilica San Valentino, which is closed. We won't be able to see the saint's remains, which have lain on or under this holy site for 1800 years. Valentino is Terni's patron saint. Young lovers come on pilgrimages. The church advertises a Betrothal Festival, a Silver Wedding Festival, a Golden Wedding Festival and a Free Guided Tour of the Basilica on 14 February. Would-be participants can book online, where they can also purchase San Valentino T-shirts and a plastic San Valentino statuette.

A group of Frati Carmelitani Scalzi – Barefoot Carmelite Monks – watches over the saint's remains twenty-four seven and were apparently doing the same in 1849. Belluzzi tells how Garibaldi's men made fun of the monks and upbraided them for their laziness and easy lives. There was even some fat-shaming. Nevertheless, in 1882, six weeks after Garibaldi's death, the friars did put up a plaque above a side door to record the hero's passing. Fortunately Belluzzi noted down what it said because, aside from the first two lines, the words are no longer legible.

In July 1849
Giuseppe Garibaldi
Venice-bound
refreshed here the glorious remnants
The citizens and the town council
marked with reverence
the great commander's footprint.
22 July 1882

Remnants of what? Perhaps the monastery objected to any mention of the Roman Republic, which was anathema to the Pope. Perhaps the plaque has been allowed to fade on purpose. Still, one can't help feeling that some mention of José and Anita would play to the monks' San Valentino racket. It's a missed opportunity.

Back in town, the *duomo* has a different kind of footprint. Beside the door, at head height, the shape of a shoe is sunk three inches into the wall. It seems in fifteenth-century Terni there had been too much loving going on. Valentino's influence perhaps. Laws were introduced to curb ladies' scandalous indulgence in fine clothes, jewels and beauty products. High shoes were particularly in vogue, to create a seductive sway beneath long skirts. This shoe shape sunk in the wall indicated the maximum permitted height of a shoe from 1444 on. Three inches. Clearly the girls weren't trekking.

The sandals we're wearing this morning have barely a half-inch of sole. We debated a month and more whether we should pack spare footwear. Even simple sandals weigh a pound or so. But you need to give sore feet some air. I imagine Garibaldi's men might have killed for a pair of Geox.

Between the basilica on the outskirts and the *duomo* back in the centre, we had to negotiate a busy roundabout, from whose grassy centre rises a hundred-foot spire of rusty, coppery metal. It's another Arnaldo Pomodoro. *The Spear of Light*. In Piazza della Repubblica on the other hand there's a moving inscription to local partisans killed fighting Nazi occupiers.

This trip, I must say, is opening my eyes; it's as if we'd been drawn into a great debating chamber where different eras have laid out their wares and staked their claims. Our own offers mostly rapid roads and empty gestures. *The Spear of Light* needs to be so tall because otherwise the passing cars would miss it. The drivers are on their phones, and will still be busy talking when they cross Ponte Garibaldi, where the partisans were shot.

Back in the cool of the flat, I get to work correcting the proofs for my article. But my body is still pulsing with summer and I can't think of anything but setting off tomorrow morning, striking up the stony hills. I'm thirsting for the sun, the heat, the sweat. And the company of the General, Anita, Bassi, Hoffstetter. And Forbes now too.

Instead of focusing on my text, I keep checking my blisters. For the nth time I enquire of Google if it's better to lance them or leave them be. Neither folklore nor sophisticated medicine seems to have resolved this conundrum. If you have to keep walking, one site suggests, lance your blisters at once. Otherwise leave them be.

On a shelf behind a glass door, the deceased occupant of our flat has left a tin with needles that might last have threaded a button in the 1960s. I hold one over a gas flame in the kitchen, then get to work. Toe by tormented toe, it's surprising how transparent the liquid is. Dewdrops almost.

Towards five I hand over the computer to Eleonora, who is equally impatient to have this nonsense of work behind us. While she translates, I use my phone to buy online storage for my photos and look through those I've taken so far. Hundreds. The scratchings in the cellar of Villa dei Romani. The terrace in Vacone. What would Garibaldi have photographed, I wonder? As Hoffstetter describes him, the

General was an obsessive observer of landscapes. No sooner had his men arrived in a new place, than he would be changing horses and off again, exploring the surrounding countryside, imagining every possible military scenario, returning to give detailed orders as to where checkpoints must be placed. 'He was tireless,' Hoffstetter remarks. Wherever there was a tower he would climb the steps to the top and gaze north, south, east and west.

Garibaldi's Google album would contain endless panoramas that only he knew how to interpret. Hoffstetter's would be full of pictures of Garibaldi, and of his beloved horses, and the interiors of fashionable cafés. Otherwise one has the impression the German would have been a CCTV man. His 500 pages are packed with details of exactly where and at what intervals he placed the sentinels each time they camped, what was in their field of view and how often they were to go back and forth to contact each other. It was a policy rewarded in Terni by the capture of a spy, an Austrian soldier in peasant clothes who had been sent south to get a close look at the *garibaldini*. By the rules of war, such a man could have been stood against a wall and shot. Many clamoured for it. But Garibaldi's severity was reserved for the unworthy among his own soldiers. The Austrian was closely guarded and forced to walk with the column during the coming days. That way he was neutralized, and perhaps also indoctrinated in the philosophy of freedom.

On the terrace, eating baked aubergine and quiche, Eleonora and I discuss *spie* – spies. It was a word frequently used at the university where we met and worked. It was known that certain members of staff would report any criticism they heard to the head of faculty. Or forward him your emails. *Spie*. 'Spies were the special curse of Italy,' observes Trevelyan, talking about the 1840s. 'Our enemies,' Garibaldi complained in his memoir, 'always found a throng of traitors ready to spy for them.'

But the evening is pleasant on the seventh-floor terrace in Terni as the sun sinks and the shadows lengthen. We have just opened a bottle of wine when Eleonora asks, 'What's that?'

It's the sound of a key turning in a lock. And now a squeak of hinges.

Spy?

'*C'è nessuno?*' a voice calls. Anyone there?

Our host's mother has come to water the multitudinous plants. An elegant woman in skirt and blouse, she unravels a hose and sets to work.

'Don't mind me,' she says cheerfully.

We offer her a glass of wine, which she declines, but then she hurries to a tub of tomato plants, washes four small red fruits with her hose and brings them to our table. They taste warm and sunny.

Eleonora enthuses on the comforts of the big flat. It was her mother-in-law's, the woman confides, directing a jet at some prickly pears. 'Poor soul.' But her son enjoys the job of renting it out. Plus their holiday home by the sea. 'We have a place near Lido di Tarquinia if you're interested.' The boy worries her, though; he still hasn't finished his degree. 'He just can't pass his English exam.'

'Have him spend the summer in England,' Eleonora suggests.

'Yes,' she says, 'we've discussed that.' Her voice becomes vague; perhaps she doesn't want her son to go away.

'If you wanted to stay a while in Terni,' she proposes, turning to a row of geraniums, 'you could pay for the apartment by giving him lessons.'

I smile. Eleonora tells her we have to be off on our travels at dawn. Once again she explains our project and lists the towns we've walked through.

'Stroncone!' the lady cries. 'I have a surgery in Stroncone once a week.' She's a doctor.

We enthuse over the beauty of Stroncone, the sadness that these beautiful medieval *borghi* are almost depopulated.

'Only the old people left,' she observes.

'We've noticed an awful lot of old people's homes,' Eleonora agrees.

'Ageing relatives,' I suggest, 'keeping the *borghi* alive with their dying.'

My humour isn't appreciated. Our hostess shifts her attention to a lemon tree.

After a short silence she says, 'You must be a professor. Right?'

'Is it so obvious?'

'I like to guess what people do.' She waves the hose back and forth. 'Not an economics professor, I don't think.'

'No.'

'Not mathematics.'

'Never in a million years.'

'Or history.'

'Why couldn't I be a history professor?'

She shakes her head. 'History professors are boring!'

'I love history.'

She lingers over an agave.

'Philosophy!'

'I wish.'

When I tell her I am, or was, a professor of translation, she again says how nice it would be if I could teach Francesco.

She circumnavigates us now and starts to pour water into the roots of a big wisteria that sends its tendrils along the railings and up the pillars to the eaves.

'About Garibaldi, though. There's a story about my great-great-grandfather, if you're interested.'

'Please!'

'It seems one day he went out, here in Terni, to buy some tobacco or something, you know how men do, and never came back. That is, he came back ten years later. He'd joined Garibaldi and stayed with him for all those years.'

'Fantastic,' Eleonora says.

'Except ...' I open my mouth to make the obvious objection, but catch a warning glint in Eleonora's eyes.

'My grandmother was very proud of him, her grandfather.'

The truth is, Garibaldi never kept an army together for any longer than the time needed to fight the battles that had to be fought. What was this man doing for ten years?

'Be hard to disappear like that today,' Eleonora offers.

'Thank God,' says our hostess, thinking of Francesco perhaps. She coils her hose. 'Just leave the keys on the table. And *buon viaggio*!'

We lay out our clothes and prepare our backpacks. In bed we read how Garibaldi put Forbes and his 900 men at the head of the Second Legion, where most of the desertions had occurred, and had him lead the column out of Terni in the early evening. Not as an honour, Belluzzi says, but for fear that if the Englishman went last the angry populace would throw stones at him.

PART TWO

Hope

DAY 8

9–10 July 1849 – 1 August 2019

Terni, Cesi, San Gemini Fonte, Carsulae, Acquasparta – 16 miles

Cesi

'Venice-bound', says the plaque on the Basilica di San Valentino. But when he stopped in Terni Garibaldi had no clear idea where he was heading. Venice was the last city where a revolutionary government was hanging on, but tremendously difficult to reach. Two hundred and fifty miles away. With the high Apennine chain between, then the barrier of the Po Delta, miles and miles of marsh and deep-water channels. Plus the obstacle of five Austrian armies, one of which had the slowly starving *Serenissima* in the grip of a tight siege, aided by a well-equipped Austrian fleet blockading any approach from the sea. For the moment it seemed easier to head for Tuscany, trusting advice that the Tuscans were ready to rise at any moment, if only someone would lead them.

So dawn sees us walking north and slightly west out of Terni beside a single-track railway line, heading first for Acquasparta, then tomorrow Todi. As ever the Spanish are beyond the hills to our right, the French beyond those to the left, while the Austrians are now in Foligno to the north and east of Todi. And all these foreign armies are feeling bullish because the war is going their way; all are enjoying regular meals, decent beds and laundry services. Garibaldi has to move fast if he's to squeeze between them. Meanwhile, we're trying to get used to using our trekking poles in the proper fashion. Before sleeping in Terni we watched three YouTube videos in which expert walkers tell you how it should be done.

Of course I'd got it wrong. I'd been setting my poles down every other step. Instead you have to do it every step. This means moving your arms pretty briskly. We experience a clumsy half-hour in the grey early light, tripping on our poles and feeling stupid, but by the time the sun is up, we have it. Back forth, back forth. You feel the difference at once. The need to move the arms with every step locks you in a rhythm. The support of the poles straightens the back. The weight of the pack eases. All of a sudden, we're not walking, we're marching. And we've fallen into step, our poles are striking the ground in synch. From now on, even when one is behind and the other ahead, we will know from the sound of our poles that we're moving together. It brings a special intimacy, something soldiers must know all too well.

Leaving Terni in the evening, the *garibaldini* marched just two miles to Cesi, a small *borgo* up the hillside to our right, setting up camp beside an adequate spring and stopping for a few hours' sleep. But water wasn't all they drank. 'At eleven o'clock,' says Hoffstetter, 'we were surprised by a deputation of citizens bringing us a huge barrel of the best wine I've ever tasted.' Drinking, he was able to smile at the dismay of Forbes's men – 900 of them – when they discovered there would be nothing to eat until the next morning. And they couldn't believe it when they saw that the great Garibaldi would be sleeping with them on his saddle blanket under the stars. 'They'll get used to it,' the General laughed.

He was wrong. Forbes's men deserted in even greater numbers than those who'd survived the siege in Rome. The cavalry in particular, Ruggeri remarks, were sorely tempted by the money they could make selling their horses. But desertion wasn't always a wise choice. Many were picked up by the French and would spend long years in prison.

A steep track of chalky rubble draws us upwards through scrub of pines and brambles to a cluster of houses on a ridge. It's a first opportunity to take the rubber tips off our poles and thrust the sharp points into the stones. This brings new knowledge of the ground – hard, soft or crusty – a direct transmission of landscape to nervous system.

A half-hour later we are just wondering why the delightful Cesi has not been awarded *borgo più bello* status when we realize there is no café. There are shady alleys with little tunnels and fancy brick paving, plaques to long-dead benefactors and a street with the charming name of Santa Maria della Bottega – Saint Mary of the Shop. But no café. So soldier on.

Still heading north, we descend the hill slantwise to San Gemini Fonte, source of one of Italy's most famous mineral waters. Tall railings surround a pretty park beside industrial buildings of Fascist inspiration. All closed. But round the corner on the fast main road by the petrol station, Le Ragazze del Coyote Ugly is doing brisk business. Above the entrance, they have a glossy still from McNally's film: nightclub girls in red corsets. KITSCH CAFFÈ another sign announces. Inside, behind the bar, stands what Italians call a *stangona*, a tall, solid, flagrantly sexy woman. Her hair is ash blonde, her lips are mauve and she has a bunch of men buzzing round her. When I ask for orange juice, she enquires in a deep voice if I have ever tried it mixed with lemon. It will give me more zing, she promises.

Carsulae

From contemporary New York to ancient Rome is but another mile of scorching trail. Garibaldi, Hoffstetter and three or four others were galloping together across these low hills on a reconnaissance mission when they ran into an ancient stone arch rising from the parched grass. They had set off from Cesi before dawn, travelled twenty miles north and east, then circled west before returning. Worried about an enemy attack, they were pleased to find the hills thick with bushes and frequently broken with stony landslides. No place for a regular army. But the landscape 'didn't only please the military eye', Hoffstetter remembers.

> Gilded by the rays of the rising sun, amid the lively green of the vineyards, rose Cesi, Terni, Narni and San Gemini, while from distant mountain vapours ever more castles emerged around the wide horizon. On the spot where we were riding an old Sabine city had once stood. Scattered here and there, in this lonely, secluded place, lay broken fragments of great millstones, wells and columns. A stately arch rose alone in the midst of the ruins. The General passed under this arch on his horse. Did this cloaked

man, I wondered then, lack anything but a helmet to be a Roman consul? Garibaldi was solemn and taciturn. No one dared say a word. Everyone was dreaming. And in truth our lives, our doings, were as extraordinary and poetic as lives can be. Fatigue, hunger, thirst, privations and dangers of every kind – and then the most sublime joys of the spirit.

I wanted to pass under that arch myself, if it was still there. I wasn't expecting sublime joy, but maybe we could savour, in distant echo, that curious apprehension of anointment that Garibaldi evidently felt at moments like this. Throughout his life people had assured him he was destined for great things. He believed them. Sitting astride his horse under the Roman arch, he was inviting his men to dream.

The scatter of white stones that are the ruins of the Roman town of Carsulae lie like old bones to the left of our track. Surrounded by iron railings. On the right is a modern reception centre. Inside, behind an impressive stone lion, the three or four staff have nothing to do. There are no visitors. We pay our five euros and are told that before visiting the site we would do well to watch the introductory video. Since this is being shown in a cool dark room, we do so.

It's impressive. First there are all the usual computer reconstructions of amphitheatre and baths, forum, necropolis and arrow-straight Roman road, then comes the dramatic enactment of a major battle fought right here between opposing Roman consuls. So we have the pleasure of seeing men in red cloaks and silvery helmets galloping into battle. And I was struck by the thought that for thousands of years the warrior on his horse remained the fastest and most flexible agent of death, so that there was a substantial continuity from the classical era right down to our Garibaldi moment in 1849; then an abyss between those times and our own. In eight days' walking, we have yet to see a man on a horse.

To enter the ruins you slip your ticket into an electronic reader and go through a turnstile. Today it's broken and we just push through. Perhaps it's always broken. Beyond, we're in a wide expanse of parched, wispy grass and old stone blocks. There's no relief from the sun. When we reach a stone arch it is suspiciously high above the ground, perched on top of a low wall, so that you can't imagine riding a horse under it. Nevertheless we climb up and take photos of each other, trying to feel some connection with the past.

Further down the hill, three people on their knees under floppy hats must be archaeologists on a dig. We start to walk towards them and are quickly warned not to pass a red plastic ribbon stretched on the ground. A woman in shorts and bra gesticulates. Eleonora tells them we're looking for the arch that Garibaldi passed under in 1849. 'Was it that one?' A man shakes his head; even at this distance I can see the look of pity on his face. Isn't it obvious, he asks, that that section was recently rebuilt? The one intact, authentic Roman arch is at the northern end of the settlement. Over there.

So we walk back whence we came, then a few hundred yards along a bigger path made of shiny old boulders half covered with grass. And finally, there it is. A grey arch, ten feet wide by twenty-five high, made of neatly squared blocks with no cement. We stand under it, knowing this time that the hero really did stop his horse here, while his companions watched and wondered. Beyond the arch, around the sunken tombs of the necropolis, are a dozen hardy oak trees that very likely witnessed the scene. As unimpressed then as they are today.

We sit on a bench in the shade with the fierce heat and old stones all around. All the people who lived and loved and fought in Carsulae are utterly gone. For some reason this makes us feel extremely affectionate towards each other. We hug and I recite a few lines remembered from my English O level.

> The champaign with its endless fleece
> Of feathery grasses everywhere!
> Silence and passion, joy and peace,
> An everlasting wash of air—
> Rome's ghost since her decease.

Robert Browning, I tell Eleonora. 'Two in the Campagna'. She remembers the opening to *The Garden of the Finzi-Continis*, where the narrator visits some Etruscan tombs with friends and family, and one person observes that the Etruscans have been dead so long it's as if they never lived. But a little girl replies, 'Now you say that, you make me think the Etruscans did really live their lives, and I wish them well, like everyone else.'

Wishing the Romans well, we return to the reception centre, where the man behind the ticket desk tells us of a woman in Cesi whose great-great-grandmother kept a diary in which she recorded cooking a *crostata* for Garibaldi, which he very much appreciated.

The *garibaldini* spread out right across the valley below Carsulae, claims Belluzzi, who carried out interviews in all the villages. They were seen in Cesi, San Gemini and Casteltodino. Garibaldi kept them here a full day while he waited for the bread that still hadn't arrived from Terni. Also Ugo Bassi had run up a fever and had to be carried into Cesi in search of a bed. And there were problems with the mules.

'The mules,' Hoffstetter tells us 'were carrying 20 cartridges for every soldier, that is 74,000 cartridges in 74 cases, meaning 2 cartridge boxes each for 37 of the 90 mules we now had. About 130 pounds weight.' But 'the cases were hung on ropes over the sort of wooden harnesses they use in these parts. So at every stop the cases had to be taken off the harnesses, then the harnesses off the animals, to give them some relief, and it took far too long to put them all back on again.'

What the men were trying to do now was to make harnesses that could be removed and replaced at speed, in a single unit.

'Unfortunately, we couldn't load the animals any further,' Hoffstetter complains, 'because they were already worn out with the extreme heat and most had sores as a result of the wooden harnessing. The stench of the exposed sores was so strong that everyone kept away from them.'

On occasion some loads had to be shifted to the spare cavalry horses, which threatened to compromise their military usefulness.

'It's not easy to handle mules,' Hoffstetter continues. 'They get restless. They kick and bite. So every mule needed two soldiers, one to lead it, one to keep a check on the ammunition cases. And it had to be the same two men, always, for each mule, since if you changed them, the animals got even grouchier. So the men leading the mules were put on double pay.'

Of money and soldiers' pay, more anon. Suffice it to say that twenty-two years later Garibaldi would found, in Turin, the Royal Society for the Protection of Animals, which in 1938 was transformed into the present-day National Authority for the Protection of Animals. Perhaps the stench of those mule sores was not in vain.

I noticed the beginnings of a sore myself that day, walking the last four miles to Acquasparta. In the groin. And foolishly ignored it. We were set on reaching a trattoria for lunch, and wondering what the feverish Ugo Bassi must have thought when Garibaldi went to visit him in a private home in Cesi and told him there was no question of them waiting for him. He would just have to catch up if he could, when he was well.

Acquasparta

'You don't need air conditioning,' a small old man tried to persuade us. 'It's really very cool in here.'

We looked into a small stuffy room whose shutters were drawn against the afternoon sun. Our man was wearing a flat cap of white cotton, as might an aristocrat on his yacht.

'There's a fan.' He pointed to two big blades revolving overhead.

'We'll take the room with the air conditioning,' Eleonora said.

This is the first hotel we've stayed in on the trip. Bar Albergo Martini. It's been recently refurbished. The corridor carpets are bright green. The rooms have wrought-iron bedsteads, modern versions of old designs. Below them is the bar, dark and wooden, and outside a half-dozen tables with old men playing cards under an awning and arguing as old men always do when they play cards in Italian bars.

We wash our clothes and hang them to dry, slipping the hooks of coat hangers into the slats of the open shutters, and strike out to explore another of *i borghi più belli d'Italia*.

Acquasparta is a worthy winner. The heraldry of the *contrade*, the town's old districts, is gracefully played up. The central piazza has their coats of arms displayed on coloured shields between medieval arches. More shields, marble this time, have been set in the elegant paving as you pass from one district to another. 'Contrada Porta Vecchia', says one. 'Contrada San Cristoforo' another. And the spirit of the *contrada* is not just a thing of the past. That it's still alive you can see, ironically enough, on the death notices, the small black and white posters Italians display when people die. 'Contrada del Ghetto,' one proclaims. 'All *contradaioli* – members of the community – are close to Raffaela, Claudio and Teresa for the loss of their beloved Ada.'

Other less attractive aspects of the past are also alive in Acquasparta. 'Here we sell *Africano*,' says a notice on the door of a *gelateria* showing a grotesquely caricatured head of an African woman with rings round her neck and huge lips. *Africano* is a coffee. Grabbing an espresso in the main piazza, we find we're drinking Tiziancaffè, a brand produced in San Gemini. The name is advertised in bright red letters across our napkins together with an illustration of a steaming cup of coffee; above, a big-breasted black woman carries a broad shallow basket on her head. Coffee beans spill directly from her basket through the red lettering into the cup of coffee beneath. From Africa to the Contrada San Cristoforo; the exotic possessed in safety at home.

The sense of belonging is so important in Italy. On the main thoroughfare a brand new plaque has been raised to Federico Cesi, 'Roman prince and Duke of Acquasparta', who in 1603 at the grand age of eighteen formed, in Rome, the Accademia dei Lincei (Academy of the Lynxes), Italy's most famous scientific academy. Freedom to question orthodoxy was Cesi's manifesto. The young duke was a botanist who pioneered the use of the microscope to examine plants. Galileo Galilei became his club's most prominent member and was supported by the academy throughout his trial for heresy. But our plaque is not interested in the long history of papal opposition to scientific progress. 'Galileo came here to Acquasparta,' it proudly proclaims, 'in 1624,' and although most of Federico Cesi's work was done in Rome, *i suoi resti mortali riposano tra noi* – 'his mortal remains lie here with us'.

This is what matters. Where they put your bones. As Garibaldi's bones would one day be buried, against his will in hallowed ground after a Christian funeral. After death you must accept where you belong, or where society wants you to belong. Independence is over. The plaque to Federico Cesi was placed as recently as 24 March 2019 and is clearly part of the town's bid to make itself interesting to the cultured tourist. 'We used to get more people,' the old hotelier with the white cap tells us when we return to the Bar Albergo Martini. 'From abroad as well. Swiss particularly. They came in coaches and went walking round here, like you are. But a few years ago, just when we renovated the hotel, they stopped.'

Upstairs, checking if our clothes are dry, we discover Eleonora's sports bra has fallen from its hanger onto the awning above the grizzled card players outside. It's flaming pink, fearfully garish. How embarrassing is this? The bra is four feet below the window ledge and the men four feet below that, guffawing and bragging and drinking glass after glass of red wine as they deal their grubby cards through the endless summer evening.

'Go downstairs,' I tell Eleonora, 'walk out of the bar, then turn and look up.'

As soon as she's out of the door, I extend a trekking pole and lean out of the window. I slip the tip of the pole under a bra cup, and as she appears I flick it out, hard. She reaches up and catches it.

'The old guys didn't even look up,' she laughs.

DAY 9

11–12 July 1849 – 2 August 2019

Acquasparta, Colvalenza, Todi – 13 miles

Colvalenza

There are towns you don't see until you're almost upon them, so that you wonder if you will ever arrive – Terni, for example – and others you see from afar, imagine you will be there very soon, and instead they hover in the distance, slightly nearer, slightly nearer, but still surprisingly far away, and now there's a valley you hadn't seen that must be crossed, a gorge even, so that the sight of those towers and battlements, always looming, always beyond reach, becomes a mockery. Todi is this kind of town, a big medieval settlement, high up, not on a ridge but on the very top of a conical hill so steep it was impossible, in 1849, to get wheeled carriages up the streets.

But whichever kind of town it is, the kind that hides or the kind that teases, it will be a different place if you arrive on foot at the end of a long and dusty walk. Different, I mean, from the town you would have found had you arrived by car, or bus or train. Your body is differently attuned. Your thoughts, your needs. Todi, when finally we passed under the arches of its outer walls, was at once a refuge, a source of shade, a visual delight. In particular I needed a pharmacy.

The landscape is gentler north of Acquasparta; the hills curve softly, as though sculpted by the plough lines that turn them brown or ochre. On the skyline a farmhouse peeps from a cluster of lindens. A shale track leads through tunnels of overhanging willows. This was the day when the Brazilian maverick Bueno, who was supposed to be providing an advance guard with his cavalry, contrived to disappear, so that both Garibaldi and Hoffstetter wasted hours trying to find where he'd got to, only to discover he'd never bothered to leave San Gemini. He was disgruntled because, unlike Major Migliazza or Colonel Müller, he hadn't been chosen for the more adventurous missions, making contact with the Austrians in Foligno or the French in Civita Castellana. One thing Garibaldi couldn't hide was an indication of those he trusted and those he did not. But Bueno's disobedience almost proved disastrous.

Life is full of unexpected discoveries. After a couple of miles we cross the main road, the *superstrada*, hoping for refreshment at the little village of Colvalenza. Who would have thought that this insignificant Umbrian settlement could be home to one of the most spectacularly ugly buildings I have ever seen. In the 1950s a Spanish nun, María Josefa Alhama Valera, announced that God had told her to build a basilica at Colvalenza. Water would be found here, she prophesied, deep beneath the basilica, water that would heal pilgrims from cancer.

A Spanish architect was engaged and duly offered the worst that early-60s design could dream up, a massive central building formed of a dozen cylindrical brick silos supporting a flat concrete roof and boasting a dramatically protruding porch and plaza area of the kind one expects to find at a Las Vegas Hilton. In case anyone travelling in the vicinity might miss the sight, a slim brick campanile rises a couple of hundred feet beside the basilica, topped by slabs that look like the radar arms on airport control towers but are meant to represent Christ's cross. Closer to the ground is a huge photo reproduction of María Josefa Alhama Valera, otherwise known as Maria Esperanza of Jesus.

Water was indeed found more than 300 feet below the sanctuary; a number of large baths were built, coachloads of pilgrims were bussed in and miracles occurred. But the greatest miracles of all were, first, an 'incredible rain of money from heaven, in the presence of many witnesses' and, second, the appearance of a cardboard box with 40 million lire in it. In both cases the sums exactly corresponded to the amounts required to pay the restless building workers.

Nearby, in the Bar Marisa, a man assures me that actually the sanctuary was financed by General Franco, who like many dictators saw the advantages of this kind of religious fervour. While Eleonora is in the bathroom I try to find corroboration of this unpleasant slur from Google, but there is none. It does tell me, though, that Pope John Paul visited the sanctuary in 1981, shortly before Maria Esperanza's death, and that the church now boasts a relic of John Paul consisting of a piece of cloth soaked in his blood.

'Incredible,' Garibaldi remarked, 'that in these modern times people believe in miracles and cling to relics.' He was referring to the miracle of the Neapolitan San Gennaro, whose congealed blood, held in a small glass globule, will liquefy, or not, at three appointed periods of the year, according to whether the saint is happy, or unhappy, with the state of affairs in the town. In September 1860, when Garibaldi arrived in Naples during the triumphant campaign that ended in Italian unity, the holy blood seemed reluctant to liquefy, and the Neapolitans were beginning to draw their conclusions. Garibaldi let the priests know there would be serious trouble if San Gennaro didn't oblige and the following day the blood liquefied.

Todi

I'm enjoying the small miracle of the recovery of my feet, which if not blister-free are only mildly sore. On the other hand I'm cursing myself for not appreciating more quickly that the rapidly worsening irritation where right thigh meets groin must be a fungus. I know, dear reader, one should not mention these unpleasant details, but I feel I owe it to the *garibaldini*, who with their woollen shirts and difficulties with hygiene, must have suffered much worse.

The need to purchase some anti-fungal cream makes it all the more tantalizing when Todi appears in the distance, seemingly so near but actually a couple of hours away. We're walking along a high ridge on the east side of the north–south valley and the main road. For one long stretch our narrow track is perfectly straight, with lines of olive trees in the dry grass each side. On and on, straight, straight, straight. With Todi floating up ahead like a hallucination or one of those model cities that saints raise up to God on silver plates in Renaissance paintings.

Garibaldi also saw Todi from a distance and wondered why he hadn't received a report from Bueno as to whether it was safe to enter or not. His plan was always to arrive in a town before the main body of his men to reassure the local authorities and organize accommodation and food. He hesitated, then got Hoffstetter to send a company of dragoons ahead, just in case. Galloping up to the town, the horsemen surprised an advance guard of a hundred Austrians, who took one look at the advancing redshirts and withdrew. In the town people scrambled to get the band together to come out and greet the *garibaldini*.

Now Todi floats over a field of sunflowers, all turning their big round faces towards us in golden mockery. It hovers and shimmers and never seems to be any closer. Until at last there is the steep climb down into the valley, under the *superstrada* – filthy puddles, tin cans and urine smells – and then the even steeper climb up into town, the stoniest, most intensely medieval town I have ever visited.

We have booked into an ex-convent, Hotel Casa Vacanze SS Annunziata, which, at the time of booking, I wrongly believed to be where Anita had stayed for two nights. In fact she was at the Monastery of the Cappuccini just a few hundred yards away; Garibaldi had a straw hut built for her in the garden, so as not to offend the monks with her female presence.

It's the pleasant female presence of Alessandra who meets us at Reception. Since the convent's website offers a 'Profile of the Typical Guest' which begins, 'Singles, priests, nuns ...' and finishes with 'boy scouts, girl scouts,' I was worried that eyebrows might be raised at the odd couple we are. Not at all. Alessandra is all smiles and spinsterish solicitude. To oil the wheels, Eleonora confides that three of her aunts are nuns. Alessandra tells us what a pleasure it was to work with the Servants of Maria Riparatrici, but they left the convent last year, handing over its management to a Perugia-based consortium. They were too old, too few. All over Italy convents are closing.

Nevertheless, the SS Annunziata remains exactly as it was when the Servants of Mary were here. Alessandra leads us to our room through winding corridors, past a grand refectory whose long wooden tables sit under the frescoed lunettes of a low vaulted ceiling. Then halls, chapels and more corridors. Big white walls, brass lamp fittings, impeccably polished items of furniture. Whatever one thinks about the church's hostility to the Risorgimento, it's hard not to feel a certain melancholy seeing these once-busy spaces now echoey and abandoned.

Out in the streets we search for a cash dispenser. Not all Italian shops and bars accept credit cards. Thinking of the ease with which one refreshes one's wallet these days, I realize it's time for a word on the *garibaldini* and money. Who was paying for their long march?

They had a 'war chest', Hoffstetter says, with enough paper money to pay the soldiers and to buy food for about four weeks. This wad of cash had been given them by the constituent assembly on leaving Rome and was readily accepted in Tivoli and Monterotondo during the first days of their journey. Garibaldi prided himself on paying for food rather than requisitioning. He didn't want bad blood with peasants and shopkeepers.

However, once the French got a grip on the capital, they demanded that all paper money issued under the republic receive their official stamp in order to be legal tender. When Garibaldi heard this, Hoff-stetter claims, he had his money taken back to Rome on horseback and submitted to the authorities for stamping by people who would not arouse suspicion, then returned to his escaping army. It's hard to believe, but I haven't been able to find any other account of how they dealt with this emergency.

In any event, on arrival in Todi, aware that Roman paper money would be worthless when they reached Tuscany, Garibaldi persuaded the local authorities to accept what he had left in exchange for coin. He asked for 1000 *scudi* – the gold coins of the Papal States – but the councillors were only able to give him 728 because, on hearing of the rebels' arrival, the chief tax collector, Tommaso Mancini, had that very day dispatched all the town's money to the Austrian authorities in Perugia. Garibaldi threatened to have the man shot, but relented. The alliance between local bureaucrats and foreign occupiers was a serious obstacle to national self-determination. The Austrians astutely under-stood that by financing the pet projects of local bigwigs, they could win their loyalty and stifle any incipient patriotism.

These days a small town hardly has any independence inside the nation state. You don't find a modern town council discussing foreign policy. But in 1849, partly because of poor communications, partly because of the long Italian tradition of the independent city state, the governors of a place like Todi were used to making strategic decisions. On seeing the city's walls and elevation, Garibaldi, in Belluzzi's version, proposed to the councillors that his men might stay and defend the town against both the French and Austrians. In Hoffstetter's account, on the other hand, Garibaldi actually warned his aide-de-camp that any thoughts of staying and fighting in Todi would be a terrible mistake. They would be trapped and eventually thrashed. But whatever was actually said, Todi's councillors were not enthusiastic. They insisted that the city's defensive walls were not sound. They did not want the place to become a target for cannon fire. And you suspect that very likely Garibaldi was just testing the temperature of patriotic fervour, aware that fear of a fight would make the councillors more willing to shell out some money to get them on their way. In the event, the *garibaldini* handed over a pile of deserters' weapons and ammunition to pay for their food and board, even two cannons that Forbes had dragged from Terni. They also managed to persuade the town's civil guard to give them 200 modern rifles in exchange for older ones. Then all afternoon the men queued up at the town hall with requests for medicines and fresh soles for their shoes and grooming brushes for their horses, so many requests that the magistrates dealing with them gave up trying to keep account. In the end, the records suggest it cost the town about 3000 *scudi* to host the *garibaldini* for just two days.

On the gracious central piazza outside the town hall, with the pinkish-white *duomo* at one end and the pharmacy I'm so in need of at the other, Garibaldi watched two dogs, one very big and one very small, fighting ferociously on the flagstones. The big dog was like the Austrians, he announced, the small one his column of rebels. A gathering crowd cheered on the little dog.

Meantime, Anita in her straw hut in the monastery garden, received the city's 'most distinguished ladies' and very likely told them the story of how she came to be there. Having left Garibaldi in Rieti, in April, after she fell pregnant, and taken refuge in his family home in Nice, she had begun to worry about the bad news coming out of Rome. Eventually she decided, without telling her husband, to go back and join him. She had taken a boat to Genoa, another to Livorno, then proceeded, entirely alone, by coach and cart through Austrian-occupied Tuscany down into Lazio. On 26 June, with the siege of Rome entering its last days, she walked incognito through the French lines – My husband is wounded, she told them – and found her way to Garibaldi's headquarters in Villa Spada, then under French cannon fire. Hoffstetter was impressed by the General's spontaneous joy on seeing her. 'Dear Anita,' Garibaldi later wrote. 'I pressed her to my heart. It seemed everything was just as we wished. My good angel had flown to my side.'

One wonders what the fine ladies of Todi made of this. No doubt they asked about Anita's three children (a fourth had died in infancy), presently in Nice. Very likely they marvelled at a woman who could drop her domestic duties like this, while pregnant too, and likewise at a husband who did not order his wife to go home, but respected her choice. Did they pick up a whiff of freedom on that hot summer after-noon in the makeshift straw hut in the monastery gardens? Of love even? Anita asked if someone could kindly give her a more comfort-able saddle; the South American type she was using was no longer practical with the belly she had. And someone did. Again and again, reading about this march, about the mingling of sedentary townsfolk and vagabond patriots, one can't help feeling that the generosity so many ordinary citizens showed was the fruit of a deep yearning to live the lives they were afraid of.

The pharmacy was closed for its long lunch break. I would have to wait until four. We ate at a trattoria named after Jacopone of Todi, a thirteenth-century monk and mystic who preached the virtues of poverty to rich Pope Boniface, was imprisoned for it and wrote many wonderful *laude*, rhyming religious poems, which were popular for centuries. Somehow Eleonora knew all about Jacopone and insisted we visit his tomb in the church of San Fortunato. One descends steep stairs to the crypt, elbow to elbow with French and Japanese tourists. 'Here lie the bones of the Blessed Jacopone,' says a stone in Latin, 'who, mad for the love of Christ, mocked the World with his new art and conquered Heaven.'

Still the pharmacy wasn't open. So we climbed the stairs of the town hall where Garibaldi traded paper money for gold *scudi*, and wandered round the civic museum. I bet, I told Eleonora, there will be a painting of someone serving Todi on a plate to God. And there it was. Or they were. Two paintings. In both cases three bishops offered up the whitish stone skyline on a big wooden tray. It was just the kind of message of humble subservience that Garibaldi hated. Christianity undermined a man's courage, the General reasoned, inclining the peasants to think this life was less important than some improbable afterlife, and 'heaven their homeland, not Italy'. But he would have appreciated the glass cases full of tiny Etruscan bronzes showing gesticulating male figures beside captions explaining 'Mars in attack' or 'Hercules in attack'. Also an illustrated map from Renaissance times showing Todi in the centre – a cluster of towers on a mountain – then all the many little *borghi* in the city's jurisdiction, scores of them, each shown as a few *palazzi* perched on a little hill with the Tiber and its tributaries snaking between. Every single *borgo* is drawn differently, carefully, lovingly – Colvalenza, Acquasparta, Cesi, Cappuccini, Villanova, Massa – and even the hills are carefully distinguished by shape and steepness. You know at once the thing was drawn by someone who had done a lot of walking.

I had hoped the museum would have a section on the Risorgimento. It was relegated to a gloomy corner between two rooms; on the wall, a list of the citizens of Todi who took part in the wars of independence, together with a page of explanation. There was only one proper exhibit. Or there would have been. In a glass case on a small table was a sheet of A4 paper bearing the following bilingual message in bold lettering:

LA SELLA DI ANITA GARIBALDI È IN RESTAURO
ANITA GARIBALDI SADDLE IS UNDER RESTORATION

It seems the distinguished ladies of Todi had kept the saddle she left behind, so that now any passing visitor can examine the leather she was finding so uncomfortable between her thighs. Or could, if it wasn't being restored.

Thinking of discomforts, we returned to the pharmacy, picked up some anti-fungal cream and dashed back to the cool of SS Annunziata for an hour's repose. Meantime, on the road east to Orvieto, one of Garibaldi's cavalry patrols caught up with a convoy of carts carrying 5000 fowls and 50,000 eggs, destined, according to their travel documents, for the French army in Rome. It was fair game. Taken back to the monasteries where the men were billeted, this generous injection of protein somewhat reconciled the monks to their unwelcome guests. 'What merriment!' says Hoffstetter. 'The kitchens steamed all day. Wine was brought up from the cellars.' Priests and soldiers ate heartily together, and still the men would have boiled eggs in their pockets for the march to come.

A march that was worrying us. A march we knew would be one of the hardest. We ate in the square, or car park, which is Piazza Garibaldi, another place with a parapet looking out across the valley below. There were chairs outside Il Grottino, a sort of cave in a stone wall offering toasted panini. But no beer. We could order beer from the *birreria* next door, we were told; they wouldn't mind bringing it to us.

But the chief feature of this dinner was the statue of Garibaldi that kept watch over the square. It's a beauty. He stands on a high plinth beside an Opel Corsa, his bearded chin tucked down to watch us eating our vegetarian sandwich. He has a round military cap and his famous poncho, which I have now discovered he said he wore partly to hide his dirty shirt. His hands are joined at the waist to rest on the pommel of his sword, the point of which divides his feet. The right foot is thrust forward while the weight rests on the left, the body half turned, a pose that wonderfully conveys that mix of readiness and calmness that all observers attributed to him, even in the most difficult moments.

Behind, by the parapet, is a majestic cypress that Belluzzi claims was planted in 1849 to celebrate the hero's passing. It's a good four floors high now, rising just above the old *palazzo*. The statue has aged, gathering a crust of grime and pigeon shit; the still growing cypress has a wonderful lushness, shining like a dark candle over the landscape beyond. But of the two it's Garibaldi who looks the more alive.

Todi was the moment of decision. East, directly to the Adriatic, the road was blocked by the Austrians in Spoleto. North, to reach the sea at Ancona or Rimini, the road was blocked by the Austrians in Perugia. West to Tuscany, the road was blocked by the French in Orvieto. Or perhaps not. Perhaps they hadn't reached Orvieto yet. Cavalry had been sent to find out. Garibaldi would wait a day for their news, moving his men just a few miles north to keep his options open till the last moment. Naturally, other cavalry had been sent out in all directions to create confusion. If there was no further communication, he told his commanders, they were to rendezvous four days hence in Cetona, Tuscany.

Then Müller's news arrived. The French were approaching Orvieto, but were not there yet. So the column would march west. But not along the main road, where the eggs had been seized, which ran beside the Tiber and the shores of Lake Corbara. To be surprised down there on the flat between the lake and the hills would be fatal. Instead they would climb a thousand feet and more to cross the rugged plateau to the north. And our problem was that there is nothing up there; no *borghi*, no cafés, no shelter for twenty-five miles. With another very hot day forecast. My rash and blisters. Eleonora not feeling at her best. And the first and only place we'd found to stay was not in Prodo, a tiny village towards the far side of the plateau where the *garibaldini* camped, but a holiday farm well beyond, just short of Orvieto: Poggio Boalaio.

Were we up for such an arduous walk?

We ordered another beer to talk it back and forth. The light was falling. Above us Garibaldi tucked his beard in his chin and watched. It was hard not to glance up to him from time to time.

'Let's do it,' Eleonora said.

DAY 10

13 July 1849 – 3 August 2019

Todi, Pontecuti, Prodo, Poggio Boalaio – 23 miles

Pontecuti

Order of the day – no photos.

We've taken to a little role-playing. It fills time on the road. I wanted to be Hoffstetter. He's the one I identify with, a man anxious about his foreign accent, always worried about logistics, always seeking to impose his agenda.

Eleonora wouldn't hear of it. She couldn't be Garibaldi, she said. Or the expansive Ciceruacchio. Or the holy Ugo Bassi, who is anyway still in bed in Cesi. But she refused to be Anita either. Anita pregnant, Anita with a shadow hanging over her – 'perhaps like the light of the setting sun she foresaw her death'. Eleonora is not superstitious, but she doesn't like to tempt fate. So I had to be Garibaldi and she Hoffstetter. 'Deep down you know you want to be *il Generale*,' she told me.

Over breakfast by a coffee machine in the empty, echoey convent, I gave my order of the day. No photos except with the General's explicit permission.

Taking photos is slowing us down. Our marching rhythm is broken. We have a long day ahead.

'It will be a hard order to impose,' Hoffstetter feels. 'The country is so beautiful.'

'I expect my men to be disciplined, Gustav.'

Your pack, they say, is as heavy as your fears. And today we are afraid, with peaches and tomatoes and bread and cheese and various emergency rations weighing us down. And there will be even more weight when we fill our water bottles at the fountain just outside the convent door. These outside sources offer sweeter, fresher water than you can get in a hotel bathroom. At 5.30 we close the heavy door behind us and walk out in the dark morning. The fountain is dry. Nothing comes out.

'I can't believe this. Why wasn't it checked?'

'Marocchetti's fault,' Eleonora says. The real chief of staff.

Whatever the case, we can't tackle the main walk over the plateau without water. 'We didn't find a spring till we got to Prodo,' Hoffstetter records. Fifteen miles away. The door to the convent is locked and it's far too early to ring the bell.

'There'll be a shop or a café,' Eleonora thinks. 'Permission to take a photo of the departure?'

We leave the city by the northern gate, then circle round the western wall to the south and the road descending to the Tiber. So we have the valley falling away to our right and medieval walls looming to our left when, in the dawn light, for the first time in my life I see a badger. A black ball spins on the green bank under the walls, shows a flash of white snout and scampers off into a hole at the base of the bastion. I stop and stare, hoping it will poke its nose out again. It doesn't. Eleonora reminds me that we're supposed to be making good time. Refusing to budge, I whisper an anecdote from Garibaldi's 1859 campaign against Austria. Leading volunteers through the dead of night on a mountain path between Bergamo and Brescia, he halted the whole column to listen, cupping an ear. The men feared they had stumbled on the enemy. Instead it was a nightingale.

The badger doesn't show. My thoughts return to our water shortage. I am getting seriously worried and a little irritated that Eleonora is so relaxed.

'You're not in character. Hoffstetter would be extremely concerned.'

'Hoffstetter would have sent horses off in all directions.'

The road curves steeply down to the Tiber through cypresses, oaks and brambles. At last, right by the bridge in the small settlement of Pontecuti, at a quarter to seven, there's the miracle of a café with the charming name of Il Ponte delle Fate – the Bridge of Fairies. Even more charmingly, it's open. We push through the door, surprising four grizzled farmworkers over their breakfast, and purchase two 1.5-litre bottles of water.

The bridge was built in the seventeenth century, so we can be sure it's the same one the *garibaldini* crossed, the only bridge for miles in either direction. We sit on the parapet for a moment to gaze at the muddy Tiber sliding south under the arches. Ten days ago we had been sitting beside the same river at Ponte Sisto, below the Gianicolo. We've covered all this distance on foot. For the first time I'm aware of a feeling that I can only describe as accumulation. It has been creeping up on us for some time; an awareness of the uninterrupted intensification of physical contact with the land. Perhaps immersion is a useful word. Or continuity. Even purity. It is hard to pin down new feelings. With it comes an edge of anxiety. We don't want this accumulation to be interrupted. We want to go on and on walking across the unbroken landscape, never surfacing from its enchantment.

Beyond the bridge the main road runs left and right along the Tiber valley. But opposite a narrow lane strikes straight up the hill to the high plateau. 'This good road,' wrote Trevelyan in 1907, 'did not exist in 1849. A roughly paved bridle-path climbed steeply through the thin oak copses of the mountain, and enough of it still remains for the modern pedestrian to experience for himself parts of the route by which the half-starved and thirsty men made their way.'

Trevelyan is laying it on. The men were hardly half-starved after all those eggs and chickens. 'We almost never went hungry,' Hoffstetter assures us. Our trailblazer app indicates sections of path that I suspect correspond to that old track, but I sincerely doubt we will make it to the Poggio Boalaio holiday farm if we take them. Garibaldi had had to remain in Todi to resolve some last money issues, so it was Hoffstetter who commanded the column that day, with orders to go as far as possible towards Orvieto and to camp in a safe place. 'Our road,' he writes, 'was nothing but a steep narrow mountain path that frequently disappeared altogether. Fortunately, we had a good guide. The General's lady rode at the head of the column, which stretched out for miles since we were often forced to march in single file. But we had a magnificent view of Tuscany to one side and Romagna to the other, since we were walking for the most part on the mountain ridge.'

He's wrong about the views. From the top of the plateau you look south back across Umbria to the now-distant Lazio and north again across Umbria, perhaps with glimpses of Tuscany to the north-east. Romagna is too far away to be seen from here. The German Hoffstetter, as Trevelyan remarks, never quite got his Italian geography straight.

Our first magnificent view came towards nine at a turn in the road and a scatter of houses called Quadro. Here we found two wooden benches and a picnic table between tall cypresses. Behind them, looking back whence we'd walked, Todi's distant skyline was in silhouetted profile against the dark Apennine chain behind. A hazy romantic sight. You felt you could reach out across the Tiber and lift the town off its hilltop onto a silver tray for golden-robed clerics to offer up to the Almighty. We munched bread and white peaches then moved on, conscious we'd managed only a quarter of our march.

Conscious too that we were not going to visit all the places the *garibaldini* passed. Ruggeri, for example, strayed some miles north with a group of cavalry to an isolated monastery and asked the monks for bread. They said there was none. This seemed strange, and the officer walked boldly into the building. Passing a line of prayer cells, he came across the communal oven. At this point a door opened and a monk unleashed two ferocious dogs, one of which leaped on the cavalryman and set its teeth in his clothes. Things might have ended badly had not the yelling and snarling alerted a companion who shot the dog dead. Entering the room whence the dogs had come, the soldiers found enough bread for a hundred men.

Prodo

Onwards for three hours, constantly up and down, where deep gorges, dark with lush vegetation, score the plateau. Otherwise the land is parched blonde, with occasional old farmhouses, for the most part abandoned, though one place has dazzling white bedding hanging from an upstairs window. Or there are wide fields of stubble with a scatter of cylindrical straw bales. Distant hills in blue haze. A heavy, humming heat now, full of crickets and cicadas. Small purple butterflies fluttering or still. Feathery grasses. A leaning signpost at a tiny crossroads has four blue arrows: Orvieto, Prodo, Todi, Montecastello.

With nowhere to stop and no photos allowed, the rhythm of our poles on the cracked tarmac casts a spell that cancels time. On and on we walk. And begin to hum. To whistle. In time to the click of the poles. Old songs. Even symphonies. Eleonora studied music and has an excellent memory. The Pastoral has just the speed. Who would have thought? She knows it all. 'And did those feet,' is good too, 'in ancient time.' The morning hymns by and, towards eleven, the General grants permission for photos. A thousand and more feet down to our left, Lake Corbara has appeared. A distant patch of blue. These precipitous slopes are designated the Tiber River Park; at the bottom the river flows through the lake, which gathers the water draining off the plateau. Prodo should not be far now, the one village on our way.

We're not expecting much. 'A miserable village,' Hoffstetter wrote. 'Here, in this "gash of the wind-grieved Apennine,"' Trevelyan works it up, 'they spent the night below the old castellated hamlet of Prodo, that seems to shiver with the fear and poverty of centuries.'

It's hard to imagine much shivering in August. Nor is there any wind today. But we're beginning to wonder what on earth this village will look like. There's no sign of it yet. Unusually for Italy, not a single *campanile* pricks the skyline. No distant domes or turrets. We're on top of a wide world that is all dry ditches and stunted olive trees stretching on and on, with the great drop to the Tiber on our left and hills on all horizons.

Quite suddenly, there it is, clustering just beneath the level of the plateau, as if it had slid a few hundred yards into the gorge, stopping just in time on the brink of a precipice. A small huddle of houses and towers. We turn down towards it, hoping for nothing more than a little shade to eat our lunch in. Instead providence plays another of her generous cards; we are marching into Prodo on the one day of the year when it's buzzing with life.

The road dives down to the little *borgo*, then twists in a hairpin to climb up and out again. From the tip of that twist, the village's one piazza opens, a broad space of cracked asphalt between modest pink and ochre facades, with the grey masonry of a castle rising at the end. But what matters is it's full of white awnings where people are setting up stands to sell food. Cheeses and salamis are hanging in the shade. There's even a café.

'What's everybody celebrating?' we ask the barman, ordering *cedrata*s.

'Don't ask me.' He's burly, gruff, bending down behind the counter, searching through dusty bottles. 'None of this has anything to do with me.'

There are two tables. Plastic tablecloths with sunflower patterns. In a corner an elderly woman is arranging her artworks for sale. Thick slices of tree trunk with model villages on top, each miniature building a chunk of wood, their roofs, pieces of bark. And you can recognize Prodo! She's got it dead right. You realize that this business of imagining the community in clustered isolation must be an archetype of the Italian imagination: a circle of buildings turned inwards on a piazza. Us.

'A lot of us ex-Prodo dwellers are trying to do something for the old place,' she says. She's called Graziella. 'We organize this fair every summer.'

Outside, we ask the men sitting at a long table if they would mind ducking a moment so we can take a photo of the plaque behind their heads. 'ORVIETO,' it says, 'that saw the legendary hero Giuseppe Garibaldi 14 July 1849 ... On the first centenary of his death.' Which is to say, 1982.

'Funny it doesn't mention Prodo.'

'The barman isn't pleased,' Eleonora deduces, 'because the village is being run from Orvieto.'

The men at the table are excited when we explain why we took the picture.

'He stayed in the castle,' one enthuses, pointing to the pile at the end of the piazza.

'Same as San Francesco centuries before.'

'Perhaps they slept in the same bed,' Graziella suggests.

'Saint and hero.'

'Both crazy!'

We nod and smile. Garibaldi didn't sleep in the castle. Starting hours after the others, he didn't catch up till long after dark. Hoffstetter had found a space beneath the castle walls, a broad ledge beside a steep drop, and had the men set up camp there. It was sufficiently secluded for fires to be lit without being seen. A rare treat. And there was a spring of 'the best possible water'. Anita put up her tent on 'a protruding rock near the spring' and cooked. She was anxious about José riding in the dark along such a dangerous path. Hoffstetter assured her that he had posted men at intervals all the way. The beloved husband arrived at eleven, inspected the camp and complimented Hoffstetter on his security arrangements.

We complimented the locals on their stands and bought a piece of Cacio cheese. There were tables under a small marquee and we sliced our rolls and tomatoes beside a group of French schoolchildren eating chickpeas and bacon from plastic bowls. All the revellers were outsiders, their cars parked on the road near the bend. Middle-class metropolitan folk, suffering from the heat. Come nightfall the place would be empty again but for the bats and owls.

We tried to inspect the castle, but it's private property. Disappointed, we followed a path round it and looked down to where the *garibaldini* camped. To one side, in the thick trees, there did seem to be a flat space before the plunge. But the sun was at its zenith now. We went back to the bar for ice creams. Here, for all his grumbling, the local man was doing a brisk trade in mortadella sandwiches. A woman asked him for the key to the bathroom. 'It's clean,' he told her. 'There's even paper!' 'So, was it clean?' he demanded when she came out. 'There was no paper,' she said. '*Pazienza.*' Everybody laughed.

After a kind morning, a cruel afternoon. Leaving the *garibaldini* to sleep, we tried to save a mile or so with a short cut across a gorge. Towards the bottom the path became overgrown and impenetrable. We had to climb back out, cursing, and use the road.

Expecting it would be downhill from here, we discovered that actually the road snaked up and up. Towards three it was so hot we had to find shade. We crossed fifty yards of dry weeds and stretched our groundsheet under an isolated oak tree. It was hypnotic, on our backs gazing up through dark branches at the blazing sky. A wasp stung Eleonora between two fingers. She stood and screamed. The creature buzzed and threatened. Now our socks were full of burrs and our ankles itched from something in the grass.

A car stopped by a tiny wayside shrine. In the middle of nowhere. It's always a pleasure to think of the locals lavishing devotion on these sacred places, sweeping away the dust, bringing flowers, stopping a moment in prayer. Two Singhalese women opened the boot to pull out an assortment of cleaning equipment. They set to work as if it were another office.

At 4.30 there was a café at a place called Colonnetta di Prodo. Here our tiny lane joined a bigger road for the descent towards Orvieto. A dozen motorcyclists were laughing over beers. A boy strutted among them with a microphone, yelling tuneless songs, shouting stadium slogans. He was clearly challenged in some way or other. The bikers mocked him. Something hostile was brewing. Bringing our drinks, the proprietor yelled – *basta basta basta* – at the boy. His son perhaps. Every few minutes a couple more bikers would roar up and a couple would leave the bar and roar away. The air was hot and dusty.

Eleonora phoned the holiday farm, who said no, they didn't serve food. We asked after a grocer's and were told they didn't open till six. A long siesta. Heading down the slope, we realized what the bikers were up to. Two by two they were racing up and down the road, an interminable series of curves and hairpins. These were big bikes roaring at top speed, the riders' knees brushing the asphalt as they leaned into the bends. Twice we had to jump onto the narrow verge. Nettles and ferns. Two miles of this. It was deafening, frightening. On a short cut between two hairpins, Eleonora was again stung by a wasp. This time on the calf. Not her lucky day. This time the sting stayed in there. A black dot in sunburned flesh. The leg swelled.

At last there was the turn-off to the left and just half a mile to go. Another short cut brought us to the farm not by the main gate but through the back of a cluttered barn, where a bald, barrel-chested man was tinkering with a tractor. Two dogs trotted at his heels. Another ordeal for Eleonora. The more she shrinks back from them, the more the animals love to sniff her.

It had been a long day. Twelve hours on the road. We needed rest. Eleonora needed that sting pulling out. But first we would have to meet our extraordinary hosts.

His name was Sante. 'From Todi?' he cried, wiping oily hands on a rag and inviting us to ignore the ABSOLUTELY NO ENTRY sign on his barn. 'Todi! We thought you were walking from Orvieto.'

He led us through the barn, then outside between low cages – rabbits, tortoises, guinea pigs – past aromatic pens – piglets, ostriches, geese – beside more spacious paddocks – donkeys, lamas, sheep and long-horned cows. Meantime, dogs and cats, ducks and hens, ran free through a scatter of farming tools, tables, benches, barbecue trays, bikes, snaking yellow hosepipe, shrubs and bushes and vines and ivies and of course plump terracotta pots with lavender, agave, rosemary.

'You have your work cut out,' I said.

'Haven't had a day's holiday in fifteen years!'

A yellow house appeared across a thirsty lawn. But Sante wanted to show us the view. Beyond the building, the lawn sloped down into a field and a fabulous panorama opened up. Somewhat below, five miles across the wooded valley and still contained in the ring of its medieval walls, the city of Orvieto simmered atop a perfectly round hill, the remains of an old volcano. You could make out the big cathedral, a slender bell tower, a fortress. It was a view to die for. A vision.

But now Signora Ernesta has arrived. At once you know who's boss. Lean and light, with a boyish, bespectacled face under a tousle of short white hair, she talks ten to the dozen. She says it is all too easy to die from a wasp sting. Anaphylactic shock. Sante had to be taken into intensive care a couple of years ago. 'We nearly lost him.' She usually bakes a cake for all her visitors, she says, but has just had a hip replacement. 'There's too much to do!' She hobbles headlong, full of nervous energy.

Leading us up the stairs to their flat, which is at the top of the house, she points to the ostrich eggs that she paints with sunflowers and poppies. And the pebbles, the gourds, the goose eggs. We are given two pebbles turned into ladybirds. She gives all her guests a pebble, she explains. 'How long ago was the sting? Do you like my guinea pigs? You're still in the danger phase, I fear.'

There are cages in the middle of the kitchen. On low tables. Two guinea pigs and a chinchilla. I have never seen a chinchilla before. It looks like a giant Topo Gigio. Eleonora is trying to be polite. She has a gut loathing for all rodents. A lamp has been made from a painted ostrich egg. Signora Ernesta turns it on. She has talent. 'So difficult not to break the shells!' she wails. Every horizontal surface is crammed with cactus plants. Every inch of the walls is papered with drawings of flowers. Attached with Sellotape and pins. A shelf overflows with documents, files, pencils. A row of painted mugs over the fireplace. A row of painted flowerpots round the walls. I get the same anxious feeling I have in the crockery sections of department stores. We still have our packs on.

Ernesta is talking about how they set up the farm. How they love animals. They want people to experience the countryside. It's hard to find replacement ostriches. Or lamas. 'Could we buy some food from you?' Eleonora asks. 'O carissima, why didn't you say!' She rushes round picking up eggs, pasta, bread, zucchini, plums, a big bottle of 'Sante's beer'.

There are four or five flats. Ours is on the ground floor with a French window leading straight onto a terrace. It's where the dogs like to sit. They won't go away. Eleonora is irked. Using the needle provided by the dead mother-in-law in Terni, I dig out the sting. It's in deep. It takes time. On her stomach on the bed, Eleonora shrieks. 'Imagine it's a bullet, Gustav.'

'The hell with Hoffstetter!'

A dog noses open the door and patters into the room. It has a limp, like its mistress, and a nervy, incontinent look about it. 'Get that thing out of here,' my beloved yells, 'before I shoot the beast.'

DAY 11

14 July 1849 – 4 August 2019

Poggio Boalaio, Orvieto – 5 miles

Orvieto

Every day Eleonora receives an email asking her to review the place we stayed at the night before. Since her mother runs a B & B, she knows how important such reviews are and writes them dutifully, erring for the most part on the side of generosity. So far she's given nine or even ten out of ten to everyone. Watching her do this, marvelling that she's willing to take the time to answer all the questions, I wonder what kind of review Garibaldi would have given for the hospitality his men received in Orvieto.

Having arrived late in Prodo, the General was back in the saddle before dawn, checking out the surrounding countryside with his aide-de-camp. When a shepherd wouldn't respond to their call but scuttled away between the rocks, Hoffstetter drew his pistol. Garibaldi told him to put it away. 'We don't speak German, do we?' he called to the man, rather comically given the company he was keeping. 'We're not out to tax you or to steal your sheep. We're on your side. Your countrymen.'

Soon enough half a dozen shepherds appeared. 'The General always got the best out of these encounters,' Hoffstetter observes. 'In no time at all people were falling over themselves to tell him everything they knew about the enemy.'

But the shepherds couldn't tell them whether the French were in Orvieto yet. It was midday before one of Müller's men arrived to say they would not be in the city until the following morning. Meantime, there was an execution. A soldier had gone into a peasant's house, threatened the family with his gun and stolen a chicken. Says Hoffstetter. Belluzzi, who is always afraid we will think Garibaldi too harsh, adds that the man raped a young woman in the house. The General had no hesitation. *'Evviva Garibaldi!'* the soldiers yelled as the shots rang out. 'You can be sure,' Hoffstetter comments, 'that those who yelled the loudest were gnawing on a stolen chicken themselves. Every day it is clearer that not all the men who joined us are of the best, and this wandering around the countryside isn't helping.'

'It is so admirable, isn't it,' Belluzzi tries to put things in perspective, 'that men inspired by love of their country, subject themselves to every sort of suffering for their cause, driving themselves on without ever a bed for the night or the chance to wash themselves or their clothes.' How frustrating, then, 'when they find themselves rejected, despised, derided because a few villains have brought disgrace upon them'. He quotes a letter from Major Migliazza, commander of a party of cavalry that had stayed behind to keep an eye on the Spanish. Migliazza writes that he's been wasting days chasing groups of deserters using their guns and Garibaldi's good name to take food and horses. He's recovered a mule and some munitions sold illegally and consigned five culprits to the authorities in Acquasparta. 'My men wanted them shot, but I wouldn't.'

It must have been frustrating too, when, after four hours' march from Prodo down to the banks of the river Paglia beneath the walls of Orvieto, Garibaldi heard from his advance guard that the authorities in the town had closed the gates and wouldn't let him in. A delegation of Orvietani arrived and explained that they were willing to bring bread and meat, but with the French arriving ...

'Garibaldi received the delegation in silence,' Hoffstetter records. 'He didn't deign them a single word.' Afterwards, he sent cavalry to find which of the three gates could most easily be broken down with their cannon.

Our morning was easier. With a room already booked in central Orvieto, we treated ourselves to a late breakfast and didn't leave till after seven. The day's walk was short and simple. An hour downhill.

Then across the valley – over the river, under the autostrada, under the high-speed railway – then another hour uphill. Easy. All the same, starting when the sun is well up is harder. You have no momentum to take into the heat. You feel you can't breathe, you're short on energy. Looking up at the walls rising huge and solid from the volcanic rock eight hundred feet above, we stopped a moment and saw there was a funicular railway. A bright red carriage was sailing up the steep gradient with immense ease. Should we?

No.

Both Hoffstetter and I had extremely positive experiences once we actually got into Orvieto. As evening fell he had scouted round to the northern gate, which seemed the easiest to attack. But on a whim – 'drawn by the lure of forbidden fruit' – he decided to ride right up to the gate. Surely they wouldn't shoot. 'Who goes there?' yelled the guard. 'One of Garibaldi's officers,' the German replied. And the gate opened at once. The guard started apologizing. Actually the gates were only pulled to, he said, not bolted. They didn't mean any offense. 'Orvieto is a beautiful city, a really Italian city,' Hoffstetter comments. And he rode in up cobbled alleys, 'sure to find himself a nice café'. Minutes later he was surrounded by boys fighting for the honour of holding his horse while he sipped his espresso and smoked a cigar.

The only disturbing thing was that the streets weren't lit. The authorities had imposed a blackout. But now people began to gather round the German and shout, *'Evviva Garibaldi!'* The lights came on. The ice was broken. Another delegation was sent down to the river and this time simply begged Garibaldi and his officers to come up to town. Which they did. Now the place was ablaze with lamps and torches. And Garibaldi said he would overlook their earlier discourtesy in return for 'a small contribution in money'. When the General got back to camp, Hoffstetter remembered, 'I'd already been asleep three hours.'

As soon as you're inside the thick old walls of Orvieto you see what the German means by 'a very Italian town'. The city is more luminous than Todi. The mix of reddish stone and pink and ochre stucco creates a lively atmosphere. All along the main thoroughfares there are tables and benches against the walls, pleasantly shaded under white awnings. You're in an antique sitting room open to the sky.

In one of the first cafés a young man encouraged us to try his *torta a testo*. A *testo* is a cast-iron or terracotta cooking dish with a lid specially made for baking *torte*, which can be sweet cakes or salty pastries. The *torta a testo* looks like a little white pizza with a scattering of goodies on top, vegetables and cheese. But my young man earnestly explained how utterly, but utterly different this Umbrian speciality was from mere pizza, thanks to the use of fresh yeast, energetic kneading and the many hours that the pasta is left to settle before baking, not to mention the magic of the cast-iron *testo*.

There was no way out. We had to try it. And he was right, it melted in the mouth, saltiness wonderfully cut by the citrus sharpness of an icy *cedrata*. We chatted. We talked Garibaldi. I told him how the good citizens of Orvieto, ashamed of their initial coolness, took Garibaldi's men all the food that the French had pre-ordered for their arrival. Thousands and thousands of rations. Of *torte a testo* perhaps. He laughed and asked me where I was from.

We were at the till. It was time to pay. I smiled him a wry smile. 'Surely,' I said, 'surely, it's obvious where I'm from. Isn't it?'

He shook his head. 'Verona? Trento?'

Out in the street I punched the sky.

Eleonora was laughing. 'How deaf does the guy have to be not to hear your accent?'

Once free of our bags, we walked round the walls of the town to get the lie of the land. It's surprising how few gates there are to the world outside, how high up and closed in you feel. Garibaldi had set guards at the southern gate, where the French were expected to arrive. Müller with his party of cavalry was just a mile or two ahead of them, shepherding the enemy along almost. Over to the east, the way we came this morning, there were cavalry patrols up on the hillside and another group of men who had stayed in Prodo. They were waiting for Aristide Pilhes, commanding fifty or so cavalry, left in Terni as a distant rearguard. Then Luigi Migliazza, who took a group of cavalry north from Terni through Spoleto and Foligno right up to the walls of Perugia to give the Austrians the impression the column was headed that way. One of his men was shot dead by monks as they rode past a monastery. Also Raimondo Bonnet, who took another cavalry party north from Todi, pushing beyond Perugia towards Lake Trasimeno.

All of these men and their companies of cavalry were now expected to catch up with the column for the march into Tuscany. Though as soon as he was back, the valiant Müller would be sent off again, this time due west to the Tyrrhenian Sea, to create the impression that the General was planning to escape on a ship, perhaps from the port of Orbetello. Sometimes I'm agog at how much Garibaldi is keeping track of, how many things Hoffstetter is finding time to write down.

They didn't waste any energy visiting churches of course. But in the end it's the Orvieto *duomo*, more than the panorama of endless hills, that suddenly gives me a sense of the enormity of the General's task and the power of the forces opposing the Risorgimento.

Enter any Italian town and you soon come across a road sign with a list of the local churches. Santa Maria Annunziata, Santi Apostoli, San Francesco, San Giovenale, La Madonna del Velo, Abbazia dei Santi Severo e Martirio. Invariably it will be a long list, rich with allusion, history and myth. San Giacomo all'Ospedale, San Lorenzo de' Arari, Santa Maria dei Servi. The arrows beside the names point in every direction. Sant'Agostino this way, Santo Stefano that, Sant'Andrea the other. The Church is ubiquitous, its buildings striking and captivating. For every plaque to Garibaldi and his brave crew, there are countless monuments to bishops, cardinals and popes, all of them implacably opposed to any political change.

The Orvieto *duomo* is also breathtakingly beautiful, a miracle of collective vision and individual craftsmanship. To anyone arriving from whatever point of the compass, it rises massively above the rest of the city, drawing the visitor to the central square, where it dwarfs everything in sight. At once you understand that it is an object spread across time, across centuries, styles, trends, tendencies. Romanesque, Gothic, Siennese, Florentine. It absorbs them all. Its whitish-pink stone hosts sparkling gold and turquoise mosaics; huge bas-reliefs are thronged with arms and legs, necks and shoulders; there's a magnificent rose window and an army of Apostles alert in their niches; winged and horned animals launch themselves into the air; right in the centre, a bronze lamb stands precariously on the apex of a triangle.

What can one say? Change here is merely accretion, greater and greater density. Century after century. More and more confident affirmation. More and more wealth. More and more beauty. More and more power. Uncannily, the whole enormous pile seems about to lift off from its volcanic base into the blue summer sky. It is so graceful, its columns so slender and as if twined with ivies thirsting for light. Its three great triangles above the arched doors, then again three smaller slenderer triangles above those, draw the eye up to heights that bristle with ornamented spires and gesturing figures. And everywhere there is narrative, everywhere symbol, everywhere meaning. Founding myths. Messianic prophecies. Suffering and sacrifice. Mother and child. Sin and redemption. Heaven and hell.

How utterly, overwhelmingly convincing this must have seemed to the peasants of centuries past. And not only the peasants. How much more present and important than a ragged band of men with an unlikely political project. Unity? What did that mean? Freedom? To do what? And even if for some perverse reason you hated the Church, nevertheless how unmovable it must have appeared, how invincible. To argue with the force that created the Orvieto *duomo* you would have to argue with history, with God.

At the entrance, a great stone font tells you there is never any lack of water for the faithful. Inside, in the airy vastness, with its kaleidoscope of frescoes, amid altars, tombs, saints, candles and relics, you know at once that the only possible response is submission, devotion. On your knees! As we gaze at painted miracles around the walls, a French woman invites her young daughter to kneel before the Virgin, put her hands together, bow her head. '*Oui, comme ça.*' Both woman and well-groomed child enjoy the thrill of worship.

'We'd better go,' I tell Eleonora, 'or the enemy will be at the gates.'

Directly opposite the *duomo* is the civic museum. Here, as in Todi, horses and warriors ride around rows of Etruscan amphorae.

'Departure of the hero on his chariot', says a typical caption. Sharp black shapes raise swords against bright orange backgrounds. Or there are lovers. Men and women twining together. One vase has fighting on one side, lovemaking on the other. Another mixes the two. 'Duel between a warrior and an Amazon', says the caption. But step to the window that looks out across the square and the only thing you can see is the great facade of the *duomo*: the saints, the Apostles, the gold and the blue.

How hard it is to find a steady position between two such compelling visions, how difficult to bring all of reality into a single frame.

Late afternoon, we follow the walls to the north of the city to take a look at tomorrow's route. A broad valley bakes in bright sunshine, with steep slopes east and west. Leaning out from the wall, you feel hot air rising from below. There's a brooding, dark green intensity to it all. We'll be headed to the little town of Ficulle, lost in a haze of hills to the north. A good defensive position in case the French try to attack.

The morning after his city revels Garibaldi waited a dangerously long time before getting his men on the move. He wanted to gather in Pilhes and Migliazza with their hundreds of cavalry. There was a rumour that Migliazza had been killed. But then he turned up. Likewise the rearguard from Prodo. But no Pilhes. Nor Müller. Still the General waited. Then someone reported that many of the men were fording the river to sneak into town for some fun. Garibaldi ordered an immediate departure.

It was mid-afternoon. The hottest moment. Hoffstetter and most of the cavalry stayed back to round up the partygoers and stragglers. 'So I was two hours behind the main column,' he writes. 'And we were barely a mile out of town when the French arrived. Major Cenni, behind me, almost fell into their hands.'

The French, however, finding there was nothing left for them to eat, did not have the energy, after their steep climb to the city walls, to launch themselves straight down again after the well-fed figures disappearing in the distance. Anyway they were nearing the limit of their sphere of influence, the Tuscan border. To move north was to risk a clash with the Austrians.

We watched a Frecciarossa high-speed train streaking up the valley. Florence-bound. If Ficulle was fifteen miles away and the Freccia travels at 150 mph, it would be leaving the little *borgo* on its right in six minutes' time. A walk that would take us six hours.

DAY 12

15 July 1849 – 5 August 2019

Orvieto, Ficulle – 15 miles

Ficulle

'I was born,' Garibaldi wrote in 1837, 'to bust the balls of half humanity.'

Papal balls, French balls, Bourbon balls, above all Austrian balls.

Austria, or rather the Austrian Empire – guardian of the status quo, pillar of privileged propriety – was in 1849 what Germany would become after 1870, what the Holy Roman Empire had once been, the ultimate power in Europe. Its territories comprised present-day Austria and Hungary, the Czech Republic, Slovakia, Slovenia, Bosnia, Croatia and parts of present Poland, Romania, Ukraine, Moldova, Serbia, Montenegro and of course Italy.

Garibaldi's first clashes with the empire came in 1848. Milan had rebelled against Austrian domination in August, then, when help from Piedmont was withdrawn, found itself fighting a war it couldn't win. Freshly back from South America, Garibaldi was placed in charge of a thousand volunteers and won two battles near Varese, north-west of the city, before being obliged to withdraw and escape to Switzerland in the face of greatly superior forces. The man commanding the Austrians was Baron Konstantin D'Aspre, who in a letter to his superior Field Marshal Radetzky expressed surprise at the 'outlaw's ... initiative and energy'. In July 1849, as Garibaldi left Orvieto, heading north, the same man, Konstantin D'Aspre, was the effective ruler of Tuscany, based in Florence. With 30,000 men at his disposal. It was his balls Garibaldi now meant to bust.

D'Aspre was a hardened campaigner. Born in 1789, he had fought in the Napoleonic Wars; in 1815 it was his daring attack that had finished off Joachim Murat's army north of Naples, guaranteeing the return of southern Italy to the Bourbon kings. In 1832 he was involved in the repression of patriotic revolutions in Parma, Modena and Bologna. In 1840 he had put an end to a student uprising in Padua with gunfire and wholesale bloodshed. In 1848, retaking Vicenza from Italian patriots, he had the town sacked as a reprisal. In 1849, retaking Livorno, he again had the town sacked with the loss of 800 lives. Any Italian involved in the conflict was shot without trial. There were 317 executions. Surrender, for the *garibaldini*, was not an option.

In the early 2000s an Austrian historian and Italophile, Franz Pesendorfer, pieced together all the communications between Austrian generals in Italy during Garibaldi's march. Published in 2007, this is material that Hoffstetter, Belluzzi and Trevelyan would dearly have loved to get their hands on. Day by day, we have D'Aspre in Florence, communicating with Radetzky in Monza (north of Milan), General Gorzkowsky in Bologna, Major General Hahne in Rimini, General Strassoldo in Ancona, Archduke Ernst in Urbino, Colonel Paumgartten in Perugia, and Colonel Stadion, who has been sent south from Florence through Siena to find the rebels. Occasionally, ministers in Vienna and even Emperor Franz Joseph himself are brought into the conversation. A lot of horses are galloping back and forth.

In contrast to the officialese of the exchanges and the endless repetition of long honorary titles, the *garibaldini* are referred to brutally as scum, riff-raff, thieves. To be exterminated. When they begin to pop up simultaneously in many different locations, the Austrian generals deduce that the rabble has split up. Only later do they appreciate that their actions are coordinated. The reports they receive during the first week of Garibaldi's march give the group's size as anywhere between 3000 and 18,000. 'Our spies are hopeless,' Paumgartten laments.

At this time, however, the Austrians were more concerned with preventing further rebellions in the cities they had recently reoccupied than in launching an all-out attack on Garibaldi. They discuss blocking actions to prevent the rebels escaping to the sea, east or west. Troops and munitions are moved around. They complain that with the *garibaldini* active on so many roads, many messages are not getting through. In particular it has become almost impossible to communicate with the French. D'Aspre begins to wonder if the French haven't deliberately let Garibaldi escape so as to bother the Austrians. He orders all civilians in Tuscany to hand over any weapons in their possession. He threatens house-to-house searches and severe punishments. And he writes to Field Marshal Radetzky, vowing that he will wipe out this mutinous rebel as soon as possible. In his memoirs French General Marcellin Marbot described D'Aspre as 'smart, but temperamental'.

The most striking thing about the correspondence, though, is the language it is written in. Since Pesendorfer's book is published as a parallel text, with German to the left and Italian to the right, the reader is constantly made aware that in 1849 most of northern and central Italy was governed by people who did not speak Italian. And who had a low opinion of the Italians. The highest praise the Austrian generals afford to any Italian individual or community is that they are 'passive'. Needless to say, the local Italian regimes, including the despotic dukes and grand dukes whom the Austrians were propping up, were treated with carrot-and-stick tactics. They could keep their positions and privileges so long as they toed the imperial line. A great deal of wealth was transferred to Austria. Never once in all this correspondence is there the remotest hint that the men they were chasing might be driven by love of their country, or that the intimacy between a people and their land might justify a struggle for independence. 'Unhappy Italy,' D'Aspre writes, 'when will it be free of these villainous troublemakers?'

How can a person be unhappy, Garibaldi told Hoffstetter at one point in their march, when you live in a country as beautiful as Italy? The answer was, if you are homesick for somewhere else. Climbing steep slopes away from Orvieto, Hoffstetter reports being cheered and refreshed by a thick hedge of oaks, either side of a narrow path. 'Suddenly I was transported to my home country,' he remembers 'and there welled up within me a yearning such as I have not felt for a long time, so that I rode along slowly and mechanically far behind the others.'

We managed to be unhappy in a different way leaving Orvieto. Convinced that at 6 a.m. in August there would not be much traffic, we decided to do the first four miles of our walk in the valley, along the main road, then strike up towards Ficulle on the Via Cassia Antica, an old Roman road, now a path, that once linked Rome and Florence.

We were wrong. By seven we were walking beside a steady stream of vans and trucks. It was too late to change route since there was nowhere now to cross the triple barriers of railway, motorway and river running in parallel a few hundred yards to our right. I become extremely anxious in these situations. There was no space for pedestrians, and since the road was constantly bending I insisted we keep crossing, so as always to be on the outside of the bend, as visible as possible. I also insisted that when we were facing oncoming traffic I should walk ahead, and when we had the traffic hurtling towards our backs I should walk behind. That way I was always the one, so to speak, in the firing line. This behaviour bemused Eleonora, who just could not feel the danger.

Back and forth then, in the growing heat, for two and a half hours, scuttling across the road, changing positions as we did so, me behind, me ahead. Was this chivalry? I see the coming accident so clearly: an overtaking vehicle will suddenly be forced wide as the truck it is passing swerves to avoid a cyclist, and it comes ploughing right into me. It's a disturbing thought, but infinitely preferable to the vision of that same vehicle ploughing into Eleonora. Why? Is it that the mental pain in that event – her killed or maimed – would be worse than the physical pain if the car ploughs into me? I'm not sure. Perhaps I want to be the one most at risk, because I stupidly imagine I'm the one taking most care. I wonder, in battle, how many soldiers reasoned like this. Certainly there was always someone ready to throw his body in front of Garibaldi at the crucial moment. The idea of losing him was too painful.

To get some relief we added a half-mile to the walk by taking a diversion through an industrial area. On a support column of the high-speed railway someone had written SEMPRE COL PUGNALE TRA I DENTI – Never without my dagger between my teeth. 'A forbidden weapon, an Italian weapon,' Garibaldi wrote, 'that the foreigner condemns, as though the bayonet and scimitar he has bathed in innocent blood were any nobler than a dagger plunged into the breast of a tyrant.'

A few yards further on, a Roman viaduct actually passes under the higher viaducts carrying the railway and autostrada. That is, a half-dozen elegant stone arches, sprouting weeds from every crevice, are dwarfed by the great concrete structures of these contemporary thoroughfares. It's extraordinary how little the pattern of human endeavour has changed.

At last we reached the locality of Monterubiaglio, where we were to leave the main road. Just before the junction there was a filling station with a little café. We sat outside, calming our nerves, watching a young black man washing people's cars in the stifling heat. Every person of colour we have seen since Rome has been engaged in menial activities, picking fruit, pushing decrepit folk in their wheelchairs, scrubbing floors. The Roman viaduct was no doubt built by slaves.

Getting up from our coffees, we find our glasses and hats. Leaving at dawn, we walk hatless, without our sunglasses. And I love this. I feel freer without a hat, happier seeing the world in plain light. But by nine the glare and the heat are too much. And this moment when we pull out the hats always brings with it a feeling of getting serious, knuckling down to the long haul. We have 1500 feet to climb.

Our app now takes us on one of its most adventurous, vagabond peregrinations through the backyard of an olive oil mill, under the railway, along scrubland by the river, past a group of men who might be Gypsies smoking in the shade of tall bamboo canes. A chorus of barking in the distance grows louder all the time. Louder to the point of deafening. We have to walk through an acre and more of ramshackle dog kennels, assorted wire pens and corrugated-iron roofing. The animals are going wild in the heat, hurling themselves against rickety wooden gates. They are the pets of the provincial middle classes, left behind as their owners head for Majorca or the Seychelles. At last we're on a narrow walkway over the autostrada – cars racing south to Rome, north to Florence – and beyond that, open country.

The climb is gentle but steady, the landscape softly rolling, more uniform and homogeneous than on previous days, vineyards laid out like carpets, whitish soil freshly ploughed. The Via Cassia strikes diagonally upwards, following the direction of the valley but rising steadily. It's an unusually broad track of white stones between low bushes, straight and inexorable as the Romans loved. I won't pretend you can hear the chariot wheels, but you might occasionally find yourself listening for them. The hillside draws us in, and we settle into a rhythm – one hour, two hours, three. There's really nothing to look at, nothing to photograph. Just the warm odorous air, the crunch of the stones, the rasping of cicadas. Then, suddenly, a beast crosses our path.

About twenty yards up ahead, it bursts out of the thick bushes to our right and shoots into the thick bushes to our left. What was it? We stop and listen. Not a sound. Not even cicadas. It seemed too big to be a dog, or fox. Too small to be a deer. Too sleek to be a boar. Who knows what company we're keeping on the hillside here?

We push on, alert for another surprise. But nothing; no one passes. Only lizards at our feet, hawks circling above. Since the track is broad, we're able to walk side by side, which is always a pleasure. Perhaps I should have said that since Eleonora is deaf in her right ear, when we're side by side I'm always to her left. We don't have to think of this. It happens, like so much else when one walks: the length of the step, the swing of the trekking poles, the in-breath, the out-breath. We march on. The tug of the slope is steady, the white stones beneath our feet are always dazzlingly the same; all bushes are the same bush and the sky stretched over our heads is rigorously the same milky blue sky from horizon to horizon. Today I feel I could walk for ever.

Then it's over. Two hairpins, an olive grove, a stop sign, and we're turning onto the road into Ficulle. We're suddenly tired. There are a few modern houses, then the old drystone structures of the little centre. No stucco. No frills or balconies. Rich pinkish-brown colours, as if the soil had been pulled up into walls. A medieval tower. A Bar dei Motociclisti, a plaque with a few lines from Dante's *Inferno* that allude to the town. Ficulle's claim to fame.

The *garibaldini* arrived here late. The night was dark. A hedge of hawthorn had to be cut down to open the way into a field where the men could lie down. Great attention was paid to placing lookouts in all directions. The locals offered their help. Anita cooked a rice soup. 'It was still hot when I arrived,' Hoffstetter remembers. 'Yesterday the dew soaked us to the skin, and tonight the same story.'

'All the traditional values have been lost here,' our B & B host laments. He's in his forties, his wife beside him. They let us into a tiny terraced house at the top of stone steps brightened with pink geraniums. Yes, it was his parents' house. They passed away. He wouldn't want to sell it even if anyone wanted to buy. Which they never would. Who would buy in Ficulle?

The man is earnest, nostalgic. His name is Luca. No one plays in the street now as he did as a child. There's no community any more. He lives in Orvieto these days, runs a factory in the industrial estate we walked through. As he speaks, his wife is pulling back curtains, opening cupboards, turning on the gas. She runs upstairs. The ground floor is one chintzy room with kitchenette. Steep stairs lead to a bedroom barely big enough for the bed, then there's a ladder to a loft and roof terrace. Thick stone and closed shutters have kept the place cool, if not airy.

Luca is agog at our journey. 'I'm so envious.' He can barely take a week's holiday, he says. 'Last year an Australian woman stayed here for three months. An artist. Determined to change her life. So courageous. 'We'd love to do the same. We'd love to help Ficulle recover its old spirit. People work too hard. Then one day you go mad.'

His wife comes back downstairs, a reassuringly fleshy, practical woman. She listens to her husband with a mix of sympathy and alarm.

'I'm sure our guests would like to take a shower,' she says.

In the afternoon, with a little detective work we find the field where the *garibaldini* slept, now an open space beside a sports centre. Having

157

gone to bed at midnight, Hoffstetter woke, he says, soaked with dew, at 3.30 to the sound of trumpets and drums. In the pitch dark, the camp was on maximum alert, in case the French should attack from Orvieto, or the Austrians come down from the hills. No one could understand quite why neither enemy had made the killer move.

'In a war like this,' the German reflects, 'there's no point in fussing over strategic places like Perugia, or commanding converging roads. You have to find the enemy and attack him where he is.'

The truth was that the Austrians had been waging a campaign that involved retaking rebel towns, one after another. Undisturbed by any opposition in the country, they marched their big armies and heavy guns to the next town on the list, where the local rebels obligingly waited to suffer their inevitable, glorious defeat. As in Rome. Now for the first time D'Aspre and his fellow generals were facing a determined non-local volunteer group on the move. They weren't sure how to respond.

Two oxen were butchered and cooked. The French didn't show. They were leaving it to the Austrians. Relieved, the *garibaldini* came into Ficulle to enjoy themselves. Wine was provided. 'Everything about them,' Belluzzi heard tell years later, 'their looks, behaviour, chatter, suggested a collective joy. No one showed signs of suffering or fatigue.'

Can this be true? According to Ruggeri, morale was low, though there is no talk now of desertions. Perhaps the unhappy ones had already gone, and the remaining 2500 were the better for it. Or perhaps the men were pleased that Ugo Bassi was back. The monk had caught up, quite where or how none of my sources say, but people in Ficulle remembered him. They also remembered Garibaldi sitting on a stone bench surrounded by excited children. 'When you're ready, little Italians,' he told them, 'you can play your part.' Later, a farmer came and kneeled at his feet, complaining that some soldiers had damaged the property he rented from the Church. Garibaldi was in his tent. He told the man to stand up and reassured him he would be compensated. All the while, 'the General was unwinding tallow-soaked rags from the many bleeding sores on his feet, without ever complaining or cursing'.

We read this passage before falling asleep.

'What is tallow exactly?'

'Boiled animal fat,' Eleonora said.

'If only I'd known.'

DAY 13

16 July 1849 – 6 August 2019

Ficulle, Salci, Palazzone – 13 miles

Salci

We talk about all kinds of things in our long hours on the road, but one subject keeps coming back: fear. Banally, fear of traffic, fear of dogs, fear of not finding a bed for the night. More seriously, the fear that keeps everyone in their places in life: fear of not finding another job if I leave this one, fear of not having enough money if I leave my partner, and so on. Fear is the great enemy of freedom. Any self-respecting despot knows this. Konstantin D'Aspre was no exception, promising calamity for anyone who supported the cause of Italian self-determination.

But how humiliating, Garibaldi always insisted, to live in a climate of fear, governed by despots, and even worse foreign despots. If only everyone would rise up, these tyrants could be chased away. And of course there had been a moment when the people did rise up. In January 1848 the Sicilians had chased out their Bourbon masters. In February the Neapolitans forced their despotic king to give them a constitution. A week later the Tuscans chased out their duke, and in March the citizens of Parma and Modena did the same. Most spectacularly of all, Milan and Venice chased out the Austrians.

So there are moments when fear is collectively overcome; one group's bravery inspires another's. The trick is to capitalize on those moments, because they don't last. Courageous today, people may be craven tomorrow; putting your life on the line day after day is exhausting. At the point we're at on our long retreat from Rome,

Garibaldi was already thinking of the 1848 revolutions as a missed opportunity, already talking of having to wait ten years or more for a similar wave of popular feeling to offer a second chance. Yet a glimmer of hope remained that the people of Tuscany might be persuaded to go back to the barricades. There was a large liberal community in Florence, and in other Tuscan towns. He thought it worth a last throw of the dice.

The night of 16 July 1849 gives us a chance to see how Hoffstetter reacts to fear. Garibaldi had led the main column out of Ficulle towards 4 p.m., leaving the German in charge of the rearguard. There was concern that Aristide Pilhes and his company of cavalry had still not rejoined the group, nor sent word. Garibaldi headed north and west back down into the main valley, the broad Val di Chiana. However, at the village of Carnaiola, while it was still daylight, he turned east, along the bank of a small river, as if planning to climb into the Apennines in the direction of Perugia. Five miles on, he crossed the river and under cover of darkness and thick woodland turned back due west towards the Tuscan border, pitching camp before midnight under heavy rain at the tiny *borgo* of Salci.

It was the first rain of their march. In Ficulle, Hoffstetter had forty cavalry, twenty infantry and orders to make them as visible as possible while there was still daylight, for the benefit of the French to the south, then to leave as soon as it was dark. Pilhes did not show. The night was black. The men had strict orders to move in silence, since the enemy might be close. None of them knew the area. 'We were entirely in the hands of our guide,' Hoffstetter worried, 'who could easily have led us back to Orvieto without our realizing.'

Down in the valley the land was flat, criss-crossed by ditches and canals. There were no houses and no cover. In the distance, bonfires lit the night. Hoffstetter was convinced they were Austrian campfires. The guide assured him it was something the peasants did in August, for the fields. At a bridge they were joined by a second guide. The rain began to fall, a torrential summer storm. The ground turned to mud. Uncannily, the fires burned on. And despite the rain the men were tortured by thirst, not having found anywhere to drink in the dark. It had been another scorching day.

Now a third guide was to join them near a farm with three houses. Hoffstetter thought the buildings would offer some protection in case of attack. He could not believe the Austrians would not take advantage of their being exposed as they crossed the valley. And of course the houses would have water. He ordered the men to knock, quietly, but the peasants wouldn't open up. The doors were barred. The men began to shout. 'We only want water.' Nothing. Hoffstetter had them smash the windows. Now there were voices from upstairs. 'Just wait while we get dressed.' The men waited. The rain was pouring down, the night pitch black, their guides uneasy. Still the peasants didn't open their doors. A man's voice called that he couldn't find his trousers. 'Just hang on.'

Convinced an attack could come at any minute, the German lost patience. 'Get some straw,' he shouted. 'Let's burn this hovel down.' Immediately, the farmhouse door opened and a man appeared saying he always had trouble finding his clothes in the dark. 'Have pity.' Realizing now that they meant him no harm, he was suddenly euphoric. 'Forget water, everybody, let me bring you wine.' But the men wanted water. And Hoffstetter wanted to get moving. If he missed the appointment at Salci he didn't know where Garibaldi was going next. No sooner were they marching again than a mule loaded with rifles collapsed in the mud and got tangled in its halter. Panicking, the creature brayed so loudly half the countryside must have heard.

'We walked on exhausted under the relentless rain,' Hoffstetter concludes his account. 'I had brought with me the owners of the three houses, threatening their families that if the enemy followed us they would never see their loved ones again. Many of the horses stumbled over bushes and fell into ditches, betrayed by riders so sleepy they couldn't keep their eyes open. We reached Salci at one thirty, drenched to the bone.'

I had looked forward to somehow sharing this unhappy drama. Instead we had one of our most idyllic mornings, and at exactly

6.54 a.m. I took what became for us the iconic photo of our entire trip. Having set off before dawn we were in a narrow lane down in the valley with open fields of sunflowers on both sides. The plants were shoulder high, thousands upon thousands of them, all lifting and turning in regimented synchrony towards the point ahead to our right where the sun was topping the ridge in a brilliant dazzle. I was walking a few yards behind Eleonora and took a photo on the move of her striding into this sunflower sunrise. How it happened I'm not sure, but the picture is at once brooding and golden, and her posture, thrusting forward with her poles, conveys a kind of quiet boldness. There is not a shred of fear in it.

We chose to pass on Garibaldi's diversion up the river and back down again. Even without that we had a thirteen-mile hike. Again we crossed over the autostrada and under the high-speed railway, moving easily westwards on chalky tracks through brush and copse, beside sluggish irrigation canals. There was not a single hill to climb this morning, and towards ten a lawn opened up to the left of our track and we found a handsome pile of brick battlements, a tower, a spire, a grand arched gate and a smart red sign with the legend, BORGO DI SALCI.

It is empty, abandoned. No one has lived here for thirty years. But back in the 1840s, Salci was emblematic of that vocation for fragmentation that has dogged Italy since the fall of the Roman Empire. With a cluster of buildings around a single piazza and just three hectares of land wedged between Tuscany and the Papal States, Salci was an independent duchy. Before Napoleon's invasion of Italy in 1804, it had minted its own money, recruited its own army and applied its own border tariffs.

We went under the arch into the big square piazza, closed on all sides but for the narrow gate we had come through. There was no one around. There is no paving, just grass. The buildings are half noble *palazzi*, half old farmhouses. There is a round brick well, a peeling church facade, a pretty loggia and a white stone shield with a coat of arms. The whole atmosphere would be one of romantic decay and pleasant rural calm were it not for the bright red signs shouting from every doorway. *VIETATO L'ACCESSO. FABBRICATO PERICOLANTE.* No access. Building unsafe. One somewhat smaller plaque announces:

PILOT PROJECT AWARD, EUROPEAN COMMUNITY
Year 1990, Projects presented 1138, Winners 26, Italy 3
Salci contribution, 118,000 ECU

We sit in the shade of the well to eat a peach and contemplate this information. Bureaucrats in Brussels waded through 1138 projects, in order to select 26. Meaning 42 projects were set aside for every winner. Endless documentation. Thousands of hours of work. They then shelled out a trifling 118,000 ECU (the virtual currency that later became the euro) presumably to keep Salci from falling down. Looking around, it's obvious that at least ten times that amount has been spent to preserve this state of decrepitude. Similarly, on the tiny road over the plateau from Todi to Orvieto, we saw a plaque recording a European contribution of €40,000 for a project that must have cost millions. Yet only the EU gets to broadcast its benevolence. No doubt a condition of the award.

Of course every power uses patronage to consolidate loyalty. The rector did it at our university, the Austrian Empire did it, so it's hardly surprising to find the EU doing it. And it works. One of the fascinating aspects of the Brexit debate was the number of British people who spoke enthusiastically of EU financing for this or that local initiative; it made them less eager to return to a more independent state. Similarly Austrian patronage made the authorities of many towns in central and northern Italy less eager to push for Italian unity. But in both cases – the EU and the Austrian Empire – all patronage was amply paid for by local taxes. Italy was a net contributor to the empire, as it is now to the EU.

'Surely, though,' Eleonora reflects, 'Garibaldi would have been a Remainer, wouldn't he? He was an internationalist. Proud to be a citizen of four or five countries. He fought for the French against the Prussians in 1870.'

'He was the only general on the French side to win a battle, two in fact, against the Prussians. But he was fighting for the right of the French to govern themselves.'

Opposite the well, on the wall to the left of the stone gate, the inevitable plaque reads, '16 July 1849, Giuseppe Garibaldi rested here, hounded by the enemy'.

That same day the enemy, Konstantin D'Aspre, was contemplating the imminent return to Florence of Grand Duke Leopold II, whose state the Austrians had retaken for him after the revolution of the previous year. It was important, D'Aspre agreed with Field Marshal Radetzky in Monza, that the duke wear an Austrian military uniform for the celebration. And the Austrian flag be flown.

We weren't hounded by anyone but couldn't stay the night in Salci because there is no accommodation. Eleonora wondered what was the point of spending money on the place if nothing was to be done with it. Indeed. We pressed on and, forty minutes later, beside our chalky track, found a sign in Italian and English that read, 'ANCIENT BORDER. PAPAL STATE, GRAND DUCHY OF TUSCANY'.

Palazzone

Hoffstetter raves about Tuscany.

> Surprising indeed is the difference between Tuscan and Roman villages. While the inhabitants of the latter would scamper away terrified at our approach, or stand there staring at us amazed and awkward, in Tuscany people come flocking joyfully to greet us, bringing us wine along the road and offering themselves as guides. In short, we seem welcome. Anyone who has had occasion to observe the Roman villages west of the Apennines, then all at once to arrive in Tuscany, will soon agree that a military government does not corrupt people as profoundly as a regime of priests.

What changes did we notice in Tuscany? Certainly, if the word picturesque didn't exist, you'd have to invent it for Tuscany. It is incorrigibly beautiful in an entirely reassuring way. The landscape has nothing of the savage harshness of Lazio or Umbria. Every photo is a postcard. The vineyards and fields are more carefully tended. One is grateful for well kept paths, well kept verges. Each low hilltop boasts its charming clump of cypresses and cedars half-hiding, half-framing some tower, farmhouse or chapel. You can understand why tourists flock here. Everything is perfectly composed: an English dream of quaintness in a Mediterranean climate.

We were walking through rich agricultural land with discreetly opulent villas, tastefully renovated farmhouses, sparkling swimming pools. And people were indeed more friendly. They waved to us from behind the wheels of expensive cars. It's a curious little side-to-side wave that I don't recall seeing before in Italy. As if they were all members of an extended royal family acknowledging your dutiful admiration. A man on a horse appeared, the first horse and rider we had seen. It was a handsome chestnut animal, glistening in the sunshine. The rider, in his early forties, had shiny boots and spurs, a big man, well fed and bare-chested, sporting a leather Tuscan cowboy hat. Sweat trickled off a tanned paunch. He smiled complacently and waved that wave, turning into a stone gate and trotting away down a private avenue of shady cypresses.

Tuscany was less attractive when it came to booking accommodation. In Ficulle, Eleonora had had long phone conversations with various holiday farms and gated villages along Garibaldi's route.

'At that price no, *mia cara*. No, no, no. We might find you a *buchetto* [a little hole] for a hundred and fifty, but ...'

Eleonora explained that in two weeks on the road we had never paid more than ninety-five.

'But where have you been, *mia cara*?' the woman demanded. 'Oh Lazio! Oh Umbria. *Per favore!*'

For days to come Eleonora would mimic the contempt with which this well-to-do lady had pronounced the names of these unfashionable poverty-stricken regions.

'Tuscany,' the proud woman had declared, 'is a different world, *mia cara*. A different world.' And she gave an example. 'If an apricot in Umbria costs fifty cents, in Tuscany you can be sure it costs a euro.'

How many times and with how many variations would we repeat this formula in the days to come!

'If a *cedrata* in Umbria costs two euros, in Tuscany you can be sure it costs six.'

'If a Cinquecento in Umbria costs a thousand euros, in Tuscany you can be sure they drive a Porsche Cayenne.'

And so on. With occasional *mia cara*s thrown in.

'If in Umbria they want a pound of flesh, in Tuscany, *mia cara*, you can be sure they bleed you dry ...'

But eventually we do manage to find a reasonably priced place, a couple of miles to the west of our route, in the village of Palazzone, where we arrive, after just six hours walking, towards midday. Immediately, turning into the main street, we're amazed how different it feels. The stone is the same as in Ficulle. A pleasant pinkish brown. With no stucco. The architecture is the same. But everything here is sharper and neater. The flagstones have been swept Swiss clean and are all laid perfectly flush. The walls are all rigorously pointed. Wherever there is a straight line – the vertical edge of a wall, the horizontal passage of a gutter or cable – it is straighter than in Ficulle. Not to mention Vacone or Mentana. Everywhere you look, it seems someone passed by ten minutes before with a vacuum cleaner.

On a table in the street, outside a pretty café, we read the Tuscan newspaper *La Nazione* and learn that a Moroccan was stabbed with a penknife in Florence, but was unwilling to tell the police who attacked him or why. That two Bulgarian women were arrested for stealing the backpack of a Japanese man at a café in the Mercato Centrale. Florence again. It seems only foreigners generate news. Needless to say, on the front page of the paper Salvini is doing all he can to stop another boatload of Africans landing on the southern Italian coast.

In Palazzone foreigners are of a different kind. As we eat, a big BMW with German plates draws up in the empty street some three yards from where we're sitting. It doesn't look out of place among the old rural buildings. Years of expensive advertising have got us used to the vision of luxury engineering in picturesque surroundings. But the driver has left his engine on. A diesel engine.

Time passes.

'What would Greta say?' Eleonora asks.

'He's keeping his engine on because he needs the air conditioning,' I observe.

'He's waiting for someone, perhaps,' Eleonora guesses.

Meantime, our bruschetta doesn't taste so good in the presence of diesel fumes.

One complains less these days. It's fear again. But today the *garibaldino* spirit is with me. I jump to my feet and go to the car.

The driver is middle-aged, clean-shaven, wears a white shirt. At first he doesn't notice me. I have to stoop to the window. Now it winds down. I feel the cool air flowing out and he no doubt the hot air drifting in. Unthinking, I address him in Italian. 'Could you turn your engine off, please, if you're going to be here for a while? We're eating.'

Like so many Austrian soldiers in 1849, the driver doesn't speak Italian. He looks blank. I repeat the request in English. He frowns, doesn't say anything, but buzzes down all the windows and turns the engine off. I return to my seat.

But now the atmosphere is poisoned by a certain unpleasantness. He is sitting there stony faced, just a couple of yards away.

'I'm beginning to feel violent,' Eleonora observes.

'Like when someone won't open up their farmhouse to give you a glass of water?'

'Something like that.'

At last a woman steps out of a door opposite. She's smartly dressed in white skirt and red blouse, with a big straw hat on blonde hair and an elegant leather handbag under her arm. The BMW's windows buzz up. The engine starts, the woman climbs in. And you realize that this old Italian house, once humble, now immaculately spruced up, is occupied, perhaps owned, by foreigners. This is why, or one of the reasons why, the whole area feels so different from the area around Ficulle. It's being turned into an international leisure park. When your old relatives pass away in southern Tuscany, there is no problem finding a buyer for the property. Walking towards B & B Madonna del

Carmine, we get a little confused with the street plan, which doesn't seem to correspond to our app. Seeing a young man jogging despite the intense heat we ask the way. In Californian English he says, 'Sorry, I don't speak Italian.'

The Biancolini family on the other hand are born and bred citizens of Palazzone. 'In 1992 our parents left their jobs to build our future,' write the brother and sister who now run the B & B on their website. The old folks realized, that is, that the future for natives of the area was that of catering for tourists.

They do it beautifully. Our room is spacious and comfortable, the terrace balcony full of flowers, the garden shady and fragrant. There's a small swimming pool. You can lounge beside it, popping into the restaurant for an ice cream whenever you want. As darkness fell, we were the first at the tables under the pergola. The Biancolini brother, in white shirt and fancy black and purple waistcoat, served us with a curious irony, a wry twist to his lips. Every servility seemed very slightly overdone, or acted out, as if he were only playing at being a waiter – the waistcoat was a costume – and our roles might easily be reversed, him the lord and us the servants.

'You wonder if it's really generosity,' Eleonora reflected, 'or whether deep down they actually resent having to depend on you.'

'Who cares?'

'Right.'

But the *garibaldini* did care. The burning question for them over the next few crucial days would be, were the people of Tuscany really on their side, or was their hospitality just a show?

DAY 14

17–18 July 1849 – 7 August 2019

Palazzone, Cetona, Sarteano, Chianciano Terme – 20 miles

Cetona

If it was a show it was a good one. In brilliant sunshine after the night's heavy rain, a small party of cavalry galloped into Cetona to check out security. It's a spectacularly picturesque town, a walled cluster high up on a ridge, topped by a monastery and tower. The people hurried down the slopes en masse shouting, *'Evviva Garibaldi, Re d'Italia!'* The mayor was with them. This time the whole community was united. They insisted that the General and his men all come into the town and sleep in their homes.

Here's Belluzzi: 'What a milling of bodies, what excitement in the streets and houses of the lovely little town, especially around the old well spurting jets of plentiful fresh water from its artistic spouts! Oh, the happy throng crowding around, the men eager to wash themselves and their dirty clothes after so many days of punishing marches! The local men and women looking on smiling and doing all they could to meet the soldiers' every request.'

It's one of the rare moments when Belluzzi lets slip that he himself was once a *garibaldino*. 'If the reader has ever been in such a situation, he will know how wonderfully rewarding it is for the young volunteer to feel that people understand, how a woman's words of compassion or an older man's encouragement and even envy will caress his young ears and slip sweetly down into his eager, passionate heart.'

Born in 1839, Belluzzi had deserted from the papal army in 1859 when ordered to fight against Garibaldi. In 1866 he volunteered to fight with Garibaldi against the Austrians in Trento, then followed him in the 1867 campaign that ended in defeat at Mentana. He was captured and imprisoned. The rest of his life he would spend in Bologna as a schoolteacher and social activist, encouraging a positive sense of Italian identity and becoming first director of the city's Risorgimento Museum. His account of the retreat from Rome is his only full-length book.

'I wonder,' Eleonora asks, 'why he chose to write about the retreat, which happened when he was ten, instead of the things he experienced himself.'

It's an interesting question. We have stopped a moment to watch a flock of big white geese marching in determined formation across a rough hillside, passing through a scatter of grazing sheep. Both species endearingly express their collective spirit: the sheep are desultory, shabby, woolly, entirely content to be chomping dewy grass in the morning cool. The geese are wired up on their webbed feet, spick and span, orange-beaked, waddling forward with great urgency. You wonder if either group is remotely aware of the state of mind of the other.

'Perhaps,' I suggest, still thinking of Belluzzi, 'he was attracted by this journey, the thought of seeing so much of Italy. The same way we are. Or perhaps it was too depressing to write up that awful defeat he experienced, and too easy to enthuse about the glorious victories of the Thousand in Sicily. Everybody had done that. He wanted to visit all these out-of-the-way places, hear people's memories of forty years before. He used up all his summer holidays through the 1880s, corresponding with hundreds of people. And he travelled in company.'

'Ah.'

'He only acknowledges it once or twice. They moved in horse-drawn coaches for the most part, staying in taverns or with local politicians. He just mentions "my young friend".'

'Male or female?'

For better or worse, Italian noun endings – *amico, amica, compagno, compagna* – make it hard to disguise gender. You can't just say 'my friend'.

'Male. Towards the end he mentions his unhappiness that his friend has died.'

'Younger, you said?'

'Yes.'

We move on, sobered but also heartened to think that others have shared our fascination with this adventure. We are a species, moving through the landscape in the peculiar way our species does. And now we find that the country lane we're walking along is called Strada di Donna Morta – Dead Woman Street. We also discover, stopping to drink, that Eleonora has left her water bottle in Palazzone.

Fortunately Cetona isn't far now. Around 9.15, we march into a square which is recognisably the same place that Hoffstetter and Belluzzi describe. The well where the men washed their clothes is still there, with its 'artistic spouts', four grotesque fishy faces around a central stone column above a broad basin. 'It would be the first night and the last,' Hoffstetter observes, 'that all the men slept inside in people's homes and ate and drank their fill.'

The piazza is surprisingly big, a long, open, cream-stuccoed rectangle. There's easily room for a couple of thousand men to crowd in. Anita was admired for the way she handled her horse on the steep streets with their uneven stone flagging. Was she beautiful? 'Not at all,' remembers a certain Ettore Marziale. 'Her complexion was very dark, her features hardly regular and markedly scarred with smallpox. All the same you couldn't help looking at her with admiration and growing sympathy.' Amalia Gigli, the mayor's wife, felt the same. The two spent the day together, and she had Anita measured for clothes to match her condition; a dress of dark green silk was cut and sewn in a matter of hours.

But not all was sweetness and light that morning. A *garibaldino* managed to get himself caught stealing a gold earring from a jeweller. Inevitably, when the case was brought before Garibaldi, he ordered summary execution. He knew that many of the men had been dismayed to read accounts in Tuscan newspapers of their supposed looting, raping and stealing, often in places where they had never been. But the goldsmith and his wife were horrified. They just wanted their earring back. The wife hurried to the mayor's wife and she to Anita, and all the women begged the General to relent. In the event, he seemed glad to back down. All observers noticed he was in a special mood these first days in Tuscany. He thought the uprising was going to happen. It was now or never. 'A frenzy mixed with joy was visible on his face and in everything he did.'

He was doing a lot. He 'multiplied himself everywhere', Belluzzi says. First he wrote a polite request for money to the mayor. But then had to alter it. The mayor didn't want a polite request which, if the Austrians were to see it, might look like something he could have refused. He wanted an order, in threatening language. Garibaldi obliged but must have been discouraged by his host's fears. Now he assigned fifteen men to each of the town's gates and sent the top-hatted Forbes to occupy the monastery and keep watch from its tower. Müller returned with news of Austrian positions. Soon all the General's staff were on their horses, exploring the Tuscan countryside.

Ruggeri dwells at loving length on the tactics Garibaldi now evolved as they came closer to the Austrians. Cavalry would be sent east, west and north in considerable numbers to make contact with the enemy. Hopefully this would give each Austrian army the impression that they were about to be attacked, encouraging them to assume static defensive positions. Meantime the main column of men could move from one safe camp to the next, arousing public enthusiasm.

Something went wrong right away. Three miles north of Cetona, along the same chain of hills, is the small town of Sarteano. Garibaldi was riding there on the afternoon of 17 July when he ran into a crowd of people coming towards him with carts full of food. They were helping out their friends in Cetona, they said, with the business of feeding the 3000. But they also told the General that two companies of Tuscan soldiers were stationed in their town.

Whose side were these men on? Officially, the Austrian side. They were soldiers of the grand duke, who was returning to his realm thanks to Austrian intervention. But they were also Italians. Garibaldi didn't want to fight Italians. These soldiers, the people said, knew that they were bringing food to the *garibaldini* and hadn't tried to stop them. On the other hand, they had quickly left town, heading for Chiusi seven miles to the east, which was in the hands of reactionaries, in particular the Bishop of Chiusi, who had been spreading the most vicious rumours about the patriots. Inevitably, the more people were enthusiastic about Garibaldi, the more frightened and reactionary the establishment became. The situation was polarizing. It wasn't unusual, Ruggeri tells us, for priests to form bands of armed peasants to fight the patriots, who they spoke of as demons. Garibaldi ordered Captain Montanari to take twenty horsemen to Chiusi to see what was up.

'That evening we rode for a long while,' Hoffstetter remembers. 'Our horses were fresh and the magnificent places all around kept us out later than usual.' On return, bad news. Riding towards Chiusi, Montanari had seen and avoided a first ambush but then pushed on regardless and fallen into a second. Tuscan soldiers had burst from cover twenty paces away and fired. One man was killed, two horses went down and their riders were captured. Garibaldi was grieved and angry. He had hoped the Tuscan army could be brought over to his side. Now this would be more difficult. And he must find a way to get his men back, before they fell into Austrian hands.

The upset did not stop everyone enjoying their Cetona evening. They were used to crises and losses. The General and his staff climbed the monastery tower and studied the view beyond Chiusi to Lake Trasimeno in the north-east. Then they ate a sumptuous dinner laid on by the locals and talked till late. It was during this evening that Aristide Pilhes finally caught up with them from Terni, bringing all his men safe and sound into the fold. Glasses were raised. Then everyone slept in a bed, except of course the prisoners in Chiusi. And the dead man, whom nobody names.

We also explored the views of the surrounding countryside from the high walls around the monastery. East and west the hills stretch away in long wooded ridges. You can see how difficult it would be to keep track of anyone in this landscape, without satellites and air surveillance.

You can imagine the anxiety of D'Aspre and the other Austrian generals, wondering how to deal with a rebellion that wouldn't stay still. What most caught my attention, though, were the flowers of the caper plants, climbing up from a garden beneath the wall. Each presents a trembling butterfly of four white petals, from the centre of which a fine bristle of long purple stamens thrusts up to the light; every one of these – and there must be forty or fifty – is tinily tipped with a royal blue that clashes splendidly with the purple and seems to demand that the sun be even brighter than it already is. So all my amateurish photos are of flowers, not of the lie of the land that a military man must study. Still, I remembered how Belluzzi says that when he tracked down the places Anita set up her tent, they were invariably the prettiest spots. She liked to fill her days with beauty.

Sarteano

Military acumen or not, we now stole a march on Garibaldi, something the Austrians never managed to do. This was only because we hadn't found a place to stay in Cetona or Sarteano. We were booked into a hotel in the spa town of Chianciano Terme six miles to the north of Sarteano, nine miles from here, so we had a long day ahead of us.

In this regard, should you ever find yourself walking from Cetona to Sarteano, beware of Google Maps. It was one of the rare occasions when Google suggested a short cut, over a steep hill, that our trekking app was unaware of. It looked like an easy white stone track and we were glad of the half-mile or so it would save. We attacked the slope with energy, discussing the dilemma of the Tuscan soldiers as they were forced to choose between Austrians and patriots. Until, after twenty minutes, we ran into a chain across the road and the sign, PROPRIETÀ PRIVATA, VIETATO L'ACCESSO.

The climb had been stiff and we were invested in this short cut now. We ducked under the chain, slipped our trekking poles under our arms and walked in stealthy silence through the grounds of a handsome villa to our left, praying that if there was a dog it was sound asleep. Nothing stirred but a few faintly humming bees, lazily sampling orange and blue flower beds. We had just begun to whisper again and to congratulate ourselves on our boldness, when the track terminated in a garden shed.

There is no other way to describe it: Google's path simply went straight into an open shed full of gardening tools. Beyond the shed was a fence, and then, still climbing steeply, thick woodland with a dense undergrowth of brambles, blackberries and prickly plants. I climbed the fence to investigate. I advanced two yards, three, wielding my trusty trekking poles. Clearly there had been a path here once, and perhaps a week before I would have insisted we push on. But if there is one thing one learns following any of Garibaldi's campaigns, it is the art of cutting one's losses and changing plans in a trice. These brambles would tear us apart.

Mint, lavender and honeysuckle. That was our midday. Beetles and grasshoppers. Giant straw bales and barking dogs. A green glow under young acacia trees. The frequent stops to drink – in the shade of a barn – to wipe the sweat off our sunglasses. Little waves at waving Tuscans. A constant marvelling at the variety and density of leaves and twigs and stones beneath our feet. As compared with the vast blueness over our heads, quite empty but for a hawk or two, waiting to connect heaven and earth in a kill. Crows rising from a ploughed field, cawing, circling. And towards one, the sign, 'SARTEANO, Twinned with Gundelsheim (Germany)'. It was a *Città equosolidale*, the sign went on, meaning it promoted fair trade and solidarity; it boasted a *bandiera arancione*, an orange flag, meaning it respected the environment; and finally it was a *Città dell'olio*, meaning it was dedicated to the protection of the 'Culture of Olive Oil'. It also boasts a church with the charming name Cappella della Madonna del Mal di Capo – Our Lady of Headaches.

'Giuseppe Garibaldi, abandoned by everyone but his own great spirit, took refuge here from the foreigner's hatred, 19 July, 1849,' says the plaque by the town hall. The piazza is small, dominated by the dark statue of a First World War soldier in his heavy trench coat and tin hat. He too seems abandoned, melancholy, overdressed in the summer heat. On the *loggiato* of the town hall the four great architects of the Risorgimento, Mazzini, Cavour, Garibaldi, Vittorio Emanuele II, look down from neat round bas-reliefs with the colourful flags of the town's *contrade* beside. The narrow streets are flying blue and white streamers for the festival of the *contrada* of San Lorenzo. The ancient Teatro degli Arrischianti – Risktakers Theatre – is promising a jazz festival.

'Strange,' I remark over lunch, 'how the plaques often make it sound like Garibaldi was entirely alone, while in fact there were still about 3000 men with him.'

'I suppose,' Eleonora says, 'they could hardly write 3000 names. Do we even know them?'

'The archives in Cetona give the names and ranks of seventy-one men who made formal requests to the town hall for items of clothing and equipment. Some of the ranks are interesting. Ambulance surgeon. Herald. Quartermaster. War officer. Sanitary expert. Horse vet.'

Eleonora laughs. 'Abandoned by everyone but his horse vet doesn't sound so good. They want the pathos of the man absolutely alone, taking on the world alone.'

An hour later we met that man.

We were making our usual quick tour of the town, mindful of the six miles that still separated us from our hotel. Mindful too that we needed to fill our water bottles. Eventually, we came across a fountain in Piazza San Martino. This was little more than a widening in a steeply sloping cobbled alley, with a gnarled mimosa tree and a bench. The bench was occupied by an elderly man, the kind of primly dressed, panama-hatted octogenarian we'd seen so many times. Since he had the bench, we sat on a low wall to drink our fill of water and top up again before hitting the road.

We were just picking up our packs to go when the old man got up from his bench and walked towards us. It was a slow stiff walk, aided by angry jabs of his walking stick on the travertine paving. He was muttering. And as he came close the word *merda* was distinctly audible. Then when he was closer still. *Forestieri di merda.* Shitty foreigners. Or outsiders. *Forestieri di merda, di merda, di merda.*

Eleonora threw him a look of protest. Did we deserve this abuse?

The man stopped. There was an Ancient Mariner glitter to his eyes. 'Oh not you!' He jabbed his stick. 'I'm not angry with you, *signori*! Ha!' He managed a grimace of a smile. 'I'm angry with *il Padre eterno*.' With God Almighty.

'And why would that be?'

'Why? Why? Because he lets so many mean, nasty people go on living.'

We didn't know what to say.

'I hope they all go to hell. I hope an earthquake swallows up this town and everyone in it. Like Sodom and Gomorrah.'

'I thought you were complaining about foreigners,' Eleonora said.

The man frowned. He had a proud Roman nose, a bristling yellowish moustache. And he launched into his story. While we stood in the sunshine with our packs on our backs.

'When I arrived here fifty years ago we were all poor in this town. Very poor. But we were *signori*! We had no money, but we had our dignity. Now these rich shits have come along and spoiled everything. They are mean and nasty. I wish them all the fires of hell.'

'What have they done?'

'What?' He was incredulous. How was it possible we didn't know? 'They want me out of my house,' he snapped. 'They've bought everything. I'm the only one left. Holiday homes for tourists. *Forestieri*. And it's never enough. They've never made enough money. Or bought enough houses. I'm the last one in my *palazzo*. They play tricks on me. They stir up everyone against me. They want me in an old people's home. So they can turn the *palazzo* into a home for *forestieri*.'

'Awful,' Eleonora agreed.

The man stared wildly. 'It's my house. Understand? My house. It's the only thing I have. The only thing I can leave to my daughter. They won't rest till they've got me out. Villains!'

'What tricks do they play on you?' I asked.

His cleaning lady, he said. Every time he found a woman, they got to her and persuaded her to leave him. So he would be alone. He had been alone for seven years, since his wife died. Now he was ninety.

'Ninety!'

'Last May.'

'*Complimenti!*' I told him.

He drew himself up straighter. 'An old man of ninety,' he said. They knew he couldn't survive alone. They lured away anyone who came to cook for him.

'You should see a lawyer,' Eleonora suggested.

'The lawyers are on their side.'

I wondered if it wasn't paranoia.

'They're evil! *Il Padre eterno* is evil for letting such evil people walk the earth. May they be swallowed up in hell! Reduced to crawling on all fours. Like animals. With their snouts in filth.'

We were astonished. He looked at us, and now he noticed our backpacks, our sweat, and his eyes cleared. He prodded his stick more gently on the stone. 'Forgive me, *signori*. I never thought I would say these terrible things. But I have no one. I have bored you, *signori*. Forgive me.'

I assured him he hadn't bored us. Shocked us rather. We would think over what he had said. '*Coraggio*,' Eleonora said. We shook his hand and were on our way.

'So much,' I muttered, 'for the *Città equosolidale* with the *bandiera aranclone* and the Culture of Olive Oil.'

Garibaldi stayed a full day in Cetona, marching to Sarteano at four in the afternoon of 18 July. Fifty years on, eyewitnesses told Belluzzi that the column had announced its departure with a roll of drums. Garibaldi sat on his horse in the packed square and drew his sword to make a speech. He thanked the Cetonesi for their hospitality and offered a gift of a tricolour and a pennant of the First Italian Legion. Blade glinting in the sunshine, he promised he would dedicate his entire life to freeing Italy from foreign domination.

It was quite an event. People had flocked in from the countryside. 'The General's men were as if reborn,' Belluzzi says. 'They were spoiling for a fight,' Ruggeri tells us. Then they marched just three miles to Sarteano.

Garibaldi was not in a hurry. He needed to give his cavalry parties a day or two to reach, contact and confuse the enemy before he decided what to do next. He needed to see if this local enthusiasm could be transformed into serious military support. Ruggeri is more alive than Hoffstetter to the complicated psychology of the situation. Garibaldi knows that if he stops and fights with just his 3000 poorly armed and equipped men, they will soon be surrounded and overcome. He must have the local people on his side. On the other hand, his men have volunteered to fight, not to live on the run. They want action, victory; then home. They have got the idea that a battle in Tuscany was always the General's goal. So when is it going to happen? And they are not aware how heavily the cards are stacked against them. Garibaldi would be crazy to tell them. The mood is getting more excited and unstable by the day.

Then there were the two cavalrymen imprisoned in Chiusi. 'I feared for them in the clutches of these descendants of Torquemada,' Garibaldi writes in his memoirs. Torquemada was a fifteenth-century Spanish inquisitor. The General sent a prominent citizen of Cetona to demand their release, but the Bishop of Chiusi refused. So on the evening of 18 July, having identified a monastery involved in spreading anti-rebel rumours, he dispatched a group of cavalry to round up all the monks and bring them to Sarteano. They arrived the following morning. Twenty-four of them, according to Hoffstetter, 'unctuous and dripping with sweat'; no more than ten, according to Belluzzi, 'big bellied and unused to marching'. 'You have struck the sparks of a civil war,' Garibaldi told the monks. 'You call yourselves ministers of God, when in fact you are ministers of the Devil.' They would march with the column, he ordered, until his two men were released. And if they were not released, the monks would be shot.

A ring of bonfires was prepared at a distance of some two miles from Sarteano, to be lit by sentinels in the event of an attack. 'It is admirable,' Generale De Rossi remarks in the *Cavalry Review*, 'how meticulous Garibaldi was in preparing against all surprises.'

Chianciano Terme

We pushed on to Chianciano Terme. To our right, in the distance, across vineyards and cornfields, we could clearly see Lake Trasimeno, all five miles of it. Perugia was beyond, whence Colonel Paumgartten is sending his men towards Chiusi. To the left were the hills separating the Val di Chiana from the Val d'Orcia, and fifty miles further that way you reach the sea. Müller is heading in that direction to confuse D'Aspre. All around us were the usual hilltop villages, the sporadic winking of distant windows in the sunlight, the countryside slowly unfolding to the click of our poles.

Hoffstetter chooses that day in Sarteano to introduce a poignant addition to our dramatis personae, someone whose services would have been extremely useful when we arrived in Chianciano. Gaetano was Anita's servant. He was from Bologna and just thirteen years old, but 'extraordinarily serious'. 'When everyone else was joking and laughing,' Hoffstetter says, 'Gaetano scarcely moved his lips.' He was always on hand, his little red pony always the first to be saddled. And his job was to make sure that Anita had food to cook for herself and the General. Not just the bread, supplied by the local people, or the meat, which came from their own cattle, but fruit, vegetables, poultry, sweets even. 'If Gaetano couldn't find something,' Hoffstetter assures us, 'no one could.'

How had such a young boy, from Bologna, found himself in the Roman Republic, 250 miles to the south? We've no idea, but paintings of Risorgimento battles often show young boys carrying messages or banging drums and generally looking pleased with themselves in makeshift uniforms. The other boys, Hoffstetter says, showed Gaetano great respect and did everything he asked. If an older man or an officer made a joke at his expense, he wasn't afraid to hit back with a sharp gibe. 'But if Gaetano liked you, you might find yourself on the receiving end of a cigar when no one else had one.'

Cigars were a kind of currency among the officers. 'Good when you needed to stay awake,' Hoffstetter thought. Likewise coffee. Garibaldi did everything possible to make sure he started the day with a fresh cup. 'Bread, wine, meat and salt were not indispensable,' remarked Giuseppe Bandi who served the General in Sicily in 1860, 'but Garibaldi had to start the day with a cup of coffee.' Usually around 3 a.m.

We weren't looking for cigars or coffee in Chianciano, but a light evening meal to wind up a long day. It proved hard to find. Garibaldi didn't actually stop here; he bypassed it to the east, heading straight to what was then the far bigger centre of Montepulciano. Chianciano is a spa town that grew enormously in the post-war period when eager-to-please Christian Democrat governments made thermal spa cures freely available on the Italian public health service. Many of those who abandoned the tiny *borgo* of Salci came to Chianciano to cash in on the resulting bonanza, which ended in the 2000s, when the financial crisis came along and austerity set in. Now Chianciano is full of dowdy hotels offering full board at low prices. Our hotel offers a set menu, rich in meat, and a dining room full of elderly folk. We headed into town.

It was eight. The shops were closed. The centre of the spa side of the town is relatively new, a wide-open, 60s-looking plaza, bright with flower beds between rigid lines of trees and benches. The Hotel Continentale looks on. And the Hotel Excelsior. The Grand Hotel Ambasciatore looms. The Grand Hotel Milano isn't far away. Or the Grand Hotel Admiral Palace. Everything is grand without being inviting. A pub called Le Fonti spreads out across the plaza with a vaguely seaside sprawl of armchairs under sunshades but no customers.

'How did Gaetano do it?' Eleonora wonders.

'He kept going. He badgered the locals.'

The locals pointed us along the busy Viale della Libertà towards the older city centre. It was only half a mile.

We were tired. My feet were sore. Half a mile suddenly seemed a long way. And we would have to walk back. In desperation, we poked our noses into the kind of stained-concrete development you might expect in windswept Wigan or on the Neasden section of London's North Circular. Between closed shops there was a place called Pizza al Volo – Pizza in a Rush. In a poky room with no air conditioning a woman was putting together takeaway sandwiches. There was a fridge with Coke and beer. There was an electric pizza oven. But unlike Wigan or Neasden, stepping out of the back of that tiny room, you were on a small tiled terrace with four tables and a hugely satisfying view of the valley below. She couldn't bring the food out to us, our lady of rushed pizzas apologized, because she had no restaurant licence. On the other hand, if we just happened to eat our takeaway on her terrace, that was fine.

We sat watching the darkness steal across the fields. The food was wholesome and, as ever after the day's exertions, very welcome. The beer was icy.

'This is where Gaetano would have brought us,' Eleonora decided.

'If the young lad could find me a cigar,' I agreed, 'I'd smoke it.'

We clinked our bottles to a boy who disappears from history as soon as he's introduced. 'A few days later,' Hoffstetter says, 'Gaetano fell sick, and we were obliged to leave him behind.'

DAY 15

19–20 July 1849 – 8 August 2019

Chianciano Terme, Montepulciano – 6 miles

Montepulciano

It's only six miles from Chianciano to Montepulciano, so we were able to enjoy a proper breakfast in the Hotel Bosco while Garibaldi was on the march from Cetona. We will catch him before lunch at the monastery where he spent the night, two miles from Montepulciano, then enter the city together. Meantime, while a group of elderly folk at the table beside ours are regretting their decision to spend their holidays in Chianciano, we have opened our computer to review the important documents of these make-or-break days.

18 July, General D'Aspre in Florence to Field Marshal Radetzky north of Milan
Siena [40 miles south of Florence] is threatened. The grand duke has begged me to defend it. I am sending Major General Stadion with three battalions and a squadron of hussars. If Garibaldi is allowed to become a real power in central Italy the consequences will be incalculable.

19 July, General D'Aspre in Florence to Colonel Paumgartten in Perugia
We must put an end to the skulduggery of this rebel. Garibaldi is in Cetona, heading for Montepulciano. Take as many troops as possible, intercept him with forced marches and attack at once. Major General Stadion is approaching from Siena to assist. It is of the utmost importance that Garibaldi be annihilated as swiftly as possible.

Garibaldi is heading west towards the west coast. Yesterday I sent two companies ahead to the crucial crossroads of San Quirico [30 miles south of Siena]. However, just now I received news that Garibaldi is already in Montalcino [8 miles west of San Quirico, 21 miles west of Montepulciano]. He has beaten us to it, slipped through our fingers. Unfortunately, I can't follow him this evening because my men are exhausted.

Garibaldi was not in Montalcino and never would be. Müller was in Montalcino. Garibaldi was in Montepulciano. He brought with him a proclamation he had been working on since his arrival in Tuscany and hurried to have it typeset, printed and distributed.

TUSCANS!

Once again ...! Italy is condemned to wallowing in filth and disgrace ...! The bondage of twenty centuries goes on!!!

This generation had promised to break free, but proved false. We will not! We will not bend under the yoke of the usurpers. Shrouded in mourning and riddled with bullets, our banner has frightened the Germans at Luino, the Bourbons at Palestrina and Velletri, the French in the Roman Campagna. The foreigner fled before these children born from our country's betrayal.

Forced by the destiny of the Italian cause to choose between exile and the hardships of the forests, we have chosen the hardships, the dangers, the adversities! – if one can speak of adversity when serving such a beautiful homeland!

We have felt the generous ferment of Tuscany, this most hospitable of Italian peoples. And we have made haste towards those whose hearts beat hard in outrage, tormented and betrayed as they are! The usurpers, the servile traitors, they call us brigands! To their calumny we will answer with our poverty! We will show the scars of their treacherous bullets on our breasts.

Tuscans! While in the land of Columbus ... when I was deciding to sacrifice my life for Italy, when I was still fighting for the freedom of other peoples, my thoughts went to Tuscany – I looked to Tuscany as a place of refuge, of friendships dear to my heart – I received a gift sent to me from Tuscany in the name of Italy! A word of love that bound me to You – with the indissoluble knot of an entire life consecrated to You – consecrated to the honour of the name Italian.

With whatever band of brave men I can find, I will raise over our unhappy land the banner of redemption from traitors and foreigners; we offer ourselves now as a rallying point to anyone who is ashamed ... of the dishonour ... the debasement ... the calamity of our country!!! When the foreigner, the traitors, have divided their unhappy, tormented prey ...! we will trouble their sleep and sully their glee. With the cry of our hatred, our revenge, our curse !!! we will pursue them and put them to rout.

Tuscans! Let our battle cry be the one that you were the first to pronounce:

Away with the foreigners!

Away with the traitors!

GARIBALDI

'If exclamation marks were recruits, the battle was won,' Eleonora reflects.

To avoid the main road along the valley we struck up a path called Werewolf's Way. It ran straight and steep up a wooded gully. But someone had been stripping out trees. They had taken the trunks and left the branches strewn on the path, a carpet of thin black branches, perhaps a year old, some brittle, some springy, impossible to put your foot between but hard to walk on because they broke and scratched, or shifted, inviting the ankle to twist.

Eventually we topped the hill and there was Tuscany, beguiling as ever. I can think of no landscape more radically transformed by sunshine; it's as if the whole world were built with a play of profile and shadow, trees and towers inked against the sky, the chiaroscuro grid of the vineyards tensing the soft *sfumato* of the hills. In the distance a white path winds towards stony battlements. Everything glints. But if by chance the sun should slip behind a cloud, all the shape and life is suddenly gone. You could be anywhere.

We reached a small crossroads with one huge cypress and an iron cross beside it. The monastery where the *garibaldini* spent the night of 19 July appeared to our right. Apparently the men were well received, though none of the sources says how the monks reacted to the fact that Garibaldi had other monks as hostages.

Montepulciano came into view. Another variation on the hilltop theme. As usual we had to dive into a valley before tackling the ascent. Stopping to drink beside a bench, we read this dedication: 'In loving memory of Lieut. James De Villiers Browse Gray, Pretoria Regiment, killed in action, 30 June 1944'.

Another summer, another casualty. Responding to General D'Aspre, Colonel Paumgartten reports unidentified corpses along the road to Chiusi and speaks of information extorted from rebel deserters. Not always accurate. In a further message from San Quirico, General Stadion mentions an English spy who is supposed to be updating him on Garibaldi's movements. 'I confess I don't really trust him.' 'Could you send me,' he winds up, 'a detailed map of Tuscany, from the Tuscan Ministry of War.'

'Montepulciano,' Hoffstetter tells us,

> is a lively town in a delightful setting. It's surprising the luxury and amenities you find in these Tuscan towns, compared to those around Rome. But though for the tired soldier it seems too good to be true to be surrounded by so many demonstrations of friendship and opportunities for refreshment, the attraction soon fades once your bodily needs are satisfied. My mind went back ever more wistfully to the beautiful Roman landscape we had left behind, how its melancholy hush spoke deep to the heart. In Tuscany I sought in vain for those tall, noble figures, the fiery gaze and black eyes that only Roman women have.

Women aside, Hoffstetter's words strike a chord. For all Tuscany's easy beauty, we too are experiencing an unexpected nostalgia for the harsh countryside around Montecelio and Poggio Mirteto. It had a pathos you don't feel here. Least of all in Montepulciano. If, in Sarteano, we had run into one poor man holding out against the sharks, we sense at once there will be no such meeting today. Poverty has been removed in Montepulciano. Bought out. The town is a seamless string of beautifully restored facades, shops and restaurants, all focused on giving you an off-the-peg Tuscan experience at Tuscan prices and sending you away with a gift package of Montepulciano wine. Three bottles in an elegant cardboard box. The streets throng with middle-class folk from many nations all clutching the same trophy.

As soon as we were through the gates, we headed to the main square to sit at a table and contemplate the space where the *garibaldini* received the most ecstatic welcome of their entire odyssey. 'The column marched through the town in good order,' Belluzzi writes, 'while people yelled deafening hurrahs.' The men filed out of the gate on the north side and set up camp near the monastery while the citizens crowded round to watch. 'Garibaldi,' Hoffstetter remembers, 'placed his tent at a corner close to the monastery and soon enough was being mobbed by the townsfolk, in particular, as always, the fairer sex. The General mingled with them and quickly fell to talking with the prettiest. His wife thought these ladies' behaviour extremely inopportune and, throwing a sulk, withdrew at once into her tent.'

'I guess she hadn't come all the way from Montevideo to be cuckolded by a hussy from Montepulciano,' Eleonora sympathizes. 'Especially being six months pregnant.'

'Seems she told José she had a pistol with two bullets, one for the woman who managed to seduce him and the other for herself.'

'Why not for him!'

'He was such a lady's man, you have to wonder what would have happened to the two of them if Anita had lived.'

Descriptions of Garibaldi all have him coolly composed and magnetically attractive. Blonde, lightly bearded. High forehead, quick and

elastic in his movements. Slow to speak. Rarely expansive, rarely gesturing. 'More an English gentleman than a passionate Latin,' one
observer remarked. The kind of man who has brown eyes but everyone thinks they're blue.

'Dangerous.'

We contemplate the great brick pile of the *duomo* and the old town
hall with its battlements and tower. There is a rather grand sixteenth-
century well with columns on each side supporting a stone lintel that
bears the emblem of the Medici family. But it's hard to get a sense of
the space of the piazza. A team of men is putting up a stage in front of
the *duomo* and erecting extensive scaffolding for seats opposite. The
tourists must be entertained. The people milling on the flagstones are
not locals.

The waiter brings our *cedrata*s on a tray and asks for twelve euros.

'Are we in Milan, or what?' Eleonora asks.

In every café we've been in so far we've been trusted to pay when
we leave, Italian style. The waiter apologizes but says too many people
have run off without paying.

'At these prices ...'

Someone who tried to run off across this piazza 170 years ago was a
senior judge notorious for his pro-Austrian sentiments and reactionary
rulings. The people of Montepulciano were so excited to see Garibaldi's patriots marching through their streets they decided to take the
opportunity to lynch the man. He was caught. The General had to
tear himself away from the ladies to prevent a murder. The judge, he
decided, would be marched along with the hostage monks until he
was far enough from his accusers to be safely released.

For how long, we wonder, did these traumatic events reverberate in
the minds of those involved? Did anyone change their political opinions because of what happened that summer? Was the judge grateful
to be spared? And what of the monks, whose fate hung in the balance?
The Bishop of Chiusi had made it clear he wouldn't release his prisoners whatever Garibaldi did to his hostages: their martyrdom would be
an honour, and a huge propaganda coup for the Church. The General's bluff had been called.

Struggling to choose a place for lunch, Eleonora introduces me to her lasagne theory. The dish originated in Bologna or maybe Naples. The two towns eternally contest the honour. But it is certainly not typical cuisine in other parts of Italy. 'Yet notice,' Eleonora points out, 'how often it's top of the list on the menus chalked outside the restaurants.' It's the dish international tourists know best. Her conclusion is, if you're not in Bologna or Naples, never go into a restaurant that prominently advertises lasagne. It's a tourist trap.

This reasoning, which an Englishman like myself could never have arrived at, obliges us to pass by a good half a dozen places before settling for *pici con broccoli* under an awning in a backstreet watching a little boy practise tossing his *contrada*'s flag for some forthcoming festival. Admired from a doorway by his mother, the ten-year-old windmills his arm and hurls the big flag spinning high into the alley. The blue and green fabric flaps and flashes in the sunshine until he catches it in his right hand and makes a little bow. His mother applauds. He does it again and again, with remarkable skill and concentration, very aware of the foreigners watching from the terrace of the trattoria.

Garibaldi ate with his entourage at the monastery. The monks were eager to serve the great man at table, but Anita refused to be attended by priests. She loathed the priesthood. Perhaps having been forced to marry an older man at fourteen, then being stigmatized for living unmarried with José had something to do with it. We know so little about Anita, but every detail we have suggests formidable strength of character. 'To the first hero of our homeland,' says the inevitable plaque in Piazzetta Santa Lucia, 'and his intrepid wife, sublime model for Italian women ...'

In the afternoon I climbed the tower. One pays five euros in a gloomy foyer, after which a woman uses a ruler to tear off a scrap of paper with a list of recommendations, in English. The first reads, 'Visit advised against those who suffer from claustrophobia or vertigo.'

I suffer from vertigo, but I wanted to see what Hoffstetter and Garibaldi saw.

You climb about ten floors of stairs, round and round, up and up, as the walls narrow and the ancient masonry closes in, until for the last twenty feet there are just two old wooden ladders taking you right up alongside a big bell. You can see why they warn against claustrophobia. Everything is musty, dark and splintery. There's no room for someone to go up while another comes down. At the top a man with a handheld radio is in constant touch with a man at the bottom, monitoring the flow of visitors.

The parapet all around is about waist height. The view is stunning. But this openness and with it the invitation I feel to throw myself down has my legs turning to water. I have to lean with my back against the timber around the bell, breathing deeply. I ask the man with the radio if people ever panic, and he nods, bored. He's up here eight hours every day, he says.

When I've calmed down and am able to contemplate the country in all directions, Garibaldi's predicament becomes clear. He has launched his appeal for support and volunteers, but with Paumgartten's army approaching from the south-east things have to happen fast. If the Tuscans are up for a fight, he will take the Austrians on. If not, he must avoid being caught, which means escaping to Venice. To do that he will have to cross the Val di Chiana again, back towards the Apennines in the east.

It's a hot, hazy day, and the distant mountains are no more than a smudge on the horizon. Due east is Lake Trasimeno. To get to the mountains, should the Tuscans not respond to his appeal, he will have to cross the valley to the north of the lake where the land is flat and marshy. Twenty miles of it. If the column is caught there, the attacker will have an overwhelming advantage.

Ruggeri is the best chronicler of this dilemma. The townsfolk are patriotic, he tells us. But weary. They have seen their country rapidly occupied by Austrians. They have heard of the massacre in Livorno. Their newspapers are constantly telling them of the collapse of liberal revolutions all over Europe, the crushing defeat of the Piedmontese at the hands of Radetzky. Their leaders and wealthy classes are cautious men, when not actually in the pay of the foreigner.

Forced to make his decision on the spur of the moment, Ruggeri says, Garibaldi chooses to keep moving north and east, taking his proclamation through the small villages and towns, while at the same time keeping the Apennines in sight. The larger town of Arezzo at the foot of the mountains will be the cut-off point. The people there are famous for their patriotism. He has received intelligence assuring him they are ready for a fight. If that doesn't work out, the high Apennine passes will be just two days' march away.

Having set up camp in Montepulciano and distributed his proclamation, Garibaldi surprises everyone by ordering a 5 p.m. departure. After barely ten hours in the town. This will allow him to follow the hills north and reach Torrita di Siena at 2000 feet before nightfall. Always a move ahead of Paumgartten. From there he will be in a good position to dive into the valley.

On the tower, I'm now calm enough to take a fleeting look straight down into the piazza and along the neighbouring streets. You see masses of stone and terracotta, piled up over centuries of civic optimism. Arches and balconies, sloping roofs and bright flags. It's wonderful. Around me other visitors are speaking French and Korean, oohing and aahing. But they don't stay long. They don't seem sure what to look at or why. In the piazza an open-top minibus is picking up sightseers. A little girl complains about the heat; her mother unscrews a water bottle. Beyond the town, in all directions, the land lies blanched and scorched in the still summer air.

Returning to ground level, the Civic Museum is deserted but for a family of Germans with time on their hands. Further down the street, the Museum of Tortures seems to be doing better business, but I don't feel like parting with eight euros to have my stomach turned. As night falls, the tourists flock into Piazza Grande for their free entertainment from the freshly built stage. We're just settling down to sleep when the opening chords of *Carmina Burana* come wafting through the window; in Carl Orff's arrangement.

'Recognizable as lasagne,' Eleonora sighs.

DAY 16

20–21 July 1849 – 9 August 2019

Montepulciano, Torrita di Siena, Foiano della Chiana – 16 miles

Torrita di Siena

In Torrita di Siena we were pursued by a street-cleaning vehicle. We arrived around 8.30 after two and a half hours easy walking in low sunshine over dew-soaked hills. You have to be careful not to walk through grass at this hour or you'll spend the day with wet socks. The fields had been freshly harvested, relieved of their burdens of wheat and barley, the lines of the mowing still etched across the soft slopes.

Suddenly, a dog barks, and a flock of sheep bursts up the steep bank into the narrow lane. They clatter past us, chased by a handsome white Maremma sheepdog. The animal is grinning, tongue out, pleased with himself. The sheep, like the fields, have been freshly shorn. They press together in a nervous mass, ears pink in the sunlight. A timeless vignette. Then the shepherd appears, a young man on a quad bike speaking on his smartphone.

Torrita is a red town. Old brick facades glow in full sunshine. We're approaching the southern gate, an arch with a marvellously intricate sundial above, when a cleaning vehicle buzzes out. It's incongruous, two big green brushes whirring on the dark flagstones, yellow light flashing. It shifts direction with robotic jerkiness, attacking the nooks and crannies in the ancient paving. As soon as it's well outside, we hurry in, only to have it turn 180 degrees and chase us up the steep cobbles. We turn left to escape, following an alley into a deserted piazza, and just have time to get ourselves served outside the one café before a low droning sound tells us the creature is still after us. It feels its way round the corner, insect-like, with its extendable green brushes and cicada buzz.

Eleonora points out that the whole piazza is already spotless; there's nothing to clean. But there is a car, in the way, a Panda, parked beside the inevitable old well. The cleaning vehicle is turned off. A man in orange dungarees gets down and scratches his head. A policeman steps out of the noble building behind him, the town hall, complete with clock tower and commemoration plaques, flags and coats of arms. The two men smoke a cigarette contemplating the Panda, and now the paunchy proprietor who brought us our coffees comes out from the café in black braces and white vest, grumbling and shaking his head, his tired old dog at his ankles. He ambles over to the Panda, starts it up and drives it out of the square. Cigarette finished, the cleaner can get on with his job.

We spin out our breakfast to enjoy the silence after the pest is gone. All round the piazza the shutters are pulled to against the rising heat. The space is quietly alluring and uncannily empty, a complete contrast to Montepulciano. Now the proprietor's wife enters the scene, as thin and nervy as her husband is plump and slow.

She wipes a couple of tables, rapidly but without conviction, then sits at one, quickly turns the pages of the newspaper, shakes her head and says in a loud voice, 'The last grocer's has just closed in ...' and she mentions the name of some nearby village.

'The last grocer's!' she repeats.

'Really?' Eleonora was first to realize we were being invited to a conversation.

'We're down to one in Torrita now. Can you imagine? And that will be the next to go.'

'That's bad.'

'Soon we will have nowhere to buy fruit and veg and fresh bread.'

Her idea of conversation is a string of gloomy announcements. The village is dying. Half the houses are empty and for sale. The only people who buy them are foreigners, who only come a couple of weeks a year.

'Can you imagine?' she repeats. 'Our politicians are useless. When are they going to learn how to keep the young people here? When are they going to find money to invest in jobs?'

We had been enjoying the quiet square so much. Now its very quietness has become sinister. Feeling it's time to go, Eleonora goes into the café to pay and gets hit by a truly scandalous bill. 'As if we were in Piazza di Spagna!' She's outraged.

'I suppose,' I reflect, 'we're paying for having the place to ourselves.'

As in Cetona and Montepulciano, the people of Torrita welcomed the *garibaldini* with great generosity. As in Cetona and Montepulciano, no one responded to the call to join up. Not a single man. Garibaldi had launched recruitment drives before. He knew that people either came flocking or not at all. There is a tide in the affairs of men. It was not running his way.

Arriving in Torrita towards 8 p.m., the General distributed his proclamation, persuaded the locals to bake enough bread for two days' rations, and was on the move again at 2.30 a.m., dropping down into the exposed valley under cover of night.

Except now the rain came. It fell heavily through the night. 'A ruinous march,' Ruggeri remembers, across the muddy plain. And he offers a reflection on guerrilla warfare. The Italian terrain is suited to it, he believes: so many hills and walled towns. The military situation is ripe for it: an invading army, unloved and cumbersome. But, he goes on, this kind of struggle requires absolute conviction. The guerrilla fighter cannot afford to be lukewarm; he must never lose heart. Not even for an instant.

Were these Italian traits?

A messenger from Müller caught up with the column, bringing news of General Stadion's advances south of Siena. Some time later another messenger, this time from Migliazza, north of Perugia, brought details of Paumgartten's forces, now advancing along both sides of Lake Trasimeno. Many thousands of men. Well armed, well equipped. Towards dawn Garibaldi called a halt at the small town of Foiano della Chiana. The people came out in the rain to greet them;

the infantry were billeted in a monastery, in taverns; the cavalry wrapped up beside their horses under dripping trees.

But the *garibaldini* were not the only ones losing sleep that night. This was written at 1 a.m.

21 July, General Stadion in Buonconvento to General D'Aspre in Florence

Regarding the order to chase Garibaldi to the sea. I fear I am being drawn in that direction in order to leave Siena exposed and that he will occupy the town behind my back. Allow me to stay in Buonconvento [20 miles due west of Torrita], which offers the possibility of defending the road to Siena and leaving me in a position to attack, once Paumgartten has located the main rebel column.

Later that same day, General D'Aspre in Florence already had copies of Garibaldi's proclamation, just forty-eight hours after it was printed in Montepulciano.

21 July, General D'Aspre in Florence to Field Marshal Radetzky north of Milan

Garibaldi has officially invaded Tuscany with 4000 to 7000 men. It is very difficult to get precise information. Unable to defend themselves, the small cities have complied with his requests for provisions. It is not clear if he is intending to reach the Tuscan coast, where American ships are waiting to embark him, or to bring about an uprising. See the attached proclamation. It has had no effect on the local people, but there is some sympathy for the rebel, above all in Arezzo.

Foiano della Chiana

In Foiano Garibaldi turned down invitations from leading citizens and slept close to the men in a small house on the edge of town. A fitful sleep. A baby was born in the house that very night, and the General was invited to name the girl. 'Call her Italia,' he said.

Two hours later, Hoffstetter woke him to say that Bueno was refusing to provide more cavalry to reinforce security. Migliazza's men had made contact with Austrian forces on two different roads. Shots had been fired. Skirmishes. 'Relieve Bueno of his command,' Garibaldi ordered, but Hoffstetter feared the consequences and passed the buck to Garibaldi's official aide-de-camp Marocchetti, who did nothing. The German also feared the negative impact of marching those captive monks along. 'The canny priests would walk with their hands joined in prayer and their heads bowed so that people would feel sorry for them. In Foiano I begged Garibaldi to let them go.' The General agreed. 'I realized,' he later wrote, 'that the Church was actually hoping we would kill them.'

Sleep forgotten, Garibaldi addressed the citizens in the street from an upstairs window. The rain had stopped. 'Better times will come. Keep faith,' he exhorted. Amid all this activity he found time to give a cigar case to the young man from Torrita who had volunteered to guide them through the night. 'I was in heaven,' the man remembered forty years on, speaking to Belluzzi.

How different our walk was from theirs. Not a dark deluge, but blazing sunlight. I remember a tall pine hedge gloriously adorned with wisteria. Stretches of straight white track between neatly kept vineyards. A fragrant monotony of stubble and dry ditches. A marble Madonna enjoying the shade of an oak tree. The only ominous note was a long low warehouse selling stock from bankrupt businesses.

In the small town of Bettolle the woman serving us our *cedrata*s boasted that Garibaldi was not the only hero to have passed through here. Napoleon had once stayed a night in this *borgo*. She was impressed by our Garibaldi project and called to her son at the bar, 'Charge them normal prices!' Meantime, the television brought us Salvini, warning that his patience was running out; the country was paralysed, something had to be done. A man leaned across the bar and said, 'You can't sort out anything, if you don't use a big stick.'

We took off with our trekking poles and spent much of the next hour talking gloomily of politics. The woman in Torrita was surely right that a small town needed smart politicians and bright ideas to keep it in business. The country as a whole needed a leader and the only man who seemed to have any appetite for the job was blustering loudmouth Salvini. Everyone else was embarrassed at the very mention of nationhood, hoping that the EU would save the day.

Entering Foiano towards one o'clock, we stumbled on the very house where Garibaldi rested and the little girl Italia was born. 'With the enemy at his back ...' says the plaque under the window where he spoke to the crowd.

Once again, the General didn't hang around. By late afternoon the column, the cannon and the cavalry were all gone. He needed to put the lowland behind him before the Austrians arrived. There was still the Chiana Canal to cross, an artificial waterway running north–south, draining the waters of the marshes down into Lake Trasimeno. It was not a place to be caught.

Meantime, in the centre of town, we checked into a dim room, whose heavy furnishings had no doubt been chosen by someone long defunct. And where Garibaldi had met with birth and new life, when we went round the corner to the trattoria our landlady had recommended, we found the notice, CHIUSO PER LUTTO – Closed for mourning. Between our room and the trattoria was a church. The doors were open a crack. In the dark interior a coffin was surrounded by four or five seated figures.

Never mind. All in all, Foiano proved a more cheerful town than either Montepulciano or Torrita, one of the few Tuscan places that seemed neither a self-parody for the benefit of international tourism nor a ghost town. It was full of Tuscans. Rather than offering vaguely medieval music for a cosmopolitan elite, the evening promised a home-grown beauty contest – Miss Reginetta d'Italia. At eight in the evening we bagged ourselves seats outside Caffè La Costa di San Rocco.

This is the scene. In the centre of a labyrinth of narrow streets at the top of a small oval-shaped hill is Piazza Cavour, a generous rectangular space with the usual town hall and church, flags and memorials. In the middle of the piazza is a melancholy bronze statue of the Unknown Soldier; the man leans forward stiffly in his First World War uniform, hands pulling open the top of his shirt to display the wounds that have done for him. He has been so placed that his helmeted profile can be seen from outside the square through an arch under the clock tower. Leaving the square through this arch, you go down a flight of white travertine steps, perhaps sixty in all, between the Banca di Firenze on your right and the Unione Banche di Italia on your left, to a larger, more open square, where Corso Vittorio Emanuele meets Via Cairoli. Caffè La Costa di San Rocco faces across this square, so that from our table we can look up the steps between the banks to the sad soldier exactly framed in the arch at the top.

The girls eager to become Miss Reginetta d'Italia are going to parade fifty yards or so down the steps, leaving the pathos of the dead warrior behind them and displaying their charms to the judges and spectators seated on rows of wicker chairs at the bottom. Between the stairs and the spectators a band plays syrupy covers on a rectangle of red carpet.

But that's looking ahead. These August shows never get under way until darkness has fallen, after nine. Then the girls will be caught in a criss-cross of searchlights as First World War soldiers often were when they went over the top in night-time assaults. For the moment, what we're seeing from our vantage point, munching salad sandwiches and sipping icy beer, is some last-minute coaching. An ex-*reginetta* in white trousers and black silk blouse is instructing a half-dozen girls on how to walk down the steps, how to hold their shoulders and arms, how to point their fingers, where to look, when to smile.

She climbs to Piazza Cavour at the top, stands for a moment in statuesque silhouette below the silhouetted statue behind, then begins to move. It's quite a performance. Step by coquettish step she minces, she sways, she swings her right hand back and forth from her elbow. It takes time. She's in no hurry. She's enjoying it. At the bottom she pauses, pushes out her breasts, shows her head off in profile, first left then right, then comes past the band, looking sassily over the empty seats where the jury will be, allows herself a knowing smile, puts a hand on a cocked hip, swivels with a proud toss of jet-black hair, struts between the band and the front row, then, hand on hip again, swivels once more to walk away to the other side of the band so that now we can all get a load of her curvy back. At last, with a wiggle and a flounce, she's done.

'Così!'

It's challenging. The debutantes have a go. They're not in their smart dresses yet. Or their bikinis. They're mostly teenagers, awkward and self-conscious. Heaven knows what induced them to volunteer. Two or three mothers are present, shouting advice and encouragement. The ex-*reginetta* watches, arms folded, pouting. Occasionally she intervenes. 'Not like that, *per l'amor del cielo!*' She tilts a girl's chin up, shows her the haughty look. 'You have to conquer them!' Now she rearranges a hand on a hip, pushes out a pelvis. 'You don't want them to feel sorry for you!' The participants giggle.

'Sort of school for flirtation,' I suggest. 'How to be a vamp.'

Eleonora is harder: 'Whore more like.' She says one of the greatest embarrassments of her life was when her older brother used to organize beauty contests and push her to participate. She never would.

One girl trips. It's tough walking down old stone steps in high heels. At the tables to our left a group of adolescents snigger and groan.

'To think Anita might have ridden her horse down there.'

Faces appear at windows round the square. A man and his wife in their seventies are up on the third floor, he in a red vest, she cleaning her glasses on her negligée. There are a dozen girls practising now. The seats are filling up. New arrivals will have to stand. It may be crass, it may not be politically correct, but there is something fascinating about the show. Perhaps because the participants are so inept.

But no! One girl has it. A small slim creature in a black minidress with an explosion of curls on her head. She flounces down the steps exactly as instructed. She swivels in perfect imitation of the ex-*reginetta*, who claps, delighted. She does the strut and the final flounce with growing relish, then bursts out laughing, hands over her open mouth. All the other girls cheer.

Eleonora shakes her head. 'Would Garibaldi have approved?' she wonders. 'Is this what they did it for?'

'I suppose he'd be happy that it's Miss Reginetta d'Italia, not Miss Tuscany, or Miss Austrian Empire.'

In any event it's time for us to go. On our way back to our room, we find the door of the church still open and, peeking inside, see candles have been lit. A silver crucifix glimmers over the altar. The wake will go on all night, to the din of the band cranking out summer pop.

DAY 17

21 July 1849 – 10 August 2019

Foiano della Chiana, Castiglion Fiorentino – 11 miles

Castiglion Fiorentino

On the evening of 21 July Garibaldi saw the opportunity for an easy victory that would raise morale. The column marched out of Foiano shortly after five in the afternoon, preceded by Major Migliazza and forty of the best horsemen to check that all was safe. Garibaldi had told the people of Foiano that they were heading straight to Arezzo, seventeen miles up the valley to the north-east, but after five miles he left the main road and turned due east, crossed the big canal that presented the main obstacle before the hills and marched just six more miles across the plain to Castiglion Fiorentino on the first low ridge. It offered excellent defences in case of a surprise attack.

However, as they approached the town, Migliazza reported that an Austrian soldier had been captured carrying an important dispatch. In fact, the man was an Italian from Trento. He was wearing plain clothes, his Austrian army uniform stashed in a bag. In his possession was a message from the small Austrian garrison in Arezzo to Colonel Paumgartten in Perugia, with an urgent request for reinforcements. This message had already been delivered, and the messenger was now returning to Arezzo by post coach with the answer to the request scribbled at the bottom of the same piece of paper: 'Four companies are on the march and should arrive in Arezzo tonight.'

Garibaldi was astonished. He made it a matter of policy always to respect the enemy and consider him capable of acting intelligently, even brilliantly. But to write the response to a cry for help on the same piece of paper was folly. If they had to write anything at all, Hoffstetter observes, they could have given the man a piece of paper with the single word 'Granted'. Now Garibaldi knew that there was an Austrian garrison in Arezzo, that it was desperately weak, and that about 600 Austrians would soon be passing on the road from the south which led right by Castiglion Fiorentino. He quickly gathered a few hundred men of the First Legion under the command of Gaetano Sacchi and took them a couple of miles along the road that the Austrians must be coming along. In the vicinity of the village of Montecchio he found a small bridge over a stream and an elaborate ambush was set. The Austrians would be allowed to cross the bridge and march on for a few hundred yards, unaware of the *garibaldini* hidden behind hedges and in ditches. Then they would be confronted by a line of fire. Turning, they would be fired on from behind the hedges, while another company of *garibaldini* would occupy the bridge and block their retreat. Lines of apparent escape would be left where there were cottages beside the road, but the occupants had been moved out for the evening, substituted with more *garibaldini*.

We left Foiano before six in the morning, walking in a misty half-dark between lines of cypress trees leading to the cemetery and beyond. Here a sign written in a strange mix of English and Italian points the way to 'Foiano della Chiana War Cemetery, Tombe di Guerra del Commonwealth'. It contains the bodies of 256 British and South African troops who died when the retreating German army made a stand outside Arezzo in June 1944. Deciding not to visit, we nevertheless found it hard not to think of the carnage the *garibaldini* envisaged in setting up that ambush.

The country is flat as Flanders here. There's nowhere to hide. We crossed the Chiana Canal and turned north along *Il sentiero della bonifica* – the Reclaimed Land Path. You walk on a dyke through delicate white marsh flowers with fertile fields stretching away either side, the abrupt slopes of the Apennines closing the horizon. There are storks round the water, squadrons of geese overheard. Turning east, away from the canal towards Castiglion Fiorentino, we came across a man on a mountain bike, sweating profusely, who stopped to ask the way to a place we had not heard of. He was the only person we met in four hours' walking. Now came field after field of sunflowers, rigidly regimented, the plants alert and silent as soldiers lying in wait. Not even the throb of a tractor or the drone of a chainsaw disturbed the warm air. The countryside is rich and empty, luxuriant and melancholy.

Suddenly Eleonora was dancing. And screaming. Waving her arms, hopping about. There was something in her shirt. She'd been stung. I tried to calm her, helped her off with her pack, then her shirt. She kept squirming and wriggling. As the fabric slipped off, an angry hornet buzzed up into the air and away.

A little later she managed to laugh. 'Surprise attack!'

Nobody died in that well laid ambush. The *garibaldini* held their positions in silence through the summer night, but the Austrians didn't show. They had stopped in Cortona, eight miles away, apparently tipped off. Garibaldi was disgusted. 'The enthusiasm and joy of a few days before,' Ruggeri observes, 'turned to the gloom of disappointment, scoring a deep line in his brow that would never leave him.' The uprising wasn't going to happen.

Writing a year after the events, Ruggeri allows himself a rant. 'They call us enemies of humanity, these Austrian despots who preside over the unburied bones of our martyrs. But we reply with the words of the great exile Mazzini, "If you're so sure of yourselves, have the courage to prove you're right; give the people a free vote; withdraw for a while, now you've crushed all opposition; install a provisional government to call a plebiscite and let the people decide who they want to rule them."'

Not an appeal the Austrians were likely to listen to.

Another disappointment was the realization that, though the Tuscan garrisons billeted in these small towns invariably fled before Garibaldi arrived, allowing the festive welcoming parties that had so encouraged him, nevertheless as soon as the column moved on the grand duke's soldiers hurried back to reassert the status quo. The patriotic effusions were no more than a twenty-four-hour carnival. They had no consequence and required no commitment.

Garibaldi did not take his frustrations out on the captured man from Trento. He resisted requests to have him shot. Instead he had him put on his Austrian uniform and stand before the *garibaldini* in their camp below the city walls. 'How painful it is,' the General told his men, 'that our oppressors find Italians who are willing to fight their own countrymen. You tell me if this bizarre cap and uniform looks right on an Italian! I grant the man his life, because he's not worth the bullet that would kill him!'

'*Evviva!*' the *garibaldini* cried.

We entered Castiglion through Porta San Michele, a reconstruction of the medieval arch destroyed by the retreating Germans in 1944. The stone archangel in the niche above is a copy of the ancient wooden statue now removed to the safety of the town's civic museum. Michael stands nonchalantly on top of the devil in the form of a dragon, skewering him in the mouth with a long spear. It looks so easy.

Castiglion's ancient Etruscan fort was also largely destroyed in one war or another. But a solitary tower survives, square and bare in a stony space above the town, seven or eight storeys high. At the top, when your eyes have adjusted to the explosion of light, you have a commanding view of the plain we just crossed. It's vast and airy. All you can hear is a tinkle of cries from the big municipal swimming pool a few hundred yards to the south.

The topography of Castiglion Fiorentino is complicated. It sits on the first hill rising from the plain, but then there's a narrow valley before the hills proper. Hoffstetter was given the task of setting up the most elaborate defence arrangements undertaken so far. He fills three pages explaining his plans in case of attack from the various directions. The Austrian war machine was closing in.

We have found ourselves a billet in the valley between the town and the higher hills, which is where Hoffstetter had most of the men sleep. Our hosts are giving us the upstairs floor of their 1950s house. There are vases of dried flowers on white lace doilies and purple drapes over the windows tied with elaborate bows. Just beware of the dog, we're warned. It's a big Labrador that supposedly guards the space between the front door and garden gate. Today the sun has sapped the animal's energy, and it barely registers our passage as we scuttle out of the door and off to town again.

The one great glory of Castiglion Fiorentino is the Piazza del Municipio. It's a harmonious rectangle, perhaps forty yards by fifty, with the imposing fourteenth-century town hall looking across grey stone paving to a long elegant portico. Built in the fifteenth century and restored by Giorgio Vasari in the sixteenth, the portico has nine wide arches open one side, to the piazza, and three the other side offering magnificent views of the hills to the east. There's a café at one end of the portico, taking advantage of the shade, and a trattoria at the other; in between are the open arches with their wonderful view of the Apennines. The effect is something like being in an airy room with generous French windows over a dramatic drop. We bought a couple of apples and munched them under the portico, studying the terraced slopes where Hoffstetter placed his men so carefully. The blaze of light out there on vines and olives made the deep shade under the portico all the more delicious.

Unusually, the town hall has just one plaque on its rough stone facade. Placed there in the early 1860s, it's the same plaque you find, word for word, on every town hall in Tuscany.

XV MARCH MDCCCLX [15 MARCH 1860]

II HOURS 55 MINUTES AFTER NOON

THE SUPREME COURT OF APPEAL

MEETING IN PLENARY SESSION

IN THE PALAZZO DELLA SIGNORIA (FLORENCE)

HAVING HEARD THE MINISTER OF INTERNAL AFFAIRS

DECLARES

THAT FROM THE SUM CALCULATED

DURING THIS SESSION

OF THE PARTIAL RESULTS

OF THE UNIVERSAL SUFFRAGE

REGISTERED IN THE MINUTES

THE FOLLOWING FINAL RESULT WAS OBTAINED

TUSCANS VOTING — 386,445
VOTES IN FAVOUR OF UNION WITH THE
CONSTITUTIONAL MONARCHY — 366,571
VOTES FOR A SEPARATE REALM — 14,925
SPOILED VOTES — 4,949

AND THUS ASSERTS THAT
THE TUSCAN PEOPLE BY PLEBISCITE
DESIRE UNION WITH THE CONSTITUTIONAL MONARCHY
OF KING VITTORIO EMANUELE II

In short, ten years after Garibaldi's disappointments and Ruggeri's despairing rant, the Tuscans were indeed allowed their vote. Backed now by the French, Piedmont had declared war on Austria, and the struggling empire had no soldiers to send to Tuscany. Italian patriots in Florence forced the grand duke into exile and some months later this referendum was called. About a fifth of the population was eligible to vote. Needless to say, those nostalgic for the small states of the past claim the result was fixed. Certainly the figures look suspiciously one-sided. But many commentators have observed that Italians have a great respect for the way the wind is blowing. Suffice it to say that a month later, on the Tuscan coast, when Garibaldi started to look for volunteers for his Sicilian expedition, he soon had more than his two ships could carry.

We were reading this plaque, reflecting on its bureaucratic fussiness — no triumphalism, no patriotic rhetoric — when the big door of the town hall opened and a small crowd spilled out. It was a wedding, at seven on a Saturday evening, mid-August. Perhaps a dozen people stopped at the bottom of the four steps, turning to wait for the bride and groom. There was a moment's expectation. We stepped back a little, respectful but curious. And the newly-weds appeared. A Filipino couple. She in simple white dress and sandals, he in a blue suit, white shirt, dark tie. None of those watching was Filipino. The principal guests appeared to be the couple's employers.

Bride and groom had their photos taken, quickly, under the shady portico with the dazzling backdrop of the hills behind. Since the trattoria just a few yards away had now opened, we went to sit at a table for our usual early dinner, but were promptly told that all places were reserved. 'Ah, for the wedding,' I supposed. 'Not at all,' the proprietor told us sharply. 'I have nothing to do with those people.'

'Our clothes are wearing out,' Eleonora remarked as we prepared for bed.

Indeed, our shirts were fading. She had a hole in the side of a shoe. The tread was getting thin.

'Ten more days,' I told her.

'God willing.'

'Meantime there's another development you should know about.'

22 July, General D'Aspre in Florence to Field Marshal Radetzky north of Milan

Information on Garibaldi is frustratingly confusing, provided by frightened people with no notion of military matters ...

The rural population are in good spirits and the people around Foiano seem determined to defend themselves from the rebels ...

Garibaldi is taking a large number of hostages with him including a magistrate from Montepulciano, presumably in order to have some negotiating power if forced to surrender ...

The main group of rebels is in Torrita, though a small detachment of 70 cavalry is already in Murlo, just south of Siena. Their commander, a certain Müller, who claims to be Polish, realising that he had been cut off from the others, has presented a petition of surrender to the governor of Siena who has passed it on to General Stadion.

'No!'

'Yes.'

Müller deserted. Taking seventy men and their horses with him.

'But why?'

We lost half an hour's sleep discussing this. Why would a man who had fought a two-month siege, then signed up for a desperate guerrilla war, always behaving with great efficiency and valour, winning the praise of a leader he greatly admired, suddenly do a deal with the enemy? He can't really have been worried about being cut off from Garibaldi. On horseback these men could easily have found a way through the hills back to the main group. Just as Pilhes had. One party of cavalry which hadn't been seen since Todi finally caught up with the column late in the evening at Castiglion Fiorentino. An absence of ten days.

'Because he was a foreigner, perhaps. Deep down he didn't care.'

'And Hoffstetter? And Forbes? Pilhes was French.'

'Perhaps he just lost faith.'

'Eternal disgrace to the traitor!' writes Ruggeri, who has Müller selling his men and horses to the Sienese authorities and escaping on a ship to America. Assessing the situation in 1893, without the benefit of Austrian archives, Belluzzi chooses not to believe this. There must be some mistake, he thinks. The brave Pole was simply lost. But now we have the Austrian documents.

'Didn't you say the Austrians shot any rebels they got their hands on?'

'In fact D'Aspre was furious.'

General Stadion explains himself in a letter two days later.

I didn't negotiate an official surrender with this isolated group. I just explained to Major Müller that if his men laid down their arms I would spare their lives, except in the case of any deserters from the Austrian army. Then since they had no money I let them sell their horses, which were in a miserable state and would have been of no use at all to our cavalry. My only goal was to neutralize a bunch of riff-raff who had been terrorising the local population, the better to concentrate my efforts on the main group of rebels.

'And does Garibaldi know?'

'Not yet. But we never learn when he found out, and he never spoke of it.'

DAY 18

22 July 1849 – 11 August 2019

Castiglion Fiorentino, Arezzo – 16 miles

Arezzo

'We must die if '48 is to end with any seriousness: to have our example serve for others, we must die.'

Such were the words that the 24-year-old Luciano Manara, commander of the Lombard Bersaglieri, wrote to his lover, Francesca Bonacina Spina, in the last days of the siege of Rome. Not long afterwards, he was shot by a sniper and died after hours of agony.

Now the same dilemma was in the air. How to end the weary retreat from Rome *seriously*? How to turn this prolonged resistance into an example that would count?

Without dying.

Time and again historians criticize Garibaldi for his naivety and recklessness. 'His eternal instinct,' ironizes David Gilmour, 'was "When in doubt, charge with the bayonet."' 'He fought by intuition,' says David Kertzer in his excellent book on the Roman Republic, 'guided in no small part by emotion.' Of gentle disparagement by wise scholars there is no end. The man is made a force of nature rather than a thinking protagonist. The next few days will show how wrong this portrait is.

Not that Garibaldi was afraid of dying. 'Nothing would please me more than to die for Italy,' he said. But if a goal could be achieved without dying, all the better.

How?

One problem was that many of the *garibaldini* felt as the young Manara had. They wanted to go out fighting. The drama of battle was more attractive than the hard slog of forced marches. After 17 days and 250 miles, not to mention the siege that had come before, these were hardened men. But they were not professional soldiers. They had lives, perhaps jobs, families. Now more than ever they needed to feel there was some point to what they were doing. They had seen the pamphlet Garibaldi had published. They had seen that there had been no response. They had read Tuscan newspapers that described the patriotic cause as lost and the 'patriots' as a rabble of thieves. The only way to make sense of what they had been through would be to fight, gloriously; all their rhetoric, all their aspirations pointed that way. Again and again in his memoirs Garibaldi observes how rashly volunteers will rush into battle. The 'eternal instinct' of the bayonet charge was theirs, not his. He sought to exploit it as best he could.

So how to avoid a rout on the one hand, a meltdown on the other?

On 22 July the men were up before dawn, expecting to resume their march, but the General had them wait while he rode up into the hills and explored the possibility of heading directly east, avoiding Arezzo. The Apennines here are formed of two grand mountain chains, each some twenty-five miles wide, running up the spine of Italy – that is south-east to north-west. Between those two chains is the upper Tiber valley, some ten miles wide, the river flowing south towards Perugia. Garibaldi's concern had to be that Paumgartten, with his base in Perugia, would realize that he meant to head to the Adriatic, to reach Venice, and send a substantial force of men up the Tiber valley to cut off his route. Was it better to move now, over the rugged highlands and beat him to it? With the risk that, once alerted, Paumgartten would react swiftly. Or to head north for Arezzo, giving the impression that the town was his objective, and so draw Paumgartten up this side of the Apennines to defend it? From Arezzo there was a good road across the mountains; Garibaldi would make better speed and, crucially, at this point Paumgartten would be behind him.

'We were preparing for the climb,' records Hoffstetter, 'when the General returned around 1 p.m. and ordered an immediate march to Arezzo along the broad main road. By 11 that evening the whole

211

column was within a cannon shot of the city's southern walls.' And he adds, 'Exactly where the Consul Flaminius lay in wait for Hannibal in the second Punic War.'

'Do not go to Arezzo by the main road.'

The previous day we had stopped in a sports shop in Castiglion to buy fresh rubber tips for our trekking poles. The owner was a hiker himself. The road was dangerous and polluted, he said. He told us about a high path, 2500 feet, over the mountains. Wasn't there something lower, we asked, on the hillside above the road perhaps? We would have our fill of mountains soon enough. He said there were paths, but he had never gone that way. No one did.

'We'll try,' we said.

It wasn't easy. As always, when a path is not spectacular but simply a way of getting from A to B without using the road, people have ceased to use it. They have their cars. Almost at once we were confronted with such a forbidding tangle of barbs and nettles that we had to drop down to the road, then climb up again. Then drop down again. One particularly disheartening moment was presided over by a big white cat sprawled on the branches of an olive tree. The creature yawned in the early-morning sun. I felt like throwing a stone.

Towards 8 a.m., down on the road outside the Hotel Planet, the kind of place you see near major airports, a crowd of Indians was loading bulky suitcases into a sleek silvery coach from Krakow, Poland. Many of the women were wearing saris. A little further on, outside a factory producing terracotta pots and animals – lions, cocks, pigs and frogs – a tall Snow White gathered all Seven Dwarves under her blue cloak. We took stock in the Bar Centrale of the roadside village of Rigutino, learning from the television that Salvini was threatening to bring the government down and call new elections.

It was a hot, hot day, a day when our shoes seemed too flimsy for the paths we were on, when seventeen miles seemed interminable. The hillside was pretty, but rugged, thorny. The cicadas mocked. Near the tiny village of Santa Maria a Pigli an elderly couple tying up their tomatoes asked us where we were going. 'You're now on the old Via Romea,' they said proudly. 'The pilgrim trail to Rome. Only you're going the wrong way!' People only went south on this path.

In stony woodland higher up we did cross paths with a pair of hikers following the pilgrim trail. They had walked from Forlì, they said, eighty miles to the north; the Apennine crossing was hard, they warned, but there were convents and monasteries where you were sure of a bed every night. As they spoke, I found myself studying their backpacks, their shoes, their equipment, appraising, criticizing, wondering.

'They were carrying an awful lot of stuff,' Eleonora remarked.

'Heavy, heavy boots.'

'Good hats though.'

Arezzo appeared, blissfully below us, simmering. You can see how tempting it must have seemed to the *garibaldini*. A big rich town lying in the fertile upper reaches of the Val di Chiana, dominated by a splendid *duomo*. Evidently a place of ease and wealth. As we came down to the first outlying village, we encountered the most exotic creature of the day: a tall, slim young woman dressed only in the skimpiest green shorts and black bra, striding at high speed towards us. Her skin was uniformly dark in the pitiless sunshine, gleaming with sweat. Her hair was pulled fiercely from her face in a ponytail. She wore no hat, but had a wristwatch which she checked compulsively every few paces.

There was a peculiar grimness to this woman. Her very litheness seemed hostile. As if extreme behaviour of the *garibaldini* variety — pushing yourself in the hot sun — were now entirely disconnected from any meaning or purpose, just dogged narcissism. She passed by without returning our *Buon giorno*, then half an hour later overtook us as we entered Arezzo, still walking at a cruel pace, presumably on her way home.

'Textbook Amazon,' Eleonora thought.

'So unlike Anita.'

There were no suburbs outside Arezzo's walls in 1849. Garibaldi stopped his men a hundred paces from the city gate. It was shut.

Migliazza and his cavalry had been sent ahead to do the rounds of the walls and check the converging roads. Towards midnight the major brought his report. All the gates were closed and guarded. More importantly, he brought a man captured on the Siena road. Once again it was an Italian, this time a civilian, carrying Austrian dispatches. Garibaldi and Hoffstetter got down from their horses and went into a peasant cottage to read.

> I shall never forget the bizarrely picturesque scene in that hut; the only furniture was a tree stump on which burned a hunk of candle, shedding a dim light on Garibaldi and the rest of our party. I was kneeling by the candle, translating the dispatches, which were written in German. All round, in the half dark you could see the tanned and bearded faces of the general's staff and in a corner, half senseless from fear and guarded by two cavalrymen, the captured messenger.

The letter that Migliazza and his men had seized is not in the book of Austrian dispatches collected by Franz Pesendorfer, precisely because it never made it to the archives in Vienna. It was written by General Stadion, now hurrying towards Arezzo from the west, and addressed to Colonel Paumgartten, moving north from Perugia. Once again, the *garibaldini* marvelled that so much useful information had been made so easily available to them. Not even coded. Stadion believed Garibaldi had 4000 men, the dispatch said, and a number of cannons. Very likely he was planning to go to Venice. Stadion and Paumgartten should join forces as soon as possible to attack. Reinforcements were on their way to Arezzo from Florence, but public support for the rebels was slowing them down.

The General smiled, Hoffstetter says, on hearing all this, pleased that the Austrians were still overestimating their forces and still a day's march away. Surely, Hoffstetter told him, they should now use the cannon to bring down the gate and enter Arezzo immediately. Garibaldi pondered and asked for the messenger to be brought to him. The man collapsed at his feet, begging for his life and promising never to serve the Austrians again. To every question the General asked, the man responded with more pleas to spare his life. 'Go,' Garibaldi told him.

Italian street signs will often tell you not only what a street is called now, but what it used to be called twenty, fifty, even a hundred years ago. Whether this is a form of nostalgia for the older name, or is meant to be useful for someone returning home after a long absence, a ghost even, I don't know. Walking through Arezzo we swiftly came across these three road signs: Via Garibaldi, *già* via Sacra; Via Garibaldi, *già* via dell'Ascensione; Via Garibaldi, *già* via Sant'Agostino. Various segments of road following the old wall to the south of the city, all with names of religious inspiration, had been strung together and rechristened Via Garibaldi. No doubt he would be pleased to have won this small victory over the priests. We also found three prominent plaques to the hero, recalling his role in the Risorgimento, one remembering how he stopped in Arezzo in 1867 on the way to the Battle of Mentana. But there was no mention we could find of the night when he was in need and found the city barred to him.

We satisfied our immediate needs in the Antica Osteria Agania, arriving just before the kitchen closed at 2.30. This lively little restaurant is nothing more than a long narrow room running straight from door to counter with eight or nine tables each side. The menu, as Eleonora pointed out, makes no mention of lasagne. The aproned host, a cheerful, bearded Ciceruacchio figure in shorts and orange T-shirt, has the beginnings, under his apron, of what will one day be a noble paunch. The dish of the day was chalked on the board over the counter: LUMACHE DELLA VAL D'AMBRA – snails from the Ambra valley. We settled on *pappardelle* with greens followed by poached pears in red wine. It was one of the happiest eating experiences of our trip. We were so glad to be out of the sun.

Arezzo in general seems a happy, reassuring place, absorbing tourism without being overwhelmed by it. There's a pleasant buzz in the streets. We were staying near the Piazza Grande, which has the charm of being built round an uneven slope, the ground falling away diagonally across the big square, creating a seductive mix of stateliness and crooked movement. Everywhere flags, coats of arms, emblems, porti-coes, towers. On the corner of the piazza a small souvenir shop was displaying a T-shirt with the words *Garibaldi fu ferito* – Garibaldi was wounded. A cartoon Garibaldi with a big white beard carries the tri-colour and has his foot heavily bandaged. The words are the opening to a famous song describing how the hero was shot in the foot at the battle of Aspromonte in 1862, a wound that left him half crippled for the rest of his life. I did not buy the shirt.

And Arezzo was not at ease in July 1849. Ruggeri again is more attuned than Hoffstetter to what is going on. 'Arezzo is *italianissima*,' he enthuses. Meaning patriotic. Where the German remembers Fla-minius and Hannibal, the Italian recalls how the Tuscan town rose up against Napoleon in 1799 and the many volunteers it sent to support the '48 revolutions. He writes:

> We had high hopes. All over Tuscany citizens of every class and kind had hurried to greet and help us, vied with each other to feed us and forage our horses, to give us fresh clothes, new shoes, encourage us. All under the very noses of the Austrians. The people themselves, ever alien to the murky dealings of political parties and the skulduggery of the Jesuits, were for Garibaldi and for independence. But not the *moderates* – that infamous sect of Italians, cause of so many of our disasters; and it was this sect that came to the aid of the Austrians in Arezzo.

Antonio Guadagnoli, Mayor of Arezzo, was a moderate, meaning a patriot, but of the cautious, not-now kind: for sure let us eventually arrive at an independent unified Italy, but no fighting, please, and above all no upsets for the wealthy classes. Guadagnoli was also a poet, a satirical poet at that. This didn't prevent him summoning the town council as Garibaldi approached and convincing them that the rebels were only interested in plundering the town and that anyway any dealings with them would be severely punished by the Austrians.

In truth there were only ninety Austrians in the town garrison, many of them convalescing from previous battles. Guadagnoli proposed to put these few foreigners in control of the town's defence and bring in peasants from outside the town to serve as soldiers, since the local citizens were generally in favour of Garibaldi. His proposal passed the council by the narrowest of margins, causing fierce protests in the town. Ruggeri describes the column's arrival on the night of 22 July:

> Garibaldi went to the gate himself and was surprised to find a mixed guard of Austrians and Italians defending it ... A self-styled representative of the town, one of Guadagnoli's henchmen, in an ill-disguised funk, stuttered something about the people of Arezzo not wanting to compromise themselves with the Austrians and being ready to meet force with force if necessary, but also willing to provide food and drink and anything we needed if only we would agree to camp outside. On hearing these words, the General trembled with rage, but said nothing.

Via Cavour runs into Via Mazzini and both run parallel to Via Garibaldi all just a few yards from the Vittorio Emanuele II boarding school. It was curious, we thought, sitting in a *birreria* late in the evening, given their different reputations, how the four protagonists of the Risorgimento handled disappointments. Cavour, the great statesman and schemer, would fly into an apoplectic rage, kick chairs around, offer his resignation and threaten to put a bullet in his brain. King Vittorio Emanuele II, 'the gentleman king', would swear and blaspheme in Piedmontese dialect, dissolve parliament on the spur of the moment, order his secret police to take revenge. Mazzini, the visionary and ideologue, would sink into black gloom and talk of withdrawing into total seclusion or 'finishing it all with a rifle in hand'. Garibaldi, the supposedly ingenuous warrior, though not immune from rage or depression, was at his most alert and cool-headed precisely when everything was going awry. Standing at the closed gate, knowing that this refusal would be a huge blow to his men's morale, he kept his head.

'We could walk in there now,' Hoffstetter insisted. 'We wouldn't lose more than ten or twenty men at most.'

Garibaldi said it could wait till morning and sent everyone to sleep. Hoffstetter was disgusted.

We were sleeping in a loft at the top of an old *palazzo*. There were four floors of stairs, no lift, and once inside you had to climb a ladder to the bed. It was right under a roof that had been in the sun all day. I wished we were sleeping outside the walls.

DAY 19

23 July 1849 – 12 August 2019

Arezzo

Arezzo seemed a good place to take our first full day's break since Terni. The *garibaldini* spent a day of high drama here. Eleonora was troubled by tendinitis under her right foot. The heatwave was supposed to peak at forty degrees. And then, Arezzo is Arezzo, city of Piero della Francesca, of Cimabue, of Vasari, of Guido Monaco. There is much to see.

Yet I could not enjoy it as I meant to. I was plunged so deep in the Garibaldi story. In churches and museums I found it impossible not to see everything in relation to that adventure of 170 years before. Cimabue's astonishing crucifix in the Basilica di San Domenico made one think of the dazzle and lure of martyrdom. San Domenico is one of those places where you have to put in a coin to have the nave light up for a couple of minutes. We hadn't realized this and were craning up into the gloom where the great crucifix hangs when someone paid, and the painting glowed with its sumptuous reds and dark blues, its elegant contortions. Pain was never more beautiful. One almost understood those few *garibaldini*, natives of Arezzo, who begged the General to lead them to their deaths rather than endure the shame of a home town that had sided with Austria.

Leaving San Domenico, there was an exhibit at the door inspired by the present migrant crisis. Some children had built a model sailboat of the kind Garibaldi planned to use to reach Venice. On the white sail was written, *Speranza*. Hope.

In the Basilica di San Francesco it was impossible not to look at Piero della Francesca's *True Cross* battle scenes – the horses, the swords, the spears, the flags – without thinking of the mayhem of a band of men attacking a town. Many of the Crusaders have red tunics. A trumpeter wears a fabulously tall white hat; how not think of Forbes? One man has a sword sunk into his skull, which will be the fate of one of Garibaldi's cavalry captains, though not in Arezzo. Overall, it is the grim glamour of the scene that captures the imagination: men getting history done. Which sets off a train of thought that has been with me for some days now: that although the *garibaldini* had fought no battles since leaving Rome, nevertheless they were doing the hard work of the Risorgimento, forcing people to think, to take sides, unsettling the mental landscape as they marched across the physical.

Other scenes in the *True Cross* sequence remind you that some things never change. A man is lowered into a well to force him to talk. Where did you hide Christ's cross? Many of the *garibaldini*, deserters and stragglers, faced all kinds of brutality to get them to talk.

Climbing to the top of the town and the *duomo*, up an arrow-straight street called Piaggia di San Lorenzo, you can turn and look down to an arch right at the bottom where once there was the southern gate and beyond that, across a narrow valley, to the low hill that rises above the convent of Santa Maria delle Grazie. It was here, on top of the hill, that Garibaldi set up the rebels' cannon on the morning of 23 July, its barrel trained on the gate, ready to pound it to pieces at a moment's notice.

Hoffstetter woke at four to find Garibaldi had sent Ugo Bassi to parley. In vain. The General stood a hundred paces back from the walls, in case of snipers. Tell them, Garibaldi instructed Bassi, that if they don't want us to attack, they have six hours to provide food in abundance and enough money to keep us going. He ordered the main column of men away from the Castiglion Fiorentino road and had them assemble half a mile to the east on the hillside above Santa Maria, very visible to the town, poised for attack or flight. Hoffstetter was given the task of establishing a rearguard to defend the western valley, whence the Austrians might arrive from Castiglion Fiorentino or Foiano at any moment. Sure enough, shortly after midday cavalry scouts reported Paumgartten's men just a few miles away.

We moved on to Vasari's house, where I was immediately struck by these words from his *Lives of the Artists*, quoted on a panel in the first room:

Their names ... are being forgotten ... and will soon be altogether gone. To defend them as far as I can from this second death, and to keep them as long as possible in the memory of the living, having spent so much time looking for their works ... and made such an effort to find their stories in the accounts of older men and numerous books and archives, and having drawn profit and pleasure from all this, I decided it was right, my duty in fact, to make whatever record modest talent and limited discernment can.

The house was suffocating with heat and tourists, while Vasari's own paintings seemed rather dull after the beauties we had seen earlier on.

Over lunch we discussed their lunch. The mayor set the people to work to meet Garibaldi's demands, so that by mid-morning a stream of carts was bringing bread and meat and fruit and wine out of the town to the rebels. The Austrian garrison, Hoffstetter reflects, probably gave their blessing, so as not to risk a rebel attack before reinforcements arrived.

Many of the wealthier citizens came to Santa Maria delle Grazie to beg Garibaldi not to storm the town, but others urged the opposite: he must attack at once. There had been protests and resistance, they said, from the 'democrats' in the town, who had tried to force the mayor to open the gates. The authorities were making scores of arrests; the General must attack to protect these patriots.

'I saw people desperate, people crying,' Ruggeri says. Hoffstetter couldn't believe that Garibaldi, so famous for his can-do attitude, was not going to use the cannon. What had they brought it for? He left his place in the rearguard, where first contact with the Austrians had now been made, and went to plead with the General. The town could be taken for the loss of a handful of men, he insisted, after which it offered excellent defensive possibilities.

At last Garibaldi explained himself: 'I've been thinking the same thing, but what would we do with the wounded? We can't carry them, and if we leave them, they'll be shot by the Austrians. Arezzo may be important for morale, but nothing else; there's no question of our wanting to stay here. We'd be surrounded in no time.'

Hoffstetter objected that backing off would make a bad impression on those citizens who were on their side, and on his own soldiers too. 'They need to fire their guns!' But Garibaldi had made up his mind, 'and now that I'm in a position to consider the matter more calmly,' Hoffstetter writes a year later, 'I realize how right he was. His aim now was to reach the coast and sail to Venice, to do it as quickly as possible, with the least loss of life. Fighting would not only have slowed us down, it would have stirred up the Austrians to greater efforts and guaranteed a grim future for any patriots in the town who took our side.'

'So he did the right thing,' Eleonora observes.

'Ruggeri talks of two hundred "democrats" arrested in Arezzo and still in jail when he was writing in 1850. A survivor from Forbes's men, Francesco Manfredini, recalls how furious the men were, and says this was the beginning of the end for discipline. The General lost respect.'

'So he did the wrong thing.'

'De Rossi reckons the problem was precisely Forbes's men, who were undisciplined. Garibaldi feared that if they had to fight to get into the town he couldn't guarantee these men wouldn't get drunk and trash it – a PR disaster.'

'So there was no right thing to do.'

It was too hot to be around town in the early afternoon. Returning to our room, we passed Piazza Guido Monaco with its statue to the monk who invented modern musical notation. A little further on we found a plaque on the house where he was born, or so they claim, in 992. Below his name is a line of music with the notes spelled out: 'Ut re mi fa sol la.' Ut, Eleonora tells me, was Monaco's base note taken from the first word of an old hymn, which provided him with the names of other notes too. Then it was a case of the secular gradually replacing the religious over the centuries.

With music in our minds we whiled away the hottest hours of the day in the air-conditioned part of our loft listening on YouTube to the so-called *Inni Garibaldini, garibaldini* hymns, another case of the secular moving in on sacred territory. More than fifty songs would eventually be written in honour of the hero, or as marching music for his campaigns. But only one dates back to 1848, *Addio, mia bella, addio* – Farewell, my beauty, farewell – and it wasn't specifically written for Garibaldi. *Squilla la tromba*, begins the last verse …

> *Squilla la tromba … Addio …*
> *L'armata se ne va …*
> *Un bacio al figlio mio!*
> *Viva la libertà!*

> The trumpet sounds … Farewell
> The army is leaving
> A kiss to my son!
> Long live freedom

Did Garibaldi's men sing these words on the long retreat from Rome? None of my sources mention singing. The most famous of the hymns was written at Garibaldi's request in 1858 by the poet Luigi Mercantini. The first lines are still widely quoted:

> *Si scopron le tombe, si levano i morti,*
> *I martiri nostri son tutti risorti*

> The graves open, the dead spring up,
> Our martyrs are all alive again

The music is more melancholy than stirring. But the refrain packs a punch:

> *Va' fuori d'Italia! va' fuori ch'è l'ora!*
> *Va' fuori d'Italia! va' fuori, stranier!*

Get out of Italy! Get out, the time has come!
Get out of Italy! Get out, foreigner!

It's impossible to sing these songs today. They feel strange to the mouth and the spirit. We've tried a couple of times along the road, but after a line or two you stop and shake your head. An abyss opens between present and past; we live in quite different worlds of feeling.

In any event, on 23 July 1849 the *garibaldini* were not in a singing mood. By 5 p.m., when we left our room again, the Austrians had appeared in force at the opening of the valley that Hoffstetter had been ordered to defend and he had started to fall back slowly through terraced vineyards, shooting only occasionally, as planned. It was a holding operation; Garibaldi did not want to begin the march until after dark. There are two major roads from Arezzo crossing the mountains to the Tiber valley: one south-east to Città di Castello, one north-east to Anghiari. Plus any number of paths. In the late afternoon Garibaldi started to send parties of cavalry along all possible routes to create confusion. But the infantry, the baggage train and the cannon would only move when no one could see where they were going.

We walk down Piaggia San Lorenzo towards the old city gate and Santa Maria delle Grazie, taking in the Archaeological Museum on the way. Happily, there are storm clouds gathering. With luck, it will rain tonight and be cool tomorrow.

The woman on the ticket desk in the Archaeological Museum is sleepy and bored. The place is empty, and wonderful. But again the experience is entirely hijacked by my historical obsessions. Looking back, I find that the first thing I photographed was a glass case displaying votive swaddled baby statuettes, each a few inches of pale stone in the form of a swaddled baby. Apparently Etruscan women offered them to the gods in return for a safe birth. I would never normally dwell on such things, but thinking of Anita, in her seventh month now, the tiny noses and mouths take on a certain poignancy.

Then photographs of vases. Combat between Romans and barbarians. An Amazon with drawn sword. A fragment of war mosaic showing prancing horses. Retreating in the pitch dark, the cavalry-man beside Hoffstetter suddenly disappeared. The hillside was terraced. The horse had plunged ten feet or so. 'It really was remarkable,' Hoffstetter recalled, 'that neither horse nor horseman were hurt.'

Next, the skull of an Etruscan ox complete with horns. Knowing there would be few villages in the mountains, Garibaldi had used the money extorted from the mayor to buy more oxen to slaughter on the way.

A marvellous chimera, the museum's *pièce de résistance*: lion, snake and goat fused in bronze, and roaring. The most amazing things can be done with imagination and technique.

Finally, very curiously, an array of small bronze phalluses. What were Garibaldi's men doing for sex? Did some want to storm Arezzo in the hope of finding a woman? There's nothing in my sources. Not a hint of homosexuality. Most nights the men were marching.

It's half a mile or so from the Archaeological Museum out of town to Santa Maria delle Grazie. This is flat land criss-crossed with fast roads. A big Burger King rises from a waste of asphalt beside a petrol station. Only a couple of hundred yards away, at the end of a narrow lane, the old convent is framed by tall pines. It's very beautiful: a long, low cream-stuccoed complex with Renaissance church and porticoes. The whole place breathes peace and quiet. For centuries an Etruscan temple had stood here. Then in the fifteenth century San Bernardino of Siena brought some peasants along to hack it down and replace it with a convent. On one wall a barely legible plaque recalls that Garibaldi camped on the hillside above the building in July 1849. No details are given.

Inside the church there is a magnificent marble altarpiece by Andrea della Robbia and above it, framed in a charming terracotta twine of leaves and fruit, a fresco of a tall Madonna opening her white cloak to gather and protect a crowd of small adoring faithful. It's the sublime version of that garden statue of Snow White and the Dwarves: the old Italian obsession with a generous figure protecting the community.

Outside the clouds are thick above the hill and there's a first rumble of thunder. The light is failing. As soon as darkness fell, Garibaldi gathered his community and set off through a narrow gorge, behind the hill, out of sight of the city. First the cavalry, then the baggage, then the men, climbing south-east to the source of the Scopetone river four miles away. It's a moment when our various accounts of the march differ wildly.

Hoffstetter describes falling back as the Austrians tentatively pushed towards the Italian camp. The problem was to gather the rearguard and the returning cavalry scouts and get them out of danger, with the Austrians to one side and the town walls patrolled with hostile soldiers to the other. In the pitch dark. Garibaldi had left pickets every hundred yards or so to guide them on their way.

Something went wrong. Perhaps, thinking there was no one left, the pickets had moved on. Hoffstetter found himself lost in the gorges and valleys south of the town. He gathered his men at a crossroads and sent horses out in all directions to see if contact could be made. Suddenly there was the sound of shots. The guards on the city walls were firing into the valley. The Austrians behind them were firing. Hoffstetter ordered his men into battle formation and raced up a hill. All he could see were flashes of rifle fire lighting walls and vineyards. 'Occasionally a spent bullet fell at our feet.'

It was then that the rider beside him, Major Mosso, tumbled down the terraced hillside. One can imagine the confusion, especially since Hoffstetter had insisted on silence. Now he wondered if the hills weren't playing tricks on his hearing and sense of direction. Had the enemy encircled them? A horseman returned and said he had found Migliazza with a company of cavalry to show them the way. When Hoffstetter caught up with the General towards midnight neither had any idea what the firing had been about.

Ruggeri paints a grimmer picture: men, himself included, lost in the dark, fired on as they rode or marched by the walls of the town. An Austrian cavalry charge. Men killed and wounded. Parties of peasants sent out from the town and surrounding villages to finish off the wounded and kill any stragglers or deserters. 'Horrible to relate,' Ruggeri writes. 'Traitors sold to the enemy.'

226

Trevelyan repeats Ruggeri's version, which is excitingly dramatic. He throws in the account of a 'gentleman traveller' who 'that same week' heard peasants chanting songs in favour of the Austrian emperor, to the point that 'the hills resounded with *Evviva la corona del nostro Imperator*'. 'Such, in its effect,' Trevelyan observes 'was the political teaching of the Church in the era of Italy's resurrection.'

Belluzzi talks of a 'hellish night' that led to 'a huge number of desertions'. 'Greedy peasants scavenging for rifles and munitions abandoned in the fields ... tying up stragglers and barbarously handing them over to the Austrians who did God knows what with them.'

De Rossi, working from Gaetano Sacchi's notes, turns it into farce. 'The armed peasants on the walls, sensing the enemy was fleeing, fired for the sake of firing. The *garibaldini*, without reflecting that they were actually out of range, responded furiously, as if fighting off an attack. The Austrians, alarmed by the infernal noise and fearing they were being ambushed, joined in, firing wildly. The bloodless battle went on late into the night and it would be hard to know which of the combatants shooting in the dark was most terrified.'

Certainly it's hard to know which of these accounts to believe. Each writer has an agenda and bends his story to suit it. Ruggeri's instinct is to denigrate the Risorgimento's enemies; tales of treachery abound. Belluzzi and Hoffstetter want to present Garibaldi in the most positive light and play down any failures. De Rossi likes to look down on the confusion of amateurs with the wry amusement of the professional soldier. Trevelyan covers all the bases, somehow persuading us that it was both an infernal night and a brilliant move by Garibaldi.

The Austrian colonels and generals also twisted the truth to give positive versions of their behaviour. On 23 July Radetzky writes to the minister of defence in Vienna, telling him Garibaldi is in Todi, despite having already replied to D'Aspre's last dispatch that put him in Foiano. Apparently the old field marshal did not want to admit that the rebels had already succeeded in crossing much of Tuscany. Stadion and D'Aspre frequently exaggerate their small achievements, the length of their marches, their foresight. Paumgartten constantly plays up the problems he is facing, his fortitude and wisdom in overcoming them. On 24 July a certain Major Holzer writes to his superiors to say that he has outmanoeuvred Garibaldi and entered Arezzo with 4000 men. By the time he did so, Garibaldi, his real target, was far away in the hills.

Perhaps the most instructive moments for any writer of non-fiction are when you feel a strong resistance to the material you have found. Belluzzi didn't want to believe Müller capable of betrayal. And reading Belluzzi before reading the Austrian dispatches, I didn't want to believe it either. Denial is always inviting. The whole Arezzo episode is painful. The city had been cried up as the most patriotic in Tuscany; with Garibaldi's arrival the uprising would surely begin. How one would love to write that Garibaldi came at night, battered down the gate, and was welcomed by a wave of enthusiasm that swept away the pathetic Austrian garrison, the traitorous mayor and so on. Or again that the General's men understood perfectly the wisdom of his decision not to attack and headed into the hills with enthusiasm. But that wasn't the case. They were furious, demoralized.

Writing and reading stories, you learn about yourself, which way you want things to go. And this is all the more true of history, where some facts just can't be ignored. Garibaldi got it wrong about Tuscany. He was badly informed. He had taken a gamble and lost. He had underestimated the effect on his men. Now it was hard to know what to do for the best. On the other hand, for anyone with aspirations and optimism, disappointment is always on the cards. The General was used to it. Reaching the source of the Scopetone at 1500 feet, he had his men rest a few hours, then left before dawn, turning due east on a good road along the Cerfone valley. Venice was a hundred and eighty miles away.

PART THREE

Survival

DAY 20

24–25 July 1849 – 13 August 2019

Arezzo, Citerna – 19 miles

Citerna

Hoffstetter has a pounding headache. The sun 'falls straight as a plumb line' in the narrow valley. He can barely stay on his horse. Major Cenni has typhus. He's laid out in a carriage somewhere behind the column, protected by a party of cavalry. Word gets round that it was his carriage passing right under the walls of Arezzo that started last night's shooting. Protecting him, Major Zambianchi took a bullet in the foot that is causing him serious pain. Local notables looking for Garibaldi come across Anita crouched in a shelter of laurel branches, pale as death, cracking nuts on a stone. A cavalry scout is struck on the head, exchanging sword blows with an Austrian hussar. A doctor must be found.

In Citerna, towards evening, no one comes to greet them. Most of the inhabitants have fled. There is no one to bake bread. No forage for the animals. The gates of the convent are barred. In the Tiber valley beyond, the Austrians have a garrison in San Sepolcro, where all roads meet. An Austrian column from Perugia is marching up the valley to Città di Castello to the south. On the road from Arezzo, behind the *garibaldini*, Migliazza is skirmishing with Paumgartten's soldiers as they climb in pursuit. Wounded men on both sides. Two Austrian horses captured.

The convent in Citerna is eventually occupied. Likewise a monastery. Hoffstetter can't sleep in the garden with the others because he has diarrhoea. He passes the night shivering with fever on the floor of a filthy cell. Major Cenni is coughing in the next cell. A black night.

It's a matter of time now, surely. They are fugitives, nothing more. The locals will not support them.

It is pointless, writes Ippolito Nievo in his great novel *Confessions of an Italian*, 'to plead for freedom if one's heart is deeply servile.' The book was written in 1858 before the nationality 'Italian' officially existed. 'There are rights,' he goes on 'that have to be earned.' As a schoolboy Nievo was involved in uprisings in Mantua in 1848 and Pisa in 1849. Like many patriots he formed a scathing opinion of his fellow citizens: 'a sheep-like flock of men without faith, strength or dreams'.

Such exasperations chime with today's revisionists, who tell us the formation of Italy was a mistake, the work of a few hothead liberals, a rapacious Piedmontese monarchy and an international conspiracy of Masons. In a trattoria in Milan, a month before we began our march, I had a falling-out with two university colleagues, economics professors, who insisted that, unlike in other countries, there had been no widespread support for unity in Italy. Unity was a farce, they said. I couldn't understand these things, because I was a literary man. And English at that. 'Only a handful,' they insisted, 'actually fought.'

In which other western European countries, I countered, in the eighteenth and nineteenth centuries did volunteer armies fight for so long to rid themselves of despots and foreign occupiers? Many Germans rose up against their rulers in 1848, seeking the formation of a pan-German territory, but the main work of German unification was done by Bismarck and the Prussian army; and there was nowhere near the same level of foreign occupation. Nor the apparently insuperable problem of a state governed by the Pope and propped up by other Catholic countries.

Some 6000 Tuscans, 14,000 Romans and 14,000 Neapolitans came north to join the Piedmontese in their battle against Austria in 1848. By the time the southern campaign of 1860 reached its final battle at Volturno, the original 1000 had become 50,000. All volunteers. They fought without any assurance of pay or pensions or even medical care. In 1866, 40,000 volunteered to serve with Garibaldi in the last war of independence against Austria. At the time, the overall population of Italy was fewer than 20 million.

Yet it could all so easily not have happened, had Garibaldi been cap-tured or killed in the flight across the Apennines. Garibaldi was important because, more than any of the other patriot leaders, it was he who understood, precisely after this long and disappointing retreat, that they must drop all talk of social revolution and republicanism. They must unite around the single aim of Italian unity. It was the only way to bring the bourgeoisie on board and sever their ties with the foreigner. Supporting the Piedmontese monarchy, the patriot volunteers could then become the loyal and legitimising link between a new king and a new nation. So it would turn out in the great campaigns of ten years on. But for that to be achieved, the General needed to survive, now.

The men's change of mood after Arezzo was matched by a change of landscape. Postcard Tuscany is behind us. The country is wilder and emptier. We're climbing wooded slopes up to 4000 feet. Tall grasses and thistles, gorse and heather. Everything is poorer. Makeshift sign-posts of board nailed on wood. An abandoned hut. A few wilted flowers next to a Madonna in a dog's kennel. An exposed thorn bush twisted by the wind.

By 7 a.m. we're looking back at Arezzo, far below. A distant glimpse of Foiano and Chiantishire beyond. Castiglion Fiorentino is hidden by a dark ridge. The paths deteriorate. Dry mud, shale and stone. All rut-ted by the recent rain. Roots to trip over. Ahead, hills, hills and more hills, rolling away in long chains, all wooded, all uncultivated. This is not the route Garibaldi took. The narrow Cerfone valley is now a four-lane *superstrada*. We are outriding again. On a parallel line a couple of miles to the north.

Despite last night's thunder, it hasn't rained. The sky is a milky blue haze. There's nowhere to stop for refreshment. There are no buildings at all. We're laden with food and drink. At a certain point the trees and scrub give way to an open stretch of tall dry grass, white with flowers. The path disappears. We're feeling our way across, looking for an opening in the trees ahead, when a smell assails us. The smell of death. There's a corpse torn and rotting in the grass. A deer. Perhaps a hunter wounded it and it came here to die. Days ago. Now it's a feast for ani-mals and insects. The air is buzzing. Eleonora is nauseated by the smell

233

and indignant with the casual killers. Very likely, I reflect, we owe it to the hunters that these paths are open at all. We haven't met a soul all day.

Where to stop and eat? We're winding left and right, up and down in thick, untended woodland at 3000 feet. Stunted trees laden with lichens, choked with ivies. Dense undergrowth. Desert-dry soil, prickly with creeping grasses. Broken rocks, fallen trunks, green lizards, thick cobwebs. The kind of place a knight might go to fight a demon, in an etching by Dürer.

There's nowhere to spread a groundsheet. Eleonora is wary of wasps and hornets. I'm desperate to stop. I need sustenance. Perhaps we should eat on our feet. She's determined to find a comfortable place. It goes on. Noon has come and gone. At last providence provides. Towards the top of another hill, a scribbled sign on bare board: Il Cappello di Paglia. The Straw Hat. A restaurant apparently. Incredibly. It's a little off our path, but we head there anyway. The woods open into a couple of small fields. There are fences and farm paraphernalia. Geese and turkeys. A vegetable garden. At last a low modern ranch appears with a veranda looking down into the Cerfone valley. Lines of tables and chairs. It seems we can eat a proper lunch!

No. It's closed. There's no one about. Not even a dog. We decide to sit on the veranda and eat our sandwiches. But climbing up there we hear a tinkle of music from inside the house. The last thing we need is to be surprised by an angry proprietor. I open the French window an inch and call across an empty room. The music is louder. I call again. Two figures appear, a man and woman, in aprons, holding floury hands in the air. And a beautiful misunderstanding occurs.

The restaurant is closed because today is 13 August. 15 August is *Ferragosto*, the big summer bank holiday, traditionally a time of heavy eating. They have closed for a couple of days to prepare for a full house. They're making pasta. We explain we've walked from Arezzo and, passing by, hoped we could eat. Perhaps if they don't mind we could just sit on the veranda a while.

They don't get it. As on other occasions, the idea of people walking so far just won't sink in. They assume we've driven from Arezzo and walked up from Citerna or Monterchi, a few miles away. 'Oh, but you should have phoned and booked,' the woman cries. She's so sorry! We must feel so let down. We repeat that we were passing by chance; there's no need to apologize. But they are not listening. 'You really should have phoned. By all means take a seat, have a rest.' They can't feed us, she says, but perhaps we would like a drink.

'*Cedrata?*'

'At once!' The woman wipes her hands, disappears and returns with two yellow bottles and glasses filled with ice. She won't hear of being paid. '*Per l'amor di Dio*, you climbed all the way up here, poor things, only to find us closed.'

So we eat our bread and cheese and apples and peaches on a shaded veranda, looking down into the Cerfone valley, where the *garibaldini* barbecued a couple of oxen while Migliazza made life difficult for the advancing Austrians. Forty years later a nun in the local convent complains to Belluzzi that the rebels forced them to open up and took their bread without paying. But monks in the nearby monastery remembered with amazement that the *garibaldini* paid for everything, and paid well. A historian in Città del Castello turns up an IOU in town hall archives in which the General promises to repay a large loan in ten years' time. 'How can one know the truth,' the historian despairs, 'when everybody tells different stories.' Belluzzi makes the same complaint. He finds it hard to believe the *garibaldini* took four monks hostage in Citerna – surely they wouldn't repeat that mistake – and even harder to believe the Austrians were so afraid of being poisoned that they would ask the locals to taste anything they offered before accepting it. The only thing everyone agrees about is that the rebels were in very poor shape when they arrived in Citerna.

25 July, 9 p.m., General Stadion in Arezzo to General D'Aspre in Florence

This very moment reliable news has arrived: Garibaldi's bands, around 2500 men in a miserable state, are now in the vicinity of Monterchi, Le Ville, Citerna. Majors Zsoldos and Matinowsky will be there tomorrow and are under orders to attack at once.

'Just a big bunch of boys,' reported one local. 'Disheartened, bruised and beaten, completely incapable of facing a battle.'

We too were in a miserable state on arrival in Citerna. We had forgotten to fill our water bottles at Il Cappello di Paglia. Thirsty, we hurried. The sun was burning. Suddenly I found myself right back where I'd been climbing that last hill to Tivoli three weeks before: head heavy, eyes swimming, odd sensations of detachment. And no sign of Citerna. The road stretched on. Cracked asphalt, dusty hedgerows, scorched grass. Climbing, climbing, climbing. Until, at last, an avenue of pines announced the town. We topped the hill and found ourselves in Corso Giuseppe Garibaldi. A piazza opened to the left on the wide panorama of the Tiber valley. To the right, under a grey stone tower, the white sunshades of Bar Citerna. I collapsed on a chair. The *padrona* stood over me wringing her hands in a dishtowel. Should she call a doctor? 'How old is he?' she asked Eleonora. 'Just bring,' I whispered, 'a Coke and two bottles of water.'

Topography is important. Garibaldi chose Citerna carefully. It's a small stony *borgo* on the top of a ridge, about 400 yards long by 100 wide. There are just three parallel streets, with Corso Garibaldi, in the middle, higher up, and the other two below marking the edges of the ridge each side. To the north and east you look out across the fertile Tiber valley, six miles wide here, and the higher mountains of the second Apennine chain beyond, in particular Monte Giove – Mount Jupiter – which is directly opposite. The drop from Citerna into the plain is a steep scarp of maybe 500 feet. There are no paths or roads that way. It's precipitous. On the other side of the ridge, to the south and west, the town walls command a view of the narrow Cerfone valley and the village of Monterchi about a mile away. The Cerfone flows through Monterchi towards Citerna, but veers sharply right below it to breech the ridge on which the town stands a few miles to the east, near Città di Castello.

So, roughly speaking, in Citerna we're at the joint of a T with the Tiber running across the top and the Cerfone approaching from beneath. Garibaldi can look back along the valley that he and his men have just travelled. He can see Zsoldos and Matinowsky arrive. He can fire his cannon at them. If they want to get to the Tiber valley they will have to pass beneath Citerna, under a barrage of rifle fire from above. And on the other side of the town he has an unbroken view north up the Tiber valley to San Sepolcro, nestling at the base of the next line of mountains, and San Giustino, almost straight across the valley, beneath Monte Giove. He can't see Città di Castello eight miles to the south-east, but he can watch the road from there to San Giustino. And the road from Anghiari five miles to the west to San Sepolcro. In short, through his trusty telescope, the General can watch all the Austrian troop movements, pretty much 360 degrees.

And watch, or gaze, is what Garibaldi will now do for what Hoffstetter feels is an unconscionably long forty-eight hours. Don't they risk being trapped here? On the other hand, Hoffstetter is ill and glad of the chance to rest. And you would have to be mad, he feels, to attack Citerna. Sitting on its high ridge, surrounded by thick walls, it's impregnable. The danger is encirclement. To avoid that, Garibaldi sends his cavalry to do their normal duty of pushing against the enemy's advance guard, giving them the impression he is headed this way or that, inviting them to assume defensive positions. So his men ride to Anghiari, San Sepolcro, San Giustino and Città di Castello.

'A party of horsemen in bizarre clothes rode into the piazza,' reports an inhabitant of Cospaia, a tiny village outside San Giustino. 'They galloped around waving their sabres and rode off. Like Bedouins!'

The tactic worked, but was not without its costs. Here is a passage from *Anecdotes and Memories of the Passage of Giuseppe Garibaldi through the Upper Tiber Valley in July 1849* by the local historian Giovanni Magherini-Graziani.

A certain Cipriani Angioloni, scouting for Garibaldi near Città di Castello, was surprised and captured by the Austrians. He was beaten with sticks and tied to a stone trough in the cowshed under the barn where the soldiers were billeted, his hands trussed under his knees, like a goat. The following night the Austrians left and Angioloni was loaded on a cart. Eventually, he asked if he could get down from the cart and walk. They let him and when he had the chance, he grabbed a soldier's bayonet and in a fury stabbed as many Austrians as he could. Restrained despite ferocious resistance, he was shot in the evening at the hour of the Angelus.

Other anecdotes Magherini-Graziani tells are more cheerful. A priest whose wooden leg prevented him from fleeing barricaded his fine house against the *garibaldini*. But in the dark three men broke in and rushed up to his bedroom. 'Don't you recognize me?' cried one. 'Ciceruacchio!' the priest shouted, and the old acquaintances drank into the night. Another local man was astonished when the cavalrymen billeted in his house insisted on visiting his dying father and paying their respects. 'They were so polite,' he marvelled. 'They even made a point of not looking into my daughter's room when they passed by.'

Ugo Bassi rode into Città di Castello just before the Austrians arrived to find himself a fresh pair of trousers. They gave him red ones and he took two pistols from the town's armoury. *Evviva Ugo Bassi*, the people cried. Say *Evviva l'Italia*, he protested. He was eating in a hotel in the piazza when two cavalrymen brought him a priest who had almost drowned in the Tiber, running away. Bassi lectured his fellow cleric: the duty of a priest is to stay with his flock when they are in danger. And you were never in danger from us!

But Bassi was in danger himself: the Austrians were approaching the town's southern gate. He left his food unfinished and rode off.

We finished a plate of ice cream in Bar Citerna and left our packs there while we explored the town's three streets. Heartened by my rapid recovery, the *padrona* insisted that the one thing to see in Citerna was Donatello's terracotta Madonna. This is in the church of San Francesco, a stone's throw from the bar, though the church is locked, and the Madonna is hidden in a vestry which is also locked. You have to go to the town hall, once the monastery, beside the church, and ask to be accompanied by a guide, at a cost of five euros.

This elderly man now took over our afternoon. We found him sitting alone and disconsolate in a drab office. Our presence brought him to life. He began to talk. Nineteen to the dozen. We must understand the history of Citerna. A thousand years of it. Over the next hour he would show us absolutely everything there was to be seen and tell us everything there was to be told, before finally pulling out the huge key that would let us into the church to see the only thing we wanted to see.

Not quite the only thing. Belluzzi describes visiting the monastery and examining the opening in the southern wall, under a portico, where Garibaldi placed his cannon so that it could fire down on Monterchi. No sooner were we through the door of the town hall than I recognized the place: across the courtyard, a thick wall with big arched apertures, through which you can gaze down onto a cluster of towers and terracotta roofs where the Austrians placed two much larger and more powerful cannons, pointing up at Citerna.

Garibaldi? Our guide had seen, in the town hall archive, he said, IOUs that Garibaldi left in his own handwriting, alas later stolen by souvenir hunters. Of course people steal everything, he complained. That was why the Madonna had to be under lock and key. He patted his pocket. He had us in his power.

Fifteen minutes into the visit, he took us down stone stairs to a labyrinth of vaulted cellars under the monastery/town hall to see the huge water cistern that had given the town its name. Perhaps. The idea, back in the 1300s, was to gather rainwater through ducts and conduits, and store it in one central place. This supply, together with huge stores of grain in the cellars, would enable the *borgo* to resist a siege more or less indefinitely. We looked down into dank water.

In the church there was a huge amount to see before we could even dream of approaching the locked door and Donatello's Madonna. A thirteenth-century crucifixion. A Deposition. An Annunciation. A Madonna in Glory. San Nicola of Bari, San Carlo Borromeo, Sant'Antonio with his lily in his hand.

And how do you imagine it is, our guide asked, that a tiny place like this has so many wonderful works of art? We give up, I told him. It seemed a certain Vincenzo Vitelli, a mercenary commander of the sixteenth century who fought the Turks in Malta and at Lepanto, had a cultured lover, a *nobildonna*, who chose paintings for him to bring back to Citerna, which the Pope had given him to govern in payment for services rendered.

We moved along a line of altars. San Michele speared the dragon. The Holy Family showed off their baby. From a painted niche San Francesco looked on. 'Did you know that San Francesco performed two miracles, right here in Citerna? He freed an oak tree from infesting ants and rid himself of a woman who was bothering him. Fancy that.'

Indeed. I began to show signs of mutiny. No doubt our guide was practised in gauging exactly how much a visitor could take before moving on. In any event, he at last produced a shiny key and let us into a small, bare, white room to one side of the nave.

'*La Madonna di Citerna!*' he announced with flourish. '*Di Donatello.* In terracotta.'

She was worth waiting for. After seven years of restoration work in Florence, they had set her up in the centre of the room on a polished wooden block surrounded by low ropes. She's about four feet high, wearing a long red dress and a white headscarf. Her hair is golden. Her baby is nude and plump and his hair is also golden. The same gold. Same hair. Same skin too. The two possess each other wonderfully, his hand on her neck, her cheek touching his temple. There's a serene complicity between them, a quiet grace that spreads into the space around. It seems extraordinary that such a beauty should be locked away in this empty room, waiting for this garrulous man to turn the key.

Having found nowhere to stay in Citerna, we walked a mile east to Le Rasse, an *agriturismo* in a renovated farmhouse where the young owners gave us directions through an extensive wooded garden to a swimming pool. To our delight, this was built right on the southern edge of the ridge, so that again there was a strategic view of Monterchi. Sitting with your feet in the water you could easily imagine aiming a gun at the arriving Austrians. They marched through the night and occupied the *borgo* at 5 a.m. on the morning of 25 July, just twelve hours after the *garibaldini* had occupied Citerna high above. Despite General Stadion's order to attack, they would have seen at once the folly of such a strategy, and instead set up their cannons and prepared for a siege. Their compatriots in San Sepolcro and Città di Castello would surely soon close Garibaldi in from the north.

So the cannons pointed at each other, but didn't fire. Ammunition was scarce. As soon as night fell on the 25th, a party of *garibaldini* clambered down to Monterchi and taunted the Austrians from outside the town walls. *Mangiazucche!* they yelled in the dark. Pumpkin eaters. *Segoni!* Wankers.

On the 26th a large Austrian column from Florence, following the Arno to the north of Arezzo, arrived in Anghiari, where they immediately found themselves skirmishing with Garibaldi's cavalry. They were overwhelmingly the stronger force and soon occupied the town. Everything was in place now. Some 6000 Austrians had converged on the Tiber valley. They had their man.

We ate out on the terrace of Le Rasse, which looks out across the valley to San Giustino and the mountains. A full moon sailed through pine trees above the steep scarp.

'So how did they get away?' Eleonora asked.

DAY 21

26–27 July 1849 – 14 August 2019

Citerna, San Giustino, Bocca Trabaria, ValdericArte – 20 miles

San Giustino

How on earth did we escape? Hoffstetter wonders during the morning of the 27th. He's still feverish, still fearful he may fall off his horse. Most of all, he's amazed.

Throughout 26 July, their second day in Citerna, the General's cavalry continued their scouting and skirmishing between San Sepolcro on the one side and Città di Castello on the other. A handful of wounded men were treated in the church of San Francesco under the gaze of Donatello's Madonna.

In the afternoon scouts reported the arrival of the Austrians in Anghiari. Two battalions and accompanying heavy artillery. A showdown was imminent. The soldiers talked openly, says Ruggeri, about what to do if defeated; they knew the Austrians were taking no prisoners.

Garibaldi watched through his telescope. He was studying a road that climbs the slopes of Monte Giove behind San Giustino, directly across the valley. That road eventually rises 4000 feet to the pass at Bocca Trabaria, crossing the so-called Alpe della Luna – Moon Alps – and descends to the Adriatic. The port of Fano is just sixty miles away.

But there was no bridge across the Tiber to San Giustino. Just a ford. The soil was loose and sandy, the land flat, exposed. For a bridge, one must go to within a mile of San Sepolcro, due north, then turn back three miles to San Giustino. Surely the Austrians, who held San Sepolcro, would block his path. Garibaldi studied the situation. As yet his scouts had found no Austrians in San Giustino or on Monte Giove.

The more frequently used roads across the mountains led north and east from San Sepolcro, or east from Città di Castello.

The General told no one of his plans. He ordered an ambush to be placed at San Leo, between Citerna and Anghiari. Presumably for fear the Austrians might make a move before nightfall. But they were weary from their long climb. Then an attack was launched on Monterchi. Lots of movement, lots of firing. Lots of men assembled threateningly on the heights of Citerna, visible from below to the Austrians, who watched through their telescopes. Finally, towards evening, another attack was launched on Città di Castello. Shooting at the town walls from across the river. The firing went on intermittently through the twilight.

It was all sham. In Citerna, as darkness fell, the men who had gathered to threaten Monterchi crossed to the other side of the ridge and went straight down the steep wooded scarp to the Tiber plain beneath. No paths. No lights. A 500-foot plunge. There were accidents. Some men were lost. Some equipment had to be abandoned. But eventually they hit the road at the bottom and set off in silence.

Garibaldi split them up. Some would ford the Tiber and go straight to San Giustino. Six miles. Arriving with their boots and trousers soaked. The twenty-three-year-old Domenico Piva, later one of the famous Thousand, insisted to Belluzzi that they did indeed take the monks from the monastery in Citerna to prevent them from informing the Austrians. He remembers fat men, complaining bitterly, up to their thighs in the dark river.

The rest of the column, Garibaldi with them, approached the bridge near San Sepolcro. It was the moment of maximum tension. The Austrians, occupying the town and the road north, had left the bridge unguarded. The men crossed in silence and doubled back along the riverbank. By dawn the entire force was gathered in San Giustino, where they were greeted warmly by the locals, who 'vied with each other to bring refreshments'. Migliazza and his cavalry were sent off to scout the road over the mountains.

Ruggeri, so discouraged by the failure to attack Arezzo, enjoys a rare moment of enthusiasm recalling that night-time manoeuvre. It's true that some mules went under while fording the river and some men were lost in the dark. But the column had 'slipped the Austrian noose', and 'those who admired the General's sang froid directing operations so dangerous and so sublime, those who had shared with him the endless hardships of this little war, were immensely proud to think their names would figure in the glorious legions that he formed and led'.

But Hoffstetter simply wondered why. Why hadn't the Austrians stopped them? And how could Garibaldi have known they wouldn't? Not a shot had been fired the whole night.

'So why didn't they?' Eleonora asks.

We slipped out of Le Rasse before dawn. These are lovely moments: the deep shadows of the trees furtive and fresh, the grass dewy, air balmy, and all around an atmosphere of quiet vegetable pressure, a fragrant summery tension towards the splendour of the rising sun.

We didn't plunge down the scarp, but followed a steep road. In the fields, irrigation pumps flung jets of water across row after row of tobacco plants. Tobacco has been the main crop here for centuries. The water hissed. The *garibaldini* would stock up on cigars in San Giustino. Ahead, the silhouette of the mountains turns pink. Shepherd's warning.

This is easy walking. Flat and fast. We were eager to have the road behind us before people got in their cars. In the centre of the plain is the village of Pistrino, a nondescript, modern sprawl. More fields, then the Tiber. We didn't have to ford. There's a bridge now. The river isn't wide, but the water moves fast and cold through banks thick with bushes and trees. Silver poplars, elms, myrtle. Then, just as the sun rose, at my feet, a corpse. Not a deer, not a mule, not – thank heaven – a soldier, but a big crested porcupine. It was a noble creature, with foot-long spines and a fine snout, but its haunches were crushed and bloody. He'd chosen the wrong moment to cross the road.

Eluding swarms of surrounding Austrians,
the glorious survivors of the Roman Republic
rested here on 27 July 1849,

among villagers overcome
with reverence and astonishment.

Thus the plaque on the town hall in San Giustino. It was 7.30. Five miles behind and fifteen to go. We sat outside a café in the pretty piazza among locals enjoying their coffee. Two men to our right were discussing the sale of some agricultural machinery. 'Don't make the mistake,' one said, 'of letting friends shaft you with requests for special prices.'

'Astonishment that he had made it across the valley, I presume,' Eleonora mused. 'You still haven't told me why the Austrians let him off the hook.'

Hoffstetter didn't understand. Nor Ruggeri. The answer is to be found in a book, *1844–1869: Twenty-five Years in Italy*, by Carlo Corsi, published in 1870. Twenty-two years old at the time of Garibaldi's march, Corsi, a Florentine from a noble family, had already fought in both the Tuscan and Piedmontese armies. Later he would be a military strategist and historian. In Florence in the summer of 1849, hearing tales that the *garibaldini* were devastating every town in their path, and having relatives in the Apennine village of Sestino, where he feared the rebels were bound to pass, he and a friend decided to go and see for themselves. They reached Arezzo in a post-chaise then hired a carriage and took the road to Anghiari, thinking that this way they could overtake the *garibaldini*. But on 25 July they ran into the back of the Austrian battalions, marching up to the Tiber valley. An officer climbed into their carriage to question them. The two Florentines explained themselves. The officer told them that Garibaldi was finished and couldn't possibly make it to Sestino. He was surrounded. The Austrian unfolded a map and pointed to the positions of the various armies to prove his point. Writing about himself in the third person, the historian describes his reaction.

Corsi saw, however, that the map did not show the fine, new road that goes from San Giustino to Bocca Trabaria then onwards to Ancona. Laughing, he asked the officer who had given him that piece of paper. The Austrian answered that he had had it from the General Staff. And when he heard the reason for Corsi's laughter, instead of railing against the General Staff, the officer started saying it simply wasn't possible that such a serious mistake could have occurred, because the Austrians always kept their maps perfectly up to date.

The road had been opened in 1840. Nine years before. The Austrians weren't aware of it. They didn't ask the advice of local people, or even the Tuscan army. They hadn't stared at the mountains through their telescopes. When Stadion in Arezzo heard what had happened, he set out himself in mad haste to take command. But he did not tell D'Aspre. It was too shameful. There would be no dispatches to his commanding officer for a full four days now, from 25 to 29 July.

We were draining our coffee when an argument broke out. The man selling agricultural machinery had loudly remarked what a beautiful morning it was. An older man at the next table said maybe so, but for him the day was over. In another few minutes he would have to clock in at the town hall. Then he wouldn't exist till evening. He was not a free man. So it had been, he said, eight hours a day, six days a week, for thirty years and more. The machinery man laughed and said something along the lines of it being the other's fault if he had chosen the easy number of public-sector employment: no pressure, no risk, early retirement, endless bonuses. 'You're a slave by choice! A sponger.' 'And you're a barbarian,' the other man shouted. Insults flew – in jest, in earnest.

Magherini-Graziani records an exchange between a public employee and a free man in San Giustino on 26 July 1849, some hours before the General made his move. Officer Campi worked in the customs house, collecting duties on trade passing between Tuscany and the Papal States. Hence he wore the uniform of the so-called Finanzieri, a celebrated military corps. Crossing the street, he heard the thunder of hooves. 'I love the Finanzieri!' a voice shouted. A cavalry party galloped up; the men reined in their horses.

Campi recalls the meeting in a letter that Magherini-Graziani quotes in full. Garibaldi's scouts had just bought cigars in the piazza. They were all smoking, unkempt and wild. 'The Finanzieri never let me down!' the leading cavalryman went on. 'On the walls of Rome you could always sleep sound with the Finanzieri beside you. They were loyal. What I hate is a traitor! It was the traitors that lost us Rome. Not the French. A traitor I think I have the right to kill. What do you say?'

He reached for his pistol. Frightened, the customs man agreed. By all means, kill the traitors. The cavalryman stared at him.

'I have reason to think,' he said, 'that you are one.'

'Me? But why?'

'The way you're acting,' the cavalryman said.

'If I haven't greeted you warmly,' Campi protested, 'it's just my surprise, and the enormous regard I have for you.'

The cavalryman shook his head. 'I've just been hearing from your fellow townsfolk that at the customs house you all support the Austrians. Is that right?'

'It's a slander.' Campi was trembling now. He added, 'That's the sort of envious tale-telling public employees get all the time.'

'Give me your hand on it,' the cavalryman said abruptly.

Campi obeyed, but in his nervousness gave the man his left hand, his right being occupied with 'a good fistful of tobacco'. The cavalryman protested. Campi switched hands. Now the cavalryman leaned down and insisted on a kiss, which he gave 'with all the fire of Mars'. Then drew back. 'I'm not convinced,' he said. 'A good Italian should hate the foreigner, who bleeds us of the taxes that should be spent on the poor and on our own industries.'

'We just obey and do our jobs,' Campi pleaded. 'We have children to support.'

'Those are hardly arguments to persuade a man facing death for his country! You people are too attached to your money.' The cavalryman stopped. 'But I'm not here to change your opinions, which I respect. Think what you like, just don't betray me.'

At last it dawned on Campi that he was simply being warned not to inform the Austrians of the rebels' presence. 'Even if we wanted to,' he replied, 'they wouldn't listen.'

Bocca Trabaria

'Time to take my ibuprofen,' Eleonora sighs. We shoulder our packs and set off from the piazza up a steep narrow road. Via G. Garibaldi. It's not the road he took. That's now the main road and a motorcyclists' favourite, glowingly reviewed on numerous biker sites. We climb steeply through the village of Corposano – Healthybody – then we're striking up paths through chestnut trees laden with prickly husks, bright green in the morning sun.

We've been worrying a great deal about today's walk. On paper and on the app it looks the highest and hardest. Four thousand feet. How healthy are our bodies? Eleonora has this pain under her foot. It's troubling to be beside someone who is suffering for your project. I wonder what kind of things Anita and her José were saying to each other in those days as she began to fade. 'It's my project too,' Eleonora protests. Anita categorically refused to be left behind.

In the event, the morning is a pleasure. The ibuprofen does its job. The climb is steep but steady and the paths good. There are fields of cornflowers and cow parsley. These woods are nobler, airier. From time to time we glimpse someone mushrooming. Mushroomers are secretive folk, always afraid you're trying to discover the hidden spots where they unearth their truffles. All the same, one man coming down the path in lumberjack shirt and leather boots lets us take a photo of a big basket full of assorted fleshy fungi. They look like a catch of cuttlefish.

Back in San Giustino, Garibaldi went into the pharmacy to ask for pen and paper and wrote some orders for those who had been guarding San Leo and then the bridge at San Sepolcro. Scouts reported Austrians on the move. At 9.30 a pistol shot rang out, there was a roll of drums, and 'in good order' the men marched out of the village to the mountain road. They climbed five miles and set up camp for the day on a flat area offering 'the best possible defensive position'. This while Garibaldi waited for Migliazza's report on the road ahead.

Hours later the Austrians rolled into San Giustino. Officer Campi's colleague at the customs office, Natale Calvori, also wrote a personal account for Magherini-Graziani's *Anecdotes*. He's scathing of the *garibaldini*. 'Tough nasty types, cursing and even blaspheming, so that I drew back, not wanting to hear.' The Austrians, in contrast, or the 'Germans' as he calls them, filed by 'in typical order, putting on a good show'. However, on passing the customs house, the Austrian commander looked in, took the cigar from his lips and gave the order, 'Get the cash box.' 'At first I didn't understand,' says Calvori. 'Then I realized they meant the customs house cash and I shouted, No!'

Too late. All that money so carefully collected was gone. 'They had two lovely cannons,' Calvori adds, 'a smart howitzer, and lots of baggage wagons.'

Towards ten we passed a tower and an abandoned monastery. The path was a sort of grey grit now. Mossy rocks and tiny white and purple flowers. From time to time a fleeting deer. Then a lovely oak forest, but desperately steep and the soft grey soil crumbling under your feet, so you had to dig in your poles for fear of falling backwards. Suddenly a vast drop opened to our right and for the first time we saw the road that they took, rising from the plain below in endless zigzags. Sick as he was, Hoffstetter was impressed.

The way up to the Moon Mountains is magnificent. The road climbs in three great sweeps, each with ten or so hairpins, rising wide and solid on thick parapets of rock. The column wound slowly up in gigantic spirals, like a big beautiful snake, Garibaldi riding at the head beside his heroic wife, his chief officers right behind, recognisable from their white cloaks, ruffled by the cool mountain breeze. They were followed by the few lancers who remained from the bold ranks that on 30 April had defeated an entire battalion of Frenchmen under the walls of Rome. Then the new cavalry, two by two, their feathered hats, red shirts and assorted weaponry giving them a wild, improvised look. Light and nimble-legged, all the horses tackled the slope cheerfully, neighing and snorting. Then the baggage team, urging on forty dark brown mules, shouting, cursing and cracking their whips. Then a drove of white bulls with long, curved horns, treading warily. A short distance from the animals, the infantry marched behind. First the three much-weakened cohorts that were all that was left of the Italian Legion, led by the excellent Gaetano Sacchi. Beneath their Calabrian hats, you could still see the same bold, tanned faces that had been Garibaldi's pride, but were little more than a guard of honour now, their banner shredded with bullets, but still held high. Between these and the Second Legion, four horses pulled our only, much-prized cannon. Forbes led the Second Legion, together with his young son, the two bizarre Britons in their summer outfits, their men wearing light grey with dark kepis on their heads. At the back were the Bersaglieri and the Finanzieri, no more than a hundred men, the Bersaglieri in light blue with red trimmings, the Finanzieri with their famous peaked caps. Seeing them, I was suddenly overcome by a sharp pain, stricken with grief, my eye searching for old comrades. Where is Manara now? Where are Dandolo and Rozzat and Morosini? Fewer than two thousand were climbing the Moon Mountains, and even these must soon be lost. As if to increase my melancholy, the sun set behind us, sending its last pink rays across the fertile hills beneath to strike the white rocks above.

We looked down on the scene from Poggio del Romito, the peak, eating our bread and cheese. You could glimpse the winding road through the trees, hear the distant rumble of lorries, the drone of a bike. The day was clouding over, the air heavier by the minute, the landscape a play of light and shadow. Eleonora remembered the pink morning sky and grew anxious. I laughed and said it wasn't going to rain on us today. We turned right, down a path that dives through thick woods along the border between Umbria and the Marche, to meet the road at the pass, Bocca Trabaria.

'Garibaldi, Anita, Ciceruacchio, Ugo Bassi ... From valley to valley, these lands still hear the echo of their irrepressible yearning.'

So says the stone by the roadside at Italy's watershed. Standing in that bleak place, with cars flashing by and the valleys echoing mainly with combustion engines, the words feel like empty rhetoric. But this really is where they slept, towards midnight, after their long climb, stretching themselves out on the bare ground. 'Although it was July, a bitter wind blew across those crags,' remembered Ruggeri, 'nor stream ran or spring rose to wet the lips of the exhausted soldiers, whose memory of that cold bleak night, I am sure, will remain with them, as it has with me, all their lives.'

Those who survived.

ValdericArte

We were definitely not going to sleep beside the road, but we had had trouble finding a place to stay. In the end, way off the beaten track, Google Maps turned up the ValdericArte Creative Residence. 'THE ISLAND OF EVERLAND,' says the website.

The quick way was to walk five miles down the road, crossing the regional boundary into the Marche, then another mile, to the right, into a narrow valley where the Creative Residence seemed to be the only building. But the road was all hairpin bends and heavy traffic. Our app proposed a great elephant's ear of a diversion. Eight miles, circling east, then north, then back to the west.

Eleonora grew more and more irritated that I wasn't taking the coming storm seriously. Distant thunder boomed. I teased her. She protested: 'Don't tempt the gods!' I looked up at the sky and shouted, 'Bring it on! I'm ready!' Lightning flickered. What had got into me?

The path was easy, but long. We stepped up the pace as the thunder echoed back and forth. Four miles, five. The sky was heaping dense billows over the mountain tops. 'It won't rain on us,' I laughed. 'Never!'

We had circled right round our destination now and were approaching it from the east, descending steeply on grey shaley tracks, when two things happened at once. We realized that our app hadn't actually found a path to the Creative Residence. The last half-mile was simply a dead-straight line. It's an infuriating thing that this app does from time to time. When it can't find a path to a point you've touched on the map, it gets as close as possible, then draws a straight line. Which in this case crossed a wooded ravine. Just as we appreciated that we had a problem, with a terrific crack right above our heads, the rain came down.

We had our routine. Back to back, we raised the groundsheet on our poles to make a big umbrella. But today we were on a steep slope. And the rain fell torrentially. For ten minutes. For twenty. Suddenly the track was a stream, a landslide. Grey slime was flowing over our shoes. Then the wind rose and our flimsy shelter was tugged this way and that. The rain swept in underneath. 'Just accept we'll be drenched.' I pulled in my poles. 'Let's move.'

'Tempting the gods on Mount Jupiter,' Eleonora said. 'Not smart.'

We stumbled downhill. But quickly stopped. We had no idea which way to go. Thick woodland all around. Glimpses of peaks and valleys. No buildings. No landmarks. We had a paper map but it wasn't detailed enough. And we were cold. We were shivering. Covering each other with the groundsheet, we rummaged in our packs for our rain jackets. Trying to study our phones, the screens got splashed and went dark. Anyway there was no signal. Eleonora's battery was almost done.

'Think,' I said. 'We have to think.'

We remembered there had been a signal a few hundred yards back. We floundered up the hill again through the woods as the mud flowed down towards us. Twigs and stones and dead leaves. The whole surface was on the move. Then I understood. Since our app didn't show the residence, we had inserted a destination guessing from the address shown on Google. We must have got it a fraction to one side of where it actually was. Not as crazy as a professional army using a map ten years out of date, but not brilliant.

We were soaked. The rain wasn't letting up. My phone was still out of action. Eleonora's was on 3 per cent. And Eleonora's had the app. With the amount of mud sliding towards us you began to wonder if a tree wouldn't come down. Bending together, we made a shelter beneath our jackets. I opened my pack and used a T-shirt to dry my phone. Carefully. There. It came to life.

I opened Google Maps and opted for satellite view. It took an age to come up. We were shivering. At last the image formed. We compared it with the app which had the red line indicating the way we had walked. This gave us our bearings. It seemed if we walked back half a mile or so, a path should open to our left. So it did. An hour later we stepped, sodden, into Everland.

Stella studied fine art in France and the USA. Her mother was an artist. Her father a professor of sociology. They came from Pesaro, on the Adriatic coast. Then retreated from the world. They bought a remote ruin deep in a dead-end valley, a place monks once used as a base in summer to gather logs for charcoal. And transformed it into the kind of fabled sanctuary where wounded heroes go to be cured by elfin queens.

Herbs, colours, music and painting are the medicine. And excellent food. The rooms have different themes of blue, because 'blue is the colour that awakens creativity'. There are reworkings of famous paintings. Giotto's blue. Piero della Francesca's. Cimabue's. You can learn to make colours from plants in the valley. There is woad. There is madder. You can dye your clothes with them. You can paint, or etch, or work clay, or play the piano, or the guitar. You can gather herbs and cook with them. Or make cosmetics. You can make honey. There are common spaces full of paintings and sculptures of women. By women. The bathrooms are stony grottos with trees and ivy. A shower head hangs from a branch. Water flows out of a stone wall, on an upturned terracotta roof tile. The towels are deep blue pile. Dried lavender perfumes the corridors. A trough is sunk in the floor for dogs and cats to drink.

Most of all you can eat. There are just three tables in the sitting room. A young woman tells us she comes here every year, alone, to relax and purify her soul. A couple at the far end keep themselves to themselves. We're welcomed with a basket of home-made breads. A bottle of Trebbiano. The food comes on curious white plates they've crafted themselves, one edge scrolled into a naked woman. Dish after dish arrives. Even Angelino and Massimo, back in Paradiso, never dreamed of such abundance. A long wooden board laden with delicate savoury pastries. Big ravioli wrapped round twigs to look like the bundle a monk puts over his shoulder. A salad dish full of edible flowers. A risotto. Lentil dumplings with wild garlic. *Radicchio al forno. Patate gratinate.*

Our defences are down after the drama of the storm. Stella brings another plate. She chats about herbs and flowers and rediscovering the recipes of the Middle Ages. Her mother arrives with a soup. She talks about her paintings. About the retro furniture. The father brings more pastries. 'From sociology to medieval cuisine': he gives his biography in a nutshell.

'Studying society prompts total retreat,' I suggest.

A young man appears, Stella's boyfriend, offering an array of cakes. Tomorrow is *Ferragosto*, he says. As well as cooking for us, they are preparing for fifty guests at lunch. In the garden. Why don't we stay?

We fight a rearguard action against grappas, cordials, digestives, nuts and cakes and fruits and sweet wines, and eventually, somehow, stagger back upstairs, past candlesticks, lanterns and vases of fresh flowers into a swoon of Piero della Francesca blue, where, having eaten too much, I sleep badly. But not as badly as Hoffstetter. Worried his fever would come back if he slept in the open on the mountain top, the German proceeded along the road until he found a hut where he could wrap up comfortably in his horse blankets. 'But I was deceived. Not only was I cruelly surprised by a multitude of pestilential insects, but towards dawn they brought a cavalryman shot while scouting. They laid him next to me and proceeded to dig the bullet from his knee. Despite the icy early morning I went outside in the hope of a little more rest before another day.'

DAY 22

28–29 July 1849 – 15 August 2019

Bocca Trabaria/ValdericArte, Mercatello, Sant'Angelo in Vado – 14 miles

Mercatello

'Yet sweet illusions could still arise in fervent minds.'

So says Ruggeri of the men setting out at dawn from Bocca Trabaria. It was easy walking down a gentle valley. After seven miles they met the river Metauro flowing from the east and could drink. Another three miles and they were in Mercatello, where the inhabitants provided them 'with every kind of food and abundant forage for the animals'.

They were back in business. Hoffstetter had got over his fever and was feeling bullish. Arriving in the small *borgo* at ten they set up camp in a field by the river. 'We had rested three hours,' the German recalls, 'when news arrived that the enemy had been sighted just beyond Sant'Angelo in Vado, five miles ahead. Once again we were trapped, since we knew that forces from Arezzo were not far behind.'

It was not unexpected. Garibaldi was aware the Austrians had an army in Urbino on the Adriatic side of the Apennines, potentially blocking the path to the sea. In his dispatch of 25 July Stadion had asked D'Aspre to order Archduke Ernst, the Emperor's young cousin, who was commanding these troops, to march up towards the mountain passes. Just in case.

So the *garibaldini* were now in the narrow Metauro valley with enemy behind and enemy in front. They had missed the chance, some miles back, to take a turn north to Sestino, where the Florentine

Carlo Corsi had already arrived, on foot, from San Sepolcro. But as Corsi recalls, the Austrians arrived there soon after. 'The soldiers were so tired and breathless they could barely stand. They cursed these mountains and Garibaldi and anybody who supported him. One captain said: "This devil will dance us to hell, or to Africa at least."' But the truth was, Corsi says, 'the younger officials had begun rather to admire this bold soldier and thought him an outstanding partisan fighter'.

On hearing of the army approaching from the Adriatic, Garibaldi left Forbes to organize a defensive position against the army behind them and galloped off in haste with anyone who had a saddle on his horse to occupy Sant'Angelo in Vado before the enemy did. He never panicked, Ruggeri remarks. He was never daunted.

Since we had only fourteen miles to cover today, we decided to follow the ridge that looks down into the Metauro valley where the *garibaldini* walked. It meant a steep climb, then interminable ups and downs on a shaley, slithery path. Some slopes had no vegetation at all, just broken slate and mud. You can see why someone thought of the surface of the moon. Looking around, other ridges and mountains marched away in all directions. Stumbling down to Mercatello, it was already two o'clock when we found a small weathered stone that said, 'To Giuseppe Garibaldi, in the centenary of his passing, 28 July 1849'.

Built on the right bank of the Metauro, Mercatello is a mix of narrow alleys, spacious piazzas, grand churches and decaying hovels. The population of 1500 is considerably smaller than it was in 1849. In a café with a shady garden we saw to our surprise, above the fridge near the till, a poster announcing a Garibaldi anniversary party. Three weeks earlier.

'It was a big success,' the young woman behind the bar declared. People had dressed up as Garibaldi and Anita and Ugo Bassi and even as Austrian soldiers. When we described our trip, her eyes shone. 'And here I am,' she wailed, 'stuck making sandwiches and pouring drinks in a place where nothing ever happens.' We shouldered our bags and smiled. Out on the street it was thirty-four degrees.

Sant'Angelo in Vado

Leaving Mercatello, we were now on the road that Garibaldi and his men galloped down towards Sant'Angelo in Vado, ready for anything. Finding to their surprise that the Austrians had not yet occupied the town, they left some men in defensive positions and rode cautiously on, eastward. The valley widens here for a couple of miles, then closes in again with steep hills on both sides. It was at this narrow point that the Austrians had blocked the road. The extraordinary thing was that a half-mile before that, to the left, there was an old mule track climbing north to the small *borgo* of Lunano seven miles away. And from there, another road led down to the sea. And the Austrians had not blocked it.

Moving swiftly, Garibaldi began to set up defences on the slopes all around the point where the track left the road. Forbes was recalled from Mercatello. Scouts were sent to skirmish with the Austrians blocking the road, but the enemy were well hidden among trees and rocks and it was impossible to establish how many there were.

Children were splashing in the river below the road as we marched along the valley. The sluggish water was not inviting. We walked fast and covered the five miles in an hour and a half. The landscape is beautiful, but the traffic incessant, with no space for wayfarers. At last the sign for Sant'Angelo in Vado appeared. 'Home,' it said, 'of the Prized White Truffle'. And 'Twinned with Mar della Plata'. Garibaldi had fought some of his hardest battles against the Argentinians. Then the main road veered left to circle the town, and we could walk in relative safety to the city gate, Porta Albani.

It's a pompous thing, built in 1837, with an arched space inside where, in bold black lettering, you can read two disturbing slogans: LIBRO E MOSCHETTO / FASCISTA PERFETTO. Book and gun, the perfect Fascist. And IL CREDO DEL BORGHESE È L'EGOISMO. IL CREDO DEL FASCISTA È L'EROISMO. The credo of the bourgeois is selfishness, the credo of the Fascist is heroism.

The Fascists always claimed that their own credo was the logical continuation of the Risorgimento. Revisionists of the Risorgimento take this as proven and use it to attack the movement that united Italy. There's an obvious connection, they say, between Fascism's cult of heroism and the hero worship surrounding Garibaldi. *Garibaldi, the First Fascist*, is the title of one recent book. But Garibaldi never proposed heroism as a principle in itself. The value he proposed was national self-determination. Once that was achieved, you could forget heroics. In his novel *Cantoni, the Volunteer* he spells it out. 'Cantoni is a volunteer, not a soldier. He serves Italy the nation, not its leaders, all more or less tyrants, all more or less sold out to the foreigner ... Is the country in danger? The volunteers arrive from every part of the peninsula ... Is the enemy beaten? The volunteers go home to till the fields, or do whatever jobs will provide them with a living.'

There is an abyss between this and Fascism.

But there was another reason I was looking at the gate. I had noticed something none of my sources mention. This is not like the much older gates of Orvieto or Arezzo, where there is, or was, an actual door that could be swung shut and barred. It is simply an arch over the road that you have to pass through to enter the town. This perhaps goes some way to explaining Major Migliazza's fatal oversight when, on the morning of 29 July he failed to 'secure the gate'. 'A cart pulled across the entrance would have been enough,' Hoffstetter protested. Garibaldi stripped the cavalryman of his command at once.

Beyond the gate, Via Santa Veronica Giuliani quickly morphs into Corso Giuseppe Garibaldi, racing straight as an arrow the 300 yards to the centre of Sant'Angelo. Everything is narrow, enclosed and fast. The buildings seem tall on either side, their bricks grey-brown. Walking into town it's not hard to imagine the clatter of galloping hooves on the cobbles. The cries of the men must have boomed in the confined spaces. Gunshots and clashing sabres. Only a couple of tight side alleys right and left offer some opportunity to escape. Even the main piazza – Piazza Garibaldi of course – is only a slight widening of the space where three roads meet. It's not a place you would want to be trapped in.

Our B & B is in one of the town's finest *palazzi* by the central Caffè del Corso, whose quaint old street sign has a painted iron *garibaldino* with a red cap holding a tricolour. And on our *palazzo* too, which we chose because the claim is that Garibaldi stayed here, there is a plaque with the usual rhetoric: 'Sublime in the sufferings of his country' … 'Prophet of better times to come'. But nowhere in the square or the town is there any mention of what actually happened here.

Nor does our landlady know about the massacre. Though she is very proud of the building's connection with Garibaldi. It's a fine late-sixteenth-century *palazzo*, with noble stone staircases and generous common spaces, except we've drawn the short straw, a tiny ground-floor room whose barred window gives directly onto the space where so much blood was shed.

'I've never heard that story,' she says, offering us a glass of water in an upstairs room among the sort of old paintings that don't invite you to look beneath the varnish. We were sweating profusely. She was disconcerted on all fronts.

'There is,' she went on, 'a small monument to the *garibaldini*, and the cannon they abandoned here, along the road to Urbania.'

'Cannon?' I almost fell off my chair.

'About five kilometres away. It's just a few minutes in the car.' She frowned, remembering our circumstances. 'I could lend you a bicycle if you like.'

When I explained that the *garibaldini* marched with only one cannon and had not left it near Sant'Angelo, she was indignant. How could I, a complete stranger, know about something that happened here in Sant'Angelo, where I'd never been, and so long ago? Was I saying the cannon was a hoax?

I was conciliatory. After all she had promised to be up for 6 a.m. to serve us breakfast. 'We must go and look,' I said.

But we were too tired to walk the three miles now. Stretched on the bed in our room, we opened Google Street View and clicked our way out of Sant'Angelo, over a brick bridge across the Metauro and west into the valley, which first widens, just as Hoffstetter describes, then, after a couple of miles, narrows, the hill to the left rising sharply from the edge of the road.

But no cannon. No monument.

Eleonora got bored. I clicked back and forth. This must have been the point, I realized, where the Austrians blocked the road. On the morning of the 29th a group of Garibaldi's cavalry, pushing a little further towards the enemy, had fallen into an ambush; those who escaped said three men had been taken prisoner. It made sense there should be a monument here.

Suddenly I had it. The cannon was half hidden under trees. You had to click at exactly the right point. But there it was. A few yards of grass beside the road. An old stone memorial to the fore, then a large, more modern wall behind with a bas-relief. The cannon was to one side. Zooming in, I saw a slick Second World War howitzer.

Now it took only a moment to find out more. The wall with the bas-relief was a memorial to men of the Corpo Italiano di Liberazione who had died freeing Sant'Angelo from the Nazis in 1944. But it had been placed close to an old stone recalling the death of three unnamed *garibaldini*. The captured men had not been prisoners for long.

I would like to tell this drama exactly how it happened, but all the sources have different versions. We explored the small town and the winding streets that the General's men once fled along, diving into any doorway that would open for them. The scene by the river has a languid charm. The deep shade of the alleys is welcome. Posters promised a bank holiday concert at 9 p.m.: 'Music with Alfio, one of the Pirates'.

Towards eight, sitting outside the Caffè del Corso, we consulted a menu that was strong on white truffles. Three Arab women in burkas walked by, following an Arab man. And a large family of Indians. We hadn't seen anything like this in the mountains before.

Garibaldi spent the 28th gathering his troops on the road between Sant'Angelo and the Austrian road block. Time was needed to gather provisions because there would be no food up that mule track. Back in Sant'Angelo he searched for guides and spent time consulting them. Forbes arrived with Anita, bringing the Second Legion. The men settled down for a tense night. Twenty-four Austrian battalions were encircling them. Intermittently, shots rang out.

And Bueno chose this moment to desert. He slipped off up the mule track in the small hours. With the army's money chest. And twenty horsemen, says Hoffstetter. Ruggeri says seven. De Rossi, quoting Sacchi, says fifty. In any event, it was a severe blow. Bueno was an officer and close friend of the General's. Who could the men trust now?

'God be praised he's gone!' Hoffstetter has Garibaldi putting a brave face on it. Others describe him as deeply upset. The reactions don't seem incompatible. The two men went back a long way. Bueno was Brazilian, like Anita. A big, impulsive man, courageous and combative but hopelessly undisciplined. 'His idea of military service,' Hoffstetter tells us, 'was to ride ahead, arrive first where we planned to camp, and get horizontal.' Since Garibaldi was still hoping for news from Müller, knowing nothing of his desertion, he promoted Migliazza overall cavalry commander.

The honour would not last till lunchtime. The plan had been for an early-morning departure, but the horses and mules had to be watered, and the drop to the river was steep and exposed. It took time. Everything had to be done in the awareness that a battle could break out at any moment.

Forbes's infantry was pulled out of Sant'Angelo towards 9 a.m., leaving just Migliazza and fifty cavalry in the town as a rearguard. At ten the baggage train began to wind north up the hill, followed by the First Legion. To draw attention away from the movement, Garibaldi sent a patrol to launch a fake attack on Archduke Ernst's forces blocking the road ahead. As these men approached, the Austrians fell back. They appeared to be running. The commanding officer gave chase – foolishly, Hoffstetter observes – and was caught in a classic ambush.

'The three men remembered in the monument.'

'Right.'

But Migliazza also got caught. He had reckoned he had at least another hour in Sant'Angelo. He had scouts on the road from Mercatello to bring news of the Austrians advancing from the mountain pass. So far nothing. He told his men they could relax in the piazza a while. They could get themselves something to eat.

'Like we're doing now,' I observed. 'Right here.'

'You're winding me up,' Eleonora objects. 'Get on with it.'

'I'm trying to put everything in place. I can't understand how a guy who had done everything so right for so long could have made such an awful mistake. He hadn't even ordered the men to keep their horses saddled.'

'He was exhausted. He hadn't slept. Promotion had gone to his head.'

'Ruggeri manages to blame Bueno. For never disciplining the men. Belluzzi says the local people were very welcoming. Offering drinks and so on.'

'Get on with it.'

Hoffstetter was holding his position at the base of the mule track where the men were filing away up the hill when he saw Migliazza galloping towards him, hatless, in desperate flight, with just a few companions behind. A party of Austrian hussars had burst into Sant'Angelo through Porta Albani.

Hoffstetter and Forbes halted the retreat and organized defensive positions in the last houses outside the town in case the Austrians followed up. Migliazza called for an immediate counter-attack on Sant'Angelo. His men were trapped in there. He himself had barely managed to fight his way out. Hoffstetter said a counter-attack would require an order from the General. It was a delicate moment, with most of the men already climbing the hill and the enemy on the other side less than a mile away. Frantic, Migliazza rode off up the mule track in search of Garibaldi.

Eleonora is getting impatient. 'Tell me what actually happened in Sant'Angelo!'

Major General Stadion in Sant'Angelo in Vado to General D'Aspre in Florence, 29 July 1849

May I respectfully inform you that yesterday I followed the enemy from Borgo San Sepolcro to a few miles before Ganosa where I camped.

This morning I set out at 4 and at 9.30 came into contact with the enemy's rearguard in Sant'Angelo in Vado. My cavalry cut a number of men to pieces and captured several horses. In this occasion I must make warm mention of Lieutenant Rehak of the Reuss Hussars.

'No mention of the cock-up in the Tiber valley?'
'None.'
'And where is Ganosa?'
'Nobody knows. Stadion constantly gets the names of places wrong. But he always says how early he got up, how brave his men are and how hard it is to find provisions since Garibaldi has taken them all before he gets there.'

From our table outside Caffè del Corso we look at the small space around us where it happened. Fifty horses here would have been quite a crowd. Then the men and their gear. Saddles and blankets and sabres and pistols. A survivor described the situation thus:

They had been taking it easy, some in people's houses, some on the street. No guard had been left at the gate. The hussars, Hungarians, had surprised Migliazza's scouts, who turned their horses back to the town at a gallop. The Austrian horses were faster. How many isn't clear. Perhaps only thirty or forty in the first group. They galloped under the arch down the narrow street swinging their sabres.

Opposite us is a shop called Beauty. Then a florist's and a tobacconist's. A wine bar called Carpe Diem. And a butcher's. Belluzzi collected anecdotes. Dragged from his horse and surrounded by hussars with their sabres raised, Captain Orlandi from Perugia surrendered, was pulled to his feet and shot. The same fate awaited another officer, running out of a house. Yet another tried to fire his pistol, only to find the powder was damp. His last disappointment.

Those who avoided the first assault found the hussars had sealed both the town's gates. One man who fought his way out just in time had to have his hand amputated. Some ran into houses, where they were protected. Some climbed out of windows backing on to the river, forded the water and ran after the column. Others would still be hiding in the village a week later. One posed as a travelling tradesman and sold the Austrians 'tobacco and aniseed and other things that marching soldiers appreciate'. Responding to warnings of severe punishments for anyone harbouring the rebels, Giustino Brega, a cobbler, informed the Austrians that a man was hiding in his house. The *garibaldino* was executed. Shunned by his fellow villagers, the cobbler went mad and died.

These are experiences that change a community and force people to take sides. But the most remarkable story is that of Captain Jourdan, the *garibaldini*'s chief engineer. He was with Migliazza, strapping the saddle on his horse, when the whirlwind fell upon him. Hooves and cries and blades. Pulling a pistol from his saddlebag he shot his first attacker dead, only to be struck down by a storm of sabre blows. One sliced the nape of the neck to the bone. Left for dead in a pool of blood, Jourdan dragged himself through a house and across the river to join the rearguard.

'How he was on his feet with that terrible wound I couldn't understand,' says Hoffstetter, 'yet he stood perfectly erect and was able to tell me in a calm firm voice what had happened.' He wasn't able to sit on Hoffstetter's horse, though. Four men were dragging the captain up the hill when the enemy attacked again.

Suddenly, the Austrians were all around. 'We would have been caught, had not Forbes and the Bersaglieri counter-attacked, then held the line in a farm building till the enemy withdrew.' Finally a stretcher was found and eight men hauled Jourdan up the slope to where the *garibaldini*'s doctors were treating others. They pronounced him a hopeless case.

'And?'

'They carried him along anyway.'

'I mean did he survive?'

'We'll see.'

Eleonora shook her head. 'You're teasing.'

The Austrians followed at 'a respectful distance', says Hoffstetter, but it was not the kind of terrain where they could deploy their heavy equipment, and the *garibaldini* had the better of it now. Forbes and his men, Ruggeri says, showed tireless determination and courage. At this point the column was straggling over miles on the steep narrow track. As soon as there was open ground, higher up, Garibaldi ordered a halt, got the men to regroup and addressed them all together. Hoffstetter doesn't reveal what he said, only that he was 'cheered more warmly than ever'. Before moving on, 'the General shared his last cigar and some fruit with us'.

We drained the last of our beer and went to hear Alfio play his music. He was standing under an old-fashioned lantern a hundred yards from our *palazzo*. A middle-aged hippy in jacket and jeans, with long blonde hair. He'd set up a console for his backing tracks, a microphone and four big speakers. And he was singing old pop songs. A few people in chairs outside the bar opposite were half listening, and that was it. Eleonora sang along to *'Attenti al lupo'* – 'Beware of the Wolf'. Alfio jived, swinging his mike back and forth. There was a curious feeling about the performance, cheerful and pathetic. As if he hadn't quite given up hope an audience might turn up later.

Eleonora was still humming along as we climbed into bed. There was no double-glazing on the windows so the music was still very much with us. Lying awake, I thought of Migliazza. Reduced to the ranks, he accepted his disgrace. He didn't desert. Garibaldi let deserters slip away because there was no point, he said, in hanging on to men who weren't determined. Except in moments of battle when your comrades were counting on you; then a deserter must be shot. Over the coming days the Austrians shot any fugitives they could find. Stadion made a point of informing D'Aspre of his severity, perhaps to excuse himself for his lenience with Müller. In general the townsfolk protected the rebels, at great risk to themselves, but in the country the peasants were happy to steal the men's weapons and hand them over to the Austrians.

This reminded me – and now Alfio was singing 'A Whiter Shade of Pale' – of something I'd read in Linda Colley's great book *Britons*. When the British government launched a huge appeal for volunteers to meet the threatened Napoleonic invasion of 1797, they had expected the conservative country folk to respond, not the radicalized workers of town and factory. Instead the opposite was the case. Where people read newspapers and talked politics, where they had learned to criticize those who governed them, they could see the importance of not being overrun by a foreign power. They had a stake in the nation. When the police raided one group of political radicals in London, they found them trying to decide which regiment to volunteer for. Arguably, that patriotism earned those men the social reforms of the post-1815 years. It was the same consciousness that Garibaldi was seeking to form in Italy: the dream, the gamble, of self-government. Years later, when he visited England, he got his warmest welcome and raised the most cash among the dock workers of the north.

Alfio was still seeping through the window. The last song I remember before sleep finally ambushed me was '*Vengo dopo il TG*', 'I'll Come After the News'. It's a comic 1980s song in which a man keeps his lusty girlfriend waiting in bed while he watches the day's last news bulletin. I smiled. The news these days of course was all Brexit – another bid for self-government. And Salvini's opportunistic xenophobia. The same stuff coming round and round, century after century, in different shades of pale. And Alfio sang,

> *È la tivvù che vizia,*
> *Il fatto è che mi sfizia,*
> *Restare fino all'ultima notizia.*

> It's the TV that spoils me,
> Fact is, it suits my fancy
> To stay till the last story.

DAY 23

29 July 1849 – 16 August 2019

Sant'Angelo in Vado, Lunano, Macerata Feltria – 14 miles

Lunano

We woke to the jingle of our alarm. For some days now the *garibaldini* had stopped using a trumpet for reveille. The enemy was too near. In each company a sentry was assigned the job of waking the others.

The posh old clock in the breakfast room said ten to six when we presented ourselves to find boiled eggs already on the table. I steered clear of the question of the cannon. Our landlady was explaining that there were so many immigrants in the town because of the jeans factory. Remote towns like this, she said, needed some big industry to keep the population from emigrating. Lunano, for example, had high-quality industrial tubes. But then the local youngsters left anyway, so people came in from outside.

'Not everyone wants to spend their lives in a factory,' Eleonora observes, having escaped her own home town fifteen years ago.

By 6.30 we were on the road. Unusually there were clouds. The sun topping peaks to the east was shining beneath them. A big pylon stark above us carried cables across the river where the *garibaldini* watered their horses. The mule track was gone, or if it was there, our maps didn't give it. We followed a new road for a couple of miles, then left it where it disappeared into a tunnel.

The path was steep now, but the landscape magnificent. Rolling upland, rich with crops and shady thickets, but thrusting up here and there to higher, darker slopes where craggy outcrops look like they might be castles, or vice versa. There's a sense of vastness, distant hills, distant mountains beyond the hills, and faint peaks, even more remote, reaching into the sky. The bright sunshine enamelled everything, the pale stubble and the lush alfalfa and white flecks of isolated farm-houses. Seeing rich fields of maize, Anita wanted to stop to gather forage, but Garibaldi insisted they press on. It was a race.

We pressed on despite Eleonora's tendinitis, and towards nine dropped down into Lunano over the mouth of the long tunnel we had been walking above.

Lunano need not apply for the *borgo-più-bello* award. The castle on the hill above is in ruins. The centre is as much a car park as a piazza. 'And Anita's heart beat beside him,' says the plaque on the town hall. Otherwise there's a quietness about the place that might be leisure, but is more likely melancholy.

Macerata Feltria

Having travelled north to reach Lunano, Garibaldi now turned north-east along the tiny river Foglia. He could then drop down to Sassocorvaro and from there to Pesaro and the sea, just forty miles away. Except the paths were poor or non-existent. Their guide led the men down into a gorge and along the riverbed. I was curious to see if this was still possible, and at the first opportunity we turned off what is now a fast modern road and pushed half a mile along a gravel track past abandoned farmhouses. Just before a narrow bridge, a chain was hung across the path leading to the river and a sign told us access was Absolutely Forbidden. We climbed over and went down to the water.

Very little of it. The riverbed was twenty yards wide. Cracked grey mud with thick trees and bushes each side. The air buzzed with winged beetles and cicadas. The heat was intense. The narrow stream, just a few feet wide, meandered back and forth across the mud, forming pools among big flat stones. Dragonflies hovered. We went under the bridge and found a beaver's dam just beyond. There was a lot of woody debris about. Eleonora was sceptical, but I thought it looked possible.

Our feet slipped on slimy stones. Here and there the ground gave way and shoes sank in the mud. Then, at a bend in the river, the stream drifted towards us and we were trapped between the water and a high bank of thorns. Should we ford it? It wasn't the kind of situation where you wanted to walk barefoot. I backtracked to where a boulder seemed to offer a stepping stone, but it shifted under my weight and I ended up with a leg in the water.

Enough. This was silly. We turned back. Yet that half-hour fooling on the riverbed in the heat with the flies and the slime brought us far closer to the *garibaldini* than we ever could be on the smooth asphalt of the road. Closer to their doggedness; thinking of the mules and oxen splashing in the shallows, the horses heaving the cannon and Captain Jourdan moaning on his stretcher. Major Zambianchi's foot wound was worse by the hour so that he screamed with pain at every jolt. Major Cenni was still feverish with typhus, but recovering. Anita was fading, pale and sapped of energy. Everyone crowded into this meandering trickle of grey mud and flies, one long hot summer's day.

Approaching Sassocorvaro, a cavalry scout brought news that the main body of Archduke Ernst's army was marching on the other side of the hills to their right, the east, in order to block their descent to the sea. Garibaldi had already discussed alternatives with their guides, and the column turned sharply left, which is to say north-west, to Macerata Feltria, five miles away. It was a climb of 1500 feet, and again they followed the bed of a dry torrent. *Assai dirupato*, Hoffstetter says laconically. Rocky.

All the same, when they made it to Macerata Feltria in the early evening, Garibaldi was in excellent spirits. They had eluded the Austrians again! He feasted on roast chicken and wine provided by a deferential young priest who refused to be paid, relaxing with Anita under canvas on Church property.

The people of Macerata were welcoming and excited. True, their chief citizens had fled, but they had left orders to provide for the soldiers. Two barrels of dried cod were opened and much appreciated. A few educated men who had stayed came to offer the General their opinions as to which route might be feasible. Not the road down to Pesaro, which Archduke Ernst would soon occupy. Not the longer road to the west, through Carpegna, Pennabilli and Perticara towards

Cesena; that was already occupied by Austrian troops climbing up from Tuscany. Which left the wild paths over the mountains, past San Marino and down through Verucchio to Rimini.

Garibaldi listened and smiled and kept his counsel. There was much eating and drinking. I find no mention of the forty or so men they had lost in Sant'Angelo.

Was this unfeeling? This merriment. Was this stubbornness foolhardy? Eleonora and I are thinking a lot about the men who tramped these hills before us. We've been with them more than 300 miles now. The deserters are easy to understand. They are discouraged. They want to save themselves. But the hard core still supporting the General are of a different mettle. For them death has long since been factored in. It may come, it may not, but it's not the issue. This frees them to follow their cause and live for the day.

We don't even look for the dry torrent they took and instead climb steep earthy paths through woods and wild dry grasses, until Macerata appears below us to the right with all the air of a pretty market town in Derbyshire. From this distance even the tower at the top of the town looks vaguely English. The houses cluster on a low hill above a valley thick with foliage. A half-hour later, entering the first streets, we come across Via Ugo Bassi. Born evangelist, the priest took only a couple of hours to impress himself on the locals. Ciceruacchio on the other hand, dining in a private house, fell into an argument with a cavalry officer and challenged him to a duel. The two were already out in the courtyard with swords drawn before their companions managed to disarm them.

Again we're in one of the *borghi più belli.* A long straight street climbs to a T-junction which boasts an elaborate ironwork drinking fountain with two quaint old street lamps hanging above. Plaques abound.

Macerata Feltria, proud guardian of the remains of
the unknown *garibaldino* ... 1962

The Nazi Fascist fury of 1944 smashed this memorial stone to
Giuseppe Garibaldi, which the people of Macerata Feltria have

repaired in honour of this symbol of liberty and
independence ... 1954

From the horrendous carnage
Meditated and perpetrated
By a new and more ferocious Attila
Comes a cry of grief
Europe bleeds and weeps and
The horrified world
Stamps on the face of history
Two accursed names
Benito Mussolini, Adolf Hitler
April 1945

Shining with ideal beauty
Among the glorious defeated,
Heroic in her daring
Sublime in her sacrifice
Blessed in her kiss of love,
Anita Garibaldi ... 1908

In the gardens that look out from the town across the valley, at the
top of six steps on a high plinth between two dark cypresses, stands a
tall white Garibaldi; he's wearing loose dungarees, has a sword in his
belt, his arms folded under his poncho, his bearded face raised to the
mountains. Which is where, towards 11 p.m. on 29 July, just as his
men were settling down for the night beside blazing campfires, the
General ordered them to climb. At once.

Belluzzi's interviewees, years later, speak admiringly or disparag-
ingly of Garibaldi's impulsiveness, the suddenness of his decisions:
when he ordered his men out of Citerna at midnight; when he left
Torrita di Siena at a moment's notice; when he suddenly changed
course to go to Castiglion Fiorentino. That was how he was, they sigh.

Hoffstetter was not fooled. The General hadn't told anybody they
would be leaving Macerata Feltria, he observes, for obvious reasons.

But the decision had long been made. An hour before departure the mule men were quietly warned to start loading their animals. Then came the order to march. It caused consternation. Even resistance. Great care had been taken to make sure their position was safe. They had marched through the town and camped above it, so that the enemy would have to come through narrow, well defended streets to attack them. They had sealed the entrance, leaving a rearguard down the road, with fifteen of the boys from the Compagnia Speranza constantly running back and forth from rearguard to town gate to make sure all was well.

Some men had barely fallen asleep and didn't want to move. Others were in taverns or houses. Some of the rearguard tried to rush into the town for a quick drink or something to eat. The youngsters blocked the gate with their bayonets: the men must hold their position till the General ordered.

Hoffstetter was impressed. Officials were sent round the houses to flush out stragglers. In one case blows were exchanged. Two officers were arguing furiously over a question of protocol. These flare-ups, Hoffstetter observes, always occurred between those who had been professional soldiers and those who hadn't. The untrained volunteers would forget the proper terms of address. The trained soldiers couldn't get used to the idea that they were not in a regular army. But now a volley of shots rang out.

Were they under attack? Everyone ran to join their companies. The General had ordered this false alarm to put an end to the chaos. The arguing officers were reduced to the ranks. So in a few minutes the column was on the road, in a savage mood, climbing due west now, away from the sea, into the mountains, in the night. And it became clear why Garibaldi had allowed the luxury of campfires. Hoffstetter was left behind with a company of cavalry to keep them alight for a few more hours, so that distant eyes would imagine they were all still there.

We walked through the town and out in the same direction to where the Hotel Pitinum, a modern three-star establishment, stood up on the hillside beside its swimming pool. Yes, we were just in time for lunch, the proprietor said. Then took an age to serve us. The chef was having a day off, no doubt after his *Ferragosto* efforts of the day before. The proprietor's mother was cooking. Alone in a dining room meant for a hundred, we drank white wine and waited.

'And Captain Jourdan?'

'They left him behind. For dead, Hoffstetter thought.'

'But? And?'

'Together with another man, also wounded in Sant'Angelo and also carried on a stretcher. They were left in a hostel with a family called the Venturini.'

'But do we know if he survived?'

'Hoffstetter never found out. The other guy had already been given the last rites.'

Eleonora laughs. '*Basta!* Tell me.'

She drums her fingers on the table and looks pointedly right and left. With its marble floor and air conditioning, the room is cool to the point of being chilly. There is no sign of our food.

'OK, I give up.'

At dawn on 30 July, while the *garibaldini* were taking up defensive positions at Rocca Pietrarubbia, a monastery perched on an impregnable crag five miles up the road, two Austrian soldiers, Tyrolese men, burst into the Venturini household, smashed furniture and mirrors, grabbed the wounded man beside Jourdan and started pulling him out of the house by his feet. Jourdan was alive enough to curse them. A villager rushed in and protested that the man was dying. So the soldiers grabbed Jourdan and took him out in the street in bedclothes caked in blood. 'Goodbye, my friend,' he called to the man who had tried to stop the soldiers. 'I'm off to die. But not afraid.'

'Lots of detail here!' Eleonora says appreciatively.

'It's the version of a guy called Filippo Belli, the villager who tried to intervene. He told Belluzzi. Forty years on.'

Jourdan was questioned by General Stadion himself, who wanted to know about Garibaldi's plans. Jourdan couldn't stand up. Having been a professional soldier, an engineer in the papal army, he saluted the Austrian general respectfully but refused to give any information aside

273

from his name and rank. Stadion, who was meeting his first *garibaldino* face to face, was taken aback by the man's dignity and conviction. Instead of having him shot, as everyone expected, he not only sent him back to his bed, but for the duration of the Austrian army's stay put two guards on the door and had a black flag hung over the building to indicate it was being used as a hospital. Jourdan was then looked after by Doctor Giovanni Castellani, who filled his huge wound with lint soaked in a mixture of boiled fat and crushed rose petals. Three months later, perfectly healed, Jourdan left Macerata Feltria, to the great regret of its people, and emigrated to the USA.

'Hurrah for General Stadion!' Eleonora raised her glass.

Our *tagliolini* had arrived.

'Hurrah for crushed rose petals!'

'I bet the general didn't mention this in his dispatches, though.'

He did not. But there was definitely a change of tone in the exchanges between the Austrian commanders at this point in the saga. In mid-July the *garibaldini* were riff-raff, brigands, vandals. An irritation. Now, exchanging compliments with the French commander, General Oudinot, in Rome, D'Aspre talks admiringly about Garibaldi's ability and speed. 'Almost encircled by our battalions coming from Bologna, Ancona, Arezzo, he could still break out. He moves faster than us. He has friends everywhere.'

Stadion writes on 30 July to boast of having shot seventeen *garibaldini* stragglers. But he fears the rebels are still capable of doubling back into Tuscany and raising hell. 'At which point the only thing we can do is, at all costs, to catch up with them and launch a surprise attack.' The 'at all costs' suggests how improbable he fears this is. He thanks D'Aspre for the delivery of three state-of-the-art rocket launchers, though these have had to be carried on mules. 'It is so difficult to move things around on these miserable paths.'

'Too bad the *garibaldini* couldn't read all this,' Eleonora observes. 'It might have cheered them up.'

Two other correspondents join the discussion. Major General Hahne in Rimini and General Karl von Gorzkowsky, governor of Bologna. They have been asked to close in on Garibaldi from the east and the north, to complete the encirclement that will finally allow them to get their man. Gorzkowsky is the most senior and the most powerful. He has a reputation for ruthlessness. And he writes to the operation's overall commander, Field Marshal Radetzky, to complain of the incompetence of Stadion and Paumgartten and Archduke Ernst. 'If Garibaldi remains the shrewd and tireless commander he is, he'll get down to Rimini or Cesena long before Paumgartten or Ernst ... Then I'll have to deal with him myself with the few men I have.' He goes on to complain that rumours of Garibaldi's arrival are provoking all kinds of excitement in liberal circles in Bologna and Ravenna, with graffiti everywhere and many young men ready to join him. He demands Radetzky send reinforcements.

In Florence, D'Aspre is already looking forward to the moment when Garibaldi is finally defeated. He informs Radetzky that the Grand Duke of Tuscany has appeared in Florence at the annual Corsa dei Cocchi – a kind of chariot race – and again in the evening at the theatre, wearing full Austrian uniform on both occasions. 'It seems he is eager to know if we are satisfied with his behaviour.' Historians now agree that it was the grand duke's growing identification with his ruthless minders that would lead to him being swept away without regret ten years down the line.

Ten years, Garibaldi told people in Macerata. We will be back in ten years to thank you for your kindness.

We spend the evening studying maps. Tomorrow we are going to steal a march on the *garibaldini*. Two dramatic days of theirs will be crammed into one of ours. Because we will have the benefit of modern roads and bridges.

Our destination, eighteen miles away, is San Marino. The climax is at hand. We feel excited, but anxious too. There will be endless ups and downs. The mountains are higher again. We are fit but full of niggles – blisters, tendinitis, sunburn – and a mental tiredness is gathering. It's the sheer quantity of *world* we have had to absorb: the conversations, the sun, the landscape. The endless decisions about paths and food and places to stay. The insects. The bathrooms. The lack of bathrooms ...

Yet now the end is coming – just a matter of days – we feel anxious about that too. About returning to our normal lives. It's a strange feeling, a kind of nostalgia for adventure before the adventure is over. I wonder if the *garibaldini* felt this. As when Hoffstetter, watching the column snake up to the pass at Bocca Trabaria, thought that very soon many of these men would be dead. Everyone knew it couldn't go on much longer. The noble company must disperse. Perhaps they were expecting a *Morte d'Arthur* moment. Garibaldi's death even. One man was so disheartened, or in so much pain, he decided not to wait for the inevitable. A witness told Belluzzi how, just outside Macerata Feltria, she saw a straggler sit down on the edge of a ditch and pull off his boots. 'He inspected his feet. Then he pointed his rifle under his chin and fired.'

DAY 24

30–31 July 1849 – 17 August 2019

Macerata Feltria, Mercato Vecchio, San Marino – 19 miles

Mercato Vecchio

There we are, then, on the road at 5.45. Dawn comes later than at the beginning of our journey. It's still dark. Or rather, the road is moonlit. There's a full moon high ahead, over the hills. Then the cool beauty of it is shattered by a tractor dragging some kind of heavy clanking device to destroy the vegetation on the verge. The big vehicle has a couple of spotlights and proceeds slowly and steadily, with menacing military precision.

The road here is a long straight climb. Proceeding steadily and slowly behind the *garibaldini*, the Austrians mopped up the stragglers. Four men resting in a shed were betrayed to the enemy by the local peasants. One escaped, jumping from a window. Three were shot. Six *garibaldini* were pulled from houses in Mercato Vecchio. 'They showed me the point in the road where they were shot,' says Belluzzi. 'One dragged himself to a barn and howled all night, but the people were too scared to help.'

The bodies were burned in lime. The priest refused Christian burial. However, in Pietrarubbia another priest offered Austrian soldiers six *scudi* to spare a man's life. That's about two week's wages. The redeemed *garibaldino* gave the priest his horse. Forty years on, these stories had become fable. The peasants who betrayed the four men in their barn had stolen money from the corpses. Despised by the community, they all died miserable deaths.

So they say.

The sun, behind us this morning, brought a golden glow to a high rock face beyond fields of stubble. Pietrarubbia. It's a large monastery beneath a ruined fortress on a crest overlooking the valley that leads from Mercato Vecchio – a half-mile ahead of us now – to Carpegna three miles to the south-west. Occupying the complex during the night, Garibaldi was 600 feet above his enemies and had a panoramic view. An ambush set on the road behind was already in place when Hoffstetter passed after keeping the fires going in Macerata Feltria. Cavalry parties were sent off in the dark to Carpegna, but also northwards, as far as San Marino, and even Verucchio beyond, the main nodal point on the descent to the coast. At 4 a.m. the scouts heading to Carpegna encountered advancing Austrians.

This was one of Paumgartten's battalions under the command of Major Holzer. It had been on Garibaldi's trail since Todi. If readers are struggling with the sheer number of imperial armies marching across the Italian landscape, here is Generale De Rossi's summary of the position on 30 July.

Behind him and to the east Garibaldi now had 17 battalions, 2 artillery batteries and 3 cavalry squadrons. These were the forces of General Stadion and Archduke Ernst, now under the overall command of the archduke. On his left flank, to the west, he had 1 battalion commanded by Major Holzer, while up ahead, to the north and east, beyond San Marino there was General Hahne, with 6 battalions, 1 artillery battery and 7 cavalry squadrons.

Garibaldi decided that if the Austrians from Carpegna wanted to attack, he was ready for a fight. He knew this force was relatively small. He was in a perfect position. The cannon was placed high on the ridge and looked guaranteed to cause havoc. The infantry were deployed in lines. The cavalry were covering the flanks. A short sharp victory would get his men's tails up.

Dawn brought mist and cloud. There was rain in the air. The enemy backed off. Aside from skirmishes, the Austrian strategy throughout this campaign was to accept battle only if they had an overwhelming advantage in numbers. Both sides knew that General Stadion couldn't be far away. Around midday Garibaldi launched a fake attack, under cover of which, on the other side of the hill, the baggage train was sent back north, down through Mercato Vecchio, then on up the steep slopes towards Montecopiolo and Villagrande. A fog came down, then heavy rain, and very soon the whole column was on the move again. Rather than following the rebels, Major Holzer chose to wait for Stadion. Further east, the archduke was approaching San Marino on the far side of the Apennines.

We marched into Mercato Vecchio at seven. Four uphill miles in an hour and fifteen. Not bad. The scattered houses had that shabby weathered look that seems inevitable in poorer mountain villages. There was no sign of a centre or anything resembling a monument, but the Bar Bracci was open for business.

I pushed through a bead curtain over the door. Serving at the counter was an ancient, wizened woman, who I quickly understood must be deaf. Her one customer was yelling at her. The place was tiny. I ordered coffees, then ordered again in a louder voice. 'Due caffè! Due paste!' Under wispy grey hair, deep wrinkles relaxed in a smile of welcome. 'How nice to see a strange face in my shop,' her voice quavered. 'And so early in the morning!' I said we were walking and how thankful we would be if she could rustle us up a couple of sandwiches.

'He said he'd like a couple of sandwiches!' the customer beside me shouted. She was a handsome, severe, smartly dressed woman with a strong local accent. When I smiled my thanks at her, she didn't smile back.

I took the coffees and pastries to one of three tables outside. Looking around, we saw that we were in Via Garibaldi.

Ten minutes later, when I went back in to pay, the old lady had the sandwiches stacked and wrapped. She looked me in the eye and held the contact for a few seconds. 'I want to thank you, signore,' she said, 'for visiting our village. I wish you a lovely day and I hope you will come back some time in the future.'

It seemed excessive. But she meant it. 'And I thank you, signora,' I said 'for being open for us when we needed you.'

The other woman, who seemed a fixture, shook her head.

We should really have climbed to Pietrarubbia. The road snakes up the hill to the monastery due south. A half-hour walk, Google said. Photos showed grey stone cloisters, steep grassy paths, a derelict tower built into outcropping rock. But after the climb and another half an hour to explore, there would be yet another half an hour's steep descent, to Mercato Vecchio. Then the fifteen miles to San Marino, which by all accounts will be hard walking.

We wimped out. And I regret it. Because now, at the climax of this long drama, one wanted to stay as close as possible to the *garibaldini*'s experience. At the same time we didn't want to suffer. Really suffer. We had no cause to. No worthy cause. So that I wonder if my regret isn't more a yearning for a purpose, a real reason to climb to Pietrarubbia, the way those extraordinary plaques in Macerata Feltria and elsewhere show such a longing for some noble collective enterprise and a legendary hero to take the lead.

'However, I fear we can't really know the exact route they took,' Belluzzi observes. Descending from Pietrarubbia in heavy rain the afternoon of the 30th many *garibaldini* lost their way. The paths were awash, the streams swollen. The cloud had come down and visibility was poor. There were ravines, cliffs, thick woods, waterfalls. Everything and everyone was soaked. The main body of the troops lost contact with the advance guard. The rearguard lost contact with the main column. Our various sources all give different versions. De Rossi has the main body of men spending the night of the 30th in defensive positions on Montecopiolo, just four miles north of Mercato Vecchio and a mile short of the *borgo* of Villagrande. But with more than a third of the men missing, he says.

Ruggeri doesn't seem to know where they were, but speaks of wandering about in a vast beech wood, like children in a fairy tale. The rain had stopped. Garibaldi and some other horsemen, he says, rode tirelessly back and forth to gather stragglers and point the way. Hoffstetter talks about entering the Conca valley at nightfall. That would be north and east of Montecopiolo. Towards eleven the men rested in a high clearing, he says, in an endless forest, while he rode off in search of the baggage train, which he located towards midnight, leading the mules back in the dark. There was hay, he tells us, in a peasant's barn. But no food. No water. 'The march resumed around one o'clock, in the most splendid moonlight, and strict silence.'

If they did get lost, the men now knew that they were heading for San Marino. This tiny independent state of just twenty-three square miles was politically neutral. Theoretically neither the Austrians nor the *garibaldini* could enter it. The plan, as Sacchi understood, was to use the territory as a shield, passing quickly to the west of the city itself, so that the Archduke Ernst, to the east, on the coast side, couldn't get at them; then to turn sharply right, through Verucchio and dive down to the sea. However, a message brought during the night changed everything.

Garibaldi still had about 500 horsemen at his service. He was still asking them to perform miracles of reconnaissance and subterfuge. And diplomacy. A party of thirteen horsemen under the twenty-three-year-old Francesco Nullo had been sent direct from Macerata Feltria on the night of the 29th to ask the Captains Regent, the two leaders of San Marino, to grant the *garibaldini* safe and rapid passage. The Sam marinesi had a tradition of sheltering Risorgimento patriots from the Austrian police. However, in the chaos that was the afternoon and evening of the 30th none of the cavalry parties managed to find their way back to the column. So Nullo, who was to be a hero of the Sicilian campaign in 1860, didn't manage to bring the Regents' refusal. Any incursion from Garibaldi, wrote Captain Regent Domenico Maria Belzoppi, would offer the Austrians the excuse for an invasion and very likely end San Marino's independent status once and for all.

Having heard nothing from Nullo, during the afternoon of the 30th Garibaldi sent Ugo Bassi to San Marino to make the same request. Again the order was to ride as swiftly as possible and bring back a positive response. Again no answer had arrived as the column climbed the steep slopes north and east from Villagrande in the dark.

But one cavalry party did get through. And Luigi Migliazza's name comes up again. Barely twenty-four hours after stripping him of his command, on the morning of 30 July Garibaldi had sent Migliazza beyond San Marino to check out the town of Verucchio and warn the locals to prepare rations for them. Somehow, in the night, in the endless forest, Migliazza found the resting *garibaldini* and told the General that Verucchio was already occupied by a large force of Austrians. These were the six battalions of General Hahne. Their encirclement was complete.

As if this wasn't enough, some hours later another messenger intercepted the column on the slopes of Monte San Paolo. But not a *garibaldino*. Consoling himself with a glass of wine after the Captains Regent had once again refused the General's request to pass through their territory, Ugo Bassi looked out of the windows of the Caffè Simoncini, high up on the western side of the city, and saw in the plain below what could only be the campfires of a considerable army. Marching from Verucchio, the Austrians were already in San Marino. With or without permission. Bassi begged the café's proprietor to find a man capable of reaching the column in the dark, to warn Garibaldi not to approach the state, as planned, from the west.

The messenger's name was Francesco della Balda. When he finally found the rebels he was taken for a spy and could easily have been shot. But eventually his message got through. Garibaldi does not seem to have given Hoffstetter any inkling of all this bad news. He did not need to know.

Belluzzi made the trip from Macerata Feltria to San Marino on a donkey, during a summer holiday in the 1890s. He gives his route as Mercato Vecchio, Pietrarubbia, Ca' dei Nanni, Montecopiolo, Serra Bruciata, Monte San Paolo. He had a guide, he says, and it took ten hours. Or rather *they* had a guide; it's one of the rare occasions when Belluzzi mentions his travelling companion, and the only time he names him. He tells us that the beech forest Ruggeri speaks of must have been, according to their guide, the oak forest of Serra Bruciata, Burned Mountain. And he was determined to visit it.

I couldn't find Serra Bruciata on any map, but eventually I hunted down a use of the name on a local website. It was 3000 feet up on a ridge above the Conca valley, four miles east of Montecopiolo. Which made sense. A place that now went by the name of Cuccagna, Cockaigne. Belluzzi writes, 'So the column rested in the immense forest, where I too, together with my young travelling companion, Engineer Nerio Pancerasi, whose sudden death in Constantinople I still mourn, enjoyed an hour of the most sweet repose.'

Postponing our repose until our B & B in San Marino, we followed the road from Mercato Vecchio to Ponte Cappuccini, then began the steep climb to Villagrande. I remember a magnificent mimosa tree and an ancient man propped on his hoe in a vegetable garden that seemed tropically dense. He raised his wrinkled face for a moment at the click of our poles but did not return our greeting. Further on, in red paint on an ugly prefab that bore the legend ROAD SERVICES, PROVINCIA DI PESARO E URBINO, someone had scrawled *THE MOUNTAINS ARE PARTISANS!* It was an idea we instinctively understood. In the mountains, there you feel free.

Moments later our hearts were lifted again by the first sight of the sea. Far, far away to the right, across twenty miles of wooded hills, a long sunny sparkle lit the horizon. We stopped and gazed in thrall to powerful emotions of achievement and arrival: on foot, all the way from Rome, and now the northern Adriatic was in sight. We embraced. And Eleonora reflected that it really was too bad that, with the weather so grim that afternoon, the *garibaldini* weren't able to see it. They would have to wait for the following dawn. Hoffstetter:

We had crossed several high open fields, then, always in silence, followed a paved road in a long gully, from which we emerged, as the sun rose, to find ourselves on the eastern slopes of the Apennines.

Magnificent view! Stretching away beneath us was an endless plain, and beyond it the sea, in all its majesty. Like proud swans, gilded in sunshine, a multitude of ships ploughed a surface that shone like a mirror, while dark blue waves gently greeted the long green shore where, in a generous scatter, we could see Pesaro, Rimini, Cesenatico ... Everyone's eyes moved anxiously

283

across the redeeming deep towards the same goal, and in our souls we saw, rising from the blueness, our last star, last hope, the city of lagoons!

One surely can't see Venice from this position. But it was cheering to imagine it. He does say, 'in our souls'. And writing a year or so after the event, without the benefit of digital photographs, which so use-fully indicate the exact time they were taken, he is probably conflating moments that must have been some distance apart. The next para-graph opens, 'Between the mountains and Rimini, rising perpendicular from the plain is an immense rocky crag. The Republic of San Marino. The city covers just a small part of it, built above a sheer rock wall, while the summit is crowned with two ancient castles ... Everyone, officers and men, pushed forward in astonishment to admire this splendid picture.'

So near and yet so far. Garibaldi knew now that the chances of fighting his way to the sea were minimal. He was between a rock and a hard place. He had left Rome swearing never to surrender to a for-eign power on Italian soil. But now if he did not surrender, around 2000 tired men would very likely be massacred and shot. Not to men-tion his wife and himself. Once again, he organized his troops for the four hours' march that remained: first a 1000-foot dive into the deep gorge, at the bottom of which was the border, then 800 feet up the precipitous rocky slopes to the eastern gate of San Marino. They must arrive, he ordered, as soon as possible, before the Austrians completely surrounded the state. Then, taking just a small escort, he rode on ahead to plead with the Captains Regent himself. So he was not pres-ent when disaster struck.

Towards Villagrande, having used the road to cross all the deep little ravines that slowed the *garibaldini* down, we left Montecopiolo to our left and struck up north-east on a path that eventually leads to Serra Bruciata, now Cuccagna. It was surely the most spectacular of all our walks, a *Lord of the Rings* landscape of mountain, crag and forest, everywhere gorse and blackberries, heath and heather. The *garibaldini* must have felt they were simultaneously in a dream and a nightmare.

We walked through deep woods and across open meadows. The path was stony and rugged and hard on the feet, or it was dusty and black and soft. Sometimes grassy. These uplands are constantly changing, fluid, as if the land shifted with the shifting cirrus, sometimes soft and rolling, but then knotting up in Gothic crags, plunging into dark ravines. Or the turfy surface of a slope breaks into deep crusty scars. You can never be sure how near or far anything is because the gorges suddenly fall away where you thought the ground was solid. In a turn of the head you move from the tame bucolic of Samuel Palmer to the wild romance of Casper Friedrich. Orchard to precipice.

Meantime, the hot sun, hazy air and a general sense of vastness induces a slow stupefaction. You are at once happy and exhausted. You want the walk to last for ever and you want it to end now. Never hope, I told myself at one point, in a voice that seemed to come from some Buddhist koan, that the climb is over. There is always more. It was one of those moments when the ridge you'd set your sights on turns out to be just the beginning of an even steeper slope. The calves stiffen. On the other hand, the voice went on, never fear that the climb will go on for ever. Everything ends. Of course. So just walk. Without hope or fear. Just enjoy.

Now there was a field of dazzling white flowers, now an ascent that felt like climbing a dry mountain torrent. The trees along the way were indeed oaks, small and gnarled and alive with spiders. At last, across a ploughed field full of broken roots and pecking crows, we had our first view of the Most Serene Republic of San Marino. The city is arranged in parallel lines atop a high ridge running north–south, as if a huge ocean liner were beached in the plain just beyond the mountains. It looked so near. And it was only ten o'clock. But we would not be climbing on board till four and gone.

Pleased to have the goal in sight, we took time out to gather blackberries. Or rather, I persuaded Eleonora to join me gathering them. She had never done this before. Italians, who love to gather herbs and mushrooms and wild asparagus, for some reason ignore blackberries.

We filled our Tupperware box, scratched our wrists and shooed away the wasps.

Now there were white long-horn cattle, which made me wonder if the *garibaldini* still had any oxen with them. The big animals were sprawled in full sunshine with an air of utter resignation. A man moved along a line of beehives wearing all the gear. We had reached Cuccagna.

Perhaps there was once an immense forest here. No longer. It's a high, open plateau, with mowed pastures sloping downwards on either side of the road and a couple of ramshackle farm buildings. A woman appeared walking a dog. She took it down into one of the fields and started shouting commands. Heel. Fetch. Then came the clip-clop of three riders on horses. They had climbed up from the San Marino side and were suffering the heat. The horses too seemed sluggish and disheartened. It was partly the heat, says Belluzzi, that undid the *garibaldini* on the morning of the 31st. And their tiredness. But above all the cannon. The cannon they'd hauled 350 miles and never fired.

I was aware of having various things in my pack we had not used so far. Our emergency lightweight tent, for example, and five thick paper maps. Thinking of the cannon, I pulled a map out now and unfolded it on the grass to see if it was any help. We needed to decide whether to go fairly directly to San Marino, approaching from the south-west, where Hahne's men were camped, or, as I wanted, to climb Monte San Paolo, right ahead of us. That way we would be able to approach San Marino from the south and hopefully find the very place where the cannon's undercarriage finally snapped. And the artillerymen, so proud of their vital weapon, insisted on stopping to make repairs.

The map was no help, and our app was at a loss when it came to Monte San Paolo. The route it gave was impossibly roundabout. Google Satellite suggested that the site of the battle, at the bottom of the valley, on the very border of San Marino, was now a residential area. Eleonora said she needed an ibuprofen. Anita, I remembered, had been through hell that morning.

I looked east to where the mountain gathered itself above the plateau. A hawk was circling, gliding with wonderful grace in slow circles over the wooded slopes. Then it came down like a stone on some invisible prey.

'Let's leave it,' I said. 'We can come back some other time.'

'Citizen President,' Garibaldi told Captain Regent Belzoppi, 'my troops, chased by overwhelming Austrian armies, and devastated by forced marches across mountain and chasm, are no longer fit for battle; we have had to cross your border for a few hours' rest and some bread to eat. The men will lay down their arms in your republic, where, in this moment, the Roman War for Italian Independence ends. I come to you as a refugee; accept me as such and accept the burden of becoming guarantor of the safety of those who have followed me.'

'The refugee is welcome,' Belzoppi replied. 'This hospitable land, dear General, will take you in. Rations for your soldiers will be prepared; your wounded will be housed and cared for. In return, you must spare this land the hardships and disasters that we fear. I accept the mandate you give me to mediate; it's a humane duty and as such I am glad to undertake it.'

Could it really have been so simple? So noble? These are the words that have come down to us, first through eyewitnesses, then reported in the historian Pietro Franciosi's account many years later. Whatever the case, the meeting was interrupted by a warning that the column was under attack. Hoffstetter was beside Garibaldi.

Returning in haste, we heard shots. Despite the steep, stony, dangerous roads, we galloped headlong down towards our men. But they were running, frightened to be caught in the gorge, followed by Austrian infantry ... Reaching the steepest part, we saw the general's wife, alone, blocking the flight of the running men, cracking her whip and ordering them to stop and turn.

Having turned away from Monte San Paolo, we began our long flight down from Cuccagna to San Marino. It felt rather like slow-motion flying, as when the plane banks right and left and gradually what seemed so far below grows closer and closer. San Marino on its crag. The sea beyond. Hills and villages coming into clearer and clearer focus. Ever so gradually. One hour, two.

Our track was white stones, winding this way and that. A tractor ploughed between vines. There was a shabby little shrine and withered flowers where long ago a child had died. Donkeys trotted across a paddock wanting to be fed. A pomegranate tree was so full of fruit its branches sagged in the sun.

Frequent water breaks. More blackberry-picking. And then … providence again. Having not seen a single place of refreshment since Mercato Vecchio, we marched into the village of Pieve Corena just before one o'clock and found, with everything else closed, the Caffè ABC open, empty and well stocked with ice and *cedrata*. Sitting outside, we ate the old lady's sandwiches in the shade and rested.

Never rest till you're home and dry. That must be the moral of this tale. On the other hand, how incredibly unlucky, after dragging that cannon 350 arduous miles, that the steering bar of its undercarriage should break just as the men began to haul it up from the bottom of the last gorge towards the city of refuge. A loud crack and a couple of tons of cast iron started to slip back down the slope. The men dashed to halt it.

Clarification. If the Roman Republic held out as long as it did, it was largely thanks to the artillery men who manned the few rebel cannons on the city walls, firing for hours on end while under heavy fire themselves. These were professional soldiers. Many died. The small party that had joined Garibaldi on his long march, bringing just one small cannon, were extremely attached to their weapon, maintaining it with obsessive care, knowing it could be decisive in battle. When, towards ten o'clock of what was already a sweltering hot morning, the steering bar broke, they would not hear of abandoning it. It must be repaired.

The artillerymen had a certain authority. Their fellow soldiers were exhausted and only too glad of the break. The last four days had been an endless sleepless whirl of extreme weather conditions, alarms and endless marching. In particular they had just walked nine hours through the night. Who would not forgive a man who falls asleep in such circumstances?

Garibaldi.

Repairs took two hours. By the time the cannon was ready to move, the advance guard had already reached San Marino, while the rear-guard had long since caught up with the column at the bottom of the gorge and was resting with them. No guards had been set. The men were totally exposed, when all at once the trees above and behind them were alive with white uniforms.

Once again we were looking at a steep descent followed by an arduous climb to end the day. San Marino raises this experience to new levels of masochism. Seen from the west across the gorge, the ground falls sheer away, while on the other side you have the impression of a vertical rock face, whitish brown, occasionally mottled with bushes; you turn anxiously to your app to assure yourself there really is a path up there. Not for nothing is it called Mount Titan. Of course we could have followed the road from Pieve Corena, a busy road that snakes down to the north then approaches the city where a neck of land leads less steeply to the heights. But we were determined that at least this gorge we would cross more or less as the *garibaldini* did. Towards two, with the sun sizzling, we found the gap in the road's crash barrier where the path began and went over the top.

These are badlands. Fit for goats. You mustn't put a foot wrong. Dry, greyish grass at the top, then thicker and thicker brambles and thorns. A woodsman's stone cottage, long abandoned, in dense vegetation. Finally we heard the tiny river at the bottom. The San Marino. Would there be a bridge?

No.

We took our shoes off. 'Only a few still had shoes,' Hoffstetter observes of the *garibaldini* at this point. The air was damp with that rhubarb-like growth you find at the bottom of gullies. And thick nettles. There were snails on tree trunks and twigs catching at your clothes. You could feel the gritty squelch under your toes. But the cool of the water was delightful. We had just got our shoes back on and were ready to tackle a narrow path climbing vertically into the brambles when we heard, to our amazement, the heavy tramp of boots coming down. For a moment I shivered, thinking how vulnerable we were here.

It was a man in his fifties. 'Last time I forded this,' he said, 'I slipped and broke my ankle. You can't imagine how long before they got me out of here.'

The men's immediate instinct, Ruggeri writes, was to get out of that dangerous place as soon as possible. He offers the most sympathetic account. One suspects he was in the fighting, though he never speaks of his personal role. Hoffstetter was merely disgusted, first that the men allowed themselves to be caught napping, then that they ran. It wasn't exactly running, says Ruggeri. Or not running *away*. The officers were trying to get the men to higher ground on the San Marino side, in part to gain a vantage point where they could turn on their attackers, in part to keep the path to safety open.

This clearly wasn't Anita's impression. The first men had already started climbing. The cannon was near the bottom but repaired now and ready to roll when the enemy *Jäger* came pouring down through the trees. And began to launch their rockets. Searing light, loud bangs and flame.

The *garibaldini* ran. More than a thousand men in a tight space. Like sheep. But the artillerymen stayed put, returning rifle fire. They tried to defend their baby. They took casualties. Anita, already higher up the slope, pregnant and exhausted, turned her horse, yelled, lashed out with her whip. 'She was furious with this cowardly flight,' Hoffstetter says. 'That incomparable woman,' Garibaldi remembered years later, 'just couldn't believe that men who in the past had fought so courageously should now be so afraid.' After all, he went on, 'those famous rockets, the Austrians' favourite toy, never hurt anyone'.

Forbes distinguished himself. The ineffable Forbes in his white hat. He was beside Anita trying to stem the tide. Isolated and overwhelmed, the last artillerymen abandoned the cannon and ran. With the return of Garibaldi and his staff, some order was re-established. A rearguard was set up where the ground levelled out, while Anita was given the task of leading the column up endless hairpins to the city walls.

With the advantage of the slope, the line now held. Once again the Austrians pulled back. They didn't want to take losses. In a dispatch to D'Aspre on 1 August, Stadion presented the attack as a huge success. 'The rebels fled in total disorder at the sight of a few rockets. Their one cannon and much of their camping equipment was seized.' He does not mention his own side's failure to follow up. 'In the end, although it might have looked like a rout,' Ruggeri concludes, 'we only had a few light wounds.' Garibaldi mentions deaths among the artillerymen, but does not say how many. The column topped Mount Titan towards midday in blistering heat.

'There were two thousand of us,' wrote Captain Raimondo Bonnet years later, 'dead tired, not so much from hunger and hardship as from the disheartening awareness that the Italians had so quickly forgotten the holy cause of independence.'

Oreste Brizi, a pro-Austrian member of the San Marino elite, was beside the road watching.

One thousand five hundred infantry made up the Cosmopolitan Garibaldi Band. More than 300 men on horseback and no small number of beasts of burden. You could see boys of 12 to 15 still terrified from their last battle, when they threw down their arms to run faster; you could see horsemen walking and infantry men on horseback; uniforms of various colours and styles, filthy, in tatters, all higgledy-piggledy; heterogeneous weapons, black with rust; horses exhausted and poorly harnessed. Soldiers with daggers at their sides and cartridge belts across their chests. Like bandits. Red caps with shredded feathers, white cloaks and long beards; but no cannons, and no discipline.

Quoting this, Belluzzi is beside himself with indignation.

This writer, who is so scornful, so pleased that the ill-starred Roman Republic has finally fallen, is nevertheless obliged to confess it took only two of Garibaldi's officers at the San Francesco gate, to deter this 'unruly horde' from entering the city, steering them to the nearby convent of the Cappuccini. And in his whole malicious account he is unable to record a single theft, or killing, or even a serious argument.

It took us an hour and twenty to climb Mount Titan. Stopping every few minutes to get our breaths in the heavily scented air. At the edge of town, almost the first thing we saw was one of those big steel containers where people can donate their old clothes. I imagined the *garibaldini* dumping their filthy red shirts. Which not so many years later would become collectors' items, displayed in museums all over the land.

We dropped our stuff in our B & B, a half-mile outside the walls, showered and rested, then climbed the last stretch in the early evening. It's spectacular. From Porta San Francesco, on the city's west side, the men would have been able to look out across the broad panorama of the Apennines, and down to where the Austrians were camped in the plain. They had escaped by the skin of their teeth. The convent where most of them were housed is 200 yards to the south, just outside the walls, but entirely safe from attack, because perched, like all the city, over precipitous rock faces. Shortly after they had been led there, Garibaldi sat on the steps outside the building, borrowed a drum to put on his knee, stretched a piece of paper over its skin, and with an old stub of pencil wrote the order of the day.

San Marino, 31 July, 1849
We have reached the land of refuge, and we owe our hosts our best behaviour. That way we will have deserved the consideration due to persecution and misfortune.

From this moment on I release my companions from any obligation in my regard, leaving them free to return to their private lives, but reminding them that Italy must not remain in disgrace and that it is better to die than to live as slaves to the foreigner.

These words are now engraved on a plaque on the convent wall. Handing the scrap of paper to his officers, Garibaldi must have been perfectly aware the drama wasn't over yet. Archduke Ernst had already rejected San Marino's offer of mediation. Nothing less than total sur- render would do, he said. The Pope himself demanded it. If Garibaldi refused, he warned, the people of San Marino must expel the rebels from their city; the Austrians would then exterminate them on the slopes of Mount Titan.

DAY 25

31 July 1849 – 18 August 2019

San Marino

Ruggeri's and Hoffstetter's books are full of small mistakes. Rushed into print in 1850 and 1851, in Genoa and Turin, hastily translated in Hoffstetter's case, they have been unavailable for 150 years. No new editions. No corrections. Place names are misspelled, explanations offered that cannot be right. Sometimes Hoffstetter gets his dates mixed up. Immediately after the arrival of the column at the Cappuccini convent, he writes, '*1° agosto*', indicating a new day. I thus assumed that Garibaldi had spent both the 31st and the 1st in San Marino, and in consequence we decided to treat ourselves to a day there. In fact, the General left the city around 11 p.m. on the 31st. He had spent just fifteen hours in the place. When or if he slept we do not know.

We, however, had time for a leisurely breakfast with our Airbnb hosts, a young Sammarinese and his Russian wife. They had met couch-surfing, they said, and were just back from six months in India with their baby girl. They spoke earnestly of the need to be free, to travel, but felt that Garibaldi had made a mistake uniting Italy. The country's many states should have remained free and independent, like San Marino. When Eleonora pointed out that most of the Italian states had been neither free nor independent and that San Marino had only been allowed to maintain its republican status because it was so tiny, he assured us that sooner or later the other states would have been free. How he did not know. On the subject of the EU, he thought it necessary for its member states to surrender their sovereignty to the union so as not to be overwhelmed by the other great powers, China, Russia, the USA. To each his inconsistencies. Very kindly, he gave us a copy of *The Republic of San Marino, Historic and Artistic Guide of the City of Castles*. While I was cleaning my teeth, Eleonora found the pages referring to 1849 and read out loud:

> Without dismounting from his horse, Garibaldi rode straight to the Public Palace. The doors of the houses were barred, not a woman was to be seen on the steep streets: the 'buccaneer' was in town, the 'lady-killer', the 'red devil'. All at once, a window opened and a mother and daughter appeared. The girl couldn't contain her emotion and cried: 'Mother, that's no murderer. Look, he has the same face as the Nazarene!

Piety is in the air in San Marino. The streets are obsessively swept, the asphalt brightly painted. Blue and yellow lines adorn every kerb. You always know where you can park, or cross, or turn. Outside Porta San Francesco a tall policewoman stands beside a sentry box deciding who can enter and who cannot. She wears blue trousers, orange shirt, peaked cap and dark glasses. Has a military bearing. Her hand signs are elegant and abrupt. Everyone obeys.

Behind her, outside the walls and directly below the gate, there is a parking space for about fifteen tourist coaches. Herds climb the steps, following the abundant signs provided. Inside the gate, fifty yards across cobbles to the left is, or was, Lorenzo Simoncini's café, where Garibaldi spent most of his time in San Marino. Now, beneath a plaque that declares, 'In this house, surrounded by German arms, Garibaldi refused the terms of surrender,' a menu of the day is posted on a large board. Top of the list is lasagne. Eleonora shakes her head.

Aside from the food, we are in luck. The Pinacoteca San Francesco, right opposite the city gate, is advertising a special exhibition. GARIBALDI IN SAN MARINO. A poster features the famous print, *Garibaldi and Anita towards San Marino*, made by Roberto Franzoni in 1949. The buccaneer and his wife now look like they are starring in some elegant costume drama. Sporting smart cloaks and fancy hats, they top a hill on handsome horses. It's a parade. Among those riding behind is a second woman who appears to be wearing a fur coat. In midsummer.

We buy a ticket that covers all the state's six museums, but decide first to find the hotel, in the centre, that we've booked into for this evening. 'I'm on Greta's side,' says a poster by the door. Opposite, through glossy glass, are three shop dummies in stylish pink and grey coats. BRASCHI, FUR COLLECTIONS, the sign announces.

It was a Lieutenant Giambattista Braschi who took Archduke Ernst the message bearing Garibaldi's rejection of unconditional surrender. The archduke was camped down in Fiorentino, two miles and 700 feet below. There was no question of the people of San Marino forcing the *garibaldini* out of the city, Braschi warned the archduke, because the walls were breached in many places and the General's men were still armed.

The archduke began to place cannons and rockets on the heights opposite the ancient town.

Next to the Braschi fur shop is a window displaying Chanel, Givenchy, Dior. Then a supermarket for fine liquors. San Marino is a vast duty-free store. This is what the tourists come for. This is how it exploits its postage-stamp sovereignty. And many shops are selling postage stamps. San Marino produces them on an industrial scale. Philatelists abound. *Garibaldi and Anita towards San Marino* comes in five different values and colours. Then there's Ugo Bassi in his priest's hat, fifteen cents. Garibaldi with an ostrich feather, fifty cents. Anita, looking as if painted by Rubens, five cents.

All this would be innocent enough, were it not for the weapons. There are gun shops everywhere. Rifles, semi-automatics, Kalashnikovs. HOT SHOT, one particularly busy emporium is called. Displayed beside the guns are racks of baseball bats. But these aren't sports shops. Matteo Salvini, we have read, is seeking to relax Italy's gun laws. He's a great supporter of neighbourhood vigilante groups. 'Any soldier found guilty of selling his rifle will be shot,' Garibaldi warned his soldiers as the men tried to come to terms with the disbanding of the legions.

The tourists gaze into the windows of their choice. Girls and women, men and boys. They do not seem to be visiting the museums. Except the Museum of Medieval Criminality and Torture, which is attracting much attention. And the two picture-book castles that top the town. Here, on walkways connecting ancient stone towers, there's barely room to move. Everybody is sweating profusely from the steep climb up the cobbled streets. The views from the battlements don't disappoint. The sea is a beguiling blue haze, the hills wonderfully textured with their woods and stubble and scarps. In the larger of the two castles is a well stocked museum of weaponry. People are queuing.

But back at the Pinacoteca San Francesco, nobody. Not a single soul in the Garibaldi exhibition. The two women at the door seem taken aback when we enter. In the first room a startled guard looks up from her phone. The timeline panels introducing the show set out a clear narrative: San Marino saved Garibaldi and, in so doing, made a crucial contribution to the eventual unification of Italy. '30 July, Ugo Bassi arrives in San Marino asking for permission to cross the territory.' The panel doesn't say that permission was denied. Twice.

But the relics are fascinating. Garibaldi's saddle. One of the many, one presumes. With a fancy pommel and iron studs. Garibaldi's pistol, elaborately engraved. A camp fork, its iron prongs folding into an ivory handle. A camp spoon. A banner of the PRIMA LEGIONE ROMANA. A rubber stamp of the Roman Republic. A small silver container that was Ugo Bassi's holy-oil sprinkler. Leaving San Marino in haste, he didn't have time to pack his bag.

Above all, there's the handwriting. Garibaldi's orders of the day: decisive, sharply slanted pen strokes. 'Anyone found sleeping on sentry duty will be shot.' 'Officers must set an example.' 'The men must not be allowed to straggle.'

Archduke Ernst's response to Belzoppi's attempt to mediate is just eight lines scrawled at the top of a piece of notepaper. 'I am acting on behalf of the Pope who will accept nothing but total surrender.' Whoever actually wrote the words, in Italian, was having problems with his pen. The ink wasn't flowing. Scratches and blots. The paper bears the stamp of the San Marino government archive.

Captain Regent Belzoppi had also sent a messenger to General Hahne, the archduke's superior, in Rimini. An hour away on horseback.

Ernst, we should remember, although a cousin of Emperor Franz Joseph and a distant cousin of the Grand Duke of Tuscany, was only twenty-four years old. Hahne was in his sixties. He sent a negotiator, Adolfo De Fidler, who arrived shortly after Ernst's negative response. 'I have received your message,' Garibaldi scrawls to Belzoppi on a note without date or time, 'and would ask you to complete the negotiations in all haste.' While they were talking, the Austrians were reinforcing their positions.

Towards five in the afternoon Garibaldi was called to the Palazzo Pubblico and handed a larger sheet of paper, roughly scribbled on both sides with plenty of blots. I had to ask Eleonora to photograph it; my hand was shaking. The hand that wrote it was uncertain too. Some of the nouns are given capital letters, as if the writer might be more used to German than Italian. Some words are crossed out. Others inserted in tiny letters.

There were nine conditions. The men would lay down their arms. They would be divided according to their Italian regions, then escorted home by Austrian forces and handed over to the civil authorities. Only those accused of 'common crimes' would be punished. The Republic of San Marino would be compensated for its expenses with seizure of the column's horses, mules and equipment. All guns and money would go to the Austrians. Garibaldi would be obliged to depart for America with Anita and must promise never to return. The rebels had until midday tomorrow, 1 August, to respond. Assuming they accepted, the agreement would only come into force after the governor of Bologna, General Gorzkowsky, had given his assent, until which time there would be a ceasefire and no troop movements. As a guarantee, two representatives of the Republic of San Marino and two of Garibaldi's top officers must go to Rimini as hostages.

Reading through the terms, Garibaldi observed to Captain Regent Belzoppi that he had not asked him to negotiate on his personal behalf, only on behalf of his men. He had no intention of leaving Italy. It was humiliating, he pointed out, that only one side should be asked to provide hostages. And unacceptable that his men, once disarmed, should be obliged to submit to an Austrian escort. After thanking the captain profusely for his efforts, he asked for a clean copy to be made so that he could discuss the terms with his officers.

There is only one other example of the General's handwriting in the exhibition: three lines on a thin strip of paper. Written in sharp pencil, without hesitation or second thoughts, nor any indication of time, date, place, or person addressed, it says:

The conditions imposed on you by the
Austrians are unacceptable and therefore
we are leaving the territory.
Yours. G. Garibaldi.

How curious that 'you' is! As if the guest were seeking to save his host from embarrassment.

Leaving the museum, we drifted back to the Simoncini café, barely fifty yards away. Perhaps we could eat there, lasagne or no lasagne. But the place was full. No doubt that note from Garibaldi had been written on one of the tables in there, late in the evening. The problem, all the General's officers agreed when they got together to decide their fate, was Gorzkowsky. A Polish aristocrat now in his seventies, the military governor of the region was entirely committed to the empire. Italian patriotism directly challenged his own decision not to support Polish independence. Leading the Austrian invasion of the Papal States in 1848, Gorzkowsky had been personally responsible for the heavy shelling of both Bologna and Ancona. Hoffstetter in particular argued vehemently that the governor would never agree to Hahne's lenient terms. It was a trick. The Austrians were deploying more troops by the hour.

Trick or not, Hoffstetter was right.

From General Gorzkowsky in Bologna to Field Marshal Radetzky in Monza
This very moment I have received a communication from Major General Hahne dated Rimini, 1 August, two in the morning, according to which the whole Garibaldi mob is now in the territory of San Marino.

In relation to these rebels, Major General Hahne, acting against my advice, has undertaken a negotiation with the Republic which is protecting this infamous band.

Your Excellency will be so good as to peruse the terms and conditions attached.

To resolve this question quickly and effectively I am leaving this minute for Rimini by stagecoach.

To give more power to my Diktat – a demand for total and unconditional surrender of all this horde – I have ordered the following troops to follow by forced marches under the command of Colonel Count Creneville:

The Creneville battalion of grenadiers
5 companies
½ cavalry squadron
1 horse-drawn battery
¼ rocket battery
1, 4-horse cart and 5, 2-horse carts with munitions
The Marziani battalion of grenadiers
2 Romanian companies
½ cavalry squadron
2 mortars
1 howitzer battery

If Garibaldi does not bow to my conditions, I am determined to invade that miniscule Republic with force of arms.

Hahne felt the situation should be defused, and Garibaldi consequently diminished, whereas Gorzkowsky wanted blood. In the café, on the afternoon of 31 July, Hoffstetter and others felt sure that the governor's real intention was to capture and perhaps execute the General himself. 'As one man,' Ruggeri writes, 'the officers rejected the terms. 'Onward,' they said. 'Let's break through their lines, fighting if necessary. Then to Venice!'

★

We could not summon up any interest in San Marino's other museums. Walking past the now familiar pottery from centuries past, the interminable coins and medals, the religious relics and second-rate paintings, the only question for discussion was Garibaldi's decision. How can one not be fascinated by the psychology of decision-making? We remembered times when we had had to decide whether to leave the university, or to leave a partner, take this job or that. How hard it is. And here hundreds of lives were at stake.

After grabbing a sandwich, we walked down to the convent of the Cappuccini again. Lorenzo Simoncini had gone there personally to fetch Anita and take her to his café. She was ashen and finding it hard even to stand. In the convent grounds the men were recovering from their heroic efforts. They were anxious that the Austrian forces had moved closer. Some were crying. Many angry. 'How did they react the following morning,' Eleonora asked, 'when they heard that Garibaldi was gone?'

'We'll discuss that tomorrow,' I said. Already I felt eager to be walking again. It was a sort of hunger.

'You don't have a sore tendon,' Eleonora pointed out.

Retiring to our hotel room to escape from the sun, we went through the photographs we'd taken of the display cases in the Garibaldi exhibition. It was another lucky moment. Eleonora pointed to something we hadn't noticed during the visit: a rather childish-looking home-made album with a typewritten label. It was displayed among other books and half obscured by the butt of a rifle laid across its cover. Zooming in on the photo, we managed to read a few words, written with a manual typewriter on a white label. 'Gino Zani, BADARLON SPEAKS.' I vaguely remembered having seen the name Zani, but who was Badarlon? Idly, I typed the names in Google. A website came up at once. For the next hour we were riveted. Written in 1949, this was material neither Trevelyan or Belluzzi had seen.

'Feel like going for a walk?'

Francesco della Balda, the man who had taken Ugo Bassi's message to Garibaldi on Monte San Paolo, addressed these words to Badarlon around 6 p.m. on 31 July. 'Badarlon' – meaning simpleton hunk – was the ironic nickname of Nicola Zani, a hemp curer with a second job: he would take groups of young refugees from Lombardy and the Veneto, men fleeing conscription into the Austrian army, and guide them all the way to Rome, after which they went on to Naples and safety.

'I guessed at once what I was being asked to do,' Badarlon later remembered. The man reporting his words was his grandson Gino Zani, who wrote the story down in his own old age. And the man who put it all online in 2007, the second centenary of Garibaldi's birth, was another Nicola Zani, Gino's grandson.

Badarlon was twenty-six. He was drinking in Simoncini's café, a meeting point for liberals, when his friend Della Balda took him upstairs. 'Garibaldi got to his feet. When he heard I was to be the guide, he looked me over from head to toe. His eyes were steel. All the other officers looked on in silence. I was so flustered no words would come. Anita smiled.' Cesenatico was the destination. By tomorrow. They would have to get through the Austrian lines. 'Of course I was afraid!' Badarlon told his grandson.

Garibaldi asked the guide how much he wanted. He was always up front about money. He offered four *scudi*. But Badarlon suspected the General had even less money than he did and refused. 'In any event, I realized my friends had chosen me because, being a citizen of the Papal States, not San Marino, if I was captured, no responsibility would fall on the republic. Very smart.'

Formalities over, Badarlon made to go home, to prepare for the long hike.

'You're not leaving here now,' Garibaldi said sharply.

'But my passport's at home.'

'You don't need a passport with me.'

Since he was unable to say goodbye to his wife, she was brought to the café, briefly, with their young son Pio. The Pope's name. She just had time to notice that Anita was in a desperate state. 'Swollen up, and dressed like a man, like the other rough women who followed the *gari-baldini*.' But Anita stroked Pio's blonde curls and smiled at the boy.

Confined in the room the whole evening, Badarlon understood very little. The officers spoke in different dialects, foreign languages. There was a lot of cigar smoke. 'I did realize that Anita kept trying to persuade Garibaldi to disguise himself.' Garibaldi refused. Leading armed men, he must be dressed as a soldier. Anita asked Simoncini's wife for a peasant's dress for herself. 'To set an example,' Badarlon thought. Ciceruacchio turned up with his son Lorenzo. And we discover that Ciceruacchio wore two gold earrings, 'like a woman'. The general gathered a number of documents on the window sill and set light to them. Then they ate. 'No one spoke, they were all anxious.' A lieutenant of the San Marino army came and told them the gate would be opened at eleven. Collusion. Now Braschi, Belzoppi's messenger, arrived bringing a paper. 'The General read it, then said to everyone: "If you want to come with me, come. A good republican never gives in!"'

You have to wonder what was in that paper, coming directly from the republic's head of state. No other account of the story mentions it.

'After so many years,' writes Gino Zani in 1949, 'my grandparents' memory may have betrayed them over this or that detail. Mine too. If any of this is incorrect, I beg pardon of the historians and invite them to put it right.'

'Funny the guide's wife mentioned other women,' Eleonora remarks.

We're eating in a restaurant just outside the walls. In the open air. Which is finally beginning to cool.

'Belluzzi mentions a woman whose husband had been killed in the siege in Rome and who marched with the column as far as Terni, where she lived. And another woman, in Cetona, weeping because her lover had been killed. Also in Cetona, the archives mention Colonel Rulli and his wife making a request for clothes. Not a word otherwise. Nothing in Hoffstetter, nothing in Ruggeri.'

'Men just don't care.'

But the question bothering me is this: did Garibaldi betray his men, abandoning them in the night? Was it a disloyal thing to do?

Eleonora reflects. 'He had disbanded them, hadn't he? He'd freed them from their oath.'

'According to Hoffstetter, he was furious about their behaviour under attack. Said he didn't want to have anything more to do with this rabble.'

'Words spoken in the heat of the moment.'

'You're very pro-Garibaldi today!'

Eleonora laughs. It's unusual, she says, seeing me less than enthusiastic. I admit that to me it does seem a moral issue, leaving these men to their fate without so much as a goodbye, the very ones who hadn't deserted.

Over a carafe of house wine we talk through the various scenarios that would have been on offer in the Simoncini café 170 years ago.

'If Garibaldi had stayed and they all surrendered, would that have improved the men's situation?' Eleonora asks.

'It's hard to see how. And if he had stayed and they decided to fight, they'd most likely have been massacred.'

Only at this point did the obvious occur to me. Without Garibaldi, the men were infinitely less dangerous. The Austrians could perhaps afford to honour their preliminary agreement. At least with regard to the rank and file.

'There you are,' Eleonora says. 'Whereas if he'd stayed and surrendered, he'd have been handing a huge propaganda coup to the enemy. Without gaining anything for the faithful.'

'Perhaps I just wish he could have taken them all with him, instead of a couple of hundred.'

'I suppose,' Eleonora muses, 'he didn't think it was feasible. Getting all those men going again, after officially disbanding them. Did he leave anyone in command?'

'Gaetano Sacchi, who had been with him in South America. And commanded the First Legion throughout the march.'

'I can't see how he could be fairer. He deprives himself of his main man.'

The sunlight had turned pink. We declined a sweet. We still had a box full of blackberries in the hotel fridge. At Porta San Francesco, we looked out over the parapet across hills hardening into silhouettes, as if in a child's pop-up book. The gorge below was already in darkness.

There were no Austrian campfires tonight, but streetlights were coming on in the area called Borgo Maggiore, about halfway down the mountain and a little to the north, the opposite side to where the archduke's men had camped. Garibaldi headed there around 11 p.m. with Badarlon, Anita and a half-dozen officers. They would then wait for the others. How these last faithful few were chosen, or how they chose themselves, we do not know.

'In response to an absolute need to sleep,' writes Ruggeri, 'and unknown to their respective captains, some men had taken advantage of the hospitality of the citizens to rest in their houses, and so did not get the call. Others had given up all hope of success, considering the extreme difficulty of the enterprise.'

Returning to the hotel, we passed a rose bed featuring a hybrid named after Anita. 'A rose as symbol of hope, liberty and faithfulness, across the centuries.'

'Perhaps the word "stubbornness" should be in there,' Eleonora thought. 'She should have stayed in town.'

'Badarlon remembers she was "stubborn as a mule".'

Packing my bag to be ready for a pre-dawn departure, I decided to throw away *The Republic of San Marino, Historic and Artistic Guide of the City of Castles*. It was printed on glossy photographic paper and far too heavy. Then with that feeling of regret I always have when I part with a book, I pulled it out of the waste-paper basket and read the opening pages while we ate the blackberries.

San Marino, it seemed, owed its foundation to a woman's stubbornness. Marino, a stonecutter, had fled Christian persecution in Dalmatia in the third century and taken refuge in Rimini, where he worked on rebuilding the city's walls, but also preaching and becoming saintly. Twelve years on, a woman arrived from Dalmatia, claiming she was his wife. Marino fled to Mount Titan, whose stone quarries he was already familiar with. It took her a year, but eventually she found him up there, at which point he shut himself away in a cave and refused to speak to her. After a six-day stand-off she gave up and left. Marino climbed to the top of Mount Titan, built a church and dedicated it to St Peter. San Marino would be his town.

'Reminds me,' Eleonora said, 'of San Francesco's miracle in Citerna. Ridding himself of the woman who bothered him.'

This was something Garibaldi wasn't able to do. Everybody, Badarlon noticed in that long evening in Simoncini's café, was trying to persuade Anita to stay in San Marino, where she could be looked after. In his memoir Garibaldi writes, 'A most dear but distressing hindrance was my Anita, well on with her pregnancy now and ill: I begged her to remain in that place of refuge. In vain. That generous heart of hers disdained all my warnings, and forbade me saying another word on the subject with the accusation: "You want to leave me."'

'Crazy, crazy jealousy!' Eleonora is not so impressed by Anita as others are. 'What did she think he was going to do, run after another woman?'

'I suppose she felt insecure. She'd been left behind before.'

We both woke in the early hours with serious stomach aches.

DAY 26

1 August 1849 – 19 August 2019

San Marino, Borgo Maggiore, Torriana, San Giovanni
in Galilea, Sogliano al Rubicone, Borghi, Musano,
Cento – 25 miles

Borgo Maggiore

Garibaldi wrote his novel *Clelia, or The Government of the Priests* in 1868,
long after the heroics that led to the unification of Italy but before
Rome was added to the kingdom in 1870. His declared aims were to
remember the dead, to denounce the Church's continued possession of
what must be Italy's capital city and 'to earn some money to make ends
meet'. At the heart of the novel is a figure, evidently the General himself, named Il Solitario, who lives on a tiny island, La Solitaria. In his
sixties then, despite a life spent among men willing to die for him and
women of every social class eager for romance, this was how Garibaldi
saw himself: solitary, making tough decisions alone, ever alert to
betrayal and incompetence, obliged again and again to leave companions behind, wounded or dead, to move on, start over. Looking at the
whole trajectory of his life, it could well have been in these first days of
August 1849 that the General began to think of himself as Il Solitario.

We rose at 5.30. Perhaps our miserable night and upset stomachs
would bring us closer in spirit to those we were following. There was
a long paved walkway down to Borgo Maggiore, a drop of 600 feet in
moon- and lamplight, with a vertical rock wall rising to the right and
the hillside falling sharply to the left. As we rounded Mount Titan, the
sea was tinged with pink; it seemed extremely close.

Down in the main square of Borgo Maggiore, Garibaldi waited for
others to join him. Ruggeri was not among them. Nor Migliazza. Nor

Marocchetti. The General had insisted that Major Cenni go back and fetch Ugo Bassi, who faced certain execution in the Papal States. They waited an hour, Hoffstetter remembers, speaking in whispers while something over a hundred cavalry and a hundred and fifty infantry gathered.

Bassi arrived. Forbes was there. Pilhes, Ceccaldi, Ciceruacchio. Anita was so ill she had to be taken into a house to lie down. Garibaldi sent scouts ahead to check the way was free. We took a photograph of the plaque on the house in the square where Captain Regent Domenico Belzoppi was born. 'With great political astuteness, he saved Garibaldi from Papal and Austrian rage, thus ensuring the freedom of Italy.'

A generous assessment.

Torriana

Shortly after midnight they set off 'at a brisk pace', says Badarlon. Garibaldi was wearing his white poncho, riding about a hundred yards ahead of the main group. The guide was anxious about his visibility. 'If we run into the Germans, the first bullets will be for you.' Not at all, Garibaldi assured him. 'If the Austrians fire, it will be at the main group, not the advance patrol.'

I was far from calm on this stretch of the road. Suddenly the blackberries were back. With a vengeance. I was in urgent need of a toilet. Rounding a bend, providence provided. There was a camper park tucked under the cliff. In the park a little brick building. Emerging much relieved, I found Eleonora with a broad smile on her face. She had been studying Google Maps, which showed Il Sacello del Santo in the rocks right above us, the cave where San Marino had hidden from the woman who claimed to be his wife. You wonder what it smelled like after six days barricaded in there.

Since the General's scouts had reported that this part of the hillside was free from Austrian troops, Badarlon had chosen the fastest, easiest route. But now a 'kind of ghost' was seen, slinking off the road ahead into a vineyard. Garibaldi was quickly off his horse. It

turned out to be a 'thickset peasant in shirtsleeves'. When the man refused to say what he was about, he found a pistol at his chest. He had been asked, he said, to go up to San Marino and report on what Garibaldi was doing. By the Austrians. They were in Pietracuta, a village close to where the tiny San Marino river, flowing from the south, runs into the larger Marecchia and thence east to Rimini. Right on their route.

Badarlon took them off the road and plunged down a stream, Il Fosso del Re. The King's Ditch. It was steep. 'All stones and mud.' The men went down as quietly as they could. 'At a trot.' The infantry jogging after. No one spoke. The spy had been tied to a saddle in their midst.

We didn't feel ready for a muddy ditch so early in the morning. Staying on the road, we met a thickset man in a white shirt, braces and puttees, leading a horse by the bridle. 'It's too steep to ride on the asphalt here,' he explained. 'The horseshoes slip.' But down by the river there were paths. The animal needed exercise before the day got too hot.

Never having ridden a horse myself, I was impressed, walking alongside it, by how large the beast was, a great glistening chestnut with a pink blanket under its saddle and a magnificent swishing black tail, beautifully groomed, excitingly aromatic. From time to time it turned its head to push against its master's hand. Belatedly, it came home to me what an intimate relationship this must have been for a cavalryman, living day and night with his horse, with its strength and odour, alert to its peculiar disposition. How gratifying and involving. And what hard work. Finding food and water, checking hooves, grooming. What trust too, as the animal felt for its footing on a steep stony riverbed in the dark.

When we asked our rider if there was a footbridge anywhere to cross the Marecchia, since the road bridges seemed to be either a mile to the left or two miles to the right, in Verucchio, he launched into impossibly detailed instructions. This church. That bend in the road. We would trust, we thought, to our app, and if we had to ford it, then we would. Saying goodbye to horse and horseman, we stopped to drink a little water beside a tree teeming with apricots, all glowing gold in the seven o'clock sun.

The Fosso del Re is paved over for the 200 yards before it flows into the San Marino. To accommodate a small industrial area. This was where the *garibaldini*, in their royal ditch, must have passed fairly close to the Austrians. Unsurprisingly, their only advantage was surprise; the imperial troops wouldn't expect boldness from men who had fled so abjectly the morning before.

Finally on the flat, having descended 1200 feet, we zigzagged through woods and past factories and at last reached the Marecchia. It had taken two hours, exactly the time Hoffstetter gives. 'A river about a thousand paces wide,' he says, 'but almost dry.' It hasn't changed. We found an expanse of whitish stones before a steep bank on the far side. A wild, empty place. In the middle nothing more than a shallow stream. But there was the luxury of a little wooden footbridge.

For the *garibaldini* it was their point of maximum exposure. They hurried across the water, filed some way along the further bank to find the new path then struck up into the thick vegetation of the hillside. They had been climbing fast for some minutes 'when suddenly a volley of gunfire'.

Badarlon was frightened. 'All I had was a pistol.' Garibaldi called a halt and pulled out his telescope. In the moonlight two Austrian cavalry patrols, moving from opposite directions, had met on the dry riverbed. But why the shots? The General waited a minute or two, then ordered, 'Onward.'

We obeyed, trudging up a whitish mud track through dry, faintly scented foliage. Rocky outcrops everywhere. A medieval tower, squat and grey on the ridge ahead. San Marino a stark profile in the morning sky behind. The day was warming up.

At this point in the adventure Badarlon's version and Hoffstetter's begin to diverge, radically, and ominously. Just as they had reached the Marecchia, Garibaldi had asked the German to ride back and urge on the infantry. Some were lagging. It was dark. They needed to stay tight. When he got to the stragglers they complained about the pace. It was hard keeping up with horsemen. Just two more hours,

Hoffstetter urged, and they'd be able to ease off. Just! His account then launches into a wonderfully nerdish, military-man's reflection on the speed that light infantry can move across rough country if unencumbered with mules and cannons. 'Even poorly shod, the men were more or less matching the cavalry.' He is quite unaware that he and his beloved general will never meet again.

'Suddenly someone called my name,' he writes, 'and I saw Ugo Bassi riding towards me.' The monk had fallen asleep on his horse. He was confused, lost. Together with the infantry, they arrived at the Marecchia, but having crossed the dry riverbed they couldn't find the path up the further bank. They had their own guide, a friend of Badarlon, but he only knew the way this far. He promised to bring another local man. The group waited, exposed, by the water, on the white stones. 'There were about sixty of us, including Forbes and other officers.' The new guide eventually arrived – one wonders how these men found each other in the dead of night – and led the soldiers to the path. It was narrow. They would have to move in single file. The horses went first. But all at once an Austrian cavalry patrol was thundering towards them along the riverbed. Lancers, lowering their weapons. 'Don't shoot!' Hoffstetter ordered. It would only alert more Austrians. There was a skirmish. Two wounded men were dragged into the thick trees on the steep slope where the enemy couldn't follow.

Was this the moment when the advanced group heard gunfire? The times don't match, Hoffstetter had ordered his men not to fire. But if the Austrians had arrived earlier – as spied by Garibaldi with his telescope – how could Hoffstetter and the others have waited for their guide on the riverbed? Again and again in this long story you realize how much doesn't fit, how impossible it is to know the past. People in different places experiencing different things, their sense of time quite different, depending on what they were going through, some men knowing the territory well, some disorientated, some in pain, some thirsty or hungry, some wide awake, others half asleep, some trudging, some fighting, some fleeing. Each man had his own experience, then his own account. All we know here is that the last exchange between Garibaldi and Hoffstetter was an order to go back and ensure the men stayed together. The German obeyed, and failed.

San Giovanni in Galilea

A word on the route is essential now. The goal is Cesenatico, a small fishing port thirteen miles up the coast from Rimini, where Hahne will soon be facing the wrath of Gorzkowsky. From San Marino the obvious route, taking the best roads, involved proceeding to Rimini then north. In Garibaldi's circumstances this was impossible. An alternative would be to descend the Marecchia a little, somehow bypassing Verucchio, and then proceed diagonally across the plain. This too was risky. The men would be highly visible, constantly exposed to attack. Advised by the patriots in Simoncini's café, Garibaldi had opted to stay in the hills as far north as Longiano, then go straight down to the coast, bypassing the towns of Savignano sul Rubicone and Gatteo. This limited their exposure to about nine miles. 'If we get split up,' the General had told Hoffstetter, 'look for me near Savignano.'

As a result of this strategy, they, and now we, were travelling against the run of the land and the drift of the roads and paths. No one in normal circumstances would follow such a route. 'Up narrow tracks, across fields, along the ridges of the gullies,' recalls Badarlon. So having climbed to Torriana, we now have to plunge straight down again to the river Uso, another sad trickle in the fierce summer heat, then steeply up again to San Giovanni in Galilea. These are rugged hills, far from the picturesque beauty of Tuscany or the grandeur of the high passes. The grass is white and brittle, alive with insects. We passed a huge quarry. The whole hillside had been demolished, leaving a near-vertical cliff of zigzagging chalk-white terraces. RIPA CALBANA, said a sign. Stone breaking. But the men must have been on holiday; the only sound was the baying of guard dogs running along the wire fencing.

'We arrived in San Giovanni' – the next hilltop – 'tired, throats burning,' says Badarlon, 'hoping for a break.' Garibaldi ordered them to keep going. Their only salvation was speed. We marched and sang behind. Perhaps thanks to yesterday's conversation about women soldiers, I suddenly remembered 'Sweet Polly Oliver'. It went pretty well to the click of the poles.

> As sweet Polly Oliver lay musing in bed,
> A sudden strange fancy came into her head.
> 'Nor father nor mother shall make me false prove,
> I'll 'list as a soldier, and follow my love.'

Amazingly I can remember this word for word from singing lessons in primary school. About fifty-five years ago. In Blackpool, Lancashire. Any and every moment, I suppose, inevitably fuses the present with fragments of personal history; the older we are the greater the possibility of bizarre connections. Unfortunately, I could only remember the first verse. I sang it over and over, hoping the rest would follow. It wouldn't. It was lost. With Hoffstetter.

'*Basta!*' Eleonora yelled. 'The hell with Polly Oliver.'

'What an intolerant young woman you are!'

'And what a boring old man you are! So attached to your boring old England.'

'*Terruncella!*'

'*Perfida Albione.*'

Suddenly our voices were drowned by barking. A dozen dogs came rushing to a makeshift wire gate: Labradors, terriers, collies, each determined to bark the loudest. Astonishingly, there was a little corgi that had lost a back leg, which had been replaced with two big back wheels. It rushed around with these two turquoise-blue wheels skidding and turning, barking quite as boldly as the others.

'Reminds me,' I said, 'of Leggero.'

'Who?'

Eleonora has never heard of Leggero. She has no cause to. But he is soon to become a major figure in our story. Of course, no self-respecting novelist introduces important characters near the end. But this isn't a novel. So as we tramp on from San Giovanni down towards Sogliano sul Rubicone, where Garibaldi at last allowed his men a rest, let's take the prompt of our three-legged corgi to introduce Captain Giovanni Battista Culiolo, nicknamed Leggero 'because of his extraordinary gifts of agility and speed'.

Born 1813. On the island of Maddalena, off the north coast of Sardinia. Enrols shortly before his eleventh (!) birthday in the Sardinian navy. Serves fifteen years. Secretly joins Mazzini's revolutionary movement, Young Italy. Jumps ship in Montevideo in 1839, to join Garibaldi's Italian Legion. Fights in all the General's battles in Uruguay, losing a number of fingertips and becoming an expert artilleryman. Returns to Italy with Garibaldi in 1848 and fights the Austrians in Varese. Is arrested in Genoa and condemned to death for his desertion nine years before but pardoned at the express request of Garibaldi. Distinguishes himself fighting for the Roman Republic when the French army is initially put to flight, 30 April 1849. Murders a fellow soldier during a later battle by firing a cannon into him at point-blank range, this in revenge for the man having killed a friend of his in a duel. Given the siege situation, the authorities turn a blind eye. Is wounded in head, hand and foot during fierce fighting outside Porta San Pancrazio and left for dead when Garibaldi is forced to retreat. Survives fourteen days hiding in enemy territory before re-entering the city and collapsing in a hospital on 29 June. On 14 July, still seriously lame, with Rome now in French hands, he flees the hospital and some days later procures a horse, escapes the city and, riding day and night, gleaning information where he can and avoiding French and Austrian patrols, finally catches up with Garibaldi's column. Where exactly we're not sure. Belluzzi mentions him for the first time on this day's march, so perhaps it was San Marino. Commentators hail him as 'the most *garibaldino* of the *garibaldini*'.

'And the corgi makes you think of him!'

'Carrying severe disabilities but absolutely up for a fight.'

Sogliano al Rubicone

Towards midday, following a narrow lane, we reached a crossroads with a fingerpost that indicated Sogliano al Rubicone a half-mile to our left, Borghi three miles on and Savignano al Rubicone eight miles on. So this must be the place Belluzzi describes where Garibaldi stopped about an hour after daybreak, having marched all night. Anita collapsed on a heap of gravel. Ciceruacchio together with a few officers went into the town and found Doctor Bonaventura Sabbatini, a patriot. Food was brought out. Fresh bread and watermelons. A priest, Badarlon recalls, ran back and forth, bringing bottles of wine. Sabbatini later told Belluzzi how Anita pulled her dagger from her belt, sliced a watermelon and simply sank her face into its red fruit. She was suffering from constant, acute thirst. Garibaldi ate little, drank less and spent most of the time conferring with the locals about the route. On parting, he gave the doctor some of his cigars.

'The group was smaller when we set off again,' Badarlon observes. The gruelling walk had done for many. 'Some men took off their incriminating red shirts and slipped away into the fields.' Garibaldi let them go and pressed on, still insisting to Badarlon that they avoid all villages and proper roads. 'He began to point the way himself: it was as if he had always lived in the country here. He had the nose of a dog, the eye of a hawk.'

Everyone was tired, sweating, scorched by the sun. Many of the horses had to be abandoned; they couldn't keep up. And Badarlon speaks the only harsh words I have ever seen written about Anita. 'She made you sorry for her. But angry too. She shouldn't have insisted on following her husband given the state she was in. There was a danger we would have to stop and everyone's safety would be compromised. She was hanging on to life by her teeth. In desperation.'

Borghi

We were in a somewhat better state, but suffering nevertheless. The temperature was in the mid-thirties. We had brought no food with us today and were low on water. It was August, in an area with no tourism. Everything was closed, shutters down in the blazing sunshine. Empty streets. At last, around 1.30 in the village of Borghi we found the Bar Osteria Centrale open. Sort of. The cook was on holiday, the *padrona* explained. They weren't serving food. Only drinks. We begged. No doubt the state we were in was eloquent. The good lady sat us outside at one of a scatter of plastic tables and eventually served two huge *focacce* with half-melted cheese inside.

Nibbling, Eleonora asked me what had become of Hoffstetter.

'He's down there,' I said, pointing across the road to the plain and the sea.

'Doing what?'

'Panicking.'

Having climbed to Torriana – the first hill – and failed to find Garibaldi, Hoffstetter, Forbes and Bassi and their sixty men had decided they should head straight for the emergency rendezvous at Savignano. They descended to the river Uso and, instead of climbing up to San Giovanni in Galilea, walked along its dry bed down into the plain, arriving at 'about an hour' from Savignano while Garibaldi was still up in the hills. The General had mentioned a *canonica*, a priest's house, beside a church between Santarcangelo and Savignano. But when Hofstetter's party reached the area, no one had seen Garibaldi. Meantime the sixty men had dwindled to twenty, meaning they could hardly defend themselves, even in a minor skirmish. Bassi, Forbes and the German conferred. Hoffstetter assumed that Garibaldi had been intercepted by the Austrians, who the peasants told them had a garrison in Savignano. The situation was hopeless, he said. They should switch to civilian clothes, split up and hide. 'It seemed the other two agreed,' Hoffstetter remembers, 'but they wanted to go to Savignano first to see if it was true the Austrians were there. I waited for them to come back. In vain. They must have run into the enemy and fled for the hills.'

Hoffstetter was now alone with his young servant Ramussi, the boy who had slept on sacks of forage outside the monastery in Terni. He decided to change his clothes, find someone to buy his three horses and disappear. Belluzzi is scathing. 'Overcome by a loss of confidence as sudden as it is strange, he sells his generous horses, which Garibaldi had given him, for a mere 125 lire, buries the weapons that he says he holds dear, dresses himself in civilian clothes (brought along with this in mind?) and assisted by local patriots sets off towards Milan and Switzerland travelling the whole way by hired carriage.'

'Harsh,' Eleonora thinks.

'You can see Belluzzi is actually rather pleased.'

'That the man who was much closer to the General than he ever was, nevertheless was not a true hero?'

'Right. And there is something in what he says. You can't imagine Leggero doing this. Or Ruggeri if he'd been there. Quite a few stragglers headed for Cesenatico individually and managed to rejoin Garibaldi there. But all alone, in unfamiliar territory, surrounded by enemies, Hoffstetter suddenly remembers he is a German military man with a promising future. He doesn't need to die in Italy. So he opts for out. In the end, the reason he writes such an excellent account of the drama is that he's not as passionately engaged as Ruggeri or Belluzzi. His book is not a tract. It's a description.'

'And Forbes, and Bassi?'

Two plaques would tell the story for us. Having filled our water bottles in the café, we wrapped up a good half of our *focacce*, stowed them in our bags and set off. Borghi is a long ribbon of modest modern housing, at the end of which we found Via Ugo Bassi, and on an ugly cement wall holding up the garden of a *villetta*, these words:

> 1 August, 1849, avoiding enemy ambush,
> Ugo Bassi was given food and sustenance here
> on his way to join Garibaldi in Musano.

'No Forbes.'

'Forbes was there, just he never gets mentioned. There are no streets named after Forbes or Hoffstetter.'

Musano

The small settlement of Musano was three miles away. Always the same narrow lanes, shrivelled oaks, scorched stubble, meagre shade, endless hills. There was no traffic that afternoon. It was siesta time.

We walked in a torrid hush. First the climb up to Castellaro – a scatter of houses, cars tucked in the shade – then down again to the Rubicone, so famously crossed by Caesar, now the most meagre of trickles, its dank water barely visible through thick bushes. I took a photo of an extraordinary spider, perhaps an inch and half across, black and white, suspended in the bright air between two stalks of dead grass. At last there was a stretch on the flat, turning back alongside the river through farmland and thickets of bamboo to Musano, where, amid weeds at the edge of a car park, beside a tiny church, we found these words, engraved in stone.

> Guest of Don Pompilio Fiorentino,
> in the church close by, exhausted from his long journey,
> the great spirit Garibaldi found refreshment.
> 1 August 1849

Don Pompilio, the local priest, would spend the rest of his life talking about how generous he had been that day; it was he who arranged for the memorial to be set up. He would tell people how Garibaldi and Anita had spent the night in his house while the *garibaldini* slept in his church. However, his storytelling could not begin until after Romagna was annexed to Piedmont in 1859 and so ceased to be part of the Papal States, where Garibaldi was anathema. Before that, shortly after the General's departure in 1849, the priest held a ceremony to reconsecrate the church, which had been defiled, he said, by the infidels who had forced their way in.

In any event there was no question of a night's sleep. The *garibaldini* arrived in Musano around 1 p.m. and left towards three. It was here that Bassi and Forbes, realising the General must still be in the hills, caught up with him. They brought a handful of others. Altogether there were now about 180 men left. And Anita. We took a photo of the church – a modest, low red-brick building – at 15.30 sharp. We had been on the road ten hours. Our feet were sore and our arms and legs ablaze. Fortunately we had a place booked in an *agriturismo* in Cento, just one more mile away. We would leave till tomorrow the further fifteen miles that the *garibaldini* travelled that same afternoon.

'So when did the General sleep?' Eleonora enquires.

'It's a mystery. Looking at the whole time since they left Sant'Angelo in Vado, I can't find more than the occasional hour or two when he could have rested.'

And the heroics were yet to come.

Cento

That mile to Cento was steep. The village was another scatter of white stucco and painted railings. A suburb without a centre. The promisingly named La Quiete – 'a calm place where you can find refreshment and repose' – was just beyond the houses, on the hilltop. Stripping off for the day's ablutions, we experienced one of those strange moments when you both say exactly the same thing at the same time.

'Just one more day's walking!'

From the big garden at the back of the house our goal was now in sight. We went downstairs to gloat. La Quiete was not named in vain. The garden was a little paradise of banana trees, bristling agaves, banks of lavender, pines, cedars, roses. And towards the bottom, where the slope fell away, beyond a dozen big tables – two already laid for dinner – a low parapet.

We looked out and sighed. Far to the right, across the hills we'd walked, was San Marino, sharp against the skyline. Looking directly ahead, we had the whole Romagnola coastline spread before us: Rimini to the south, Cesenatico almost opposite, Milano Marittima to the north. From up here on the hill the three towns seemed just one long band of urban development, each centre marked by a single skyscraper.

'Oh, they all have to have their big buildings!' the *padrona* laughed, serving dinner.

We had offered to sit closer to the house so she wouldn't have to bring the food too far, but she insisted we enjoy the table with the best view. 'The skyscrapers were all built in the 1950s,' she explained. 'A sort of competition between the towns.' The one in Milano Marittima was thirty-five storeys.

Eating early, we were alone. The food was excellent. A board of mixed bruschetta and *pizzette*, then pasta with herbs and mushrooms. A carafe of pale Trebbiolo. With each dish the light faded, until there was one perfect moment when the sea and the low hills around us were in shadow while a last ray of sunshine found the high peak of San Marino.

'A last thought, perhaps,' Eleonora suggested, 'on the men we left behind there.'

Belluzzi quotes a certain Pietro Fini: 'I can't tell you of what distress, fear and unhappiness we experienced that night when word got round that Garibaldi had left San Marino.' Trevelyan has the men rushing down from San Marino to follow the General, only to be repelled by the Austrians, then climbing back up to the city, surrendering their guns and negotiating their surrender. Austrian dispatches complain that only 300 rifles were handed in, speculating that the men threw their weapons away, or sold them, or sneaked off with them, or never had them anyway. Ruggeri raves that despite the agreement permitting the men to return home, the Austrians now insisted that they go to Rimini first, promising that this was merely for administrative purposes. Eight hundred set off in a column, only to be taken prisoner as soon as they were out of the city. 'Scum of all nations,' writes Gorzkowsky to Radetzky, having seen the men himself in Rimini the morning of 1 August. 'Most of them escaped convicts from the Papal State. Many Austrian citizens, many deserters from the Austrian army. Let me know what I should do with them.' Two to three hundred hid in San Marino or escaped into the hills, Ruggeri reckons. Many were hunted down and shot. 'Send them to the fortress prison in Mantua,' Radetzky sent his orders, 'to stand trial.'

'In short, some were jailed for years, others were freed that winter. Deserters from the Austrian army were shot. All the same, largely thanks to the good offices of San Marino, there was no mass killing.'

It was a balmy evening on the terrace. I accepted the offer of a tarte Tatin. Another group had arrived. *La padrona* was hard at work. We looked down towards Cesenatico.

'Gorzkowsky was furious, of course, that Garibaldi had got away. "And with his wife," he wrote to Radetzky, "a fanatical woman in an advanced state of pregnancy."'

'Which I suppose she was in a way.'

The Austrian dispatches are a testimony to the art of buck passing. 'General Hahne,' Gorzkowsky wrote to Radetzky, 'showed total incomprehension of the nature of these *garibaldino* types.' General Stadion wrote to D'Aspre that Hahne and the archduke had let Garibaldi slip away. The rebel, he said, had been seen alone with his wife and three mules, heading for Cesena. A huge reward was offered for information leading to his capture; anyone sheltering him would be shot. 'When I am back in Bologna,' Gorzkowsky promises Radetzky, 'I will prepare a detailed report on the final phase of the Garibaldi adventure, in which I will examine the reasons why it took a turn that was not entirely satisfactory.'

After a last lingering look across the plain to Cesenatico and the sea, it seemed important to head for bed and get a decent night's sleep before the final act.

DAY 27

1 August 1849 – 20 August 2019

Cento, Longiano, La Crocetta, Gatteo, Cesenatico – 15 miles

Longiano

They stumbled on, exhausted, knowing the real action would begin on their arrival in the late evening of that interminable day, last in a string of interminable days. They must be organized. They must be alert.

We ambled off into a mild summer dawn, with our nice blue backpacks and handy trekking poles, looking forward to an easy downhill stroll, with the prospect of lunch on the beach and a swim in the sea.

For the *garibaldini* it had been a month of disappointments, a dream defeated, a terrible reckoning; for us, we both agreed, despite the discomforts and fatigue, the most exhilarating time of our seven years together.

But we could not have experienced this without them. Our happiness drew nourishment from their struggles. Behind both adventures, albeit in quite different measures, lay the thrill of freedom. There is no suggestion in the comments of survivors that they regretted their choices. They had been themselves, fearlessly. We had discovered new selves, following them. 'I can't believe how thick my calves have got,' Eleonora sighed, lacing up her tattered shoes for the last stretch. 'And how strong!'

Longiano is a medieval *borgo* about two downward-sloping miles north of Cento. All the way we marvelled at the grand show of sea and sky to our right, first a deep indigo beyond the silhouette of low hills, paling in layers over a blurred horizon, then bluing, pinking, until, at exactly 6.19, the first sliver of red fire.

They covered this ground in the mid-afternoon, the hottest moment of the day. After two hours' rest in Musano, news of their coming had run ahead of them. People were at their doors to watch. One witness recalled Anita wearing a 'Scottish dress and black feathered hat'. Can that be true? Enthusiasts came out to greet the General and warn him there were Austrians in Badia, two miles further on. He must turn east now and go straight down into the plain. There is a Giuseppe Garibaldi Roundabout at the entrance to the town, where the General made that call. 'Advised and escorted by local patriots, he eluded the Austrians,' says the monument on a mound shaded by two tall pines framing the plain and the sea beyond.

Today it was Eleonora's turn to need a bathroom. We were obliged to turn the opposite way, into Longiano. A few hundred yards of tree-lined lane led us into the old centre. On a corner a plaque remembers Cesare Masini, a guide who supposedly saved the *garibaldini* from going to Badia, taking them by a different route to Gatteo. All false, Belluzzi discovered. Masini was a megalomaniac ne'er-do-well who spent his life spinning stories of his bravery. It is the only plaque in all Italy dedicated to one of Garibaldi's guides. '*Così va il mondo!*' Belluzzi comments. 'Thus goes the world.'

The only café open at 6.40 a.m. was a smart, round kiosk outside the town hall surrounded by elegant chairs and tables, white sunshades already raised. But would there be a bathroom? '*Certo, signora.*' The barman took time out from his customers to lead Eleonora twenty yards to the main door of the town hall. Still closed of course. He produced a key. 'Follow the signs,' he told her, 'and lock up after yourself.' A strange arrangement.

Strange too to find such upmarket fare at a kiosk. Carefully laid out under polished glass were row on row of large, richly stuffed croissants. *Crema, pistacchio, frutti di bosco, mela, cioccolato.* Clean chrome was all around. The cappuccinos were lovingly frothed. Italy to die for.

Six or seven men talked loudly across the tables in strong Romagnolo accents. One in the orange dungarees of a street cleaner. All thoroughly enjoying the fresh Monday morning before work. The subjects of conversation were football and video surveillance. Just as

323

players couldn't get away with the tiniest foul, so it was impossible for any of us to move anywhere these days without being watched. One man seemed to know an awful lot about surveillance techniques. The others shook their heads, as if they too would willingly have skipped their jobs and made for the sea to commandeer boats for Venice, were it not for improvements in CCTV and mobile-phone tracking.

La Crocetta

Badarlon makes no mention of other guides, but his detail on this last part of the trip is scarce, suggesting he was no longer running the show. He had promised to stay with the General as far as the small town of Gatteo, where he would hand over to a trusted friend for the last dash. We managed to find a farm track off the busy main road and began the last descent of our trip, 500 feet down to La Crocetta. An elderly man was climbing the slope towards us, carrying a red bucket full of fat green figs, each one tipped with white sap. I asked if I could take a photo and he insisted on giving us a handful. It was 7.17. The sun was high, and he was full of good cheer. The figs were luscious and dreadfully sticky.

Things were getting more civilized now. Which is to say, restricted. We ran into the usual PRIVATE PROPERTY signs. Threatening images of dogs and guns. An abandoned farmhouse beside a marvellous bank of feathery grasses bore the sign AREA VIDEOSORVEGLIATA. I doubt I would have noticed if it hadn't been for the conversation in the café.

But now, with the hills at last behind us, we had to cross the Via Emilia. This is the old trunk road that leads from Bologna to the Adriatic, running along the base of the Apennines, the road Gorzkowsky would have travelled the evening before, 31 July, heading south to Rimini. For anyone wanting to intercept a group of men making a break from hills to sea, this was the place to watch out for them: a long straight Roman road with no cover. The town of Savignano al Rubicone, nerve centre of the plain here, was just a mile to the south. Garibaldi divided his men into two groups of ninety and told Forbes to take command of one and cross a little distance to the north.

As soon as I came to the considered conclusion that Garibaldi would try to break out of San Marino to the north and cross the plain to reach one of the small seaports, I dispatched an order to Colonel Ruckstuhl, at that time in Forlì, to march down the Via Emilia with his infantry battalion, half a cavalry squadron and two six-pound cannons and to watch the area around Santarcangelo [where Hoffstetter sold his horses]. I expressly warned him not to forget Cesenatico.

With that admirable zeal typical of Colonel Ruckstuhl, he set off on 1 August and marched 22 miles to Savignano al Rubicone [where Ugo Bassi and Forbes went after leaving Hoffstetter and before finding Garibaldi in Musano].

Thanks to the negligence of General Hahne, Garibaldi managed to cross the Marecchia, reached the heights of Sogliano, and went down into the plain via Longiano. No sooner had Colonel Ruckstuhl, in Savignano, received credible reports that Garibaldi was in that area, than he took the lamentable step of setting off for Longiano with all his men, leaving no reserves at all in Savignano or along the main road. His idea of attacking Garibaldi with all the force at his disposal was mistaken and never materialized. Garibaldi had stolen a small lead and was already beyond Longiano when he arrived.

The forced marches of the previous day [from Bologna], then this evening expedition up into the mountains, had tired Ruckstuhl's troops to the point that he did not feel it was possible to follow the enemy that night.

However, the fact that he then let his men sleep until six in the morning is quite unjustifiable. When I arrived in Savignano I didn't find a single soldier.

If Colonel Ruckstuhl had kept his head in Savignano and, using the cavalry that he had, had considered at what point Garibaldi might be crossing the Via Emilia the rebels would inevitably have been captured.

If ifs and ands were pots and pans, my mother used to say, there'd be no trade for tinkers. What Gorzkowsky doesn't mention, in poor Ruckstuhl's defence, is the role played in the affair by the Mayor of Savignano. Named after the man who famously crossed the river that ran through his town, Giulio Cesare Ceccarelli was a patriot. Receiving warnings from the Mayor of Sogliano, in the hills, that Garibaldi had passed, and again from the Mayor of Gatteo, in the plain, that Garibaldi was expected to pass through later that day, warnings that came with injunctions to alert their Austrian masters as soon as possible, Ceccarelli, in the larger, more strategic town, not only did not tell the Austrians, but deliberately put about a rumour that Garibaldi was spending the night in Longiano. In particular he made sure that people who would inform the Austrians heard this rumour. And they did inform the Austrians.

And Colonel Ruckstuhl, who had already marched twenty-two miles that day not to mention forty miles the day before, duly set off to climb a further five miles to Longiano to grab the glory of wiping the rebels out, only to find Garibaldi gone. And when in the small hours of 2 August Gorzkowsky arrived in Savignano, having travelled the ten miles from Rimini through the night, he found that Ceccarelli had gone too. Into hiding. The mayor would be relieved of his duties the same day. Finding no one to punish, Gorzkowsky launched a kick at Ceccarelli's assistant, Signor Bertozzi, who was explaining that it would be impossible to find horses and carriages to speed up the Austrians' pursuit to Cesenatico because all the town's vehicles had gone off to the market fair in Verucchio.

Comedy.

'It's funny too,' Eleonora observes, 'that though nobody actually joined Garibaldi along the way, there were always people ready to help in an emergency. Even at the risk of their careers and lives.'

Towards six that evening both Garibaldi and Forbes with their separate groups crossed the Via Emilia unscathed. Ruckstuhl had left some men on the road, but they were at Ponte Ospedaletto, a village about two miles to the north. They weren't out on patrol. We crossed the road unobserved at 8.05 a.m. in the vicinity of a huge animal-feed factory – M B MANGIMI, QUALITY THAT PAYS – a great cathedral of grey and green silos, massive steel pipes, cranes and scaffolding. A hundred yards to our right, where a small lane left the main road to cut across the fields to Gatteo, stood one of the *case cantoniere*. These simple brick houses – always a door and four windows, two up two down, always the same dull red, iron-oxide colour – were built at intervals along Italy's main highways in the 1830s to provide homes for the *cantonieri*, the men responsible for maintaining the road surface. 'S.S.N9. Via Emilia, KM 16,' said an old white identification stone on the upper storey. On the opposite corner of the lane, behind rusty railings, in the deep shade of a few old pines, another stone records the General's passing: *1 agosto, 1849*. Our app had got the route spot on.

Gatteo

Two miles to Gatteo now. Flat fields of maize, every bottle-green plant erect as a palace guard. A handsome cock crowed in the clutter of a farmyard but didn't want to be photographed. Then, right in the middle of nowhere, a sign on a post: *ZONA CONTROLLO DEL VICINATO*. Neighbourhood watch. A graphic silhouette showed a man with holster and military cap stretching his right arm round another man's shoulders while linking his left to a woman, smaller of course, holding a child.

'Odd there's not a neighbourhood in sight,' Eleonora remarked.

Gatteo is an old *borgo*, pretty but surrounded by modern suburban sprawl. Avoiding hostile surveillance, the *garibaldini* passed through the main square as the shadows began to lengthen. For Badarlon it was the end of the road. He handed over to his friend Giuseppe Rossi, who was ready, waiting. 'We'll meet again in ten years' time,' Garibaldi promised him. 'In happier circumstances.' It had become a mantra. In fact they met again less than an hour later. 'Retracing my steps, a peasant whose house we'd stopped at to drink showed me a telescope Garibaldi had forgotten.' Tired as he was, Badarlon raced back to return the precious instrument to its owner and was thanked with a 'vigorous handshake'. 'I wonder how many of those men will make it home,' he remembered thinking.

We made it to the red plastic tables of the Bar Europa and ordered two espressos. Despite this culminating moment in our heroes' drama, we were feeling a little flat. Like the landscape. Aware that we would be home all too soon. A perfunctory mood had suddenly imposed itself, as if we were stamping a last ticket. No battle to rouse us. Eleonora's tendinitis was bothering her again. The sun seemed hotter down in the plain. We rubbed cream into our calves and studied the map. Once again, while the *garibaldini* were avoiding their enemies, our key concern was the traffic: how to get to Cesenatico while avoiding the major roads.

Cesenatico

At 9.45 we crossed the Autostrada Adriatica. There was nothing for it here but to trudge over a busy four-lane overpass. With no pavement. After days of freedom in the mountains, it was back to the fear of being wiped out by van or lorry. At last the app gave us a narrow lane to the right, straight as an arrow along an irrigation ditch, flat empty fields and marshland either side. You can see why Garibaldi was wary here. A man on a horse could see to the horizon. There were a few pines in the distance along the coast, the famous *pineta*, but before that nothing.

All too soon we were oppressed by a mesmerising sense of straightness, the road stretching on and on without a scrap of shade. Telegraph poles each side, in straight lines, carrying their straight wires. Straight lines of apple trees. Straight ditches. Parallel plough lines. Everywhere that imprisoning grid that comes so naturally to man.

The day was becoming more of a challenge than we expected. The sheer scorching monotony of this exposed lane. Marching in dogged silence, we wanted it to be over now. Over at last, all this endless walking. Nothing more to say. We had both begun to check our phones compulsively for the small satisfaction of seeing how far Google's blue dot had shifted along the straight line of road.

Then, wonderfully, a waft of air brought a new smell. The sea. The sea!

We sniffed and stood tall. Finally, a sign: CESENATICO. And a last obstacle. Strada Statale 16, which is to say, the coast road bypass, taking fast traffic round the town. Our little track fed into it, but with no traffic light and no zebra crossing. There were two lanes each side, the cars speeding back and forth at tight, regular intervals. We stood for ten minutes, waiting. There was no break. It was hopeless.

We retraced our steps a few hundred yards and followed a side road that promised an underpass. And there it was. A steep dip down with sharp bends immediately before and after a narrow passage between concrete walls. There was barely room for cars to pass in opposite directions, no white lines, nothing to reassure the pedestrian. Traffic was sporadic but fast.

Mad, I thought.

'Roulette,' Eleonora said.

We were still hesitating when a runner appeared from behind us. A man was actually running in this blistering heat. With no hat. A madman. He headed towards the underpass. We called to him. 'Is it safe?' He turned, running on the spot in the road, laughing. A man in his thirties. 'You just have to take your life in your hands,' he said. 'I do it every day.'

It was now or nothing for the *garibaldini*. They hit the town around eleven in the evening, after a march of twenty-three hours. 'There were Austrian guards on the road at the entrance,' the General later remembered. 'They were astonished when we suddenly appeared in front of them. Taking advantage of their hesitation, I said to the horsemen beside me, "Dismount and disarm them." A minute and it was done. We walked into the town and took over, even arresting a number of papal police who clearly weren't expecting us.'

The police were caught asleep in their barracks. Some sources say four, some eight. The men wanted to shoot them so they couldn't talk. Ugo Bassi wouldn't hear of it. At least the commander, some insisted, a certain Vice Brigadiere Sereni. No, Garibaldi said. They would take them as hostages. It proved a costly decision.

The men advanced along the canal that led to the port and the sea. As always it's hard to know what to believe. Belluzzi writes, 'A few

German soldiers were sleeping in a kind of shed beside the canal, but when Anita and Ugo Bassi rushed in among them with pistols drawn they surrendered at once.'

Does this make sense? Wasn't Anita supposed to be half-dead with pain and exhaustion? Why ask a woman and a priest to disarm enemy soldiers when you still have 180 armed men? Not to mention the fact that they had planned for this. They had taken a rest beyond Gatteo, so as to arrive after dark. Each group, every man, had an allotted task. But then what do I know about what people are capable of in desperate situations? It was night. No doubt there was confusion. The horses clattered along the silent streets. The fishing boats were there waiting for them, tied up along the canal. The so-called *bragozzi*. Big snub-nosed sailing boats. Each could take around twenty men.

Garibaldi had the mayor woken up and demanded written permission to requisition some boats. Even in a situation like this he was concerned about legality. At least a piece of paper. Fishermen were dragged from their beds to sail the boats. Now it was a race against time to find provisions and put to sea before the Austrians arrived. Forbes was already organizing barricades at the entry to the town and manning them. He was a safe pair of hands. Everything looked good.

'One can hardly deny,' Garibaldi wrote in *Clelia*, 'that fortune had been favourable to the Solitario in many arduous adventures, but now there began one of the unhappiest episodes of hardship, misfortune and disaster in his entire life.' Or as he put it more drily in his memoir, 'Luck finally let me down that night. A storm had blown up offshore, whipping the sea into big waves breaking right at the entrance to the harbour. It was going to be well-nigh impossible to get those boats out.'

We bought fruit and tomatoes at the first greengrocer's, and the young girl serving said her father was an obsessive *garibaldino* who rode the hills on his bicycle revisiting all the places the General had passed. In our hotel, a couple of streets from the sea, the big communal dining room was full of families and pensioners sitting down to the kind of lunch that could slay an ox. We took the remains of yesterday's *focacce* plus tomatoes and peaches down to the beach, grabbed a last table in one of the busy *stabilimenti* along the front, ordered Proseccos and a litre of water and ate our lunch there, surreptitiously.

I distinctly remember the clink of our glasses. *Salute! Arrivati!* It was 12.53, 20 August, 27 days 8 hours and 8 minutes after our selfie outside San Giovanni Laterano. Exactly 630 kilometres, our app calculated – 391 miles. As I was paying for the drinks, the TV behind the counter told me the government had fallen. Salvini had pulled his party out of the coalition. He wanted elections. He wanted to govern on his own.

For someone arriving at the beach in Cesenatico today, at the height of the holiday season, nothing could seem further away than the idea of desperate men fighting to get fishing boats past a barrier of waves. Replete from lunch, we walked down to the sea through rows of sun-shades. A dazzling chiaroscuro. Babes on sunbeds. Newspapers spread on paunches. The smell of flesh sizzling in coconut oil. Cries of children kicking sand. Reaching the water, we took off our sandals and paddled in the shallows towards the harbour. Everything is tame here. The beach, seemingly endless, is protected all along by big offshore breakwaters. The water is tepid and still. The sand soft. People swim in their sunglasses, play ball as if in a pool. There are pedal boats, plastic dolphins, floating trampolines.

The port itself has been greatly enlarged since that night in 1849. A long jetty stretches out into the sea, protecting the entrance. A big marina has been built, where the rich can bring their yachts and their money. The canal has been widened. As we arrive, a smart white yacht is motoring out, its tall sail hanging limp. Turning back up the canal, a quarter of a mile almost, to where the action happened that night, we find an exhibit by the water: 'Section of the old pier, rebuilt with the techniques of the 16th century.' It's a thick chunk of weathered red-brick masonry on wooden piles. 'They were sunk to a depth of six metres.' Two of these piers, it seems, projected a little way into the sea, either side of the canal. It was here the breakers were preventing the rebels' escape.

In Piazza Ciceruacchio there are kitsch busts of Anita and Giuseppe facing each other by the waterside. Everywhere bicycles, restaurant tables, sunshades. Smart porphyry paving. Lots of investment.

Elegance. Boats chugging in and out. A big ferry to Croatia. Busy, happy, summer life. Tanned skin and bright colours. Osteria degli Inseguiti, one restaurant is called. Hostelry of the Pursued. Above an arched doorway, over a wreath of dry flowers, hung no doubt on 2 August, a plaque claims, 'Anita rested here.'

Belluzzi disagrees. Forgetting her heroics of only minutes before, he has Anita sitting out the night on the bare stone at the dockside, barely conscious of what was going on, occasionally moaning for water. The fishermen were uncooperative; they didn't want to risk their boats. The *garibaldini* were building barricades against an Austrian attack or rushing about to find food and water for the journey. The General did his sums and ordered thirteen *bragozzi* to be dragged along the canal to the harbour entrance. An unlucky number. But how were they going to get through that wall of breakers at the harbour entrance? 'Garibaldi had to wait ten hours before he could get out to sea,' writes Gorzkowsky to Radetzky. 'If only Ruckstuhl had got his men up early he would surely have captured them.'

In reality it was more like seven hours. And in Garibaldi's memoirs, of the ten pages dedicated to the retreat from Rome a full three are given over to those desperate moments. It is the only incident described in any detail. The detail of a man who grew up a sailor describing a technical problem and its difficult solution.

> The sea was now our only refuge. We had to get out there. I went on the boats and had some strong ropes tied together and attached two kedge anchors. Then I tried to get out of the harbour in a smaller boat, to fix the anchors out at sea, the aim being to use them to pull the *bragozzi* through the breakers. The first attempts failed. We jumped into the sea and tried to push the boat through. No good. We urged on the rowers with all kinds of promises. It was no good.

Anyone who has tried to launch a small sailing boat or canoe through breakers will know how hard this is. And what happens when you fail. The force of the crashing wave makes the most powerful effort seem puny. There is a tremendous rush, thousands of pounds of weight unleashed at speed. Your boat is tossed back yards, if not over-turned. Leaving you battered and discouraged.

Garibaldi kept at it.

Only after repeated, extremely taxing attempts did we finally get through the waves, row the anchors out far enough and then get them to grip. But as we were rowing back to the port, paying out the ropes, the very last, being thinner than the others and flawed, snapped. All our work was lost and we would have to start from scratch. It was enough to drive you mad. I now had to go back on board the boats and find more ropes, more anchors. The fish-ermen were sleepy and hostile. The only way to get what you needed was to slap them with the flat of your sword ...

Feeling sleepy, we rested a couple of hours in the hotel, then went for a swim. The water had a slimy feel, its surface so still it was dusty. We waded past children and their weary parents and swam out a cou-ple of hundred yards to the breakwaters. Here the water was clearer and cooler. Turning, looking up and down the seashore and the end-less sunshades, we were astonished to see San Marino still plainly visible to the south. Extraordinary to think of all the toil and territory there was between here and there.

Now came a noise. A launch, passing just beyond the breakwaters, was blasting out an advertisement for coastal cruises. The message had to be loud enough to be heard by the folks on the beach. Where we were it was deafening. '*Gente! Bagnanti!*' People! Bathers! A brash voice with a comically strong local accent conjured visits to caves, on-board fry-ups, a wide range of alcoholic drinks. Half amused, half dismayed, we swam back to the shore.

Garibaldi also took a swim. It must have been around 5 a.m. Once again they struggled to get a boat through the waves. Once again they rowed a little way out to drop the anchors. In 1896 Domenico Piva, a retired colonel, published his account of events in *Il Corriere del Polesine*, a local newspaper. As a young man of twenty-three, he had rowed with the General. 'Garibaldi tossed the anchors overboard, then dived in after them, following the rope down to the bottom to make sure they were properly fixed to the seabed. I was finding it hard to hold the boat in position and when he resurfaced he was quite far away. But he swam back to me without too much effort, sprang in, shook his long hair with one sharp energetic movement and put his clothes back on.'

'This time it worked,' writes Garibaldi in his memoirs. 'The thirteen boats were roped together. The men split into groups and boarded.'

Forbes was the last. Everyone was scrambling for a boat, to haul on the rope and get through the breakers. In these final frenetic moments the General asked Domenico Piva if he had any money, and when the young man said yes, 'He asked me to go and buy some things for Anita. "She's not feeling well. Get some sugar, some rum, some sardines, some lemons, and" – here he lowered his voice – "a few cigars for me. I'll repay you as soon as I have some cash."'

We had also run out of money and consulted Google to find the nearest cash dispenser. Uncannily, it was in Via Anita Garibaldi. Ready for a celebratory *aperitivo* before dinner, we went back to the canal, walking the length of it, this time from inshore towards the coast. Where it crosses Piazza Garibaldi a row of old *bragozzi* had been rigged up and colourfully repainted, no doubt for the annual celebrations. Their sails, ketch-shaped, were raised in the still air. Rich maroon and orange. Static and exotic. The water was glassy in the bright sunshine. The whole thing seemed unreal, oriental. On his pedestal in the centre of the square, a handsome white-stone Garibaldi looks out over the painted boats. Virile, melancholy. 'He surpassed the virtues of ancient Greece and Rome,' claims the inscription.

We drank an Aperol-spritz under a portico with a view of the statue in profile. It is the most moving of all the Garibaldi statues we saw, something to do with its balance of charisma and impotence. A sort of noble frustration. Immediately behind was a small merry-go-round, the kind of thing whose tinkling music drives you crazy on summer evenings. Fortunately it wasn't running now. Fixed to the top of its marquee canopy was a shiny white horse, front hooves rearing. No doubt the creature spins with the carousel. 'They had to leave their horses behind,' wrote the Mayor of Cesenatico, Girolamo Gusella, in his account of events. 'And with what sadness after all they had been through together. Garibaldi, much moved, kissed his horse on the forehead where it had a kind of white star, then gave it to a clerk who worked in the harbour office, Remigio Antonioli. He asked: "General, what am I supposed to do with this horse?" "Anything you like, just don't let the Austrians get their hands on it!"'

Over dinner I remembered the time I too had swum down a rope to fiddle with an anchor. Not at 5 a.m. But around 6.30. Early enough. And after a sleepless night too.

'How come?'

It had proved quite difficult to get a table along the canal. We had hoped to eat at the Osteria degli Inseguiti, but it was full. The customers lingered, at their ease. Everywhere was full. Restaurant after restaurant. August is high season. It seemed the whole town was at ease. No one felt the least bit harassed or pursued. A wonderful atmosphere that we couldn't quite tune into. We crossed to the other side of the canal, away from the centre, and eventually squeezed into a place at the Osteria Pub Maraffa, where we were served *tagliolini al limone* by a diligent young recruit, constantly weaving back and forth among the tables.

'I was nineteen. I and a friend had used holiday-job money to buy a second-hand sailing boat for 300 pounds. It had a tiny cabin with room for two sleeping bags. A so-called microcruiser. Just sixteen feet. We were sailing it along the south coast. On a shoestring. Boring old England of course. One evening we dropped anchor in Portsmouth Sound. Then we decided we should move the boat closer inshore. But when we pulled the anchor it wouldn't come up. It was stuck. I tried to swim down at once. It was too deep. My ears were bursting. We studied our chart. No apps in those days. Sure enough we were in a place with big cables crossing underneath. Was there a danger of piercing something electrical? Should we throw away the anchor and a lot of rope? But if we did, how could we anchor the boat for the night?

We consulted the tide schedules. Low tide would be at 6.30. The water should fall ten feet. So after an anxious night, I jumped in.'

'Why you and not your friend?'

'Good question. I don't know. All I remember is how black it was. And the pressure of the water, holding my breath, pulling myself down the nylon rope, and how scary digging my fingers round the iron of the anchor. There was slime everywhere and something hard. I was terrified some mega electrical shock would blow me out of the water. Just before my breath was done, in a panic, I gave it a huge yank and it came free.'

'We pulled the boats out through the breakers,' Garibaldi remembers, 'one by one, with everyone on board. Out at sea, we shared round the food that had been requisitioned from the municipal authorities. I shouted some instructions, to keep as close together as possible, and we set sail for Venice.'

An hour later the Austrians rolled into town.

We wound up our meal and headed back to the hotel. Crossing Piazza Ciceruacchio again, Eleonora noticed, high on the wall of the public library, something that had escaped us in the afternoon. It was floodlit now. A huge stone plaque, perhaps four metres by three, with a long list of names in four columns.

They were the men in the boats. I took a photo and counted them back at the hotel. Three columns of fifty. One of thirty-eight.

'Didn't you say,' Eleonora objected, 'that we didn't know their names?'

'Tomorrow,' I answered, 'we'll find out how they ended up there.'

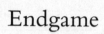

Endgame

DAY 28

2–3 August 1849 – 21 August 2019

Cesenatico, Porto Garibaldi, Lido di Volano, Lido delle Nazioni, Comacchio

Over his lifetime tens of thousands followed Garibaldi. Like a pied piper. But for every disciple, however faithful, there came the moment of separation. The General didn't play his tune – freedom, self-determination, Italy – to enchant or imprison. He bound no one and clung to no one. When you'd had enough, he let you go. Where you couldn't follow, he went on. Or you woke one morning – in Montevideo, in Rome, in San Marino – and found him gone. You were bereft. When we woke up in Cesenatico we knew at once we'd lost him.

We were overcome by a sense of deflation, a loss of impetus. We had nowhere to walk, no immediate goal. In a matter of moments, over breakfast, we changed our plans. The idea had been to chill at the beach for a couple of days, then home. Instead, like so many before us, we made a snap decision: we would try to catch him up. At least follow a little further in his wake. The wake of thirteen fishing boats with a hundred-mile voyage before them. Anita's wake. We ransacked the internet. Did anyone run boat trips up the coast? To the Marina di Ravenna perhaps. Twenty-eight miles. Or better still to Porto Garibaldi. Forty miles. No. There were no boats going north. Only tours to the south, with fry-ups. And crossings to Croatia.

Porto Garibaldi

We made for the station. We would travel by train and bus and intercept him where he touched land. We walked quickly, noticing an elementary school called *2 agosto 1849*, laughing at a poster advertising ERMES, a clairvoyant, 'Expert in bringing back a lost love.'

Our train, to Ravenna, due at 11.15, was late. The platform was an oven. The woman at the ticket office had no idea when the train would come. Or if it would come. At 11.45 it was officially *soppresso*. Cancelled. The next was at 13.15. The woman at the ticket office now thought there might be a replacement bus. At 12.00. But there might not. Buses were not her responsibility.

We waited on the plaza outside. With others. Suddenly a man was shouting. He was standing beside an old Opel Vectra opening and slamming the passenger door. He had been robbed, he cried. He was beside himself, running round and round the car, looking up and down the street. He had brought his wife to the station, he said, and parked (illegally) right outside. Returning to the car, he had found the back tyre flat. Being a practical fellow – a rough, paunchy man, in his sixties – he had set about changing the wheel. When he was done, he had found his wallet, his phone, the car keys, all gone from the front seat. He'd been tricked.

Everyone sympathized. Now he wanted to borrow a phone to call his mechanic. He asked me. I feared it might be another trick. He would run off with my phone. Or I would lend him my phone, and the bus would come and we would miss it. Nevertheless, I gave him the phone. He began a long argument with his mechanic. The bus didn't show up. 'Back to modernity,' Eleonora muttered. At every moment the General was slipping further away.

'The sun was well up when we left Cesenatico,' he writes in his memoirs. 'The weather had brightened and the wind was favourable. If I hadn't been saddened to see my Anita in such a terrible state, suffering terribly, I would have said we were through the worst and on our way to safety, in short lucky: but my dear companion's torments were too much, and likewise my regret that I could do nothing for her.'

If there was one exception to Garibaldi's rule of glorious independence, it was Anita. He was attached to Anita in a way he would never be attached to anyone else. It was nearly the death of him.

340

The main problem was water. My poor woman had a desperate thirst, an obvious symptom of whatever was wrong inside. I was thirsty myself, worn out with all the effort, and we had very little water. The whole day we followed the coast north with a good wind behind. The night too was going to be a beauty. There was a full moon, the sailors' friend, but I who had so often contemplated the moon with awe and worship, felt uneasy as I watched it rise. It was more beautiful than ever, but for us it was haplessly too beautiful. The moon proved fatal for us that night.

Having given up on the bus, we bought sandwiches and a litre of water and sat on a bench in the shady gardens opposite the station. Almost at once we felt threatened. Unshaven men of various ages and ethnicities shifted from bench to bench. They made phone calls, went to speak to other men on other benches. Drugs, Eleonora thought. We moved to a bench nearer the thoroughfare. We couldn't relax.

'The fishermen had told me,' Garibaldi goes on, 'that the Austrian navy had a squadron off the Goro promontory [at the southern tip of the Po delta, fifty miles from Venice]. However, I had no definite information. In the event, the first ship we saw was a fast brig, the *Oreste*, I think. Towards sunset, they saw us.'

We finally boarded the 13.15 train at 13.23. It was the end of our purity. We were on wheels. Motorized. The landscape flew by. Flat and dull. Marshy and industrial. We couldn't touch it. We couldn't smell it. Twenty miles, a good day's walk, was covered in twenty minutes. In Ravenna we rushed to the bus station and bagged seats up front, by the driver. The destination was Porto Garibaldi, a little fishing village known until 1919 as Magnavacca – literally, in dialect, Eat Cow, but apparently derived from the Latin *Magnum Vacum* or *Magno Vacuum*, Great Emptiness. The coast is flat and barren. Inland are marshes, then seven miles of lagoon. The bus raced north along a strip of land, on a dead-straight road, planted all down the middle with flowering oleanders and maritime pines.

In reply to our questions the driver assured us we would be fleeced in Porto Garibaldi. He was a jovial man, a Tuscan he immediately insisted on assuring us, though it was already clear from his accent. 'They have so few tourists here now, the ones they do get they fleece.' A century ago, he explained, people from Milan had built holiday homes here. Then when the roads got faster they went to the prettier and healthier places further south. Cesenatico. Rimini. With fewer mosquitoes. 'And of course, since it's poor here, the government has sent us all the scum.'

It took us a few moments to grasp what our helpful driver meant by this. Behind him a local man was nodding his head. 'The authorities here have no power,' he said. 'They can't defend themselves.' Gradually, it dawned that they were referring to immigrants. There were lots of immigrants, doing the menial jobs. What we had to do, though, he said, was see Comacchio. Four miles inland from Porto Garibaldi at the northern tip of the lagoon. A beautiful old *borgo*, a little Venice, all canals, where you could eat eels. 'Nothing but eels,' the driver laughed. 'Eels are wonderful,' the local protested. 'I drank eel broth in my baby's bottle.'

When I said we had come to see the place where Garibaldi landed, they couldn't agree where it was. 'After all, Porto Garibaldi was named after him,' the local man said. 'It's at Lido delle Nazioni,' the driver thought. 'Where the famous hut is.' That was five miles to the north. But I had read a new biography of Anita, in which the author claims they landed at Mesola beach, just beyond the Lido di Volano, a further six miles north.

'Is there a bus that goes up there?'

As soon as they had seen us [Garibaldi recounts] the brig manoeuvred to approach. I signalled to the other boats to steer a diagonal course moving closer to the coast and out of the line of the moonlight. But it made no difference, the night was so bright, brighter than I've ever seen it, that the enemy not only kept us easily in view but started firing off cannons and rockets, partly to alert the other ships in the squadron.

I tried to steer between the enemy ships and the coast, turning a deaf ear to the cannonballs coming our way. But the other boats, frightened by the noise of the explosions and the growing number of enemy ships, dropped back and, not wanting to leave them to their fate, I turned back with them.

Lido di Volano

The Hotel Ariston in Porto Garibaldi is right opposite the bus stop. We just had time to cross the road, leave our bags and drink an espresso before the bus to Lido di Volano arrived. Since there was only one bus every two hours, we had to be on board. It's a long ride into a coastal dead end. Volano is the last of Comacchio's seven *lidi* – beaches – strung one after the other up to the Po delta. The little centres are seedy, rundown. Much of the land is reclaimed, with long stretches of pine trees on duny ground. After the sixth, Lido delle Nazioni, we were the only travellers on the bus. The smell of the air, as we got down in Volano, was briny and forlorn.

I leave it to you to imagine what my position was in those wretched moments. My poor woman, dying. The enemy following us from the sea, driven with the energy of the easy victory. Us landing on a coast where there was every chance of finding more and more numerous enemies, not just Austrians, but papal soldiers too, in proud reaction after the fall of the Republic. All the same, we landed.

Where? Where *exactly*? We followed a narrow lane through dull low bushes and leaning pines. Grass poked through the asphalt of empty car parks. A garish and ramshackle *stabilimento* appeared. Flags of all nations, buckets and spades, bike hire. A large recent sign, six feet by six, celebrated, in Italian and Slovenian, but above all in bureaucratese, the European Union's funding of a bike track around the top of the Adriatic. €3,514,000. No signs indicated where the track was. Then we were on the beach. Beyond three rows of sunshades, the gritty grey sand stretched mile after mile around a vast bay. To the left, in the distance, scores of tiny white sails stood out against the dark promontory of Goro. Where the Austrian navy had lain in wait.

4 August, Birch von Dahlerup, commander of the Austrian naval squadron in the Adriatic, off the Venetian coast, to Ferenc Gyulay, imperial minister of war, in Vienna

A few minutes ago I received a report from Schiffsleutenant Scopenich, stationed off Goro; he says that on the night between 2 and 3 August his ships identified a convoy of more than twenty boats proceeding from Comacchio towards Venice. Assuming at once that this was a desperate move on the part of Garibaldi and his band, the commander of the brig *Oreste* fired cannon at the boats and chased them with launches. Most of the boats, which were in fact packed with Garibaldi's troops, were captured. From the prisoners' accounts it seems the notorious Garibaldi, with his wife, a doctor, a priest and a handful of officers, had landed somewhere between Magnavacca and Volano, where launches were immediately sent to intercept them.

We bought ice creams, took off our sandals and walked south barefoot along the beach. It's downmarket tourism here. For all the difference in climate, I was reminded of Blackpool, where I spent my infancy. Working-class families splashing in the shallows. A huge yellow duck was anchored offshore. Young black men selling necklaces and hair clips. Eventually, the sunshades ended. It was slow going on the sand, and we were completely exposed to the sun; Lido delle Nazioni, our destination, was six miles away. We switched to a path through the woods just a hundred yards inland. In the end, I announced, it hardly mattered exactly where they landed, did it?

'For sure you're not going to find any footsteps in the sand.'

'I miss Hoffstetter,' I declared. 'I felt I could rely on him to keep us in touch.'

What Garibaldi remembered was the look in the eyes of his companions as they gathered on the beach. He had lifted Anita off the boat and carried her through the shallows. There were four boats, he recalls.

Which would be seventy or eighty men. Other reports give three, others two. Others again two boats here and three further north. Forbes wasn't among them. Ugo Bassi was there, Ciceruacchio and his sons, Leggero. Various other officers and men. 'They were looking at me with the eyes of people asking what they should do.'

It was a common experience for Garibaldi. But this was the end of the road. Unable to leave Anita, he couldn't escape with them. 'Split up,' he told them, 'and seek refuge where you can.' The important thing was to get away from where they were, since the Austrian launches were not far off. 'Those friends were dear to me,' Garibaldi remembered. 'Bassi said he needed to find somewhere where he could change his red trousers. Ciceruacchio said an affectionate goodbye, and set off with his sons.' None would meet again. Only Leggero stayed with Garibaldi and Anita. Meantime, Vice Brigadiere Sereni, the hostage they had taken, ran off along the beach towards Comacchio, whence he would soon be leading a search party to capture the man who had spared him from being shot.

Lido delle Nazioni

We walked on along our sandy path in the welcome shade of the trees. Occasionally bicycles creaked by. To our left, just a few yards through the trees and over the dunes, the shore was barren, sombre. At one point there was a nudist beach. All men in middle age. Sprawled amid the debris the sea throws up. Bleached tree trunks. Rusty cans. But no fugitives. No Austrians.

There are three versions of the next crucial hours, but they have the same elements in common. The threesome: Garibaldi-Anita-Leggero. Then a man called Battista Barilari, a poverty-stricken beachcomber. A hut thatched with marsh reeds. And a huge stroke of luck in the shape of another man, Nino Bonnet. Juggle these as you will.

In Garibaldi's version, he and Leggero carry Anita across the dunes and hide in a field of maize. Anita was muttering that she would never see her children again. Her husband must provide for them. After a while, 'with no idea what to do', Garibaldi sends Leggero out to reconnoitre and Leggero comes back with Nino Bonnet, a local patriot who knew Garibaldi, was aware of the drama and had come looking to help him. Bonnet starts to lead them along the coast where they meet Barilari, who Bonnet knows. And Bonnet tells Barilari to take the fugitives to a nearby hut, half a mile inland, while he arranges transport to some safe place.

In the version of the local Garibaldi Society the field of maize disappears. Barilari witnesses the landing and takes Garibaldi directly to the hut, where two poor people give them peasant clothes to wear. Around nine o'clock Garibaldi sends Leggero off to reconnoitre and he finds Bonnet, who then arranges ... etc.

The most romantic and attractive version is Bonnet's, written up as *Garibaldi's Landing at Magnavacca: historic episode of 1849*, and published in 1887. Twenty-five years old, Bonnet was the son of a Frenchman who had set up a salt factory in Comacchio. He had fought the Austrians in Vicenza in 1848 and helped Garibaldi when he was recruiting in Ravenna later that year. A brother, Gaetano, had died defending the Roman Republic. Another brother, Raimondo, was with Garibaldi's cavalry on the retreat from Rome. We mentioned him leading an exploratory party north of Todi. Wounded, Raimondo had stayed in San Marino but sent word ahead to Nino that Garibaldi might be passing through. Bonnet was rich and well respected by the local people. In his account he describes an anxious night with a crowd of locals, together with papal and Austrian soldiers, on the quayside in Magnavacca, listening to the cannon fire out on the water. Aware, as daylight comes, that some of the boats are going to beach, he has a servant drive him north in his buggy, and is in time to see Garibaldi wading through the water with Anita in his arms. After they meet, Barilari appears ... and so on.

Eleonora and I are still discussing which of these versions makes most sense when, towards evening, we arrive in Lido delle Nazioni. The beach is busier here with much flesh on display among the sunshades. In the town itself, a sprawl of funfairs and dodgem-car circuits. Then, a few hundred yards beyond the centre, the hut. It's a tiny thing with white walls and a thatched roof, a relic from another age protected by a high fence, dwarfed by surrounding apartment blocks. The tricolour is flying, and on the fence there's a poster advertising a Garibaldi 3 August celebration: a bike ride to the various places where the heroes hid that day, a *garibaldino* band and choir, free fried fish, watermelon and wine. But when we try to get down to the beach, officially reckoned to be the place where they landed, we find only tall railings and a locked gate. It's private.

We're disappointed. There is something messy and inconclusive about our day. Trying to cheer ourselves up with a Prosecco while waiting for the bus to Comacchio, we decide that Bonnet's version can't be true. It would be too extraordinary that he, watching events unfold beside Austrian soldiers, then manages to arrive at the beach exactly as Garibaldi has Anita in his arms in the water, while the soldiers are nowhere to be seen. It's a film script. But however they met, Garibaldi reckoned it the greatest stroke of luck of his entire life. He needed a saviour, and a saviour appeared. 'I at once put myself entirely in his hands.' It is one of the sentences that most struck me, reading Garibaldi's memoirs: a man accustomed to command realizes, in a space of seconds, that he must now submit entirely to the judgement of another. And does so.

Carts, carriages, wheelbarrows and donkeys now enter the story. Bonnet comes and goes. Parties of Austrian soldiers are all around. Schiffsleutenant Scopenich reports that his men landed soon after the *garibaldini* and set off to search the dunes and woods. Gorzkowsky explains to Radetzky how he ordered the garrison in Comacchio to ransack the area. Vice Brigadiere Sereni has already arrived in the town and is ready to lead them. A 10,000 lire reward is offered to anyone who will help capture Garibaldi. Shortly before noon the fugitives leave the hut.

Bonnet moves them separately, Garibaldi in a small buggy, Anita on a white donkey, Leggero walking. Limping rather. A half-mile to the first farm. Roused by some broth, Anita begs José to shave his beard. Another mile and a half inland along tiny paths to another farm. It's five in the afternoon. Leggero climbs a tree, hides in its leaves, keeps watch. Bonnet tells Garibaldi he must give up any thought of Venice. The only hope is to the south, Ravenna, where there is a strong patriot network. Garibaldi acquiesces. But when Bonnet says that to have any chance of survival, he must part with Anita – the farmers will look after her – he baulks. Anita refuses to be left behind. 'I owe her an immense debt of gratitude and love,' Garibaldi explains. It seems he's apologising for a weakness. Bonnet sees the two will only be separated by death.

Comacchio

Our bus took us back along the coast and turned inland towards Comacchio. The marshy water of the lagoon was to our left, the great green emptiness of the plain to the right. Garibaldi, Anita and Leggero covered this ground in two boats. Bonnet had hired men to row them along the streams and waterways, without saying who their passengers were. At one point the boats had to be lifted out of the water and carried over a causeway. Towards midnight they rested, half a mile from Comacchio. It's a picturesque place of red-brick bridges and dark canals in a lovely muddle of medieval, Renaissance and seventeenth-century architecture, all paved with porphyry, carefully preserved and regularly swept, with plentiful restaurants on the waterside, swarms of mosquitoes and a very distinct smell of fried eel. We struggled, studying menu after menu, to find anything vegetarian.

'We'd have to be less fussy if we were on the run,' I observed, settling in a place whose chalkboard promised *ravioli di burrata con pomodoro*.

'But we're not on the run!' Eleonora laughed.

While we waited for our order, I studied the town's street plan and discovered that the running had ended for Ugo Bassi and ten other *garibaldini* just yards from where we sat. Bonnet had returned to town to make further arrangements for Garibaldi. Hearing that Bassi had checked into an inn, he urged him to leave at once. But the Austrians, guided by Vice Brigadiere Sereni, burst into the room as the priest tried to escape through the window.

Meantime our ravioli arrived, and with the first bite we tasted anchovies. It seems the people of Comacchio just can't resist putting

348

fish in everything. I soldiered on, but Eleonora refused. Aside from any vegetarianism, she hates anchovies. And she was hungry. Why hadn't they been listed in the menu? No need to get upset, the waitress laughed. And we had missed our bus back to Porto Garibaldi. It would be a four-mile walk in the dark. Beside a fast road.

Garibaldi had other worries, moving round Comacchio and into the lagoon to the south, with Anita stretched delirious on the floor of the boat. It was wild territory, of marsh and empty islands, places Bonnet felt sure the Austrians couldn't know or search. But at some point the men rowing the boats realized who their passengers were and what they were risking. They took fright, and Garibaldi, Anita and Leggero found themselves abandoned on a muddy island in the north-west corner of the lagoon. It was three in the morning and Anita was dying.

The night was suddenly chill. After an hour's walking we were tired and footsore. We couldn't enjoy the brooding darkness of empty water to our right because of the headlights racing intermittently towards us. At one point they lit up a stone beside the road.

IN THIS PLACE

FAR FROM HOME

THESE MEN GAVE THEIR LIVES

FOR THE FREEDOM OF PEOPLES

ANDERS LARSSEN VC

EDWARD ROBERTS

STANLEY RAYMOND HUGHES

ALFRED JOHN CROUCH

THE COMMUNITY OF COMACCHIO

REMEMBERS WITH GRATITUDE

25 APRIL 1945

We walked the last few hundred yards along Via Nino Bonnet and turned into Via dei Mille.

'Names,' Eleonora muttered. 'Endless names.'

DAY 29

4 August 1849 – 22 August 2019

Porto Garibaldi, Mandriole, Ravenna

Porto Garibaldi

'In my writings, I shall speak mainly of the dead.' Again and again Garibaldi presents his books as acts of homage. His memoirs are full of lists of dead companions. With brief notes.

'Santo N., Piedmontese corporal, hit by three bullets at Sant'Antonio, his legs broken and his face disfigured. I helped him onto his horse in the retreat, but he didn't make it to Salto. His body was found next day in the Uruguay.'

'Alessandro – from the Veneto – a good soldier and sailor, killed in Sant'Antonio.'

'Antonio – nicknamed Trentuno – from Liguria – died from cannon fire outside the walls of Montevideo.'

'*Mi duole*,' he writes – it grieves me – 'that I can't remember them all.' Or of one partisan who sheltered him at risk of his life: 'I remember his face as if it were yesterday, but not his name.'

Modern editions of Garibaldi eliminate these lists. To save space. And because they would bore the reader. It's not stylish writing. In doing so they miss the point. Freedom and independence were qualified by 'a sacred duty' to remember those who had died for freedom and independence. At least to put the names out there. One was bound, as it were, perpetually, by the struggle to be free. A pathos and a paradox. The reader was not merely to be entertained, but challenged. How do I stand in relation to these names? In relation to *so many* of them. Each with his, or her, own story.

Or, put another way: freedom was not the freedom of the individual to do what the hell he or she wanted, or to be guaranteed an entertaining yarn, it was a collective endeavour – the freedom to determine our fate together.

Those 188 names on the plaque in Cesenatico, I told Eleonora, were handed over by the Austrians in the 1880s in response to a request from the mayor of the town. They were the men captured on the boats. Belluzzi points out that many of the names were false, because the prisoners didn't want to reveal their true identities. But the number was correct. There was a man behind every name.

'So what happened to them?'

We're on the bus again, travelling south, with the sea to our left and the lagoon to our right.

'They were lucky. Because they hadn't been arrested in papal territory, they were not subject to martial law and hence an automatic death penalty. Unless of course they proved to be deserters from the Austrian army. Initially, they were taken to a fortress prison in the town of Pola on the Croatian coast. Foreign citizens and those from Italian states not controlled by the Austrians or by the Pope were released the following year. Citizens of the Veneto and Lombardy were made to serve in the Austrian army. Domenico Piva, for example, who rowed out the boat when Garibaldi sank the anchors off Cesenatico, was sentenced to seven years' service in the Austrian army.'

We had meant to explore Porto Garibaldi in the morning, but we overslept and the bus left at 9.16. We were getting lazy. The trip was all but over. Eleonora protested that, as I'd told the story, Garibaldi never actually visited the town anyway; it was the merest opportunism to change its name because he landed six miles up the coast.

'Perhaps they were fed up with the ugly "Magnavacca".'

In the event, we had just twenty minutes to walk up and down the main street and peek at the beach, noticing the inevitable monument in the centre of a roundabout, then various sentimental statues, all quite recent and evidently commissioned with tourism in mind. The best had Garibaldi, in bronze, standing in a flat-bottomed boat that looked like a punt surrounded by tall reeds. These boats were used for harpooning eels in shallow, marshy waters, and when Bonnet heard that his men had left the fugitives stranded, it was to a group of eelers that he turned. This time he told them frankly who their passengers were and paid them handsomely in gold coin. By 8 a.m. on 4 August they had Anita on the boat. She was foaming at the mouth, Garibaldi dabbing her lips with a handkerchief. It was a blistering day, and they had to move quietly through a spectacularly flat, wide-open landscape where the dazzling sky presses down on the watery earth as far as the eye can see.

Mandriole

By the early afternoon they had reached the southern shore of the lagoon, where there was a complication. Four hundred yards beyond the bank was the fast-flowing river Reno. The boats had to be hauled up, carried and relaunched. Garibaldi was begging for a doctor. He asked a woman in a cottage to kill a chicken and make some broth. Anita couldn't hold it down. One of the men ran to the village of Sant'Alberto. An Austrian patrol had just passed. A horse and cart had to be found. The destination was the Guiccioli farm near the village of Mandriole just south of the lagoon. And it was our destination too. The bus dropped us off at the Antica Romea, a café for lorry drivers in the middle of nowhere. Sky, poplars, fields and water. From here it was just half a mile's walk along a broad canal, following signs that eloquently announced, 'House where Anita died.'

From distant Brazil to north-Italian marshland. A few days before her twenty-eighth birthday, this was the end of her journey. It's a rather lovely place, a wide-open well-kept courtyard with low elegant buildings on three sides. Ignazio Guiccioli, intellectual and landowner, had been finance minister in the Roman Republic and was now in exile. His tenant farmer, Stefano Ravaglia, was a patriot. Not a person was in sight when we arrived. A purple pedal car had been abandoned beside a bench. Plaques were everywhere. The tricolour hung beside the EU's yellow stars over an ordinary front door. It wasn't clear whether it was a museum or a private house.

Garibaldi found the place packed. Saturday was payday for the labourers. The men were gathered in the yard for their week's wages. And Doctor Nannini had just arrived from Sant'Alberto. The fugitives turned into the gates around 7.30 on a horse-drawn cart; they had made slow going of the last miles on a rutted track. Leggero limped behind, keeping watch. A one-man rearguard. Having spent pages describing the drama of getting the *bragozzi* out of Cesenatico, Garibaldi devotes only a few perfunctory paragraphs of his memoirs to the two days between the landing and this fateful moment. The forty-eight hours of Anita's agony. He doesn't want to go there. He'd rather be remembering soldiers who died in battle. Or Ugo Bassi – he breaks off his tale – 'tortured by the priests, before they shot him'. Or 'poor old Ciceruacchio', executed with his two sons and seven other *garibaldini* in the village of Ca' Tiepolo in the Po delta. 'All shot and buried by Italian hands, you understand! A thirteen-year-old boy! The foreign soldier giving the orders. And you'd better obey at once or you'd be beaten.'

But these are digressions. At last he bites the bullet. 'We arrived in Mandriole, with Anita lying on a mattress in the cart. I said to Doctor Nannini, "Do what you can to save this woman!" And he to me: "Let's get her into a bed." So four of us lifted the corners of the mattress and took her to a bed in a room at the top of the stairs.'

We tried the handle of the museum, found it open and walked in. No one was around. The stairs were right in front. Beautifully renovated. Polished wood, whitewashed walls. We walked up.

'As I laid my woman down in the bed, I thought I saw death on her face. I took her pulse. It wasn't there.'

The room is modest with a window over the courtyard. The floor is terracotta. The walls are plastered, though here and there strips of the old brickwork have been allowed to show through. Cordoned off in the corner is a narrow single bed with high wooden head- and footboards curling back in carved scrolls. A dry wreath lies on the blue bedspread. Anita was gone.

Garibaldi broke down. By all accounts it was an extraordinary scene. Renowned for his composure under fire, the General howled and sobbed. He covered the corpse with kisses. Out in the courtyard everyone heard. Everyone understood. The fugitives' cover was blown. The others in the room tried to pull him away. He wouldn't let go of the corpse. Two men arrived from Ravenna, sent by Giovanni Montanari, head of a clandestine group of patriots. Garibaldi must leave with them at once. The Austrians were everywhere. 'For your children,' Leggero pleaded. 'For Italy.' Garibaldi began to rave about embalming the body, preserving the body. He got halfway down the stairs then ran back up to throw himself on her again. 'All his soul dissolved through his eyes in bitter tears,' reported one witness. He begged that she at least be properly buried. He stripped the coat off her, pulled the ring from her finger and offered them in payment. Suddenly exhausted, he asked if someone could be so kind as to give him a piece of bread.

There was nothing else to look at in the room. Downstairs, a little museum had a few mementos. A red shirt. A 1904 painting of the death scene which borders on the comic, as if we were looking at amateur actors not quite sure where to stand or what to do with their hands. Outside, in the courtyard, we found a man in his seventies talking to a young couple with a toddler. Apparently, he was the museum guard and guide; the couple were on holiday, taking a day off from the beach. The guide was shocked that we had managed to sneak in and see everything without the pleasure of his company. He had taken a coffee break and hadn't locked up. Like the garrulous man who made us wait so long to see Donatello's Madonna in Citerna, he had evidently set himself up as keeper and protector of Anita's pathos. No man must get to the heroine but by him.

We stood by while he explained that very likely she had died not of malaria but sepsis, due to the death of the foetus. The young couple listened dutifully. 'Of course they couldn't give her a proper burial. The family were terrified one of their workers might betray them. After dark they wrapped her in a sheet, carried her a half-mile into the country and dug a shallow grave.'

The guide was astonished when I added that the man who dug the grave was paid with the gift of the mattress she had died on. He looked at me suspiciously. The young man shook his head. 'Different times,' his wife observed.

We walked along a narrow lane between shady cedars to the burial place. There were low hedges around a modest monument. The grass was dry and limp. 'Here, buried in secret, lay the body of Anita Garibaldi, 4–10 August, 1849.' The man rewarded with the mattress hadn't dug deep enough. A hand emerged, and a little girl had the shock of her life seeing human fingers gnawed to the bone. The story came out with the body. An autopsy suggested she had been strangled. Garibaldi was a murderer. The farmers were accomplices. They were arrested. Bonnet was arrested. Even today, Risorgimento revisionists like to believe that Garibaldi killed her. A re-examination of the body showed no sign of foul play. The farmers were released. But not Bonnet. 'He has been taken to Bologna to be shot,' announced a local newspaper.

This should have been a quiet place, but someone was using a chain-saw in the next field. It droned and rasped. There was a smell of hay. Life goes on. The young couple appeared, having escaped the guide. They wanted to chat, and we told them about our walk. They were envious. If only they didn't have their little girl . . .

'Where next then?' the man asked.

It was a good question. We could have followed Anita's body to the cemetery in Mandriole, where it rested until 1859, when Garibaldi had it exhumed and moved to his home town of Nice. Or we could walk west to Sant'Alberto, where the General spent the night in a tailor's house and watched from the window as Austrian soldiers marched past in the street. But I felt enough was enough.

'It's game over for us.'

'We have a hotel in Ravenna,' Eleonora said.

Ravenna

It would take Garibaldi and Leggero four days to travel the eleven miles to Ravenna, moved from house to house by patriots, spending long hours in remote huts or hiding in undergrowth and fields of corn. 'You'd have to have seen it to believe how efficiently those young

Romagnoli set about saving me. How it grieves me now not to be able to consign their names to the page.'

We turned down the offer of a lift from the young couple and walked four miles to the coast on a track beside the canal. Every few hundred yards there was a wooden hut built out from the bank, suspended over the water, with poles to lower nets and pull up fish and eels. It seemed a mean way to make a living, but the huts and nets had a lovely Van Gogh look. Otherwise there was precious little to see. Waterside vegetation. Dragonflies. We had thought it might be fun to get in a last swim while we were near a beach. But again melancholy overtook us. We grabbed a sandwich in the tiny resort of Casal Borsetti, then another bus to Ravenna.

The coast is marred here by the Marcegaglia steelworks. A mile of piping, chimneys, grey walls, scaffolding, fences. Did Garibaldi guess that the stars had factory work in store for him? After Ravenna there would be another three weeks of flight, another 200 miles, westward this time. Across the Apennines again. Always in the hands of his minders. On the morning of 2 September he and Leggero were rowed out to a ship off the Tuscan coast. Once in Piedmontese territory, he was beyond the reach of Austria at last but so popular as to be dangerous to the authorities. Crowds gathered wherever he went. General La Marmora, governor of Genoa and later prime minister, had him arrested but was impressed when he met him. 'He is very discerning ... It was a terrible mistake not to make use of him.'

Allowed to see his children in Nice, Garibaldi was unable to tell them Anita was dead. He sank into depression. The Piedmontese sent him off to Tunis, but the Tunisian government didn't want him. Gibraltar rejected him. Parked on the tiny island of Maddalena, Leggero's home, he tried to recover some peace of mind before being moved to Tangiers. Then it was Liverpool and finally, in August 1850, New York. Crippled by rheumatism, he had to be carried off the boat. He declined all celebratory dinners, speeches, rallies. There was nothing to celebrate. Instead he wrote short biographical accounts of comrades who had died. Anita. Ugo Bassi. On Staten Island, to make ends meet, he accepted work in a friend's candle factory. 'I therefore spend my time making wicks and handling tallow with unbelievable skill. By the boilers the temperatures are almost Cuban.'

In Ravenna the temperature was falling. The day had clouded over and a thin drizzle was in the air. The city, with its soft yellows and greys, was as beautiful as ever. But the Risorgimento Museum was closed and looked as if it had been for quite a while. We did the rounds of the churches and the mosaics, sharing Henry James's amazement that 'while centuries had worn themselves away and empires risen and fallen, these little cubes of coloured glass had stuck in their allotted places and kept their freshness'. Returning to the hotel, we made a detour through Piazza Anita Garibaldi to check out the monument to 'the people of Ravenna who died for liberty, on the scaffold, in prison, in war or in exile and to Anita Ribeira dé Silva di Merinos, from Laguna (Brazil)'. Above a bas-relief of a woman on a rearing horse, the inscription reads, 'How well the name of Anita Garibaldi sounds here.'

DAY 30

23 August 2019

Ravenna, Bologna, Milan

As I begin these final pages we are in the fourth week of lockdown in Milan. For Covid-19. After a year thinking about freedom it has been taken away from me. Suddenly and drastically. It could be, then, that the note of wistfulness that has crept into these last chapters has as much to do with what is happening in Italy now as in 1849 or last summer. Day by day, looking at the photographs we took and the notes I made, our walk seems more and more fabulous. I study the people in the street, the packed restaurants, the open roads, with a sense of wonder.

The present changes the past. The same would be true of the event that came to be known as the Retreat from Rome. In 1849 Garibaldi would never have claimed it was anything but an abject failure. Like the whole 1848 experience. He hadn't inspired a revolution. He hadn't made it to Venice. He hadn't saved his companions. He had lost Anita. The patriots in general had lost. Venice fell to the Austrians on 28 August. The old order prevailed.

But already there were signs this assessment would change. What press had remained free in Italy, notably in Piedmont, contrasted Garibaldi's resistance with the collapse of their own armies. He hadn't surrendered. He had restored Italy's military honour. Throughout the month of August, when nobody knew what had become of him, newspapers reported sightings all over Italy, even in Venice. Historians are unsure whether these were mistakes or deliberate attempts to mislead his pursuers. On 21 August the satirical paper *Il Fischietto* – the Whistle – published a cartoon that became notorious, showing Garibaldi cocking a snoop at idiot Austrian soldiers. On 7 September the Tuscan paper *Concordia* announced with jubilation that Garibaldi had arrived safe and sound on the Ligurian coast. 'How he saved himself this time,' La Marmora wrote, 'really is a miracle.' Meantime, Europe's liberal press expressed disgust at the execution of Ugo Bassi. Buried in unconsecrated ground, his remains immediately became a place of pilgrimage, heaped with flowers, until the Austrians had the body exhumed and hidden.

Never once in the dispatches between Austrian generals is there an open acknowledgement of the failure to capture or kill Garibaldi. But there is plenty of sniping at each other's inadequacies. Posters and newspaper pages offering rewards for the 'notorious criminal' only broadcast the occupying army's frustration and enhanced Garibaldi's image. The ruthlessness that Gorzkowsky in particular showed towards Bassi and a score of others, all shot without trial, began to look like impotent rage. Stadion, writing to D'Aspre, claimed he would have finished the job, if only Hahne had let him. D'Aspre, writing to Radetzky from Florence, continued to purr about the Grand Duke of Tuscany's willingness to wear an Austrian uniform at public events. Radetzky, reporting to the minister of war, Ferenc Gyulay, in Vienna, was unimpressed; other sources had told him of the grand duke being 'visibly embarrassed' and the people cold. Just once, writing to Emperor Franz Joseph on 5 August, Radetzky uses the expression 'this Garibaldi catastrophe'. And he asks for Gorzkowsky to be moved from Bologna to the Veneto. In October he would be forcibly retired.

We would be changing trains in Bologna on our way home. But first we spent the morning completing our checklist of Ravenna's treasures. The city is unspeakably beautiful, though it's conveyor-belt tourism, with crowds and queues. We had a wait of fifteen minutes or so to climb four steps and peep over a red-ribbon barrier into the tiny mausoleum where Dante's bones lie. I was impatient, my mind elsewhere. Eleonora insisted we hang on. Dante too, she reminded me, lamented a divided Italy, overrun by foreign powers. And she quoted from the *Purgatorio*:

> *Ahi serva Italia, di dolore ostello,*
> *nave sanza nocchiere in gran tempesta,*
> *non donna di provincie, ma bordello!*

Ah, vassal Italy, home to grief
Ship without a pilot in great tempest
No lady of the provinces, but a whore!

When you finally get to the top of the steps and the open door, your eyes need a moment to adjust to the gloomy marble interior. Everything you are looking at – the tomb, a bas-relief of the poet, the decorative stone inlays – was made centuries after his death. The bones of course, so often moved back and forth lest they be stolen by others eager to appropriate the bard's celebrity, are not in view. By the time you are able to see things clearly the people in the queue behind you are humming and hahing eager for their turn.

I stepped back and we headed for the National Museum of Ravenna. A question occurred to me that I had not seen written in any book: how long had the myth of Garibaldi been in the making? Posit a ship without a pilot and inevitably you conjure up a possible pilot. An able ship's captain. Posit a country divided and overwhelmed, and immediately you conjure the man who might unite and liberate it. A valiant warrior. I remembered the famous conclusion of *The Prince* where Machiavelli tries to flatter Lorenzo Medici by imagining him as Italy's saviour: 'You can see the country is praying God to send someone to save her from the cruelty and barbarity of these foreigners. You can see she is ready and willing to march beneath a flag, if only someone were to raise one up.' That was 1514. More than three centuries later, after the events of 1849, depictions of Garibaldi began to appear that fused the iconography of military hero and messiah. A man of sorrows and miracles. However disastrous for him personally, the story of Anita's passion and death had lent him a new charisma.

Garibaldi mentions Dante three times in his memoirs. In 1838, having piloted his storm-tossed ship through reefs off the Uruguayan coast, he rowed ashore, looking for provisions, and found in a tiny isolated house a beautiful Italian poetess who charmed him by speaking of Dante and Petrarch and gave him a volume of 'the lovely poems' of the Spanish patriotic writer Manuel José Quintana. In 1848, recruiting soldiers in Ravenna (the occasion of him meeting Nino Bonnet), he says, 'Clustered round Dante's mausoleum in Ravenna, I witnessed something unique and encouraging, a truly wonderful harmony between different classes of citizens.' It was as if the presence of the great poet's bones had inspired a community spirit. 'Such a harmony is the key to achieving liberty and independence for our country, its absence the origin of all our misery.'

Austrian dispatches support his view. On 21 August 1849 General D'Aspre wrote to the new governor of Bologna, General Strassoldo, asking that the Count of Carpegna, a *borgo* to the west of Macerata Feltria, be allowed to keep his hunting rifle despite the newly imposed restrictions. The count had offered invaluable spying services and generous help to Austrian troops as they tried to nail Garibaldi in the mountains. In an earlier dispatch to Gorzkowsky, on 31 July, General Hahne had spoken of 'extremely useful intelligence given spontaneously by the Lawyer Amadei, whose pro-Austrian sentiments have led to his suffering much persecution'. It is hard to achieve independence if your potential governing class is happy to be ruled from abroad.

And the third time Garibaldi mentions Dante? The General had promised his supporters he would be back in ten years' time. In February 1859, hindsight having transformed the Retreat from Rome into a glorious act of resistance, Count Cavour, Prime Minister of Piedmont, who by all accounts loathed Garibaldi and feared his popularity, nevertheless invited the hero, now based on the island of Caprera, to form a volunteer corps to aid Piedmont in the forthcoming war against Austria. Reflecting on why he, a republican, agreed to fight for a monarchy, Garibaldi explains that the priority had to be making Italy, not its form of government: 'Wasn't that the idea of Dante, Machiavelli, Petrarch and so many of our great men?' In a string of hard-fought battles through the spring of that year the General led 3500 men without cavalry or cannon from the river Ticino west of Milan as far as Lake Garda, liberating Como, Bergamo and Brescia, and relieving the pressure on the main Piedmontese army to the south. Commanding the Austrian troops was Ferenc Gyulay, the minister of war to whom Radetzky had been reporting in 1849. Radetzky himself was dead by then. Hahne was dead, falling from his horse in 1853. D'Aspre died in

1850, shortly after replacing Gorzkowsky as governor of the Veneto. Gorzkowsky died in 1858. Strassoldo died in 1855. Of all Garibaldi's direct enemies of 1849, only Archduke Ernst was alive to regret not having finished him off when there was a chance. In a private letter Cavour wrote, in French, his preferred language, 'Garibaldi has rendered Italy the greatest service a man can render. He has given the Italians confidence in themselves.'

There was a large group of French schoolchildren in the station café in Ravenna, but it was the Italian waiter who refused to heat my muffin for me. The logic of the muffin, I told him, was that you served it warm. 'I'm not turning on a big oven for just one muffin,' he complained. Apparently there was no microwave. Nor much harmony. But never mind, the train to Bologna was announced on time. We were on our way.

Bologna

Hoffstetter also passed through Bologna on his way back to Milan and eventually Geneva. He didn't have quite such an easy time of it as Belluzzi would have us believe. Stranded near Savignano on 1 August, it took him three days, moving from hiding place to hiding place, to cover the sixty miles to the city, arriving on the evening of the 4th, right around the time Anita died. He was running a high fever and tormented with back pains and stomach aches. Parting from Garibaldi had filled him with regret. 'Separated from my General, whom I loved and admired more than anything in the world, cut off from him without a goodbye or a handshake, uncertain whether he had escaped the many perils that beset him, anxious for my companions, I couldn't sleep.'

For him too, the present situation was rapidly changing his perception of the past. 'Every day of the last months, from Rome to San Marino, presented itself anew to my spirit. Drifting in and out of slumber I thought I was in the mountains again, I saw our column disheartened, hunted down, and suddenly I sat up in bed, imagining the General had called me.'

Unable to continue his journey, Hoffstetter found a doctor and took a room in a tavern, only to be warned two days later that Ugo Bassi and a dozen other *garibaldini* had been brought into town on open carts to face public derision and soon a firing squad. Sick as he was, Hoffstetter dressed at once and left, counting on his old Swiss army papers to get him through the passport checks.

Nino Bonnet arrived in Bologna the day after Hoffstetter left. Ominously, he was placed in the same cell Ugo Bassi had occupied. But just as his appearance on the scene had been a massive stroke of luck for Garibaldi, so he now got lucky himself. Gorzkowsky was replaced by Strassoldo, who had been constantly criticizing his predecessor behind his back. Strassoldo felt Hahne had been right to take a softer approach. And Bonnet was freed. Life or death was the whim of a general.

We had given ourselves more than an hour for the change of trains in Bologna, not wishing to miss our high-speed Freccia to Milan. We walked past the waiting room where in 1980 a terrorist bomb had killed eighty-five people and went out into the big square, Piazza Medaglie d'Oro. It is one of those places where all nations and classes meet and petty crime no doubt thrives. The busy road that joins the piazza on the opposite side from the station is named after Angelo Masini, another patriot who died on the Gianicolo defending the Roman Republic. His body was never recovered.

We sat to eat ice creams on a bench facing the big iron sculpture that dominates the centre of the square. Placed between two lines of four flagpoles, alternately flying the tricolour and the EU's yellow stars, it's a portentous thing, a great round disc of rusty metal that purports to show 'the moment in which amorphous material takes the shape of the wheel, symbol of mobility and freedom'.

It was around six o'clock on a busy Friday afternoon with crowds on the move to get away for the August weekend. We were just settling into our bench when a half-dozen ragged young North African men arrived, each with a half-litre bottle of beer. One sat next to me. They called to each other across the benches, laughing and joking. Very likely they were having the same effect on the good citizens around them that the *garibaldini* would have had on people after a couple of weeks on the march, living rough. Not company you ordinarily seek out.

Two policewomen walked by. One stopped. 'You shouldn't be drinking beer here,' she said. The young men grinned. 'There's a fine of a hundred euros.' The policewoman was calm and collected. 'We don't have any money.' The boys were laughing. 'We couldn't pay.' 'Arrest me!' the boy beside me suddenly demanded. He tipped his bottle to drink right in her face and wiped his mouth with his wrist. 'I want to be arrested! Please! Do it!' The policewoman hesitated, half smiling. A dozen paces further on, her companion was beckoning to her. 'Then I'll have somewhere to sleep tonight!' he said. He seemed delighted with the idea. 'Don't let me see you here again,' the policewoman muttered and hurried on.

The men laughed. The Italians who had witnessed the scene were silent.

'I've nowhere to sleep,' the boy beside me said, matter of fact. 'I really wouldn't mind being arrested.'

'Have you been arrested before?'

'Sure. You sleep pretty well in a police cell.'

There was a short silence, as if we were surprised to find ourselves speaking to each other.

I said, 'I suppose if you committed a proper crime they'd be obliged to arrest you.'

'Like what?' he challenged.

I laughed. 'I don't know. You could have tried to kiss the policewoman. She looked nice. I think she liked you.'

He chuckled. 'There are limits,' he said. More seriously, draining his beer, he added, 'You see, I'm not a criminal.'

We set off to find our train. The high-speed section of Bologna's station is deep underground. First stairs, then a lift, then escalators, then more stairs. A great concrete cave. This so that trains can run straight through under the city. The long, famously divided peninsula can now be travelled in a matter of hours, at least as far as Salerno. But the air is cold and damp down here, and there are not enough benches. Our train was twenty minutes late.

At last it arrived and we were on board and in our allotted places. Each person finds his seat and withdraws into himself for the journey. Or herself. Any talking is between those travelling together, and is perceived as a disturbance by those beside them. Or there are loud phone conversations. The older woman beside Eleonora grimaced as someone behind her chattered on and on in grating dialect. Most passengers defended themselves with headsets, computers, games. The occasional book. Garibaldi would have found neither harmony nor disharmony here. Public space has become a purgatory where you wait to be released into the freedom of your private life.

Fortunately we were on a fast train. Two hundred miles an hour. Nobody bothers with the landscape. It's a blur. The wheel may have given us mobility and freedom, but it cuts us off from the world. Eleonora settled down to read about the political crisis on her mobile phone. I opened our little computer and tried to wrap up the Garibaldi story. In my mind at least. What had become of the men we encountered on our trip?

Doctor Nannini, who had been able to do nothing to save Anita, would be a medical officer in Garibaldi's 1860 expedition to Sicily.

Gaetano Sacchi, who commanded the First Legion during the retreat, escaped from San Marino to become a ferryboat captain on the Po, then was forced to emigrate to Zurich and later Uruguay after taking part in a failed uprising. Returning to Italy in 1856, he joined Garibaldi in the Alps in 1859, fought at Volturno in 1860, became a general in the united Italian army in 1862 and in 1876 a senator of the Kingdom of Italy.

Hugh Forbes was captured at sea by the Austrians but released after just a few months, thanks to his British citizenship. Promptly emigrating to the USA, he wrote and published the *Manual for the Patriotic Volunteer*, which led, in the late 1850s, to him being invited to train the revolutionary militia of the slavery abolitionist John Brown. But the two fell out when Brown didn't pay the colonel the sum they had agreed, after which Forbes betrayed Brown to the authorities. Forbes returned to Italy with other English volunteers in time for the second phase of Garibaldi's 1860 campaign.

Stefano Piva, who rowed the boat in Cesenatico and served seven years with the Austrian army, fought with Garibaldi in 1859 and 1860 and later became a lieutenant colonel in the Italian army. Likewise Major Cenni, who had suffered from typhus outside Arezzo.

Major Zambianchi, who was shot in the foot while helping Cenni at Arezzo, was to become one of the most controversial figures of the Risorgimento. During the siege of Rome he had ordered the shooting of a number of priests believed to be giving intelligence to the French. Recovering from his wounds in San Marino, he fled to London and Argentina, where he founded a charitable institution for the health and welfare of immigrants. He returned to Italy in 1860 to fight in Sicily, was arrested for seeking to start an uprising in the Papal States, and eventually emigrated again to Argentina, where he became a colonel in the country's army.

Francesco Nullo, the cavalryman who had taken Garibaldi's first request for help to San Marino, and was considered by all 'the most handsome' of the *garibaldini*, fought again with his General in 1859, 1860 and 1862, then turned his attention to the liberation of Poland, where he died alongside other Italian volunteers in 1863. Many streets and schools in Poland are named after him.

Of the industrious cavalry commander Luigi Migliazza, not a trace. Always generously mentioned in accounts of the retreat, there seems to be no other record of his existence.

Nor of the Pole, Emil Müller, who betrayed the *garibaldini*.

Nor of Ignazio Bueno, who deserted outside Sant'Angelo in Vado.

Egidio Ruggeri, our second diarist, is mentioned in one 1976 academic paper, in Spanish, surveying Italian political emigration to South America. In 1850 he responded to a call by the Uruguayan consul in Genoa for Italian liberals to come to Montevideo to fight the Argentinians. Ruggeri must have departed immediately after his account of the retreat was published. Certainly he couldn't have made his disgust at the political situation in Italy any clearer.

The French cavalryman Aristide Pilhes was among those captured at sea by the Austrians. His older brother Victor was parliamentary representative of the Ariège district in south-western France. A socialist close to Proudhon, Victor was jailed for starting an insurrection when it became clear that French soldiers, in violation of their constitution, would be attacking a sister republic in Rome. Aristide, returning home in 1850, tried and failed to win his brother's vacant parliamentary seat, then started a newspaper called *Le Vote Universel*. The only detailed document about him online is an extract from French police records denouncing him as 'immoral and dangerous' and listing such crimes as 'insulting a gendarme', 'jumping bail' and 'causing anarchical disturbances'.

One could go on. But it is the story of Leggero that most fascinated me as the train raced across the north Italian plain. Having accompanied Garibaldi as far as Tangiers, he emigrated to Central America. Fighting American slave traders in Costa Rica, he lost his right arm and was imprisoned. He worked as a customs officer, fought the slave traders again, was wounded again, losing four fingers of his remaining hand, then trained soldiers in San Salvador. In 1860 he rushed back to Italy for the war in Sicily but arrived too late to fight. Eventually he retired to Maddalena, married and had children, dying in 1871 aged fifty-seven. It was he who encouraged Garibaldi to set up home on the nearby island of Caprera.

Milan

I have one photo from the train ride back to Milan. I must have taken it after shutting my computer in amazement. So much mad life. Such determination to change the world. Such energy, courage and stubbornness. Such violence. My photo shows the sun setting over a distant urban skyline – Milan – with dark fields in the foreground, pylons against a pink sky and a low horizon of chimneys, power stations, factories, apartment blocks. The dull labyrinth of metropolitan life.

On arriving in Milan, Hoffstetter did a soldier's duty by his lost friend and superior Luciano Manara, going straight to visit his widow.

She was prettier than he had expected. Stories were told, tears shed, then the German returned to Switzerland, where a distinguished career as a military administrator awaited him. We hurried through the vast hall of Stazione Centrale with its aura of Fascist grandeur, down into the metro and onto a green-line train. The second stop is Porta Garibaldi. The city's northern gate had originally been named after Emperor Francis of Austria; it was here that Garibaldi entered the city in 1859 after liberating Como. As the train's doors were closing, three adolescents rushed in. They were tanked up. They had a huge boom box and turned the volume up full. In the enclosed carriage it was deafening, intimidating. They knew it and enjoyed it, shouting their pleasure. No one reacted.

Alighting at the end of the line, we were almost home, eager to see if all was well in our flat, looking forward to wearing some fresh clothes and sleeping in our own bed. How strange it felt to fish the house keys from the bottom of my pack, where they had lain untouched for the 400 miles of our walk, and find that each one turned perfectly in its lock, as if we'd done no more than gone out for a pleasant *passeggiata*.

And now I look back on all this, eight months after our great hike, from a situation where we are scarcely allowed out of the house. The *passeggiata* is punishable with fines of up to €1000. On the building opposite ours a tricolour has appeared. On two or three occasions the national anthem has been heard, words written by a man who died fighting for the Roman Republic. Our prime minister, Giuseppe Conte, having avoided an election and kept Salvini out of power, appears on our screens to tell us we are 'at war' and Italy is 'the admiration of the world'. In a flash the revisionists have disappeared. Suddenly it's clear to everyone that Italy is a nation and we are in this together. Covid-19 has revealed that the Risorgimento patriots didn't die for nothing. Yet only this morning I received a worried letter from a friend. A university professor. A cultured woman. 'Our only hope after this catastrophe,' she writes, 'if we are to avoid sliding into South American anarchy, is Germany. I fear the south and its corruption. I feel closer to the French and the Germans. I don't mind surrendering "sovereignty" to them.' Four hundred miles away, on the tiny island of Caprera, Garibaldi turns in his grave. 'Like a nightmare,' he wrote, 'Italy is weighed down by a terrible conviction of its own weakness … especially among those classes accustomed to a comfortable life.' But he added, 'A people not disposed to bend the knee is invincible.'

This story will run and run.

But let's leave ours with Garibaldi running. Smuggled to a remote point of the Ligurian coast on 2 September 1849, he surprised his rescuers by making a dash across the stony beach to the sea, pulling off his boots and paddling like a child in the water. A fishing boat was approaching. 'He looked like a captive lion whose cage has been opened,' one witness wrote. Garibaldi thanked the men with him profusely. And added, 'On the sea, I fear no one.'